Rewarding Performance

Building on evergreen principles, concepts, and strategies of performance and rewards management, the second edition of *Rewarding Performance* is a clear guide to how strategies must be adjusted to align with new realities, and programs revised to ensure their effectiveness.

Appendices dealing with the important and increased reliance on evidence-based management have been added, to provide insights into how evidence can be applied in performance and rewards management. Another major development addressed in the second edition is the rise of the "gig economy," which has challenged organizations to brand themselves as employers of choice. This new edition answers the challenge by considering the impact of this trend on performance and rewards management throughout the book, and expanding the content related to managing non-employees.

The second edition also includes a new appendix, providing a fundamental grounding in the use of statistics relevant to performance and rewards management. A chapter on contractors has been added and material on cognitive bias explores why managing people must be understood as different from managing quantitative measures. Updated figures and PowerPoint presentations make the new edition of *Rewarding Performance* an essential resource for instructors and students of human resource management.

Robert J. Greene, PhD, consults with organizations on formulating and evaluating human resource management strategies and designing, implementing, administering and evaluating performance and rewards management programs. He is CEO of Reward Systems, Inc., a consultancy whose mission is "Helping Organizations Succeed Through People." He is also a faculty member in the MBA and MSHR degree programs for DePaul University, USA, and a Consulting Principal with Pontifex, a public sector consultancy.

Rewarding Performance

Guiding Principles; Custom Strategies

Second Edition

Robert J. Greene

Routledge
Taylor & Francis Group

NEW YORK AND LONDON

First published 2019
by Routledge
711 Third Avenue, New York, NY 10017

and by Routledge
2 Park Square, Milton Park, Abingdon, Oxon, OX14 4RN

Routledge is an imprint of the Taylor & Francis Group, an informa business

© 2019 Taylor & Francis

The right of Robert J. Greene to be identified as author of this work has been asserted by him in accordance with sections 77 and 78 of the Copyright, Designs and Patents Act 1988.

Library of Congress Cataloging in Publication Data
Names: Greene, Robert J. (Robert James), 1940- author.
Title: Rewarding performance : guiding principles, custom strategies / Robert J. Greene.
Description: 2 Edition. | New York : Routledge, 2019. | Revised edition of the author's Rewarding performance, 2011.
Identifiers: LCCN 2018029141| ISBN 9781138368798 (hardback) | ISBN 9781138368804 (pbk.) | ISBN 9780429429019 (eBook)
Subjects: LCSH: Compensation management. | Employees—Rating of. | Performance awards. | Strategic planning.
Classification: LCC HF5549.5.C67 G74 2019 | DDC 658.3/225—dc23
LC record available at https://lccn.loc.gov/2018029141

ISBN: 978-1-138-36879-8 (hbk)
ISBN: 978-1-138-36880-4 (pbk)
ISBN: 978-0-429-42901-9 (ebk)

Typeset in Bembo
by Swales & Willis Ltd, Exeter, Devon, UK

Visit the eResources: www.routledge.com/9781138368804

Contents

Introduction to the Second Edition

Every organization needs to do two things: 1) determine what is needed for success, and 2) make it happen. At the most fundamental level what the organization needs is to fulfill its mission by meeting critical objectives. In order for the right strategy to be formulated it is necessary to first identify its comparative advantage . . . what the organization is or can be exceptional at doing. This enables the organization to commit resources to things that will be likely to have a large payback and that have the best chance of being done successfully. Then a strategy must be developed that will enable it to gain a competitive advantage. In almost any endeavor the field is crowded. Other organizations compete for resources by doing things better, faster or cheaper and the bar that must be cleared in order to survive gets higher and higher. In order to succeed in this competitive arena an organization must develop and execute a human capital strategy that ensures is has the people it requires.

The human capital strategy must be derived from the context within which the organization exists and be a good fit to that context. The vision and mission of an organization establish the destination and the magnetic north that can be used to navigate by. The internal and external realities influence how things can and should be done. The culture of the organization provides the context within which those doing the work function and influences how they do what is required. There is no human capital strategy that will work well in every organization . . . what works if what fits the unique organizational context.

An organization's human capital (talent) is always a critical resource. Financial, operational and customer capital are also required for success and their relative criticality varies across organizations. Despite the increased use of technology being heralded today all that is done in an organization must be created by and governed by people . . . those that are either doing the work, directing it or developing the technology that will do the work.

In order to attract, retain and motivate the talent an organization requires for success in today's competitive market it must be viewed as an employer of choice. Much as organizations brand their products they must brand themselves as employers in order to be a preferred place for talent to apply their skills and knowledge. The first step towards successful attraction and retention is to offer a value proposition that is attractive to the people the organization needs and wants. Some organizations attempt to establish their credibility as a desirable employer by communicating impressive-sounding mission statements and cultural profiles. Websites are receiving massive investments in an attempt to attract the right people, because of the increased use of web-based search activities by those seeking opportunities. Claims like "our people are our most important asset" and "we have an employee friendly culture" are common. But they are claims made by the organization, which will be recognized as potentially self-serving and which may not be believable to potential candidates for employment. Those considering the organization may instead visit websites that report the perceptions of actual employees.

When branding the organization as an employer it is first necessary to identify the type of people the organization needs and wants. People will respond positively to organizations that walk the right talk. If they seek personal development they will view organizations that invest heavily in human capital development positively. If they want short-term rewards they will opt for organizations that seem to offer premium rewards packages. If they are most concerned about doing meaningful or socially responsible work they will prefer organizations known for exhibiting corporate social responsibility and be less impressed by premium rewards. If they want to work on a project or part-time basis they will look for indications that the organization is flexible relative to work schedules . . . but also that they will be rewarded appropriately and not treated as second-class citizens. And if they are security-oriented they may be more impressed by generous benefits packages than would people more focused on short-term direct compensation.

Once candidates have been attracted by the organization's value proposition it is necessary to manage the selection process effectively. One of the most important things to do is to honestly portray what employment will be like in the organization. Decades of research has established that the most effective device for avoiding unwanted turnover in the first 12–24 months is a "realistic job preview." This entails telling the truth . . . the whole truth. It both inoculates the candidate against the likely bumps in the road and it begins the employment relationship on an honest, transparent basis. Recently, the author orchestrated a session with members of a client's executive team that resulted in lists of the "good stuff" and the "not so good stuff" associated with working in the organization. That summary was used in a recruiting brochure and put on the organization's website. It was also communicated during selection interviews. Although some seemingly qualified candidates might have been lost as a result of honest portrayal it is likely they would have left anyway, after the organization invested considerable resources in hiring and training them. False promises are dangerous . . . a recent public sector client continued to claim they rewarded performance despite giving across the board step increases every year. That hypocrisy created cynicism, rather than motivation.

The final step in the employment process is the "onboarding" of new employees. This requires proper orientation and attention to ensuring new employees know what they need to know and have what they need to have in order to be successful. By creating a formal process that is used for all new employees, the organization can ensure that there is consistency and that the early socialization of new hires is aligned with the culture of the organization. Assigning highly competent people to act as counselors should be viewed as an investment and a commitment to effectively integrating new people into the organization.

Once an organization is clear about what type of people they need and how they want them to contribute to the organization's success, it is much easier to decide what kind of staffing, development, performance management and rewards management strategies are appropriate. How effectively and appropriately the organization structures itself and designs individual roles will impact on workforce effectiveness. How heavily the organization invests in developing its people will significantly impact how well the viability of the workforce will be sustained. And how effectively and appropriately an organization defines, measures, manages and rewards performance will have a major impact on employee engagement and motivation.

Performance and rewards strategies must be consistent with the culture. Some organizations adopt a strategy that richly rewards outstanding individual performance. Others may differentiate less dramatically between individuals and tie rewards more to team/unit or organizational results. Some reward long service, with time-based step increases and generous benefit accruals. The types of total compensation packages differ based on their mix of the various components: base pay, short-term incentives, long-term incentives, equity and benefits. An organization electing to offer employment security, premium base pay opportunities tied to longevity, rich benefits and no incentives will appeal to one type of candidate. This profile is common in the public sector. Others may offer modest base pay and benefits but use performance-based short-term incentives and/or equity to motivate and reward success. This will attract those who view a "we win–you win" deal as acceptable.

The use of incentives, in the form of cash or equity, has become more widely adopted. As the economy has changed much of the new employment in the U.S. is in smaller and start-up organizations, and these are the type that may not be able to afford large fixed costs. By utilizing incentives an organization can provide direct compensation that is greater than the market average if performance is outstanding, at market average if performance meets target and below market average if performance does not meet target. Offering significant equity appreciation opportunity via the use of stock may also be a sound approach for an organization not able to offer competitive direct cash compensation and benefits.

There may be a single rewards strategy for the entire workforce. But an alternative is to design different total rewards packages for different types of employees. Given the increased national/ethnic diversity the use of a single rewards strategy for all employees can be shortsighted. And different occupations might warrant different strategies, or at least variation in mix of rewards. Most organizations offer different packages for executives and direct sales personnel. Some global organizations have different packages for personnel in countries outside the headquarters country. And some differentiate between management/key professional personnel and support personnel. Culture will influence the decision as to how much, if any, customization occurs within the workforce, as will economic realities.

Benefit design can also be such that it allows for customization. Over the last several decades the use of "cafeteria benefits" has expanded dramatically. This enables people to opt for more of what they value most and less of what they value less. The ability to sell vacation days to have better health coverage would appeal to employees with growing families who fear being financially wiped out more than they might regret taking fewer vacations. The use of paid time off pools can provide more flexibility to those with different needs or preferences. And defined contribution plans can be made more performance-contingent by varying the employer match percentage based on performance. Finally, flexibility in work schedules and/or location might be valued more than the costs. This type of approach seems to fit the increasingly diverse workforces of today. Assuming any one package could be equally appropriate for four generations or appeal to culturally diverse groups seems delusional.

All facets of human capital management must be assessed in light of the context within which work will be performed. The roles on offer must be well designed, which means effective in producing the desired results and promoting engagement by appealing to those with the talent needed. A rewards strategy that fits both the needs of the organization and that has the highest appeal to the people the organization wants and needs is optimal. These strategies can be communicated to employees and potential employees as the employer value proposition. And it is important that the proposition be communicated in the way that the desired audience will accept most readily. Clear, honest and complete descriptions of the employer brand and the components of the value proposition should be developed and then delivered via the media of choice by the intended audience. And if needs change the value proposition should be evaluated to determine whether it will enable the organization to compete for the talent it needs. "We have always done it this way" can condemn an organization to living in a past that does not fit current reality.

This Second Edition

This second edition contains much of the content found in the first edition, since the principles of sound performance and rewards management have not changed dramatically. What has changed is the environment within which organizations must function. And environmental change has impacted how effective strategies are. The effectiveness of strategies and programs is impacted by context. What works is what fits the context within which strategies are executed.

An increasing reliance on evidence when making management decisions has been a positive development in management science over the last decade. The emergence of evidence-based medicine and its success was a contributing factor to the adoption of evidence-based approaches to management decision-making. Finance and marketing were the functions that were early adopters of EBM (evidence-based management). The human resources function has followed them.

Workforce management decisions are increasingly utilizing data analytics, artificial intelligence and machine learning. Early adopter organizations have found that considerable intelligence useful in decision-making can be derived from sound analysis of data. The academic and practitioner literature in the HR field has begun to focus on the potential value of utilizing the scientific method and evidence when making decisions. This evolution is of major importance. Discussions about dealing with evidence-based management (EBM) have been added to this edition to provide insights into how EBM can be applied in performance management and rewards management. Appendix 1 on the use of data analytics and other forms of evidence will be useful to those readers who would like to verify that they are familiar with the scientific method and how quantitative analysis should be done. Reviewing Appendix 1 prior to reading the rest of the book if the reader feels the need to brush up on his or her QM skills is advisable.

The fact that workforce management deals with people has an impact on what should be accepted as relevant considerations in making decisions. There is a difference between utilizing purely quantitative evidence and incorporating qualitative evidence. Quantitative evidence can answer the *what* and *how much* questions . . . but qualitative evidence can address the *why* and *how* questions. And in order to fully understand what is related to what and the consequences of those relationships all of these questions should be answered. If a newly implemented incentive plan appears to make people exert greater effort and to focus on what needs to be done a correlation can be established. But it is also helpful to understand why the plan had that effect. Qualitative evidence can be gathered by examining attitudinal measures (what people say their reaction to the plan was) or behavioral (what the plan led them to do differently). By comparing people's attitudes to their behaviors, a much richer explanation of the motivational forces at work becomes accessible. Deriving conclusions from data is an inductive approach.

The inductive approach to discovery involves inference derived from facts. Evidence is accumulated and analyzed and a theory is developed based on the analysis. A high correlation between A and B can suggest A has an impact on B if A precedes B and there are no other plausible explanations for the behavior of B. This is the approach used when workforce analytics are used to explain relationships. Yet the complexity of human behavior results in underlying values, beliefs, priorities and perceptions impacting outcomes. A positive reaction to an incentive plan can be explained by the fact that the organization communicated the importance of some outcomes by making them the basis for awards, rather than the fact that potential rewards provided the motivation. Performance requires both effort and focus. A negative reaction to a team incentive plan can be caused by an individualistic cultural orientation, rather than a disagreement about what should determine rewards and how they are distributed. It is these complexities that make a purely inductive approach to explanation hazardous.

A deductive approach to explaining relationships involves developing a testable hypothesis (increasing pay will lower unwanted turnover), identifying the assumptions underlying the hypothesis, testing the hypothesis through experimentation and using the results to confirm/reject/modify the hypothesis. If qualitative evidence is used in the development of the hypothesis it can help to avoid a simplistic hypothesis. For example, asking people what they value and what contributes to their satisfaction recognizes the reality that several factors can have an impact. The creation of a team incentive plan can provide recognition as well as monetary rewards. It can involve participants in collaborating on how to produce better results and support collaboration. It can promote a healthy form of inter-team competition. But if qualitative evidence is not used to explore what participants view as motivational, a purely inductive process can produce a simplistic hypothesis (the implementation of the plan reduced unwanted turnover). In fact, the prospect of more money was a necessary but not sufficient explanation for the desirable outcomes. As evidence-based workforce management evolves, its positive effects will be enhanced by utilizing methods that respect the potential relevance of both quantitative and qualitative evidence.

Another major development has been the increased use of people who are not employees to do the work of organizations. This has produced what some have called the "gig economy." This trend is so pronounced that it is estimated that 40% of all work in the U.S. will be performed by people not employed by the organization by 2020. As contractors, consultants and freelancers become a significant part of an organization's talent pool the strategies used to define, measure, manage and reward performance face new challenges. When knowledge/skill is in short supply organizations must compete for the talent that possesses what the organization needs to succeed. This reality has challenged organizations to brand themselves as employers/talent utilizers of choice. The value proposition they offer to the market must result in attracting and retaining the needed talent and motivating that talent to focus on contributing to the organization's success. This edition addresses this challenge by considering the impact of this trend on performance and rewards management and by expanding the content related to managing non-employees. A new chapter (11) has been added to this second edition to provide insights into the issues created by having work performed by non-employees and how performance and rewards management strategies can address these issues.

Since 2007 the economy has been turbulent. As of 2018 there seems to be positive growth globally, although economists are divided as to how stable the upward trend will be. The decade that has passed has convinced many that their journey into the future will be more like a rafter facing permanent whitewater, rather than someone riding a roller coaster that has fairly predictable cycles. One must adapt quickly to change when facing whitewater. Historically, most rafters created a navigation strategy based on river maps and observations from the shore. But by the time the map is interpreted and the shore observations made, the path forward through whitewater has changed. So the important skills for a rafter are adaptability and possessing a wide range of capabilities that can be utilized to deal with whatever happens. It is the same with organizations. Strategies must be developed that are robust in a number of possible futures. Scenario-based planning is increasingly used to prepare for whatever might materialize.

Organizations must define, measure, manage and reward performance dynamically. Balanced scorecards are still useful in providing information about organizational performance, but although the things that are measured (financial, operational, customer and workforce performance) may remain the same, the relative importance of each and what constitutes adequate performance must be defined dynamically. As what the organization needs changes so must its offerings to the talent market. Defining, measuring and appraising individual performance must be done continuously, so that everyone clearly understands what is expected, how current performance compares to standards and what can be done to improve. Doing a once a year performance appraisal at the end of the year has always been ineffective if the required attention to continuous measurement and feedback is not paid throughout the year. The use of relevant and accurate evidence is also required if those appraised are to believe they are being treated fairly and appropriately, both with respect to their appraisal and the rewards accompanying it.

Because people are a unique resource, it is important to understand their characteristics. Research in the fields of neuroscience and behavioral economics has told us a lot about how people process information and make decisions. The research has identified numerous types of cognitive bias that everyone is subject to. Those that are the most impactful in workforce management are discussed in this edition. It is important to recognize that people's perceptions are their reality and if bias causes perceptions to be inaccurate people will still act on what they believe to be truce. Recognition of bias and discussing it with employees can minimize the gap between perceptions and reality.

At the end of the chapters of this edition there are scenarios intended to have the reader reflect on and apply the principles discussed in the chapters. The author would welcome reader responses to these scenarios and encourage a dialogue on issues that are difficult to resolve.

Author Biography

Robert J. Greene, PhD, SHRM-SCP, SHPR, GPHR, CCP, CBP, GRP, CPHRC

Greene is the CEO of Reward $ystems, Inc., a consultancy whose mission is "Helping Organizations Succeed Through People." He is also a faculty member for DePaul University in their MBA and MSHR degree programs and a Consulting Principal in Pontifex, a consultancy dedicated to effective management in the public sector.

He consults with organizations on formulating, executing and evaluating human resource management strategies and designing, implementing, administering and evaluating programs that support strategy and contribute to the effectiveness of a workforce and to the success of an organization.

He was one of the principal designers of the PHR and SPHR certification programs of the Human Resource Certification Institute and the CCP and GRP certification programs, of the American Compensation Association (now WorldatWork). He was the first recipient of the Keystone Award, bestowed by the American Compensation Association for attaining the highest level of excellence in the field.

The first edition of *Rewarding Performance: Guiding Principles; Custom Strategies*, published by Routledge/Taylor & Francis in 2011, was written for those seeking a more in-depth treatment of effectively defining, measuring, managing and rewarding performance, as is this edition. His second book *Rewarding Performance Globally: Reconciling The Global – Local Dilemma*, co-authored with Fons Trompenaars, focuses on managing a global workforce. It was published by Routledge in 2017. His third book, *The Most Important Asset: Valuing Human Captial*, deals with principles and strategies relating to all aspects of workforce management. It was published by Routledge in 2018. The books have been supplemented by over 100 articles and book chapters on topics related to effective workforce management. Designing and delivering training on workforce management globally has broadened his perspective and has taught him valuable insights into how organizations can best utilize the talent they use to fulfil their mission. During 2017 and 2018 he wrote over 100 LinkedIn posts, all of which were intended to be addresse topics that are currently at issue. Readers are encouraged to visit LinkedIn/In/RewardSystems and to share their views on the topics treated. Books are valuable, but the dynamic environment requires constant assessment of strategies to ensure they remain viable.

Acknowledgements

This second edition is the result of over five decades of experience in industry and consulting. Since the publication of the first edition the feedback received by those reading it has been helpful in recognizing developments in management. Both editions are attributable to the contributions of many. My parents and my brother, Richard, during their lifetimes encouraged me by providing support and a nurturing family. My wife, Dorothy, and my son, John, provide that same kind of support today, while encouraging me to write and offering their perspectives. My two granddaughters Grace and Alice inspire me to do something meaningful since I so want them to be proud of their grandfather.

A number of valued colleagues and friends acted as reviewers during the development of both editions. Denise Rousseau included me in the Evidence-Based Management Collaboration, which expanded my awareness of how decision-making can be improved. Wayne Cascio increased my understanding of how psychology can be applied to Human Resource Management. John Boudreau and Ed Lawler provided insights into how talent is managed when work is performed by people who are not employees. And the value provided by the people who inspired and contributed to the first edition continues to inform me. All of these people have earned my gratitude and friendship.

The opportunity to share knowledge with those who function as researchers, practitioners and consultants as a part of my consulting practice has enhanced my knowledge and understanding. My colleague Pete Ronza at Pontifex has shared his deep knowledge of workforce management in the public sector and allowed me to apply that knowledge by working with him.

Interaction with students of management has enriched my knowledge as well, and teaching has been a rich source of learning and personal development, as well as opportunity to give back to the profession that has been so good to me. My service as a faculty member for DePaul University in their MBA and MSHR degree programs, in the U.S. and internationally, has enabled me to develop a network of researchers and academics. The members of that network have helped me to increase my understanding of the concepts and principles underlying sound workforce management.

My involvement with the American Compensation Association (now World at Work) and the Society for Human Resource Management over the last 30 years has provided me with the opportunity to define the body of knowledge in HR, develop a certification program, design and teach professional development programs and speak at their conferences. This has given me exposure to thousands of HR practitioners and enriched my understanding of the issues they deal with.

All of my experiences have resulted in a firm belief that the most important asset for any organization is its people, which is the focus of my third book *The Most Important Asset: Valuing Human Capital*.

Part I

Guiding Principles

Each organization presents a value proposition to current and prospective employees and enters into an economic and psychological, if not legal, contractual relationship with employees. The talent utilized may consist of employees and outsiders who offer their knowledge and skills in varying ways. The terms of the contract with people doing the organization's work will include a philosophy about how performance is defined, managed and rewarded. If the terms are mutually understood there is less chance of misunderstanding and conflict, which can lead to poor performance or unwanted turnover.

The principles that determine how the employer manages performance and rewards will play a critical role in guiding the formulation of strategies and programs. And in order to be effective the performance and rewards strategies must be well integrated with the staffing, development and employee relations strategies, to produce a human resource strategy that is effective and appropriate to the context.

Part I explores how organizations can develop human resource management strategies that are a good fit to their context (Chapter 1). It then addresses the process of formulating performance and rewards management principles that will support the effective execution of the human resource strategy (Chapters 2 and 3). The importance of choosing guiding principles to guide the development of strategies and programs is a central theme. Lacking guiding principles, an organization can develop local strategies and programs that are not integrated with the business strategy and with each other, potentially creating inconsistencies and conflicting interests across the organization.

Chapter 1

Human Resource Management Strategy

Performance and rewards management strategies and programs must fit the context within which they will operate. What works is what fits. They must be consistent with and supportive of the human resource management strategy, which in turn must be consistent with and supportive of the organizational strategy. Prior to discussing the principles of sound performance and rewards management, it is therefore necessary to describe how an organization develops an effective and appropriate human resource management strategy. The HR strategy will guide the development of appropriate and effective performance and rewards management strategies, as well as integrating those strategies with the staffing, development and employee relations strategies adopted by the organization.

The human resource management strategy utilized by any organization must first and foremost produce the desired results at the individual, group and organization-wide levels. In order to accomplish this it must drive the effective creation and application of the required intellectual capital by:

- defining, evaluating and shaping a culture that is appropriate;
- designing an organization structure and employee roles that fit the context;
- formulating staffing and development strategies that produce the workforce required;
- formulating performance and rewards management strategies that motivate that workforce to work towards organizational objectives;
- integrating all strategies and programs that impact workforce management in a manner that is fair, competitive and acceptable to employees.

Figure 1.1 provides a model for formulating an HR strategy that will produce a good fit with an organization's context. This model can guide the design of a human resource management strategy and can also be used to evaluate the current effectiveness and appropriateness of an existing strategy. Once an effective strategy has been formulated it can then be used to evaluate how well policies and programs support the strategy. The model must be dynamic. If any of the contextual characteristics change, the HR strategy should be reassessed. The degree to which the HR strategy is made specific will also depend on contextual characteristics. During stable periods it may be well defined. In times of uncertainty and/or rapid change it may be in the form of a general direction, to be in sharp focus only when a direction is clear and new objectives defined. This demands a dynamic strategy that is administered by continuously assessing the environmental and internal realities and by reallocating resources in a manner that keeps the organization on its desired course.

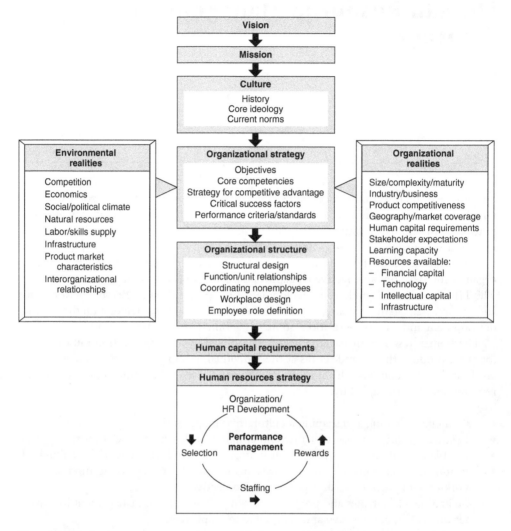

Figure 1.1 Aligning human resources strategy with the organizational context

Formulating an HR Strategy That Fits the Organizational Context

To ensure alignment with the context, several key characteristics of that context must be defined.

Vision/Mission

The *vision* of an organization defines the organization's desired future: the desired end state it is focused on producing. The *mission* of the organization defines the role it intends to play in producing that end state. The example below from the utilities division of a major city illustrates how the vision and mission might be defined:

Vision: (Our City) with reliable power and safe, clean water available to the entire population, contributing to a healthy, high-quality standard of living.

Mission: To generate and distribute power and to purify and distribute water to the entire population, reliably and in a cost-efficient manner.

The vision statement serves as a "magnetic north" that can guide the organization. It can provide a purpose for its existence and define what it needs to accomplish in order to be successful. The mission statement defines the role of the organization in making the vision come true. An often heard mission statement is "to maximize shareholder value." This unidimensional definition of performance may be defensible for private sector, for-profit organizations, and it is likely to be viewed as appropriate by the party at interest that is being served by this approach. On the other hand, if it results in short-term maximization of resource utilization it can jeopardize the long-term viability of the entity. Or, if it results in low pay and lack of job security for employees, the organization may be unable to attract and retain the workforce required to produce financial success. Therefore, it is critical to integrate how an organization defines performance with its mission.

The CEO of a publicly traded organization must pay attention to the external constituencies that have an interest in the well-being of an organization and in how it conducts business. Conflicting views on the part of these constituencies can make the mission difficult to reconcile. For example, Sam's Club has been criticized by the public and (more silently) by the government, for low pay and for not providing benefits to many of its employees. The organization is seen as too focused on shareholder return, at the expense of the employees. Its direct competitor Costco has been criticized by Wall Street analysts and shareholders, for pay levels that are too high and benefits that are too generous, which lower shareholder return. Dilemmas such as this are common for executive management when attempting to align HR strategies with business strategies.[1] The Sam's Club–Costco example demonstrates equifinality – that there are numerous feasible paths to success.

Culture

The *culture* of an organization defines how its members see the world; it is a function of their beliefs, values and priorities. Edgar Schein defined culture as how an organization resolves problems of external adaptation and internal integration.[2] Organizational culture impacts how members of an organization behave. The culture of the workforce is also critical in shaping employee behavior. A formal articulation of the desired organizational culture can help to align all constituencies. Below is an example of how key elements of the aforementioned utility's culture could be defined:

Culture: Reliability in serving customers and executing processes is the primary goal of all employees and organizational units. All employees will be expected to perform well as individuals, while contributing to the effectiveness of those they work with and to the effective functioning of their unit. Safe, reliable and affordable services are the primary measures of effectiveness. Rewards and career progression will be based on competence and performance. Long service will be rewarded through recognition programs and company loyalty to the employee, assuming that they continue to perform and that they maintain the skills and knowledge required. Ingenuity and creativity are valued, as long as they are consistent with safety, reliability and cost-effectiveness standards. Individual contributions to the effectiveness of their unit and of the organization are valued and will be rewarded.

This summary leaves a lot unsaid about how an employee should behave when presented with a particular set of circumstances. But it establishes the importance of safety and reliability and commits everyone to valuing both service and performance, as well as committing the organization to adhering to established principles and values. It provides information about how performance is defined, how it will be measured and what will be rewarded. It sends the message that a "performance culture" is going to be pursued.

It is important for each organization to define and evaluate its culture to determine if it is optimal given the vision/mission and the realities it operates within, as well as the nature of the culture(s) of its workforce. Appendix 2 provides a process that enables an organization to define and evaluate its culture. It also addresses issues associated with the workforce culture, specifically occupational mix and generational mix.

Environmental Realities

The *environmental realities* faced by an organization at a given point in time should be considered when formulating its strategy. The economic, market, social/political, legal and competitive conditions will play a major part in determining the feasible approaches to accomplishing organizational objectives. For example, organizations attempting to use contingent incentive compensation awards to motivate employees worldwide may find that in some places the approach is not accepted, or even legal. And the condition of the infrastructure needed to support operations may render an otherwise attractive strategy impossible to execute. Failure to perform regular environmental scans and to consider their impact on the organizational and human resources strategies can be a recipe for disaster, particularly if operations are dispersed globally.

The environmental realities must be identified and their impact assessed. An example of a summary of environmental realities for the aforementioned utility might be:

> *Environmental realities*: Governmental support is available to provide long-term capital for constructing the necessary power generation and distribution and water purification, processing and distribution infrastructure. Private capital is available at premium rates. Major corporations may have their own facilities to provide their power. Utilities from other areas are free to provide alternative power sources owing to deregulation. Regulatory control precludes denying power or water based on consumer ability to pay, and customer dissatisfaction will subject the organization to scrutiny by regulatory bodies. Environmental impact of operations will be monitored by public and private agencies.

A summary of environmental forces identifies the critical realities faced by the organization and assesses their impact both on strategy and on how operations are conducted. It is important to ensure that how an organization defines, measures and rewards performance is reasonable when externalities are considered. Setting performance objectives that require being first or second in every business may work for General Electric, but would not be believable for a minor player in an industry, which lacks the resources to achieve the average performance level of competitors. Obviously unattainable performance standards would not motivate the workforce, instead promoting a sense of futility.

Another environmental reality that has become critical for many organizations over the last decade is the availability of critical skills. As technology races forward in areas like data analytics, cyber security, artificial intelligence and machine learning a severe shortage in data scientists and other related occupations has been created. Much like the desperate shortage of network IT personnel in the late 1990s, due to Y2K, organizations have had to "rent" skills rather than buy. This has created a new challenge . . . how to deconstruct work into manageable modules that can be contracted out to people who are not employees. Talent platforms have come on the scene (UpWork, Top Coder and the like) that offer to find the needed skills and to connect talent to organizations to perform short-term projects. In order to compete for the best contractors an organization must brand itself as a desirable entity to do business with, much the same as it does when attracting employees. Contracts must be designed that will attract talent and offer them rewards that are viewed as fair, competitive and appropriate. This is a much different challenge than employing talent on a longer-term basis. And yet another challenge involves integrating what is done by employees and contractors, to ensure the units are compatible and work together to produce the desired result.

Organizational Realities

The *organizational realities* existing at a given point in time will also have a critical impact on what the strategy can be, how it can be executed and what performance levels are achievable. The characteristics of the organization and its business(es) will be dynamic, as will the resources it has available. As organizations grow it becomes increasingly critical to formulate policies and systems that will enable the growth to be controlled. The human capital requirements are particularly relevant to the human resource management strategy. It does little good to build a state-of-the-art microchip plant if the available workforce does not have the knowledge, skills and abilities to operate it effectively.

The SWOT model addresses organizational realities by identifying strengths and weaknesses, providing the guidance to ensure the strategy employed builds on strengths and minimizes the impact of weaknesses. Using the aforementioned utility as an example again, a summary of internal realities might be as follows:

> *Organizational realities*: Adequate technological knowledge exists within the workforce to operate and maintain the facilities and supporting systems. Outside engineering, consulting resources are available for design work exceeding the existing skills and staffing levels, partially funded by governmental agencies. Operating capital meets minimally acceptable levels. The current workforce is resistant to a major infusion of technology if it results in reduction of jobs. Over one-half of the workforce is in need of continuing training in new technology. Employees believe they are entitled to continued employment and annual adjustments to pay levels.

When performance criteria and standards are developed it is critical to demonstrate that they are achievable and that existing realities have been considered. It is also critical to ensure that the rewards that go with various performance levels are reasonable and competitive.

Strategy

Once the vision and mission of the organization have been established, the culture defined and the environmental and organizational realities identified, the next step is to formulate a strategy that will enable the organization to achieve its objectives. Successful organizations concern themselves with both *comparative advantage* and *competitive advantage*. *Comparative advantage* is determined by evaluating what the organization is best at and where it should focus its resources (e.g., build high-quality products that customers will purchase, based on quality rather than on price vs. be a low-cost provider of lesser-quality products). In order to test the feasibility of a strategy the core capabilities required for successful execution of the strategy must be defined and the existing capabilities assessed. Many strategies are not implemented because organizations are not capable of doing what is needed, so it is critical to realistically assess the feasibility of adopting a strategy.

Once core capabilities have been identified and their existence confirmed, the next step is to decide how they will be deployed to produce a *competitive advantage*. The critical success factors must be identified and the appropriate performance criteria and standards defined. One of the critical prerequisites for producing motivation and alignment in the workforce is a clear definition of what is needed and a clear understanding by each person or unit of how they must act to facilitate attainment of the organization's objectives. Using our utility example once again, a summary of the strategy might read as follows:

> *Strategy*: To be the preferred provider of power and water for commercial organizations, by providing more peak capacity than they can afford, and by demonstrating superior reliability. Lower rates will be charged consumers and will be funded by the ability to charge higher commercial rates, as well as government subsidies for low-income customers. Localized distribution of power will be done by cooperatives who purchase power and collect income from customers. Water will be controlled from collection to distribution. Maintenance functions will be centralized and available to cooperatives on a contractor fee basis. The competitive advantage of the organization will be gained through operational excellence, which requires efficiency, reliability and speed.

Unfortunately, many organizations decide their strategy is "to be better than everyone at everything." It is unlikely that all other organizations are so inept that such an approach is possible. This definition of strategy can cause resources to be applied in a dispersed fashion, often rendering the organization ineffective at everything. The most popular strategic management models mandate that an organization make choices about where the focus will be and where excellence is required. The Treacy and Wiersema model[3] presents three alternatives: operational excellence, product leadership or customer intimacy. This model mandates that choices be made between them. Although an organization must be at least competent in all three it should seek primary competitive advantage by emphasizing one. Once the choice is made the strategy will provide direction to those formulating a human resource management strategy.

An Operational Excellence strategy has led Walmart to identify their key occupations as logistics and information management, while a Customer Intimacy strategy leads "competitor" Nordstrom to put customer service personnel at the top of their list.

Another competitor, Costco, may try to be an innovator by providing a more limited selection of high-quality products, priced between Walmart and Nordstrom. By identifying which functions are critical to the successful execution of strategy, an organization can focus its resources when staffing, developing and rewarding those people who will have the largest impact on organizational success. The selection of an Operational Excellence strategy by the utility being used as an example helps to provide a focus for allocating resources, particularly those related to the workforce.

Structure

The *organizational structure* is directly related to strategy execution. The structure is the architecture of the organization and must be reflected in the human resource management strategy, since it defines the roles of functions/units and employees and also the relationships between the parts of the organization. Much has been written about the end of hierarchy and the emergence of the "network" organization—a parallel to the way information technology has evolved over the last two decades. However, some would argue that there is still room for well-defined, hierarchical structures, particularly when reliability is a primary focus. The description of the utility's philosophy relative to structure might be:

> *Structure*: Staff functions will be centralized and be outsourced when cost and quality dictate. Power generation, power distribution and water/waste water purification and distribution organizational units will be centralized and be fully staffed by permanent employees. Teams will be utilized for field maintenance and construction.

Although this sounds very "Roman legion-ish" and out of date in today's world, one might consider the impact on the population if the utility moved to self-directed work teams focused on ingenuity and operating autonomously. Failure to integrate activities and to control operations closely to ensure they conform to regulatory requirements and sound practice could result in a lot of sick or distressed people, owing to unsafe water or an avalanche of power failures. Autonomy and innovation can certainly be valuable, but the degree to which employees are given free rein should be guided by the strategy and kept within the desired control parameters defined by the organizational structure. A software design firm focused on leading the way in new technology would certainly choose a structure that differs substantially from the structure of the utility used as an example in this chapter. Project-focused teams with fluid membership are apt to be the unit of choice for the software firm. In contrast, the utility is likely to use departments delineated on organizational charts, supported by specific job descriptions that establish the responsibility for critical tasks.

Structure is a major consideration in the development of the HR strategy, much as an architect's plans prescribe the type of materials needed and how they must come together in order for the entity to function appropriately. It should have a major impact on how the organization defines and measures performance.

A fundamental question that every organization must ask itself is what strategy will be the most effective for performing the work. Figure 1.2 illustrates the options for doing the work.

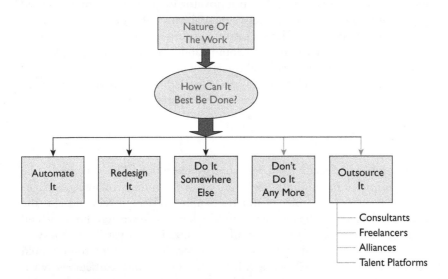

Figure 1.2 Developing a strategy for effectively performing the work

Some things can be automated, particularly if the process can be defined in algorithmic terms. If the "how" can be fully specified, automation may be able to do the work more efficiently and accurately. In recent years software has been used to assist physicians in exploring alternative treatments as well as diagnosing illnesses from data on symptoms. Payrolls have been widely automated and diagnostic models have been developed to do things like screen résumés to determine who is qualified to perform a role. Job design has a rich literature and the characteristics of what constitutes a sound job design are widely understood. Work can be performed in different locations more easily due to enabling technology, which opens the door to offshoring work to locations where qualified people can be employed at a much lower cost. But work may also be relocated to gain other advantages. Silicon Valley is a talent rich ecosystem that has attracted many organizations despite the high cost of living and of talent. The most overlooked alternative is not doing the work at all. Re-engineering re-entered the management literature a few years back with the message that organizations cannot afford to keep doing work if its value is less than its costs.

A last option is to have someone outside the organization do it. Chapter 11 deals with all types of non-employee sources. The emergence of the "gig economy" where already at least 40% of work in the U.S. is performed by parties who are not employees. This reality can raise major issues about the continued adequacy of workforce management strategies and programs.

Human Resource Management Strategy

The organizational context and the strategy utilized by the organization must be considered when defining human capital requirements. The human resource management strategy must be designed to produce a workforce that can execute the organization's strategy and do so in the organizational context. The strategy must enable the organization to staff operations with the right kind of people, develop those people so they are able to do what is required, define and measure performance in an appropriate manner and reward individuals and units based on results realized. The utility used throughout as an example might define its HR strategy by describing the strategy in each of the functional areas as follows:

- *Staffing*: Management and professional personnel will be hired based on their education and experience and their fit to the organization's culture. Newly graduated professionals will be from the top one-quarter of their class. Those performing permanent core functions will be hired on a permanent full-time basis, supplemented by contractors on major projects involving non-recurring work or non-core activities. If an adequate supply of the talent required is not available the organization may contract out work to be performed by people who are not employees. The impact of allocating work to "outsiders" must be considered, since it may negatively impact the morale of employees and lead them to believe that the "good work" is being farmed out.
- *Development*: Technical personnel will be developed using internal training programs, augmented by periodic formal education at external institutions. Management training will be provided internally, using a planned development curriculum. Staff professionals will be trained both internally and externally, based on need. Operating personnel will be trained internally, using structured certification programs and on-the-job training. Developmental assignments will be utilized to broaden the capabilities of selected employees and to enhance the career management programs.
- *Performance management*: The performance of the organization will be measured against established standards for customer satisfaction, operational measures and financial measures. Each division will have goals established and will be measured against them. Employee performance will be appraised annually, and their rating will drive base pay and incentive levels. Contractors will be evaluated by measuring results against established objectives. The level of performance by a contractor will impact the likelihood of the person being used in the future.
- *Rewards management*: The total compensation package will meet or exceed the average in private industry. Direct pay levels will be 10–15% above market for high-performing technical, professional and managerial personnel. This will be achieved by setting base pay levels at 95% of market average and providing incentive award opportunity of 15–20% of base pay. All other personnel will be paid competitive salaries, and outstanding performers will be eligible for larger pay adjustments and significant cash incentive awards. An annual performance-sharing plan will provide the opportunity for all employees to earn cash awards, based on organizational performance. The benefits package will provide adequate protection from major threats to their standard of living (illness, disability, pre-retirement death, unemployment and retirement). Defined contribution retirement plans will be utilized and benefit program options will be offered on a flexible basis, driven by employee choice.

Contractors will be rewarded based on contractual terms established in advance. Their performance level may have a direct impact on their current cash compensation and the relationship between performance and rewards may differ between employees and contractors.

This summary of the utility's HR strategy establishes its value proposition—it becomes its "brand" as an employer. The HR strategy must define how people will be selected for employment, how they will be developed and how their performance will be defined, measured and rewarded. From the organization's perspective the HR strategy must establish how its human capital will be deployed to support its strategy and to meet its objectives.

The integration of the components of an HR strategy can best be illustrated by an example. A mature organization with a long history of sustained success had maintained an HR strategy that was based on the following functional strategies, which were aligned with each other:

- *Staffing*: Fully qualified candidates were hired when the demand dictated.
- *Development*: Minimal investment was made in development; specific skill training was conducted when current needs dictated doing so.
- *Performance management*: Current results compared to established standards determined the performance rating.
- *Rewards management*: Pay levels were at or above market. Base pay rates and adjustments were directly tied to current performance. No equity or long-term programs were utilized.

The culture of the organization was one that supported treating employees as bundles of skills, who were rented for the duration of the need for those skills. Security was viewed as an individual responsibility. This strategy worked until there was a spike in demand for the products provided by the organization and by its competitors. This led to a huge increase in the demand for critical skills, creating a shortage of supply. The organization was unable to fill orders. Leasing temporary help, using contractors, enticing people out of retirement, substituting capital equipment for labor and other initiatives moderated the shortage but at great cost. Once the year-long demand surge passed, the organization rethought the viability of its HR strategy into the future. A new HR strategy was formulated that contained the following components:

- *Staffing*: People with the innate ability to grow were recruited into entry-level roles. If higher level work could not be performed by the current workforce in the short term the use of outside contractors was considered. The balance between employees and contractors was determined by the demand and supply of skills.
- *Development*: The investment in training and developmental assignments was increased for employees, accompanied by a commitment to continuously develop people. Workforce planning was initiated so that future needs could be forecasted and met. Development for contractors was considered when there was a shortage of available talent, with the decision being based on costs and benefits.
- *Performance management*: The singular focus on current results was moderated by an increased focus on employee competence, with more emphasis on breadth of capabilities. Development plans were linked to performance appraisals.
- *Rewards management*: The competitive pay posture was modified to position base pay levels at prevailing market levels and to provide incentives that delivered above-market direct compensation levels if organization and individual performance warranted it. Base pay rates were tied to skill acquisition for some jobs. Long-term incentives were used for management and cash profit-sharing plans for all employees. Contractors were given competitive contractual commitments regarding their rewards.

The new culture viewed employees as valuable assets that warranted investment. By investing in people the objective was to promote retention, so the organization could not be held hostage by ups and downs in the external environment. But when the use of employees to perform all work became impossible or not optimal contractors were considered as an alternative way to get the work done.

This organization moved from one HR strategy that had a long history of success to one that would produce better results in the changing environment. Both were internally integrated and rather than changing one thing (such as pay) to respond to a need the organization rethought all parts of the strategy to ensure that they would not work against each other. The ultimate folly is to change the parts independently: the result could be hiring for A, developing for B, defining performance as C, rewarding D, all the while hoping for E.

Aligning HR Strategies across the Organization

Increasingly, large organizations are composed of a number of businesses, which the organization desires to manage as separate entities, at least initially, if there are compelling reasons to do so. For example, if an organization acquires another in similar lines of business, but with a customer base that is loyal to the acquired organization's "brand," the acquiring organization may leave management in place and let that business set its own direction. Conversely, if the acquisition is aimed at merging the two organizations in order to gain economies of scale, integration and homogenization may be the order of the day. Banks in the U.S. have been going through mergers for the last several decades, and much of the attraction of acquiring other banks was predicated on the belief that they could reduce the number of branches and the size of the workforce while maintaining the combined revenue levels.

Very diverse organizations may continue to operate their different businesses separately. An organization the author worked with was an aggregation of businesses that seemed to have been chosen to maximize the contrasts between them. Management wished to formulate and administer a single overarching human resource management strategy that regulated how it managed management and professional personnel. The belief was that people who were moved across businesses gained a broader perspective and that those who could succeed wherever they were moved were the leading candidates for progression into executive management. This raised the issues of internal continuity within the businesses and in some cases made it very difficult to design and operate performance and rewards management programs that were a good fit to local contexts. An accountant or financial analyst in one of the businesses who was promoted into a slot that was now covered by a different corporate HR strategy experienced relatively dramatic changes in the way their performance was defined and measured and in the way their rewards were managed. This often caused major discontinuities in pay level, since an accountant who worked in the specialty steel business and moved to the poultry business would be at a salary level that was well above that of the new peers in the lower-paid business. However, the organization dealt with these adjustments, based on the belief that the integrated corporate HR strategy had advantages that outweighed any difficulties experienced. There was a development fund at the corporate level that could be used when the organization placed a highly paid employee in a business that maintained lower pay levels. The "excess" being paid the person being put on the development assignment was absorbed by the fund so the receiving division was not penalized.

Mergers and acquisitions present very large challenges relative to HR strategies. When Daimler and Chrysler "merged," the new CEO of the combined organization was paid substantially less than his new subordinate in the U.S. organization. Illustrating how global differences in culture can impact such combinations, the new CEO felt he was unable to raise his pay since it would be socially unacceptable in Germany. There was no reporting in the business press as to whether lowering the pay of the U.S. organization had been considered. Selecting a new HR strategy when multiple entities are merged can be accomplished by selecting one of three options. First, one of the HR strategies can be selected as the new common strategy. Second, the HR strategies can continue to be different from each other. Finally, a new HR strategy can be formulated, perhaps adopting the best features of the pre-combination strategies. Perhaps the most difficult challenge with any of these is dealing with cultural differences.

An insurance company the author worked with acquired another insurance company. The combination was a dream from a business perspective—at least on paper. The customer bases and the product lines were both complementary and synergistic. It was obvious to decision makers that the merged organization would be a much stronger entity on both the customer and the product dimensions. However, culture was considered only after the decision had been made. The acquiring entity was staffed at relatively lean levels, had competitive base pay levels and aggressive incentive programs and had a very "What have you done for us lately?" attitude relative to performance. The acquired entity was an overstaffed, happy family organization, with pay levels that were substantially below market, and performance was defined as staying with the organization for another year. The contrast could not have been more challenging if someone had deliberately chosen opposites. An appropriate and effective HR strategy was the key to a successful combination, and it took three years for the transition to the new strategy. Some people left voluntarily and some involuntarily, but the organization survived the transition because they laid out the culture, strategy and structure they wanted going into the future and formulated an HR strategy to fit that context.

Performance and Rewards Management

A successful HR strategy must result in the type and level of performance that enables the organization to meet its objectives and fulfill its mission. In order for employees to perform there are four prerequisites: 1) they must be able to do what is required; 2) they must be allowed to do it; 3) they must want to do it; and 4) they must know what "it" is. In order to facilitate the required level of performance by individuals and units, the HR strategies and programs must be appropriate, as described earlier. In Chapters 2 and 3 global principles for defining, measuring and rewarding performance will be addressed. In Part II custom strategies for different employee categories are discussed. Part III deals with managing performance and rewards.

The Implications of Cognitive Bias

There is one more significant challenge that must be faced when managing performance and rewards. People are prone to cognitive bias. This bias taints their perceptions and since their perceptions are their reality and they act upon their perceptions it is important for organizations to deal with bias. Over the last two decades a considerable amount of research on cognitive bias has been done by those in the Neuroscience and Behavioral Economics fields. The findings are convincing . . . everyone is subject to a number of biases. Being knowledgeable about the types of bias and the impact they might have is critical and it is important for management and employees to recognize they exist.

In excess of 50 different kinds of bias have been identified. The discussion here will focus on those which are apt to have the most impact on the way employees view their treatment by their employer.

Perhaps the most impactful bias is that people think they are better than they are. There is four decades of behavioral research that supports this. An example is the finding that if an employee is guessing their ranking based on performance in a group the median employee will believe they are in the 75th or 80th percentile. This has a very significant impact on the way an employee might view an accurate and fair performance appraisal. The bias makes the accurate rating seem unfair and since the employee's rewards are in some way tied to performance this has severe implications. It is not clear how much of the bias can be moderated if employees are made aware of the research . . . they might easily assume it does not apply to them. But it is prudent for organizations to make the attempt.

People are biased when they attribute outcomes to the causes. Research shows that employees tend to attribute success to their efforts, while believing failures are the result of uncontrollable external factors. Regrettably, managers who would be rating performance tend to be biased in the opposite direction. Again, when training employees and managers in performance management it is important to emphasize the importance of getting attribution right. If an employee's output is less than standard but was the result of a shortage of resources or an unreasonable deadline it is the responsibility of the rating manager to recognize that and consider it in the appraisal.

Another bias is the tendency to attribute a larger share of group results to one's self than is the case. Research shows that when members of a group estimate their contribution to an outcome their estimates will be closer to 200% than 100%. This is a variance of the "think I am better than I am" bias but is more relevant in team structures.

A significant misperception is common among managers when they are asked if they are providing adequate relevant and helpful feedback on an employee's performance during the performance period. The typical response is that the manager is providing adequate feedback, but the typical employee believes (s)he is unsure about how they are doing and what they could do to improve. That results in year-end blame often being assigned to someone who was not aware they were not doing exactly what is expected. There is also an issue about the type of feedback being given and how it is received. An employee who needs coaching but gets evaluative feedback becomes frustrated, since (s)he knows his/her performance is not fully satisfactory but does not know what to do about it. And repeating "you are just fine" does not meet the objectives of one trying to do better.

Another bias is relying solely on quantitative data rather than considering qualitative data when appropriate. When this occurs things that can be easily measured can take on an importance that is outsized relative to true importance. Managers often balk at making subjective judgments since they are more easily challenged by those with differing perceptions. Yet rating a Customer Service Representative solely on number of transactions completed without considering customer satisfaction may encourage employees to forget about an important part of their job.

People have a tendency to make premature judgments. First impressions often cloud perceptions of an employee's competence or performance. Although no one likes to admit it, tall or attractive people are generally judged more favorably and people that look like us or share similar interests are easier to judge positively.

When people do not know how others are rated or compensated they tend to believe that things are more unfavorable to them than they really are. Pay secrecy has a dark side, in that I will believe subordinates and peers are doing much better relative to me than they are and that superiors are doing worse. This impacts not only one's sense of distributive justice but also may limit career aspirations, since it is believed the rewards for taking on more responsibility are less than they are.

There is a tendency to underestimate the impact of national/ethnic culture on people's beliefs about what is fair and how things should be done. Often, U.S. managers are shocked when employees who originated in collectivist cultures reject pay being based on individual performance and prefer more egalitarian distribution. This issue will be explored in greater detail in Chapter 10 dealing with global workforces.

The tendency to accept information that agrees with what we already believe or that we wish were true more readily than conflicting information is a bias that makes managing people more difficult. This perhaps more than any other bias impacts our judgment when it comes to making evidence-based decisions. If we reject or ignore evidence that does not support our beliefs we are limiting our ability to make sound decisions. And this is impactful on many aspects of performance and rewards management. If a manager holds an employee responsible for something but the employee believes there was no way to control the outcome a conflict is created. Even if the organization does extensive surveying of market rates and establishes a competitive pay structure it is common for employees to disbelieve their pay range is appropriately competitive.

The fact that there is no known "cure" for cognitive bias means it is necessary that those who manage performance and rewards acquaint themselves with the research on the types of bias, anticipate how bias may cause difficulties and aggressively communicate their existence and that perceptions are distorted if they are.

Application of Principles: Chapter 1

An organization has sought your advice as to whether a change in their business strategy warrants changes to their human resource management strategy. The organization has been a low cost provider of software for routine business applications. It now wishes to develop products that utilize the newest technology and be first to market so premium pricing is possible. What implications do you believe this change might have on the effectiveness of the components of the human resource management strategy . . . staffing, employee development, performance management and rewards management? Why?

What difficulties do you anticipate during the transition from one strategy to the other?

Notes

1 Cascio, W., "The Economic Impact of Employee Behaviors on Organizational Performance," in *America at Work*, Lawler, E. & O'Toole, J., Eds. (New York, Palgrave Macmillan, 2006).
2 Schein, Edgar H., *Organizational Culture and Leadership* (San Francisco, CA, Jossey-Bass, 1985).
3 Treacy, M. & Wiersema, F., *The Discipline of Market Leaders* (Reading, MA, Addison-Wesley, 1995).

Chapter 2

Performance Management
Guiding Principles

What you *measure* and reward you most surely will get more of.

(Unknown)

If your people are headed in the wrong direction, don't motivate them.

(G. Odiorne)

One of the critical components of a human resource management strategy is how effectively and appropriately performance is defined, measured and managed. Getting the definition of performance right, at the organization-wide, unit and individual levels, is a key to aligning resources and people to achieve the organization's objectives.[1] It is also the basis for rewarding employees for their contribution to organizational success.

The first guiding principle of performance management is to define performance in a manner that fits the organization's context and its objectives. The definition of performance must also enable an organization to measure results and to compare the actual results to what is required. And performance must be defined, measured and managed in a way that is viewed as fair and appropriate by employees, as well as by other parties at interest. Performance management is a major component of the psychological contract entered into by the employer and the employees. If the employer defines performance using criteria that are unacceptable to employees, or if the employer sets standards that are viewed as unreasonable by employees, there will be conflict. That conflict can reduce the employee's motivation to meet the organization's expectations. Psychological research has found that self-serving bias causes each party to a contract to feel that they have fulfilled their side of the bargain completely, while believing the other party has not done so fully.[2] Employees will tend to attribute failure to outside influences and success to their own efforts. Managers are subject to viewing things the other way around. These biases are part of the human cognitive process and cannot be fully eliminated. But by defining and managing performance in a mutually acceptable manner an organization is more apt to generate employee commitment and motivation.

The definition of performance should specify the criteria used in that definition. And the measures used to indicate the level of performance must not be deficient or contaminated by irrelevant factors. An example of a deficient measure of product produced would be only to consider quantity, without considering quality. An example of a contaminated measure would be to include personality as a factor when appraising a back-room accountant who is not required to engage in interpersonal communication in order to do the job. The definition of performance must also be focused, to avoid an "everything is critical" message that diffuses employee efforts and creates more confusion than results. Individual performance is often defined at least partially by setting specific goals. One goal may be for the employee to do his or her job well, and this same goal can be repeated each performance period. There may also be goals established that pertain to the current performance period, such as installing a new piece of software or completing a segment of a project. Goal setting has been shown by extensive research to be effective in motivating improved performance when there are specific needs to be focused on.[3] The use of goals will be discussed in more detail later in this chapter.

Many believe that if something cannot be counted it cannot be measured. This is not true, since many critical results can be evaluated based on someone's subjective opinion as to how good they were. The preference for numeric measures is not misguided, but in some cases it is not practical. Evaluating how well a customer service representative dealt with a difficult customer often cannot be done by measuring only the result, which would be the level of customer satisfaction. If the customer is still dissatisfied after the representative listened respectfully, accumulated all the facts and correctly applied company policy, then the results were not good but the behavior exhibited was what the organization had defined as appropriate. And since the representative could control only behavior it can be argued that the person's performance was good. Judging the appropriateness of the behavior is measurement, albeit subjective. Southwest Airlines has always held that the customer is not always right and will defend an employee when customers are unreasonable and the employee behaved appropriately. By doing so the organization equates appropriate behavior to performance.

Another critical issue is the design of roles employees are expected to play and the nature of the contribution required from them as they fill the roles. Traditionally, roles have been defined as "jobs," which are a set of duties and responsibilities that remain constant over extended periods of time. The job of accountant can be defined by a written description, that specifies what that role entails currently. Job design has been the subject of extensive research over the last several decades, confirming that a well-designed job is an important precursor to effective performance. Job descriptions will consist of reporting relationships, primary responsibilities, duties and qualifications and sometimes performance criteria and standards. Employees are typically hired on the basis of their fit to the qualifications and they have their performance evaluated against established expectations. But organizations also structure work and assign it to teams, where individuals are expected to become competent in all duties performed by team members. One type of team is the project team, which is managed using a project plan. An accountant may work on segments of a project, either full-time for a period or part-time, making the incumbent's role different than the traditional accountant job temporarily, even though the person is doing accounting work.

Ensuring roles are designed and defined in a manner that fit organizational needs is a pre-requisite for effective performance management. Employees must clearly understand the performance expectations and accept them as reasonable and appropriate. If a job requires a wide variety of responsibilities it may be difficult to find qualified candidates. Long-service employees may reshape a job, picking up related tasks requiring a variety of knowledge and skills over time, making it difficult to find people to fill the job as it really exists. Although it is convenient to assign a variety of duties if they are very different in nature the job may become an inefficient way to get the work done. For example, if an engineer is assigned tasks related to project administration, such as keeping track of time spent by team members and the costs of materials, the person may be overqualified for some of the work, thereby unnecessarily increasing costs. The time of skilled people is expensive and if some of the work included in the job can be done by people with lesser qualifications and lower pay rates having the person do this work is inefficient. It also makes it difficult to appraise the incumbent's performance . . . if the person is a brilliant engineer but not especially competent at bookwork. Engineering work should be given more relative weight when performance is appraised. Managers should be trained in the fundamentals of good role design and also of sound organizational structures, so that they can organize their area of responsibility in a manner that is cost effective and that gets the work done efficiently.

Managing performance effectively is one of the greatest challenges faced by those responsible for doing so. Once performance is defined and measured it must be evaluated. And then the consequences of different levels of performance must be determined, communicated and appropriately linked to the evaluation. Much of the angst employees feel about having their performance appraised is due to their uncertainty about whether this will be done fairly.

Performance can be defined in terms of results, behaviors or both. Measuring results in quantitative terms has its advantages. It reduces the subjectivity required. But quantitative measures are not available for many jobs and in some cases what can be counted is not as important as what must be judged subjectively. Although measuring behaviors has been criticized, because of the subjectivity involved, behavioral measures can be used for most or all jobs. Besides, they can ensure results are produced in a manner that is safe, legal and consistent with organizational values. And they can take into account the amount of control an employee has over results. The results versus behaviors debate will no doubt be eternal. But in most cases using both where appropriate seems to produce the fairest and most acceptable outcomes.

Research has identified three aspects of "justice" (fairness): distributive justice, procedural justice and interactional justice.[4] *Distributive justice* deals with how appropriately evaluations and outcomes are distributed across individuals, even though an employee may also compare the appraisal result to what (s)he feels is fair. Equity theory posits that employees will compare their outcomes (performance rating, rewards, promotion and recognition) to the inputs they bring to the job (education, experience, effort and other qualifications).[5] They compute the ratio of their outcomes to their inputs and then compare that ratio to the ratios of others. They then judge whether they are being treated fairly on a comparative basis. For example, if all customer service representatives in a department are paid at the same rate and receive the same pay adjustments, those who view their qualifications, effort and results to be superior to others will feel distributional justice is lacking.

Procedural justice is judged based on whether the process used to arrive at decisions about distribution was fair and appropriate. Who made the decision and how they made the decision are both evaluated. If the employee feels the appraiser was biased, was not fully aware of the employee's performance or made poor appraisals then feelings of injustice will result.

Interactional justice is judged based on the communication received and how it was interpreted by the employee. The level of trust between the employee and the appraiser will also impact the perception of justice, as will the manner in which the employee was treated. If communication is inadequate an employee may feel they have been evaluated based on criteria that differ from what they were told would be evaluated. And if the employee does not know what entered into the decision this will typically result in suspicion about its credibility, and is likely to lead to the conclusion that the process was unfair. As equity theory suggests, employees will compare their evaluations with those of peers. If an employee does not know how others were evaluated relative to him or her a guess will be made and this will be likely to be more negative than actual outcomes.[6] Interactional justice is important because when it is perceived to be at high levels it mitigates negative employee reaction to distributive and/or procedural injustices.[7]

It should be noted that employee perceptions about justice will be their reality. If their perceptions differ from what is actually occurring they will still act on what they believe to be true. Cognitive bias plays a role in distorting perceptions and it is prudent to invest in communicating the impact of bias. Very few training programs dealing with performance management include a dialogue on the impact cognitive bias has on perceptions and this omission can widen the gap between what employees think and what is real.

In order for good decisions to be made when evaluating performance it is mandatory to define performance clearly in advance, ensuring the employee understands the criteria and standards that will be used to measure performance. There are four prerequisites for performance, whether by an individual employee or a group. The person(s) must: be able to do what is required, be allowed to do it, want to do it and know what "it" is. Figure 2.1 illustrates that the motivation to perform at the individual level is a continuous cycle, dependent on expectations, beliefs, past experience and wants/priorities. This model incorporates expectancy theory, goal-setting theory, equity theory and reinforcement theory, which are the motivational theories that have received strong support in research studies.

Criteria for Producing Motivation

Knows What "It" Is

The most important prerequisite for an employee being motivated is knowing what the organization needs and wants ("it"). The number one factor impacting employee satisfaction and effectiveness, according to the Gallup database dealing with this subject, is "knowing what is expected."[8] Research suggests that managers typically think their employees know what their goals and priorities are, but that employees often believe they are doing what they think is best, lacking a clear understanding of what will be viewed as good performance. In addition to knowing what is expected, it is also critical to ensure that employee efforts are aligned through common or complementary objectives, rather than disconnected objectives that may be in conflict with each other. Having highly motivated employees working at cross-purposes with each other is a recipe for chaos.

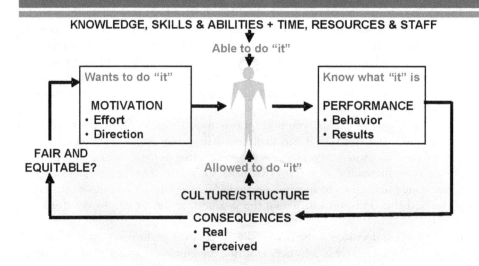

Figure 2.1 A behavioral model

Performance can be measured against performance criteria and standards related to the assigned job. It can also be defined in terms of specific objectives and goals. For employees with responsibilities that are recurring, the emphasis will be on how well those responsibilities are performed. An assembler on a production line may have only one criterion: do the job well. A design engineer may move from project to project, with his or her role in each varying. The engineer's performance may be evaluated based on results versus standards on a number of projects, with the standards being expressed as measurable goals (e.g., cost, quality, timeliness). There is a large body of work relating to goal setting, with Locke and Latham recognized as the principal contributors to the study of goal setting.[9]

A distinction should be made between objectives and goals. Objectives are stated in terms of a desired result. An objective might be "Improve customer satisfaction." A related goal could be "Increase the percentage of positive customer ratings from 75% to 85% or better." The characteristics of effective goals are many: they should be clear, specific, challenging but attainable, under the control of the employee and important. If there are multiple goals they should not conflict with each other and there should be relative importance weights established for each, so the employee can set priorities. The goals must be viewed by the employee as appropriate and legitimate, given his or her beliefs and values.

Locke and Latham also stress the importance of credible and timely feedback on performance against established goals, which not only reinforces what needs to be done, but also provides interim progress reporting. The feedback can also help the employee make any necessary adjustments to the methods being employed to reach the goals. This is particularly valuable when the employee is operating in uncharted territory and trying to find approaches that will produce the desired results. Goals must be time specific in most cases, even when continuous improvement is being pursued. The goals may be established in a participative manner or assigned by the manager, but if they are assigned Locke and Latham recommend explaining why goal attainment is necessary, in order to facilitate acceptance by the employee.

How goals are set (unilaterally assigned by the manager, set by the employee or determined jointly) can impact employee acceptance and motivation level. Any one of these approaches may fit a particular situation. If an employee must meet specific standards and the way in which this must be done is specified (assembly line worker) the goals tend to be set for the employee. It is rare for employees to set goals that will be the basis for performance appraisal without any managerial input. Given individual differences in knowledge, skills, abilities and self-efficacy this approach can easily result in a focus that is not aligned with organizational needs or not aligned with the goals set by other employees. Some degree of employee participation is much more common, since it facilitates acceptance of the goals and commitment to reaching them. But the approach should fit the nature of the work, the nature of the workforce and the context within which work is performed.

Able to Do "It"

If an employee lacks the knowledge, skills and abilities required to do what is expected, and/or is unable to exhibit the desired behaviors, that person will not be able to perform. Expectancy theory posits that if the employee believes the necessary knowledge, skills and abilities are lacking there will be no motivation to expend the required effort.[10] It is also important for the employee to *believe* he or she is competent, since a feeling of inadequacy will preclude expending the necessary effort. The term that is widely used in the research literature for this form of confidence is "self-efficacy."[11] It is therefore necessary that the staffing and development strategies result in having qualified people filling all roles and to ensure they are confident in their ability to perform at the required level. It is also necessary for the organization to provide the required resources to enable a competent employee to succeed, including the required training. Depriving someone of the time, staff, funding and support will trump good intentions and a willingness to expend the necessary effort. As already mentioned, employees will tend to attribute poor performance to external factors that are beyond their control, while raters tend to attribute that performance to the employee's ability or motivation.[12] This disconnect sets the stage for disagreement about whether performance standards are reasonable. It is critical that managers attribute the level of performance to the correct cause. There are guidelines for deciding whether causes are internal (attributed to the employee) or external (attributed to the environment).[13]

Past success or failure will impact the employee's belief in his or her ability and can influence the willingness to attempt to achieve a performance goal. Past successes tend to increase self-efficacy and make the employee willing to set higher goals. Past failures will have the reverse effect. And making the goal public can increase the employee's commitment to expending the necessary effort. If employees are treated as if they are capable of achieving the desired results it will positively impact their self-confidence and become a self-fulfilling prophecy.[14]

Allowed to Do "It"

The culture of the organization will impact an employee's willingness to expend the necessary effort and to focus it on the right objectives. A bureaucratic "follow instructions" culture will often prevent employees from taking the initiative and using their judgment on the job. Supervisors who are overly controlling cannot expect employees to take the risk associated with exercising discretion. This is not to say that anarchy is the ideal setting for high performance, but rather that the culture should fit the way the organization wishes employees to behave. Getting approval for large expenditures may be appropriate; requiring five levels of signatures may not. On the other hand, if legal issues are involved the five signatures may be required. And if organizations operate globally they should recognize that in some cultures employees are expected to act only with specific instructions from their supervisor, making "initiative" a questionable factor to use for rating employees.

Wants to Do "It"

Performance is a function of both ability and effort. An able employee will not expend the required effort if he or she is not motivated to achieve the desired results. Expectancy theory posits that the degree of motivation will be directly impacted by the probable consequences of doing something and by the desirability of those consequences.[15] If an employee believes that high levels of performance will not be recognized it is unlikely the effort required to perform will be made. If the consequences of recognized performance are believed to be undesirable or unfair the motivation to perform will not exist. For example, high performers often find that their "Outstanding" rating on their performance appraisal results in little or no additional reward. And equity theory suggests that if the others that a high-performing employee carried during the year get the same or nearly the same rewards this will create a perception of inequity and the result will be diminished motivation for the high performer.[16] One of the difficult challenges facing management is convincing employees that performance standards are fair on a relative basis. Employees are inclined to believe their standards are more demanding than those of peers.

In order to produce the desired performance at the individual, unit and organizational levels the performance management strategies and programs must support the overall HR strategy and must be effectively administered. But in order for the investment to be made in sound programs an organization's management must recognize that effectively defining, measuring and managing performance are critical to success. Management commitment to investing in sound performance management that incorporates a broad definition of organization performance is often difficult to obtain. Organizational "success" in the private sector has traditionally been equated to financial results, at least in most developed countries in the West. Western organizations are principally financed through the equity markets, causing capital providers to focus on the short term and to withdraw their investment if they do not like what they see in quarterly profit and loss statements.

And U.S. accounting principles exacerbate the difficulty of having human capital recognized as a resource. They treat any investment in human capital as a short-term expense, which reduces profit, and do not allow the organization to record asset value to offset that expense. Although much work is being done on recognizing and valuing "intangibles,"[17] making major investments in things such as employee development will be treated negatively from an accounting perspective, no matter how much it is needed for the future viability of the organization.

Despite the obstacles presented by accounting principles, the popularity of the "balanced scorecard" (BSC) concept has resulted in organizations becoming more aware that it is prudent to invest in the workforce.[18] The Learning and Growth measures included in the BSC model have furthered the cause of those who would have effective human resource management listed among the core capabilities of successful organizations. Further work on "scorecards" to evaluate human resource management programs is also contributing to the recognition that non-financial resources are critical to organizations.[19] The ultimate test of the importance of an HR strategy is whether or not good strategies contribute positively to return on investment.

Human resource strategies and programs can play a major role in facilitating performance. Table 2.1 illustrates how strategies and programs can impact the four prerequisites for performance at both the individual and the team/group/unit level. Defining, measuring and rewarding performance effectively are a key process, but must be supported by appropriate role design, selection and development, as well as a culture focused on performance.

One of the most overlooked aspects of performance measurement is that performance is likely to be uneven over time. This is due to the dynamic context within which individuals and groups work and to human nature. Individuals vary within a year, month, day and even hour in how productive they are and in the quality of their work. Everyone has good days and bad days. But measuring performance using an annual performance appraisal means taking an "average" of productivity, quality and dependability, in order to arrive at an overall rating for the administrative period. Supervisors who attempt to do appraisals only once, at the end of the year, face a daunting task—arriving at a rating that accurately reflects performance over the year and that is accepted by the employee as fair and appropriate. This point will be made repeatedly in this book, since it is so critical. *Employees must know what is expected and how well they are doing every day.*

Some employees exhibit a narrow range of performance, being relatively consistent in their focus, effort and persistence. Others exhibit performance that if plotted would look like a sine wave on an oscilloscope, varying dramatically in amplitude. How an employee whose performance is outstanding half of the time and unacceptable half of the time should be rated relative to an employee whose performance consistently meets standards is a difficult question for a rater. The nature of the work and how critical consistency is will have an impact on the answer. Some work requires consistency, while other work demands flashes of brilliance. But if interim measurements are not taken and fed back to the employee, the relative importance of consistency and innovation will not be understood by the employee, impacting the probability that the rating will be accepted. Behavioral research on motivation and performance is increasingly focused on performance over time, rather than in a static fashion, as well as attempting to consider intention, for purposes of projecting future performance.[20] Yet there is no simple way

Table 2.1 Impact of Human Resource Strategies/Programs on Performance

Prerequisite	HR Initiatives to Facilitate	Needed for Individual Performance	Needed for Group/Unit/ Organization Performance

Able to do it	Selection
	Placement
	Development
	Role/job design
		Right persons hired
		People utilized well
		Training adequate/timely
		Resources adequate
		Role design appropriate
			Interpersonal and conflict
			    management skins exist
			Necessary knowledge exists
			    within the unit
			Processes required skills

Allowed to do it	Culture
	Role/job design
	Nature of
	    management
		Support for exercising
		    appropriate autonomy
		Resources adequate
		Role design appropriate
			Group structure appropriate
			Individual roles clearly defined
			Roles integrated/not conflicting
			Oversight appropriate

Wants to do it	Rewards
	Recognition
	Culture
		Rewards tied to
		    performance
		Behavior and results are
		    both appropriately
		    rewarded
		"Heroes" are high
		    performers
		Intrinsic satisfaction
		    provided
			Competition at individual level
			    does not drive rewards
			Performance criteria/standards
			    do not conflict with norms/
			    values
			People experience intrinsic
			    satisfaction from group
			    success

Knows what "it" is	Vision/mission
	Culture
	Performance
	    model exists
	Management
	    communication
		Clear direction
		Values stated
		Objectives clear
		Performance criteria and
		    standards accepted by all
		Communication channels
		    open/feedback
		    provided continuously
			Clear direction
			Values stated
			Objectives clear
			Performance criteria and
			    standards accepted by all
			Communication channels
			    open/feedback provided
			    continuously

to translate a dynamic measure into a static rating. The best that can be done is to make performance measurement and feedback a continuous process.

Defining and Measuring Performance across Levels

A performance model that defines criteria and standards at each level should be developed by every organization. This process typically begins by defining what performance is at the organization-wide level, then at the unit/group/team level and finally at the individual level. A performance model enables the organization to define what it needs in order to perform at the desired level, and then to distribute the responsibility for achieving specific goals to units and then to individuals. This "cascading-down" process enables those responsible for achieving results at each level to assign objectives to subordinate units that will "add up" to success at that level. Figure 2.2 links the performance measures at the three levels to the key performance indicators associated with critical success factors. As with performance management strategy, performance measures must be derived from the strategy of the organization and what it defines as its core capabilities.

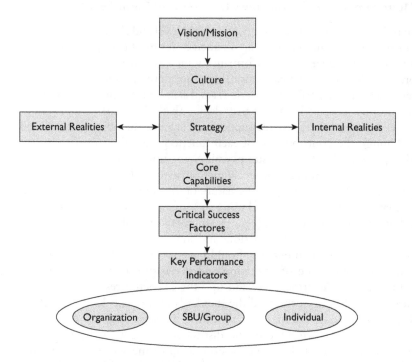

Figure 2.2 Performance management model

Performance management at the various levels differs in nature. Performance at the organizational level requires linking objectives to the strategic business planning and budgeting processes. Organizational measures have traditionally been focused on financial performance and total shareholder return, recognizing that the key constituencies focus on those types of metrics. At the unit level the focus is more often on operational measures, although financial measures are also commonly used. At the individual level performance may be defined in terms of ongoing responsibilities and activities, specific objectives, behaviors or a combination of the three.

Performance Management at the Organization-wide Level

As already noted, organizational performance has been defined more broadly in recent years, largely owing to the popularity of the balanced scorecard concept. Last year's financial performance will always be a critical metric for organizations. If it is not acceptable it threatens the viability of the organization. Yet there are two problems with measures such as ROI, EBITDA, profits and the like. First, they are historical in nature and may not give any indication of what is happening currently or what is likely to happen in the future. Second, they are focused only on past results and do not consider whether they have been achieved in a manner that is sustainable. The other types of measures used in the balanced scorecard model are customer measures, operational measures and learning/growth measures. The relative importance of each will vary across organizations, and the creation of a scorecard is an activity that must be customized to the individual organization.

Performance Management at the Business Unit/Group/Team Level

Unit performance is the next level below the organizational level and above the individual level. The performance criteria and standards are defined in terms of team, departmental, divisional and/or business unit goals. Unit performance is increasingly being defined using the balanced scorecard philosophy. Organizational measures are cascaded down to the next level in order to set specific performance criteria and standards for units. In order for an organization's customer goals to be met it may decide that sales, marketing, production, R&D and other functions must provide support and achieve the objectives assigned to each of them. Though the contributions of each function may differ in nature they should be aligned to produce the desired result overall. Some units will not have all types of measures. For example, the human resource function may be focused on measures relating to workforce effectiveness, owing to the nature of the contribution it is expected to make. Sales and marketing may be evaluated using customer measures. Production may be evaluated based on operational measures (e.g., productivity or quality).

At the next level below the corporate functions and strategic business units the divisions, departments and other defined entities should have specific performance criteria and standards related to their scope of operation and the nature of the contribution they are expected to make. It is critical to "add up" the expected results for each of the units, to ensure that if they are produced the standards of the next level up will be met. An example is the national sales manager allocating the sales target to the district sales managers, who would in turn allocate the district sales target to the individual sales representatives in each district. In order for each level to meet its sales target the level below would have to meet its goals in aggregate. And although the dollar sales may serve as the primary metric for determining incentive compensation, each level of manager would be likely to have other performance criteria that would be evaluated to determine their performance. Criteria such as effective introduction of new products, customer loyalty, developing sales personnel and the like would round out the scorecard for evaluating the managers.

Michael Porter was one of the early spokespersons for adding lateral measures into performance measurement at the unit level.[21] Owing to the interdependencies between business units and functions in today's complex organizations, it is necessary to manage horizontally as well as vertically. There is a need to integrate the activities of the various parts of the organizations, so their efforts are synergistic and do not conflict with each other. This is perhaps the most difficult type of measure to integrate into a performance model, since it is rarely possible to "cascade down" or "add up" performance targets when crossing functions and businesses. Yet integration is critical. One of the strategies is to ensure that functional and business unit executives have organization-wide performance as a significant factor in measuring their performance and in rewarding that performance. This is discussed in more detail in Chapter 4.

Performance at the Individual Level

Defining, measuring and evaluating performance at the individual level must be done in a manner that fits the nature of the work performed, the characteristics of those performing the work and the context within which they operate, particularly the culture of the organization and of the employees. In some organizations and in a number of cultures there is a belief that loyalty and service should be valued, and that acceptable contribution during the current year equates to a "Pass" grade in a "Pass–Fail" system. This is not necessarily a sign of weak management, since remaining with the organization, showing loyalty and doing what one is asked may be what the organization defines as what is needed.

It is also important to recognize that employees from some cultures do not accept differentiation based solely on relative contribution of individuals. Whether the employees come from different parts of the world and bring their culture with them or whether the organization operates in locations with different cultures the result is the same—diverse beliefs within the workforce. The cultural contrasts between operations in different countries (e.g., Japan and the U.S.) may result in debates as to whether performance should be defined at the aggregated or at the individual level. Cross-cultural issues are addressed in more detail in Chapter 10.

The criteria and standards used in evaluating individual performance tend to be much less quantitative than those at the unit or organization-wide levels. Often, it is the judgment of a supervisor about the quality of performance that is the only available metric. In other cases behavior is compared to rules and policies, and performance is defined as adherence to these directives.

> A bank teller cashes a check without following established policy and the act results in a loss to the bank. A tradesman follows the example of a seasoned veteran and bypasses the safeguards when repairing a machine, saving repair time and enabling the machine operator to operate it at higher speeds (unsafely). A software designer takes a shortcut by using old modules, causing the new software package to perform below standards. A newspaper reporter submits a story critical of a large company's ethics without adequately verifying sources, causing embarrassment when it was not warranted.

These are all illustrations of poor performance. How they are dealt with will determine whether the results are learning and improvement or demoralized employees who feel victimized. Many supervisors, particularly those without appropriate training, would chastise the employees in ways that will be perceived as personal attacks ("Your judgment was poor," "You must not care about the well-being of your fellow workers," "You do these things because you don't care about quality," "You just want to find fault with corporations," respectively). These reactions will not be likely to result in performance improvement, but rather will probably produce defensive behavior. It is also likely that the employee knows the rater has no idea of what they care about, making the attribution of poor performance to personal traits an attack on the character of the employee.

A manager trained in sound performance appraisal practices would deal with the teller by first establishing the *result* ("The bank lost money"), then attributing it to *behavior* ("You failed to adhere to the policy you had been made aware of") and then suggesting a plan that will result in learning (getting mutual agreement on why this happened and how it can be avoided in the future). This approach does not suggest that the employee's personal traits are deficient. It also makes it possible for the employee to learn, because there was no perceived attack on the employee's worth as a person. In addition, a trained supervisor would have made sure the employee knew clearly what the policy was governing check cashing so that the correct attribution is made as to why the failure occurred.

The production worker might be punished in some fashion for performing an unsafe act despite knowing better, but the seasoned worker must be dealt with as well. The software designer could also be sanctioned for inappropriate behavior (the more cruel approach would be to punish the whole team and let them handle the individual discipline). The reporter must be adequately trained in source verification and be made aware of policies governing accuracy.

Performance appraisals based on personal traits (appearance, judgment, etc.) unfortunately had a long run in U.S. industry and were the most common approach for some time.[22] This happened even though the method has had a long history of failure in litigation and had been shown to produce a negative impact on future performance. Trait-based approaches typically consist of a form requesting a series of check marks relating to personal traits, with no supporting comments to establish the linkage with job-related results and behaviors. They are generally used by organizations looking for a shortcut or failing to realize the importance of accurate appraisals. These organizations almost always will fail to adequately train evaluators in the objectives of performance appraisal and in the techniques for doing it successfully.

Employees can easily be provoked into challenging management judgments, particularly those impacting performance ratings, pay, career progression or personal reputation. Trying to make do with flawed instruments such as trait checklists is bad practice, as is turning loose untrained appraisers. Even if poor execution does not end in litigation, having employees feel their appraisals are unfair, unclear or personally indicting does not contribute to effectiveness. Finding fault with performance appraisal methods and processes accomplishes little, however, save to explain why managers often dread appraisals or view them as an HR plot to keep them from doing their job. The author recently read a book promoting the abolishment of performance appraisals, mostly to convince himself that he was open-minded. The proposition in that book was that appraisals could be made unnecessary by following a list of prescriptions that were provided. Any organization able to create the utopia they described would be successful beyond imagination and indeed would not find performance appraisals necessary. The author knows of no such organization.

Any performance appraisal approach, in order to be successful, must be guided by a philosophy that values both the employee and performance, must involve sound methods and processes and must be administered by skilled appraisers. It is also critical that performance appraisal be viewed as a part of the larger process of performance management and that effective performance planning and development are prerequisites for effective performance appraisal. It is typical for performance appraisals to impact pay, career progression, retention and other important personnel actions. Since appraisals impact critical decisions about people they warrant considerable investment to ensure they are conceptually sound and operationally effective.

Performance appraisal must be treated as a necessary but not sufficient part of the performance management process. Performance *planning* is the first step in performance management. It prescribes the criteria and standards (expectations) and communicates them so all parties to the process understand them. *Measurement and feedback* are the second step in performance management. They must be a continuous activity, beginning with the performance plan and ending when appraisal is done. *Development* is the third step and must also be continuous, attributing performance variation to the causes and taking actions to promote effectiveness. *Appraisal* is the last step—it determines what happened, why, and what to do about it, as well as triggering the administrative consequences established by policy. Appraisal also acts as the linkage between determining what happened during the last performance period and setting expectations for the next period, as well as prescribing what developmental actions are needed and the strategy for increasing future effectiveness.

In order to develop an effective system, all parties must first understand that appraisal is nested in a larger performance management system, with continuous looping (from planning to measurement/feedback to development to appraisal and back to planning). If the appraisal process is viewed in isolation it often results in the appraiser and the employee trying to reconstruct what happened during the year at the end of the year. This is too late to do anything about problems and it is almost impossible to have the parties come up with the same scenario. The two parties will almost certainly have different recollections of what happened and why. And the earlier mentioned bias that makes employees prone to taking credit for success and attributing failure to other causes will exacerbate the differences in the rater and ratee perceptions. So, if appraisal has not been a continuous activity throughout the period, engaged in by both employee and supervisor, it too easily becomes a "year-end blame allocation" session.

The mandatory prerequisites for effectiveness are: planning at the beginning of the period, continuous measurement, feedback and development throughout the period and meaningful appraisal at the end of the period. Without all of these critical elements employees are playing a game called "bowling in the dark." This game incorporates a dark curtain hung halfway down each alley, obstructing view of the pins. This simple change totally changes the experience—you roll the ball, it disappears, you hear some noise and the ball comes back, and you do it again. Players lose interest quickly for two reasons: 1) they do not know how they are doing; and 2) they do not know how to get better. Too many employees believe they are bowling in the dark, demonstrated by the high ranking of "knowing what is expected" in the Gallup poll[23] and the low incidence of employees feeling they receive the feedback they need.

Over the last few years the literature was flooded with stories of organizations that had abandoned formal year-end appraisals and replaced them with performance discussions during the year. This was a reaction to the research results that showed a large majority of appraisals were viewed as ineffective. But this "either–or" mindset is inappropriate. As mentioned earlier, continuous measurement and feedback is a pre-requisite for success. So a "both–and" approach is what is necessary. Formal appraisals provide a linkage between performance and rewards and they also establish a defense if there is a legal challenge that contends pay discrimination. It is unlikely that managers will keep complete performance "diaries" that document the discussions during the year, thereby leaving the organization with no evidence that pay actions were based on performance, rather than personal characteristics such as age, gender, race or how well the appraiser likes the employee. And it is difficult to believe that a jury will take the word of the appraiser that the employee was fully apprised of his or her performance continuously throughout the year and that pay actions were based on a fair assessment of performance. Poorly done performance appraisals can be a liability when an organization attempts to show that termination, discipline or the absence of a pay increase were warranted and were not the result of discriminatory behavior. So they need to be done well. But if appraisals are not done there must be complete and accurate documentation to demonstrate that frequent performance discussions have occurred and that employees have been continuously aware of what is expected and how well they are doing.

Many HR practitioners and managers believe finding the right performance appraisal form is 95% of the battle; experience shows it is more like 5%. The factors that actually have a significant impact on the success of the appraisal process are:

1   clear performance criteria and standards, which are related to the job/role and are communicated clearly at the start of the period;
2   adequately trained appraisers and appraisees;
3   continuous measurement and feedback;
4   developmental activities occurring throughout the period, to remedy poor performance and to build on good performance;
5   performance appraised based on job-related results and behaviors, rather than personal characteristics;
6   attribution of good or poor performance to the actual causes;
7   formulation of plans to correct poor performance and to build on good performance in the future.

One of the most overlooked or underemphasized characteristics of sound appraisals is the relevance of the criteria and standards to the individual employee. Relevance must be established from both the organization's perspective and the employee's perspective. There are performance criteria that vary from critical to insignificant, depending on the particular circumstances. For example, performing work in a safe manner may be a critical factor when appraising the performance of someone fusing explosives, while being relatively unimportant for clerical employees. Attendance for a software programmer working on extended projects may be important only if absences from the physical work site impact the project schedule or the progress of others. Yet attendance for an operator in a customer service center may be critical if absence results in a degradation of the level of customer service. And some criteria, such as ethical behavior, cannot be scaled from outstanding to unacceptable. In the case of ethical behavior, performing in a manner that is not consistent with the required minimum standards should be considered unacceptable . . . the rating should be expressed in a binary fashion.

Another consideration is how performance criteria or performance objectives are weighted, based on their relative importance. If an employee has five performance criteria and three objectives, the relative importance and impact of each must be determined in order to be able to combine them into an overall rating. Failing to provide clear importance weights results in less focused motivation, since the default assumption is that they are of equal weight. And priorities need to be adjusted to fit the current realities, which may result in the criteria and importance weights being adjusted during the performance period, in order to remain relevant.

Even though a manager defines performance expectations clearly at the start of the performance period, continuously measures results and provides relevant and useful feedback during the period and evaluates performance accurately at the end of the period the acceptance of his or her employees will also be impacted by their individual perceptions. A fundamental question facing someone responsible for appraisals is whether performance should be rated against established standards or against the performance or peers, or both. Ranking is a technique that bases an appraisal on how an employee's performance compares to that of others. When raking is used there is a danger of creating a competitive system and if cooperation and mutual support are needed there may be a conflict in the minds of employees. Should they focus on looking better than others, which can result in failing to help those struggling or in withholding their best strategies, which might improve the competitor's performance? Another difficulty with ranking is that if incumbents are not doing similar things it makes it difficult to make comparisons. Rating each individual independently on a performance scale is another approach. If four rating levels are defined, such as "Outstanding," "Significantly Exceeds Standards," Fully Meets Standards" and "Does Not Fully Meet Standards" an individual's rating is based on a comparison to those standards. But it is still challenging to define the rating level descriptors in a manner that makes rating reasonably objective, since interpretation can vary across raters. And employees often challenge a rating based on their own interpretation of the words. If performance standards are expressed quantitatively (number of units produced per hour or quarterly sales in the territory) this challenge is not as pronounced. But measuring "ergs of original thought" for research scientists may be a stretch. There will be further discussion in Parts II and III about the mechanics of performance management for the different types of employees.

In order to develop effective performance appraisals it is necessary to determine what they are to be used for. Performance appraisals should measure how well employees carry out the responsibilities of their jobs and/or meet their assigned objectives. Performance appraisals should not be used as the only basis for career planning and management. The best technician may not possess the characteristics and skills required to be a supervisor—and may not wish to become one. If the organization wishes to assess an individual's potential for other roles it is important to use a tool that will do that effectively. Trying to use the appraisal for multiple applications, particularly those for which it is not suited, will lessen its effectiveness in doing what it is designed to—measure performance in a defined role. Some organizations conduct two separate assessments annually. One is to measure performance over the defined period and the other to determine development needs and to do career planning. The first is backward looking and the second forward looking. Doing the two assessments at different times allows a better focus on performance and its consequences, separated from career planning and development. Performance appraisals can then focus on job-related results and behaviors, while the career assessments can examine personal traits and competencies and project how well they fit alternative roles. An employee who consistently performs in an outstanding manner may be considered a good candidate for promotion . . . but only if they excel at the things that will make them successful in another role.

Although it can be argued that the performance of every individual is important the reality is that some roles and some individuals contribute more to organizational performance. The concept of "return on improved performance" was developed by Boudreau[24] and is helpful in deciding how critical the contribution of different roles may be. Figure 2.3 shows the relationship between improved performance and value to the organization for two roles in a Disney park. The Mickey Mouse role requires adequate performance but is tightly controlled by a handler and rigid rules of behavior. It could be argued that rating the performance of Mickey characters should be binary . . . fully meets standards/ expectations or does not fully meet standards/expectations. But the Sweeper is also the customer service deliverer in the park, guiding visitors, dealing with their issues and the like. So every incremental improvement in Sweeper performance is apt to deliver added value to park operations. There are some roles that argue for a curve that bends sharply

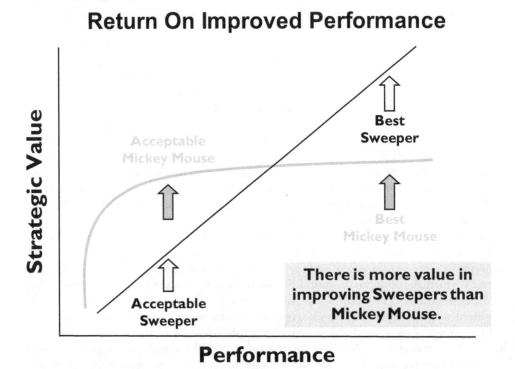

Figure 2.3 The value of improved performance

upward, indicating that each added increment of performance adds a greater percentage of value added. Bill Gates of Microsoft once stated that the best programmer was worth up to ten times what the next best programmer added in value. Recognizing the relationship between improved performance and added value for each role can help an organization decide how performance is measured, evaluated and rewarded.

Evidence-based Performance Management

Over the last few years, the practitioner literature has contained numerous articles on how workforce analytics, artificial intelligence and machine learning tools can be used to improve workforce management. As organizations recognize that data scientists are capable of turning data bases and other forms of information into intelligence about what happened, what is happening and what might happen this is going to continue. There is also a parallel body of literature on whether machines and technology will result in broad scale displacement of people, causing massive unemployment. What seems to be the consensus is that an increasing amount of work will be done by software. Whether this results in increased or decreased employment will be dependent on how organizations design and assign work. Algorithms are rule-based tools that enable software to do work that can be fully prescribed much faster and more error free. So any work that can be fully prescribed is certainly a candidate for automation. On the other hand, when judgment is required due to the need for flexible responses to complex situations, it is more difficult to routinize work fully. Direct customer contact interjects human characteristics into the arena and people do not operate on a perfectly logical basis. Experienced workers can develop heuristics, which are "rules of thumb" that suggest how a particular issue might be addressed. They are not fully prescribed and sometimes they are not useful if the situation has unique characteristics.

The "do it with people" or "do it with robots" decision is one that must be faced by organizations faced with competition. In many instances, if another organization can do what one does faster, more cheaply or better the chances are that the competitor will be the winner. And if using technology produces that advantage it is the logical choice.

During the 1990s a number of automated performance management systems became available. Some enabled a manager to check a box that represented the rating, which led to the system generating standard language supposedly supporting the rating. Some even inserted the appraisee's first name, an attempt to make it seem personalized. The difficulty with this type of automation is that it seems to relieve the manager of the obligation to provide job-related results and behaviors that supported the rating. Yet U.S. law recognizes job-related results and behaviors as the only valid measure of performance, and standard language fails to reflect what actually happened. Automating the record keeping aspects of appraisals can increase efficiency. Over automating can render the process invalid. A rating is meaningless without support for it. The narrative to support a rating should provide specific examples of how job-related results and behaviors impacted results, thereby providing a rationale for the rating.

Evidence that can be useful in managing performance can come in many forms. Appendix 1 addresses quantitative methods discusses statistical techniques that can be tools for guiding decisions. For example, if an organization implements a performance management system it must be concerned that equivalent (equally challenging) performance standards are applied across managers and units. Working with a large municipal utility with over 1,000 employees, I designed a performance appraisal system to support a move from time-based step progression of pay rates to a performance-based system. Before there were tangible consequences tied to ratings we conducted a "dry run" of appraisals. Upon analyzing the ratings we found that the Operations Director rated 1% of the division's employees "Outstanding," while the Public Relations Manager had rated 60% of that function's employees at that level. Although it is possible that both were applying equally rigorous performance standards, a decision was made to conduct extensive training that would equalize the difficulty of the standards applied by managers. This is not to suggest there should be a forced distribution of ratings across raters . . . that is arbitrary and no doubt produces invalid results as well. The same magnitude of difference was found across supervisors and managers under the directors. A process was implemented that required "calibration sessions" at each level. After all the supervisors reporting to a manager had done preliminary ratings the manager called them together to integrate the ratings with each other. Once those were reconciled the managers reporting to each director went through the same process. And the head of the utility capped it off by having the directors integrate their ratings.

It is not possible to completely eliminate the differences between raters in how they view a specific level of performance. But investing in a process to minimize distortions is one of the best investments an organization can make. The analytics enthusiasts would rate this type of treatment as mundane no doubt but there has not been any quantitative method yet discovered that would improve on it. And the reason is that performance ratings, although they might carry a numerical tag, are subjective judgments agreed to by relevant parties as the most acceptable. The perception that an answer is the best available consensus is the gold standard.

Another quantitative analysis that is relevant involves developing correlations between personal characteristics and performance outcomes. When Staffing selects new hires or employees to be promoted/reassigned they seek factors that can predict success. Validating selection processes and performance appraisal programs requires a demonstration that specific qualifications and personal characteristics are good predictors of success in a new role. U.S. employment law is used to challenge systems that produce statistically significant adverse impact on classes of people protected under legislation and regulations. The Griggs vs. Duke Power case produced the concept of "bona-fide occupational qualification" that states that selecting people or providing preferential treatment (such as a larger pay increase) based on qualifications that are not required to provide a reasonable chance of success are invalid. The fact that black candidates were rejected based on their lack of a high school diploma even though the company could not demonstrate that the diploma was a valid requirement resulted in a finding that Mr. Griggs had been rejected inappropriately but that ruling also set a legal precedent. Predicting what it takes to perform adequately in a job requires an in-depth assessment of the duties and responsibilities and deriving qualifications and hiring specifications that define the minimum requirements. It is also necessary to define what constitutes acceptable performance. The validation process almost always involves a longitudinal study, enabling the company retrospectively to assess whether the selection criteria were in fact requirements.

A debate about whether executive performance is highly correlated with organizational performance has been raging forever and may always be a source of conjecture. Organizational performance is influenced by many factors, including economic, political and sociological conditions in the environment and isolating just how much impact variations in executive performance have is difficult. Some organizational cultures emphasize that it takes everyone to create success, while others attribute outcomes to a few key people. If it is believed that the level of executive performance is critical for organizational success then it is critical that candidates for key roles be selected using criteria that strongly predict performance. The fact that a CEO candidate was a successful CEO at other organizations is certainly a form of evidence, but the degree to which the context at the new organization is similar to where the success was experienced should be considered. If the organization is facing the need to slash costs, trim product lines and restructure, selecting a candidate who was successful growing new/emerging organizations may be a gamble. And when past success was dependent on different things than future success the usefulness of background information on the candidate declines.

Many forms of evidence are anecdotal and lack hard data for analysts to crunch. And the expectation that the probable performance of a new entrant can be predicted with a high degree of accuracy is probably overly optimistic. What is important is to treat all data, all opinions, all forecasts and all experience as forms of evidence.

There is value in attempting to search broadly for relevant evidence to support performance management. Even though human judgment is needed to supplement quantitative evidence that judgment can be improved by combining it with objective evidence. Opinions of experts with extensive experience are valuable and become even more valid when supported by other forms of evidence.

In Part II the principles underlying sound performance management will be applied to various types of employees. Given the differences in the nature of the work performed, the characteristics of the people and the context within which the work is done it may be necessary to use different approaches to performance management. Alternatives will be evaluated for their fit to the local context and recommendations made relative to effective strategies.

Application of Principles: Chapter 2

The following is a description of performance relative to criteria and standards for an employee.

> *Productivity:* Employee has significantly exceeded standards established for the amount of work output. All work has been completed on time or before deadlines.

> *Quality of Work:* Quality of work has been uneven. Some work had errors that resulted in significant rework, although other work was of the highest quality.

> *Dependability:* Employee has been late or absent from the assigned workplace frequently but has been willing to stay past work hours when present and when activity levels were high.

The organization uses three rating levels when appraising performance: significantly exceeds standards, fully meets standards and does not fully meet standards. The employee is rated on each of the three criteria and then on an overall basis.

Would your ratings vary across the following jobs?

Voice Center Operator

Software Designer

Milling Machine Operator

Explosive Device Assembler

Accountant

If your ratings would vary depending on the job which criteria would be likely to be critical? Why would the nature of the job influence your ratings?

Notes

1   Lawler, E., *Pay and Organization Development* (Reading, MA, Addison-Wesley, 1981).
2   Rousseau, D., *Psychological Contracts in Organizations* (Newbury Park, CA, Sage, 1985).
3   Latham, G., *Work Motivation* (Thousand Oaks, CA, Sage, 2007).
4   Greenberg, J., "Everyone Talks about Organizational Justice but No One Does Anything about It," *Industrial/Organizational Psychology*, 2 (2009), 181–195.

5 Adams, J. S., "Injustice in Social Exchange," in *Advances in Experimental Social Psychology*, vol. 2 (New York, Academic Press, 1965).

6 Lawler, E., *Pay and Organization Development* (Reading, MA, Addison-Wesley, 1981).

7 Greenberg, J., "Everyone Talks about Organizational Justice but No One Does Anything about It," *Industrial/Organizational Psychology*, 2 (2009), 181–195.

8 Buckingham, M. & Coffman, C., *First, Break All the Rules* (New York, Simon & Schuster, 1989).

9 Locke, E. & Latham, G., *A Theory of Goal Setting and Task Performance* (Englewood Cliffs, NJ, Prentice-Hall, 1990).

10 Adams, S., "Injustice in Social Exchange," in Berkowitz, L., Ed., *Advances in Experimental Psychology* (New York, Academic Press, 1965).

11 Bandura, A., "Self-Efficacy: Toward a Unifying Theory of Behavioral Change," *Psychological Review*, 84 (1977), 191–215.

12 Bernardin, J., Hagan, C., Kane, J. & Villanova, P., "Effective Performance Management," in *Performance Appraisal*, Smither, J., Ed. (San Francisco, CA, Jossey-Bass, 1998).

13 Wood, R. & Mitchell, T., "Managing Behavior in a Social Context," *Organizational Behavior and Human Performance*, 28 (1981), 356–378.

14 Latham, G., *Work Motivation* (Thousand Oaks, CA, Sage, 2007).

15 Lawler, E., *Motivation in Work Organizations* (San Francisco, CA, Jossey-Bass, 1973 and 1994).

16 Lawler, E., *Pay and Organization Effectiveness* (New York, McGraw-Hill, 1971).

17 Lev, Baruch, *Intangibles* (Washington, DC, Brookings Institution Press, 2001).

18 Kaplan, R. & Norton, D., *The Balanced Scorecard* (Boston, MA, Harvard Business Press, 1996).

19 Huselid, M., Becker, B. & Beatty, R., *The Workforce Scorecard* (Boston, MA, Harvard Business Press, 2005).

20 Dalal, R. & Hulin, L., "Motivation for What: Multiple Dynamic Perspectives," in *Work Motivation*, Kafer, R. & Chen, G., Eds. (New York, Routledge, 2008).

21 Porter, Michael, *Competitive Advantage* (New York, Free Press, 1985).

22 Bernardin, H. & Beatty, R., *Performance Appraisal* (Boston, MA, Kent Publishing, 1984).

23 Buckingham, M. & Coffman, C., *First, Break All the Rules* (New York, Simon & Schuster, 1999).

24 Boudreau, J. & Ramstad, P., *Beyond HR: The New Science of Human Capital* (Boston, MA, Harvard Business Review Press, 2007).

Chapter 3

Rewards Management
Guiding Principles

What you measure and *reward* you most surely will get more of.

(Unknown)

Effective and appropriate rewards strategies contribute to an organization's ability to attract and retain the personnel they need and to motivate employees to contribute to the organization's success by performing at the required level. The total rewards package represents what the organization provides to employees in return for them rendering their services (commonly called total remuneration globally). It includes direct compensation (base pay and variable pay), indirect compensation (employee benefits), career opportunities and work environment. It is also a critical part of the psychological contract between employees and the organization and communicates to employees the value the organization places on the role they play and the contributions they make.[1]

Total remuneration represents a cost to any organization. For some it is relatively small. An oil refinery may have workforce costs that are only 1% of total operating costs. Organizations that are capital-intensive, like a refinery or an airline, can exercise more flexibility in how much they can spend on employee remuneration. Conversely, labor-intensive organizations, such as banks, may have remuneration costs that are 70% of operating costs, limiting their ability to pay employees at competitive levels. The author worked with a labor-intensive credit card processing center that was across the street from an airline reservation center. The credit card operation had reconciled itself to its inability to pay as well as the reservation center and recognized that its employees who were very sensitive to pay probably had employment applications on file across the street. When I conducted a salary survey in Atlanta, Delta Airlines paid substantially more than the norm, again due to the nature of its business, as well as a stated philosophy that people made the airline special.

Direct compensation is given that label because it is paid directly to an employee and is monetary. *Indirect compensation* (a.k.a. benefits) is paid into trusts or to insurers/governments and is therefore an indirect form of compensation from the employees' perspective. The other things of value an organization provides include both extrinsic and intrinsic rewards. Extrinsic rewards include, in addition to direct and indirect compensation, a secure and desirable work setting, as well as the full utilization of the employee's skills and opportunities to learn and to progress in one's career. Intrinsic rewards come in the form of satisfaction from the work and/or personal growth and are experienced by the employee. The organization can facilitate, but not provide, intrinsic rewards.

It is important for an organization to recognize that employees and potential employees will evaluate the entire employer value proposition when making decisions about joining and staying with the organization. They will also consider the total package when forming their opinions about how fair, competitive and appropriate their rewards are. At a strategic level organizations should consider everything provided to the employee and not make the mistake of treating direct and indirect compensation as totally separate things, to be managed by different functions, based on entirely different considerations. However, it is also advisable to consider the objectives to be served by offering each of the forms of rewards and to recognize that different forms are best suited to accomplishing specific things.

The first step in formulating a rewards strategy is to identify all of the components of the total rewards package that might be used and to formulate objectives the organization might have for utilizing each form of reward. Table 3.1 provides a list of possible objectives an organization might have for each of the forms. Organizations that do not go through this process of deciding what each component is intended to accomplish often find themselves with multiple plans aimed at accomplishing the same objective, objectives with no plans suited to meeting them and plans designed in a manner that renders them ineffective in accomplishing what the organization needs. It is also prudent to consider what objectives employees might have for each form of compensation and to consider that during the strategy formulation process. The two "wish lists" may differ significantly, so it is up to the organization to manage the tension between its objectives and those of employees in a balanced fashion.

For example, the organization may prefer a direct compensation package that contains a significant portion of variable pay, to keep fixed costs at a manageable level relative to revenues. Conversely, employees may prefer high base pay levels, to provide a stable income. The organization may prefer a defined contribution plan to serve as a retirement program, while employees may prefer to have a defined benefit pension plan. By defining the objectives for base pay, variable pay and retirement plans the decision about the relative mix of compensation forms and types of plans can be based on a strategy that is linked to both organizational and human resources strategies.

Formulating a Direct Compensation Strategy

Direct compensation is the largest cost component of the total rewards package for most organizations. It is typically one of the largest controllable operating costs and is the most visible to employees. Effective direct compensation strategies must contribute to realizing the organization's vision/mission, meeting the organization's objectives and maintaining the viability of the organization's workforce. They must also fit the environmental realities, organizational realities, culture, strategy and structure. Finally, they must be integrated with the organizational strategy, the human resources strategy and the indirect compensation strategy.

- *Contribute to realizing the organization's mission and to meeting its objectives*: It is critical that the direct compensation strategy supports and contributes to fulfilling the mission. Programs must support the strategy and must be designed in a way that encourages stability in key skill areas, provides incentives to perform at high levels and aligns employee interests with organizational objectives.

Table 3.1 Objectives for Components of the Total Rewards Package

Components	Possible Objectives for Component
Base pay	Provide standard of living consistent with market pay levels. Encourage growth in knowledge/skills. Encourage career progression. Reward individual performance in assigned role.
Short-term variable pay	Provide opportunity to earn additional direct compensation. Encourage teamwork to achieve group/organization results. Act as communication vehicle for business education. Reward results made possible by individual contributions. Make portion of total direct costs variable, based on results. Provide competitive total direct compensation opportunity.
Long-term variable pay	Retain key employees/skills. Encourage teamwork and focus on organization performance. Act as communication vehicle for business education. Provide incentive to perform in the short term in a manner that will result in sustained long-term performance. Provide employees a stake in long-term organizational success. Act as a vehicle for considering ownership when legal status makes equity participation possible.
Employee benefits	Provide competitive package to facilitate recruitment and retention of critical skills. Design competitive programs to best meet both employee and organizational needs. Protect employee income stream against illness, disability, pre-retirement death and retirement. Provide adequate time off.
Work environment/ career opportunities	Enable employees to work in a nurturing and stimulating work environment, enabling them to grow and feel secure. Provide career opportunities that enable employees to do what they do best, to fully utilize their capabilities and to pursue interests.

- *Fit environmental and organizational realities*: The political, social and regulatory environments impact the kind of pay system that is acceptable to key constituencies. The economic environment, including the supply and demand for critical skills in the relevant labor market, will have an impact on what the organization must pay in order to be competitive. And these two may be in conflict. For example, organizations converting their mainframe computer systems to client server network platforms may find the competitive rates of pay for specialists in this new skill area do not fit well with the pay rates for other employees, thereby raising issues concerning the employment of these specialists (versus hiring them as contractors or outsourcing the function). A hospital may find that the relative pay levels between medical professionals and IT personnel are causing dissatisfaction and feelings of inequity for the medical staff, who view themselves as being the people who are essential to the organization performing well. These realities must be accommodated in the direct compensation programs and in the way they are administered.
- *Fit the culture*: The cultural orientation prevalent among workers will impact their perceptions about what is fair, competitive and appropriate with regard to rewards.

Some national and occupational cultures emphasize individualism and applying one set of rules to all in the same way, while others believe the group is the dominant consideration and that rules should be varied according to the situation. Pay based on individual performance is dominant in individualistic cultures such as the U.S. and the U.K., but it is inconsistent with what people view as appropriate in collectivist cultures such as Japan and most of the Latin and Arab countries. Organizations that do business across country borders or that employ people from different cultural backgrounds must consider employee reactions to how they determine rewards. If they do not, they run the risk of having their programs viewed in a negative manner, thereby reducing their effectiveness in motivating performance and satisfaction. Occupational differences also warrant consideration when deciding how to reward people. Some occupations, such as engineering, focus on innovation and are project focused, while others, such as accounting, focus on consistency and reliability. This strains the ability of the organization to administer a single strategy that fits everyone. Some suggest that including audit personnel in a profit-sharing plan could provide motivation to produce the desired result (more profits), while the incumbents should be focused on the correctness of accounting procedures and their application, rather than becoming felons as a result of producing the desired result illegally. The behavior of U.S. bankers in the 2005–07 period resulted in disastrous outcomes for the financial system, due to ill-conceived incentives that created financial products that were deeply flawed but highly rewarding to individuals.

- *Be well integrated with the organizational and human resource strategy*: The way in which people are paid will impact the effectiveness of the staffing and development strategies being used by the organization. If the kind of people hired, the way they are placed and developed and the way in which they are paid are in conflict with each other, it will render the human resources strategy ineffective. For example, people hired for customer service-focused roles are typically hired for their interpersonal skills, and are trained to place the customer first. But if they are then paid based on minimizing the cost of customer service, the alignment of the functional strategies within human resources will be poor and results will be impacted. Call center operators can handle a large volume of transactions if they are abrupt with customers or if they do not take the time to get the information necessary to serve the customer. However, this behavior may be inconsistent with what the organization wishes to focus on.

In summary, the effectiveness of direct compensation strategies and programs is determined by how well they are aligned with the context within which they must operate. What works well in another kind of organization or in a different part of the same organization may not work the same way when transplanted. It is the responsibility of management to ensure that compensation programs support organizational success and are consistent with the personality of the organization, as well as being a good fit to the context.

Formulating an Indirect Compensation Strategy

Employee benefits exist to protect employees against the major hazards to their standard of living. These hazards include: 1) illness and the associated medical costs; 2) pre-retirement death or disability; 3) unemployment; and 4) retirement. Benefit programs may be government provided, employer provided as a result of government mandates or voluntarily provided by employers. Employers in the U.S. voluntarily provide a wide variety of benefits as a competitive device to attract and retain people. Since discretionary programs are an economic cost, the strategy should be to select those who provide a high return on investment. The "return" can sometimes be measured only in intangible terms, such as increased employee satisfaction. But research has shown that increasing employee satisfaction leads to reducing unwanted turnover. Increased satisfaction can also increase employee engagement, which tends to improve attendance and may improve productivity.[2] It is reasonable therefore to consider intangible outcomes as being a part of return on investment.

There is also the issue of "perceived value"—value in the eyes of employees. Increasingly, organizations are building employee choice in selecting benefit programs, in order to increase the perceived value that results from a given expenditure. Flexible benefit packages are created by offering all employees the same amount of money to spend on benefits and allowing them to select the mix of programs within the cost constraints. For example, all employees may be required to take the basic level of protection with regard to medical insurance, but allowed to select higher levels of protection by purchasing the enhanced coverage. Other options may include "selling" some of one's accrued time off and using the credits to purchase other benefits. Increasingly, organizations are utilizing employee total rewards statements, which are individualized. These statements communicate the economic value of all forms of remuneration, but employees are given the opportunity to create the mix of rewards that will produce the maximum amount of perceived value for them.

One of the philosophical issues each employer must face is whether the organization has a responsibility to provide some form of retirement income, beyond mandated contributions to a public retirement fund, such as social security in the U.S. The most prevalent philosophy, at least in the U.S., is that an adequate retirement income stream should be the result of: 1) the public retirement program, to which both employer and employee contribute; 2) personal savings; and 3) an employer-provided retirement plan. The employer-provided plan is funded by the employer, the employee or a combination of both. There has been a major shift in the type of plan that employers support, however. Until the last four decades the most common plan in the U.S. was a defined benefit pension plan, managed by the employer or by a union. There has been a dramatic decline in defined benefit plans and a rapid rise in the use of defined contribution plans, most often to control long-term liabilities and investment return risk. This shift has changed what is viewed as competitive relative to employer-funded retirement plans. The arguments in favor of defined contribution plans include the simplicity of administration (at least relative to defined benefit plans) and the limited liability the employer is exposed to. On the other hand, shifting from a defined benefit plan to a defined contribution plan shifts the risk that there will be an adequate retirement fund from the employer to the employee. And there is substantial evidence that the typical employee underestimates what will be needed for a comfortable retirement. This prompts them to save too little and to contribute too little to defined contribution plans, even when the employer matches contributions generously.[3] How paternalistic an employer is will impact the organization's philosophy relative to its obligations to ensure the employee's income stream is adequate. And its philosophy will impact the decision about replacing defined benefit plans with defined contribution plans.

A common practice relative to paid time off is to allow employees to roll over unused vacation and/or accrued sick days from one year to the next. In the U.S. a change in accounting practice some 30 years ago mandated that accrued time off be booked as a liability, impacting the financial statements. This caused some organizations to review their time-off policies. One approach, used by this author when reviewing policies with clients, is to ask what the purpose is for offering paid time off. The answer relative to vacation credit is that it enables employees to refresh themselves. But if the vacation is not taken then how is this purpose served? The answer relative to sick leave is that it enables people to accumulate credits when they do not need them, thereby having them available when they are. A major illness in a specific year may cause an employee to need more days than are accrued that year. But the practical result is that employees tend to view this as an entitlement and to augment vacation days by attributing the absence to sickness. The creation of paid time-off pools has been used by many organizations to minimize the need for the employee to have to lie about the reason for an absence.

Executing the Direct Compensation Strategy

In order to execute the direct compensation strategy, it is necessary to design programs that will support it. Base pay strategy will be discussed first, followed by variable pay strategy.

Base Pay Strategy

Base pay is the largest component of the total compensation package for most employees. The exceptions most often are direct sales personnel and top executives in organizations that utilize variable pay and equity plans heavily. Wages and salaries represent the largest controllable cost item for many organizations, and failing to manage them effectively is a sure ticket to poor financial performance. Base pay is also the foundation for total compensation, since it establishes the standard of living for employees. It serves as the primary indication of the value the organization places on the role an employee plays and on the contributions the employee makes. Employees often view their base pay as the measure of their personal worth by the organization, even though this is not intended. For this reason the subject elicits great emotion and is often the source of conflict between the employee and the organization. It is therefore critical that base pay rates are viewed by both the organization and by employees as being:

- internally equitable;
- externally competitive;
- affordable and cost-effective;
- legal and defensible;
- understandable;
- appropriate for the organization;
- appropriate for the workforce.

There are three primary approaches to determining pay.[4] The first, *pay for the job*, is based on the role an employee plays in the organization and how well they perform that role. The second, *pay for the person*, is based on what the employee brings to the organization, in the form of knowledge, skills, abilities and behaviours. The last, *pay for results*, typically is not delivered in the form of base pay, but rather utilizes variable pay programs to reward employees based on output. Results-based pay is most often used for sales personnel and employees focused on production of goods or services that are measurable in quantitative terms.

The literature in the compensation field seems to be on a continual search for the ideal answer, the one quick fix that will address the challenges of paying people in a manner that elicits their best and that attracts and retains the best people. This quest is, of course, futile, and the answer to "what is best?" is "what fits." What fits the organization (or specific portion of the organization), what fits the employees (or category of employees) and what is both effective and affordable may be "all of the above." Therefore, the compensation practitioner must understand all the approaches, assess the context and fit the program to that context.

Employees who have other employment options must feel that both their pay opportunity and their pay level are equitable relative to other employees and competitive with what other employers pay if they are to be expected to join the organization and remain with it. Most organizations develop formal structures as control devices to use in administering base pay. Pay structures consist of job grades (or "levels") and pay ranges, which are assigned to each of the grades. Jobs are placed into grades based on their relative internal value, and pay ranges are based on competitive pay levels. If employees feel they are inappropriately graded they will believe they are being treated inequitably. If they feel the ranges for their assigned grade are inadequate they will consider their pay opportunity to be non-competitive. Rarely do employees feel their jobs are graded too high or that their pay rates exceed competitive levels—and feelings of overcompensation can be easily rationalized away.[5] If they feel undervalued and/or underpaid, the organization will have a difficult time controlling turnover and sustaining high productivity. One of the most prevalent cognitive biases is that people think they are better than they are . . . against standards and relative to other employees. This makes it more challenging to get employees to accept their pay as fair and competitive, even when it is from an objective viewpoint. Another bias is that employees attribute successes to their efforts and failures to uncontrollable external factors. As a result, employees feel they should be rewarded for success and not penalized for failures.

Establishing Internal Equity

Most organizations use some type of job evaluation process to assign relative internal values to jobs. Ranking the jobs from high to low, classifying jobs into predetermined levels and scoring jobs using quantitative point factor plans are all methods used to develop an internal job worth hierarchy. There are numerous texts that describe the methods and processes available for this purpose.[6] Organizations that have considerable workforce longevity or that are predisposed to fill jobs through internal reclassification are wise to focus on equitable relationships between job values. Employees who are in the organization for extended periods tend to focus on internal relationships. As a result, job evaluation systems are used widely in this type of organization, particularly point factor plans that establish "scores" based on criteria relating to the skill, effort, responsibility and working conditions associated with each job. These four generic factors are a part of the U.S. laws governing discrimination and should be considered if the organization is going to be successful in defending its internal relationships between jobs. This is particularly important if jobs are gender segregated. However, this approach to developing a job worth hierarchy requires a significant amount of time for initial installation and for maintenance. Some employers create "internal labor markets,"[7] which are intended to have people enter the organizations only at specific levels, usually the entry level. The large public accounting firms have used this approach for professionals historically, as have consulting firms. And many organizations use this type of philosophy with their trades and operating jobs. For example, a utility may establish pay progression systems that do not increase pay solely on seniority, but rather use a skill-based system that rewards the attainment of competence and/or obtaining job-related credentials, such as licenses.

Pay surveys are widely used for determining competitive pay levels: that is their principal purpose. But they can also help the organization establish relative internal job values, particularly in smaller organizations where the number of jobs is limited and there is valid market data available. The first step in designing a market-based pay structure is to use survey averages for the jobs as proxies for "job values," which serve as the basis for assigning them to grades. The logic behind this is that the collective wisdom of all organizations as to what to pay incumbents of jobs is a credible basis for assigning them a relative value. Jobs are grouped into grades based on both their relative market value and the internal relationship between the jobs. Jobs of similar value are grouped together in the same grades and those with unlike values placed in different grades. Once the preliminary grade assignments are made it is prudent to evaluate whether these assignments reflect internal equity. If not, adjustments can be made.

It is also necessary to align the grade placements to reflect the specific characteristics of the organization. For example, one organization may value the legal function at a lower level than survey averages would mandate. This may be reasonable if higher-level activities, such as litigation, are outsourced. This might also be the case for its information technology function. As a result, the top legal executive and the top IT executive might be placed in a lower grade than dictated by the survey averages, to reflect the realities of the way responsibilities are allocated and to reflect internal equity. Internal values are a function of how *central* an occupation or job is to the primary business of the organization and how *critical* it is to the performance of the organization. Critical care nurses may be valued more highly than programmers in a hospital, even if surveys show the programmers command higher rates of pay in the market. If the organization differs significantly from other organizations included in surveys it may consider using a formal job evaluation system, since internal equity becomes more critical as the usefulness of market averages for grade assignment diminishes. It is necessary to consider both internal and external realities no matter what approach is used.

The number of grades in a pay structure should reflect the characteristics of the organization developing the structure. An organization might use more or fewer grades than is typical, depending on how hierarchical or flat its reporting structure is. The number of grades used for professional jobs will be impacted by how many levels the organization has defined in job families. A job family is a set of jobs involving work of the same nature but performed at different skill and responsibility levels. An example would be associate programmer, programmer, senior programmer and programming project leader. Flat organizations with few reporting levels and with few levels in job families might need fewer grades; more hierarchical organizations could need more. If jobs in Grade 4 report to jobs in Grade 5, it would probably be unwise to combine these two grades, even if the average market rates were felt to be relatively close together. Formal hierarchical levels should be separated in grade structures, to reflect responsibility differences, unless the organization believes the number of levels is excessive and needs to be reduced.

An approach called "broadbanding" has been tried by organizations, with mixed success. This approach uses far fewer grades and much wider ranges. Organizations using this approach have had great difficulty when they lack adequate managerial skill and budgetary discipline, since the ranges provide little control over salary actions. The principle underlying the creation of any pay structure should be that it *reflects and is consistent with both the structure of the organization and its culture*. If a structure with fewer grades and wider ranges fits the context then that approach should be considered. If the organization has a hierarchical structure the appropriate structure may elect to have more grades and narrower ranges.

Many organizations find that placing all jobs into a single pay structure is difficult and choose to create multiple structures. Some separate businesses that differ in the type of workforce they employ or in the way they structure roles. One business may require more vertical differentiation, while another may be relatively flat. There may also be a reason to separate occupational groups if the organization feels it must compete in different labor markets or the manner in which pay is administered differs.

Establishing External Competitiveness

Once the organization has created a job grade structure that reflects internal equity it can utilize prevailing market levels to establish pay ranges. Some organizations utilize a competitive posture that dictates setting pay range targets (midpoints) at average market levels. Others set them above market averages, in order to attract and retain the best people. And some may set them below market average, using variable compensation to make up the difference. Organizations operating in different geographic areas may consider a different set of ranges for each of their facilities, particularly for support personnel. The labor market for support jobs is local, while markets for management and senior-level professional jobs are regional or national. Consequently, it is common for organizations to have separate pay structures, with ranges reflecting prevailing pay levels in the relevant labor markets.

Survey data demonstrates the significant impact of organizational size on pay levels for management jobs. A hospital might use survey data from other hospitals of similar size (e.g., based on the number of beds). A manufacturing organization might compare with other manufacturing firms having similar levels of gross sales and/or that provide similar products. Although using data only from organizations of similar size makes sense for management jobs, it is also important to consider geographic differences in pay levels. A more refined basis for classification would be a special sample of survey participants who were of similar size *and* who were located in the same geographic region or in areas having similar pay levels. For non-management jobs perhaps only the local area data would be utilized, since the labor markets for blue- and white-collar support personnel tend to be local. For professional jobs regional data may be used for entry-level jobs and national data for senior-level jobs. Industry data might also be looked at, with no consideration given to organizational size, since programmers in small organizations do not necessarily make less than those in larger ones. The decision should be based on where people come from and where they might go, based on historical experience with hiring and turnover.

Pay ranges consist of a minimum, a midpoint and a maximum. The midpoint is considered to be the targeted pay level for people holding jobs classified within that grade who have full command of the skills required for their jobs and who perform at a fully acceptable level. The minimum and maximum represent the least and the most an organization is willing to pay for jobs in that grade. The midpoint is typically set at a level that reflects the average of the market rates of jobs within the grade, unless the desired competitive posture is to pay above or below market. The midpoints of pay ranges are most often determined by averaging the market averages for the jobs in the grade. Once the midpoints for each of the grades are calculated they should be adjusted to produce appropriate percentage differences between each of the midpoints. There is no "correct" midpoint difference, although it is common to have smaller differences in the lower end of the structure and larger differences in the higher grades, since each career progression tends to be more significant for managers and professionals than for those in clerical and operating jobs. Midpoint differences of 7–8% are common for support jobs, while differences of 15–20% are more common for professional and supervisory or middle management jobs. At senior management levels the differences are larger, often 25–35%, with the size of these differences determined by how vertical the reporting structure is.

The salary range spreads (between minimum and maximum) also vary. Ranges of 50% at the top, narrowing to approximately 35% at the bottom, are common. Spreads of this magnitude typically work out administratively, providing adequate opportunity for salary growth as an incumbent moves from entry-level competence to mastery. If the range is too wide, control over pay rates is sacrificed. However, if the range is too narrow, it is difficult to adequately reward those who distinguish themselves in their command of job skills and/or performance compared to expected standards. Each organization needs to make a decision about the width of its ranges, and culture will play a role, as will the manner in which pay actions are administered. Since the economy in the U.S. started to decline in 2007, salary budgets became much smaller than had been the case in the 1990s and the prior decade. A decade later they are still generally less than 3% of payroll. If ranges are 50% wide an employee starting at the minimum of the range may take eight to ten years to reach the midpoint in organizations that are performing reasonably well. In organizations that struggled for extended periods during the downturn employees may not have moved up further into the range at all. This calls into question whether range widths that were suitable when budgets were larger are still appropriate. If the use of variable pay increases, as it has been doing in many organizations, it could be prudent to tighten base pay ranges and to reward performance with a combination of base pay adjustments and performance cash awards. This would also enable organizations to limit fixed cost compounding and make it easier to deal with vacillating revenues.

Pay Rate Determination and Administration

Once an organization develops its pay structure(s) it must decide how to set and administer individual base pay rates within the ranges. There are many alternative approaches to administering individual rates. Some organizations believe it is desirable to differentiate dramatically between high performers and those who do not contribute as much. Others feel longevity should determine pay differences between incumbents of the same job. The approaches selected should fit the nature of the work, the workforce and the context within which the work is performed.

SINGLE RATE/STEP RATE PROGRAMS

Unionized organizations often make the assumption that single job rates or time-based "step rate" structures are their only feasible option. This point of view is frequently the by-product of the nature of the bargaining relationship, as well as the unwillingness of employees to trust management to appropriately administer pay based on performance. Union-free organizations also use time-based pay plans, however, because such plans are prevalent in their industry or in the local labor market. This practice is most prevalent in public sector organizations. There certainly may be obstacles to making performance-dependent pay systems effective. The biggest obstacle is that a sound performance management system must be in place in order to be able to pay for performance effectively.

The pressures to deliver high-quality service at a "reasonable" cost exist in most organizations in today's environment. Management often believes that people will not be productive when performance does not impact pay. When an employee's rate of pay is based solely on how long he or she has held a job, the employing organization will typically have difficulty controlling payroll costs and motivating employees to perform well. Under a time-based system, an employee must only survive on the job for a sufficiently long period of time in order to be paid substantially above the average market rate for the job. As a result, time-based pay raises costs without making cost increases contingent on the organization receiving the benefits derived from high levels of performance. It also sends a strong signal to employees that performance does not matter, which will typically send better performers elsewhere where they will be paid for their contribution. It encourages those who are left to play it safe and to maintain their membership in the organization above all else. Organizations that have been using time-based pay for a number of years often have most of their employees paid at the top rates in the schedule, which translates into a high-cost workforce. And even though their costs are high they may still get complaints from these very well-paid people that they only receive increases when the step schedule is adjusted. This situation is even more troublesome if a significant number of these employees are not performing well in their jobs.

Given these disadvantages, one might wonder why any organization would use time-based pay. There are reasons for doing so in some environments. Time-based pay allows an organization to predict costs with more certainty than does merit pay. It also avoids the difficulties associated with performance-based differentiation. Time-based pay works best under the following conditions: 1) when jobs require on-the-job experience in the organization to become competent; 2) when many jobs are repetitive and routine, with small variation in performance possible; 3) where a collective bargaining relationship exists and there is not a high level of trust between the union leadership and management; 4) when employees do not believe managers are able or willing to fairly administer a merit program; 5) when budgetary limitations and/or customer rate pressures require that costs are predictable; and 6) where there is concern about potential litigation and/or employee disagreement relative to performance appraisal ratings and the size of pay increases.

VARIABLE TIMING STEP RATE PROGRAMS

An organization that has a large percentage of its employees in jobs with short learning times and that involve limited performance variability (the kinds of job that best suit time-based pay) still has options for recognizing very good or very poor performance. The variable timing step rate approach incorporates a provision that allows managers to recommend double step increases or early step increases for those whose performance significantly exceeds standards. It also enables the manager to deny or delay step increases for those whose performance does not meet expectations during a performance period. Although this system provides a limited number of choices relative to the size and frequency of increases, it can help organizations acknowledge significant performance differences. It does mandate that performance criteria and performance standards be established and that individual performance be credibly measured using those standards. If a formal performance appraisal system does not exist, there is a danger that the option to vary the size of increases will be used arbitrarily or in a discriminatory fashion. The lack of sound measurement also leaves the organization open to challenge and even litigation.

A number of organizations have used the variable step rate system as a transitional device to move from time-based pay to performance-dependent (merit) pay. This is a way to phase into performance appraisal gradually, since only exceptional and unacceptable performance need be reliably identified. On the other hand, many organizations make it very difficult for managers to do anything but give a single step increase on schedule. Managers who attempt to vary from the schedule are often burdened with an additional mountain of paperwork and are made to feel like misfits. It does not take them long to revert to a de facto time-based system if this happens.

COMBINATION STEP RATE/MERIT PAY PROGRAMS

Organizations with large numbers of employees working in jobs with prescribed learning times but in which incumbents can vary performance significantly once the job skills are learned, may wish to consider an approach that combines time-based and performance-based pay. This combination program provides step increases to the range midpoint or job rate based on time, though there may be some variability, as described in the prior approach. Once the employee is being paid at the rate for fully competent incumbents, further increases may be subject to a performance test. The employee who is paid appropriately at the range midpoint/job rate and who performs at a "fully meets standards" level will have his or her pay rate adjusted only when the pay structure is adjusted. That employee will stay at the job rate as long as performance stays at that level. An employee who "exceeds standards" or is "outstanding" may move above the job rate.

This approach works well if the organization finds it difficult to differentiate between employees based on performance while they are learning the job. Once an employee is paid at the job rate, it can be argued that "fully meets standards" performance does not warrant increases above that level. It is assumed, of course, that the job rate is set at a level consistent with pay levels prevailing in the relevant labor markets and consistent with the organization's competitive posture relative to the market. On the other hand, those who perform at higher levels have the rest of the range available to them.

Employees whose performance declines below the level that justifies their current pay rate would receive no, small or less frequent increases, which would over time realign their pay rate to reflect their contribution. This is consistent with the philosophy of *paying* for performance, rather than *giving increases* for performance. If an employee is already paid at or above the level justified by performance, no further increase may be warranted. A disadvantage of the combination approach is that it necessitates effective communication about the "change in rules" when the job rate is reached. An even greater potential disadvantage is that it places considerable pressure on the performance appraisal system of the organization. Since something significant is now at stake, employees will subject the performance appraisal methodology and the process to greater scrutiny. Another consideration is the spread of existing pay ranges. If the prior pay system utilized relatively narrow ranges (30% from minimum to maximum, for example) the organization may wish to widen the ranges somewhat when adding the merit zone. This allows for most of the existing steps to remain steps and tends to minimize the perception that the organization is "taking back" guaranteed increases to pay. On the other hand, that may be precisely what the organization wishes to do, particularly if previous ranges were very wide and the top steps were at indefensibly high levels.

PERFORMANCE-BASED (MERIT) PAY PROGRAMS

A third option is to make the transition to a full merit pay program. A merit pay program utilizes pay ranges with no predefined steps within them. The range midpoint is typically the targeted pay level for "fully meets standards" employees who have a full command of the knowledge, skills and abilities required to perform at a satisfactory level. Often, there are also "penetration points" defined within the range for each performance level, and the rate at which any employee's pay rate moves to the target is based on that employee's performance. For example, only sustained outstanding performance will move an employee's rate into the upper quarter of the range, and those who have not attained full job mastery may be limited to the lower quarter of the range. See Figure 3.1.

The salary increase guide chart shown in Table 3.2 illustrates the philosophy underlying merit pay. It prescribes the largest increases for high performers paid low in the range and the smallest (or no) increases for those paid high in the range and whose performance does not warrant that pay.

Employees who perform well but who are at or near the top of the range often feel a small increase (as a percentage of pay) is not fair. But since that person is being paid substantially (e.g., 15–20%) above market and the organization has a right to expect high performance for the high rate of pay a small or no increase is fair. Theoretically, the organization has a right to ask for a refund if performance drops off, even though it is unlikely to attempt collection. Employees who perform well and who are paid in the lower part of the range should receive larger increases, expressed as a percentage of their pay, for two reasons: 1) they are attractive to competitors and could easily become dissatisfied with being paid below market; and 2) an increase of a certain dollar amount will be a larger percentage of pay for those lower in the range than for those in the upper part of the range (simple arithmetic). Compensation practitioners must make every effort to communicate this philosophy to everyone and to train managers in the administration of a true merit plan. A sound performance appraisal system is a key to successful merit pay programs. Another key is ensuring managers have the skills and knowledge required to appraise performance effectively. Much of the difficulty experienced in making performance appraisal effective is a result of under-investment in managerial training and employee communication. The lack of attention to developing a credible process and convincing employees that it is equitable also contributes substantially to failure.

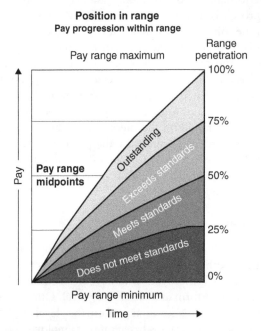

Position in range
Pay progression within range

Pay range maximum

Range penetration
100%

Pay
Pay range midpoints
Outstanding
Exceeds standards
Meets standards
Does not meet standards

75%
50%
25%
0%

Pay range minimum

Time

Figure 3.1 Progression within pay range

There has been a running debate for several decades about whether pay for performance motivates higher levels of performance. Edward Lawler, one of the most prominent researchers in the field, answers critics who suggest that extrinsic rewards diminish intrinsic rewards and therefore do not positively impact performance:

> It has been argued that pay for performance usually causes dysfunctional behavior and that people are not motivated by money, but by intrinsic rewards. Both of these arguments cannot be true. If pay motivates dysfunctional behavior it clearly affects behavior and must be important enough to affect performance. If pay were not a motivator, it would not prompt any kind of behavior, dysfunctional or otherwise.

Table 3.2 Salary Increase Guide Chart

Performance Rating	Lower Third	Middle Third	Upper Third
Outstanding	9%	7%	5%
Significantly exceeds standards	7%	5%	3%
Fully meets standards	5%	3%	0–2%
Does not fully meet standards	0–2%	0	0
Unacceptable	0	0	0

He goes on to say that:

> it has been reported in the literature that pay incentives cause employees to hide work, build the wrong products, optimize short-term profitability, cheat customers and give poor service. But the dysfunctional behaviors are the fault of poorly designed pay systems, not evidence that pay cannot be an effective motivator. Individuals do these dysfunctional things because, quite simply, their pay plans reward them for it.[8]

This viewpoint, supported by research, suggests that pay for performance will motivate behavior; what is critical is to define performance in a manner that equates to desirable results. One concern about merit pay is that in some contexts it may promote competition between individuals, rather than cooperation and supportive behavior. If the nature of the work is such that supportive behavior is required, more emphasis can be placed on contribution to the effectiveness of others or the unit when doing the performance appraisal that determines pay actions, as discussed in Chapter 2.

PERSON-BASED BASE PAY PROGRAMS

An approach that differs significantly from the options already discussed is "person-based" pay programs. This label is somewhat misleading, since an employee's base pay rate is not totally based on competence in the assigned role. Competence is important for purposes of classification. An engineer *competent* to perform at the highest level of complexity should be classified into a level in the engineering job family that reflects the level of work (s)he can do. And competence only establishes *potential to perform* rather than *performance*. So competence is used to classify the person, but performance will drive the individual's pay rate. So competence leads to classification into a pay range and performance leads to a pay rate within the range.

Person-based pay programs pay employees for what they *can do* rather than what they *are doing*. An engineer could logically be paid for the relevant knowledge he or she commands, even though for extended periods the work performed does not require these qualifications. A mechanic may be paid for the number of job-related skills he or she has mastered, even though some of them may be rarely used. The best applications of the various types of person-based pay are in units where: 1) the work is highly interdependent; 2) cooperative or supportive behavior is required; 3) flexibility of work assignment is needed; and 4) the skill or knowledge utilized is reasonably stable. Organizations using quality circles, work teams and other forms of employee participation find that employees tend to make greater contributions when they are motivated to increase their job knowledge and their skills.[9]

Care must be taken to ensure that relevant skills or knowledge can be defined and that mastery can be determined reliably before a person-based system is adopted. Particular attention should be given to the process by which competence is measured and to who makes the assessment. When skill-based pay progression is used peers and supervisors may find that saying "no" to an increase has a negative impact on morale, and they may decide to operate the system more like a seniority program. The organization must also ensure that a payback will be forthcoming from a multi-skilled workforce, since the average pay levels will typically rise as incumbents mature under the system. In order for productivity to be maintained there must be some offsetting benefits, such as lower staffing levels. A person-based pay system may not work for all occupations within an organization.

There was a great deal of discussion about "competency-based" pay in the late 1990s, although there was little actual adoption of this approach. The most common models attempted to develop levels based on behavioral competencies and then to classify individuals into these profiles. Two major problems presented themselves: 1) the criteria tend to be both complex and abstract, thereby making it difficult for managers to use them reliably; and 2) developing competencies that could be validated by tying them to jobs is enormously expensive. There should also be concern about paying for potential rather than for performance. Some highly competent people contribute little. Performance requires both ability and motivation.

Variable Compensation Strategy

An organization must ensure its total direct compensation levels (base pay plus variable pay) are equitable, competitive and appropriate if it is to compete effectively for the right people. Even if its base pay structure has been equitably and competitively established, the organization may find that competitor organizations pay incentive awards that make its total direct compensation levels inadequate. Market surveys are useful for determining total direct compensation levels as well as base pay levels, since this information is typically accumulated and reported. Most incentive compensation programs are designed using "target award levels." These targets are incentive award levels expressed as a percentage of base pay that will be paid for meeting the business plan or established objectives. Scales are then created that allow for incentive awards that are less or more than the target.

The pattern of incentive plan targets most frequently employed across industries is to have increasing amounts (as a percentage of pay) "at risk" in the form of incentive as one moves up from lower to higher levels. A typical profile would be to set the CEO's incentive target at 50–100% of base pay, top functional executives at 25–50% and directors or department managers at 15–30%. There are wide variations in actual target percentages between industries, so industry data should be looked at where appropriate. Also, one must be careful not to judge incentive plan design by levels reported in surveys in a given year. A more credible basis is to evaluate incentive targets for each job that reflect the "typical" or "planned" incentive award. The incentive awards in a given year can be impacted materially by the economic conditions prevailing in the organization's industry.

If an organization decides to set both base pay and incentive pay levels "at market," the differences between average base pay levels and average total direct pay levels from the survey provide a measure of average cash incentive awards. Market incentive levels for specific jobs may not align well with the grade assignments a specific organization establishes, because of the very different variable pay components for different occupations. For example, sales jobs typically have higher incentives but lower base pay levels than professional or management jobs. It is therefore necessary to consider taking sales jobs out of the base pay structure and placing them into a separate structure. This is discussed more fully in Chapter 7, which deals with sales personnel.

An organization may decide that incentive compensation does not fit its culture or that management is not comfortable with its ability to measure individual performance in a defensible manner, particularly with the pressure that a cash incentive plan puts on this process. That organization could elect to set its base pay structure at competitive total direct compensation averages and not use variable pay at all. This strategy has a downside, since it makes compensation costs fixed, rather than being tied to performance (which will impact the ability to pay). It also lessens the motivational impact of the pay program, since poor performance will incur, at the very worst, no increase, which is not much of a penalty if an employee is already paid at or even above competitive levels. Finally, it actually results in direct compensation that is more generous than competitive levels, since the total amount is guaranteed and in fixed cost form, while incentives paid by competitors are at risk, paid only if criteria are met.

Another organization may decide to set base pay levels significantly below average total direct compensation levels and to provide a large incentive opportunity. This strategy, if properly implemented, would provide below-market total direct compensation levels if performance is poor, at-market compensation levels if performance meets standards, and above-market compensation levels if performance exceeds expectations. Using variable pay aggressively does enable the organization to reduce costs when results are poor, but it also places a great deal of pressure on the performance measurement and incentive award determination criteria. Each organization must be sure that the risk–reward trade-off in the direct pay package is viewed as fair and competitive. Figure 3.2 illustrates these two contrasting strategies.

Another approach is to establish base pay and variable pay strategy in a manner that is tied to performance, using a form of "breakeven chart." Most organizations wish to tie total direct compensation levels to organization performance, which makes the rewards affordable. Figure 3.3 illustrates the range of options: all base, all variable or a combination of base and variable. For example, an internal auditor might have an all-base-pay direct compensation package, a sales representative might have an all-variable-pay (commission) package and a manager might have a package that combines base and variable pay. The manager would begin to receive variable pay after a certain level of performance was reached. He or she would make somewhat less than if on an all-base package if performance was below target but would make substantially more if performance exceeded target significantly.

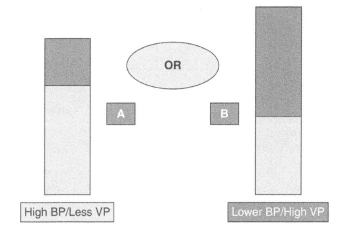

Figure 3.2 Alternative mix strategies

The organizational level at which performance should be measured and rewarded will have an impact on the types of incentives considered. If the organization wishes to elicit individual behaviors and/or results, then some type of individual incentive program would be the most feasible. If, on the other hand, work is of a highly interdependent nature or cooperative or supportive effort at the work team or organizational unit level is needed, then some form of group incentive program would be likely to fit the best.

There are different *individual incentive* approaches:

1   *Using cash awards to recognize performance, rather than using increases to base pay.* For individuals who reach the top step in time-based programs, an organization can still offer annual cash awards to exceptional performers and those who must be retained. This approach can also be used when base pay rates have gotten too high relative to some standard (i.e., market average) and must be controlled to prevent further escalation.

2   *Using cash incentive awards to supplement base pay increases for outstanding performers.* No matter how base pay rates are administered, it is sometimes desirable to have tangible, short-term reinforcement of outstanding behavior or results. Using cash awards enables the organization to bypass the established annual cycle of reward allocation and to make payouts close in time to the behavior or results being rewarded. For example, awards may be paid when a project is completed in an outstanding manner, deemed to be deserving of something beyond what the base pay administration program can provide.

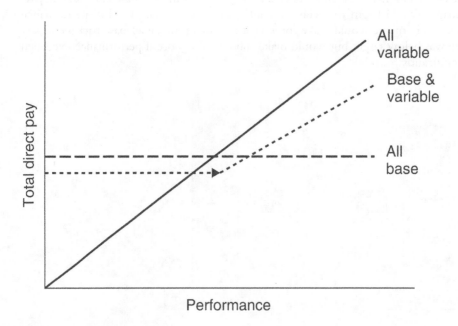

Figure 3.3 Strategy: total direct mix

There are also a number of *group incentive* approaches:

1   *Gainsharing*: formula-based incentive programs that use measures such as productivity or cost and that share gains with employees—such a system often works well in production operations;
2   *Cash profit sharing*: formula-based incentive plans based on profitability and that share a percentage of profits with employees—this system can apply to all employees and can serve as a "shared destiny" plan;
3   *Group/unit incentives (performance sharing)*: objective-based incentive plans that identify criteria, set standards and measure results against standards.

It may also be advisable to add some form of long-term incentive compensation to complete the annual direct compensation package, at least for the key executives. Several types of programs are commonly used, but they typically break down into cash-based programs and equity-based programs. Long-term cash plans are very similar to short-term incentive plans, except that the measurement period and/or payout frequency is longer than one year. There has been increasing usage of long-term cash plans in the U.S. since the early 1990s, but these plans are still not prevalent in some types of organizations. Privately held organizations often use cash plans that simulate how an equity plan would operate, in order to keep their total compensation packages competitive with those of publicly traded organizations.

Equity-based plans are of many different types and can be exceedingly complex in their design, but they can be categorized under three types. Purchase plans enable employees to buy stock, often assisted by the organization and sometimes at a price below fair market value. Restricted stock grant plans award stock to selected employees without any cash investment required of the recipients, although vesting in the shares occur only when time/performance thresholds are met. These plans are almost always limited to very senior executives (no more than 1–2% of employees in larger organizations). Stock option plans are by far the most commonly used equity-based long-term incentive plan; over 90% of the Fortune 500 companies use them. However, in the early part of the new millennium changes to U.S. tax law made the value of options chargeable against earnings, and a number of organizations moved from options to restricted stock or other types of share plans. Also, the economic downturns in 2000–02 and 2008–09 caused stock prices to plummet, making options unattractive, since their exercise price exceeded the market price. Restricted stock retains some of its value, as well as having retention power, so Microsoft and other human capital-focused organizations switched from options to restricted stock grants.

Equity plans have been popular because the equity markets in essence fund the gain realized by option holders. Additionally, gains realized at the time of exercise can be a tax deduction for the organization and there is a positive cash flow at that time. On the other hand, options have value only if the price appreciates, and there have been many tales of woe, particularly in organizations where this device has been overused. As with short-term incentives, each organization must decide whether long-term compensation plans make sense given its objectives and its culture. If stock ownership is closely held, the use of equity plans may not be possible or not desirable from the perspective of current owners.

A guiding principle is that what is rewarded is what is needed and desired. Variable pay can promote cooperative behavior among individuals and groups, but can also promote competitive behavior. Direct sales personnel who operate independently from each other are often paid based on their own results, and management often encourages competition among them. But members of teams who are specialists in different fields may be unable to deal with the challenges on their own, lacking the full range of knowledge and skills. This argues for encouraging cooperative behavior, which leads to rewards based on a team result. And if the objective is to create a "shared destiny" among all employees the level of measurement may shift to organization-wide performance, sending the "We are all in this together and each needs to contribute in their own way" message.

Indirect Compensation Strategy

Although direct compensation is the largest component of total rewards from a cost perspective, indirect compensation has become a significant cost to organizations and managing it effectively is critical. The U.S. Chamber of Commerce does surveys of benefits costs in U.S. organizations, expressing the costs of each component as a percentage of base pay. There are also surveys done by consulting firms that compare the benefit levels provided by employers. In order to decide whether the benefits package is effective an organization needs to consider: 1) costs; 2) benefit levels; and 3) the value placed on the benefits by employees. An employer may spend a lot of money on benefits and may spend it effectively, producing a high level of benefits. However, if the package provided to employees does not meet their needs, the organization will not get credit for its investment. Since the only reason for providing benefits is to satisfy employees, this makes it critical that there is alignment between what is given and what is desired. The enormous diversity in twenty-first-century workforces makes it difficult to provide a single package of benefits that fits everyone's needs. The traditional benefits package offered by U.S. organizations prior to the late 1900s was designed to fit a male employee who had a spouse who was not employed and 2.1 children. That profile fits a very small percentage of employees in most organizations today. As organizations began to realize that employee needs were becoming more diverse, the concept of providing a flexible benefits package became more attractive.[10]

Providing a "cafeteria"-style (flexible) approach to benefits involves creating a list of alternatives that employees can choose from to best fit their needs. If the organization allocates a total value of benefits it is willing to provide to each employee and calculates the cost of each option, employees can make choices from the available alternatives. For example, there may be multiple levels of health care protection available, each with a cost to the employee. This enables the young single person to choose the basic package and the person with significant family responsibilities to opt for a more comprehensive package. Another common provision is the ability to sell accrued vacation back, generating money to use on other more valued benefits. In theory, this maximizes the satisfaction of each employee while providing the organization with a method that controls cost. The variety of benefit programs has widened as more organizations have become comfortable with the administration required and as IT systems have become available making it possible to keep track of the variety across employees.

There has been a long-running debate about how an organization with direct compensation levels that are less than competitive and indirect compensation levels that are higher than those prevailing market levels will be viewed by job seekers and current employees. Will the total rewards package be viewed as competitive? That will depend on the relative value a person places on direct versus indirect compensation. Someone who places a high value on security and/or who plans to remain with an organization for a long period may view the low direct/high indirect mix as very attractive. Someone who values spendable income highly and who is highly mobile will view the package as unattractive. It is therefore incumbent on organizations to tailor the value proposition they offer as an employer to the type of employees they wish to attract and retain. In some countries the majority of benefits are either mandated by law or provided by the government, but in the U.S. the laissez-faire approach leaves employers largely free to decide what they provide.

The dramatic movement from defined benefit to defined contribution retirement plans was noted earlier. The increased usage of defined contribution retirement plans has presented a way to tie benefit levels to performance. The plans most commonly used in the U.S. involve an employer match to employee contributions, although some are totally employer funded. If the employer has committed to providing matching funds it is possible to make the terms contingent on organization performance. For example, the employer may guarantee a match of 50% of employee contributions up to a maximum of 6% of their base pay. If the organization meets its business plan it may increase the match to 75%, and if performance is at a very high level it might match 100% of the employee's contribution. Regulations and tax codes in the U.S. mandate that plans treat all plan participants in the same way, and there are limits placed on how much of employee contributions can be matched if highly paid people contribute considerably more than lower-paid people. The performance-based matching feature can provide additional encouragement for people to contribute, as well as focusing their attention on organization performance.

Non-monetary Rewards Strategy

Employees and potential employees will scrutinize the monetary rewards package to determine if they are being rewarded equitably, competitively and appropriately. But they will also consider the other terms and conditions of employment offered by an organization. As the economy becomes more globalized, job security has become an increasingly important condition of employment for many people. Although organizations often proclaim that employees are their most important asset, they sometimes behave as if employees were their most dispensable asset. Whenever economic conditions worsen there are widespread terminations in the U.S. (as in 2000–02 and 2007–12). Much of this approach to aligning costs with revenues is due to the fact that employees are largely a fixed cost. Most of their rewards package is in the form of base pay and benefits, both of which are difficult to reduce without violating laws or devastating employee morale. Employers with a significant portion of their direct compensation package in the form of variable compensation are somewhat better off, since they can credibly defend the disappearance of incentive payments in order to lower costs and avoid layoffs. But this is typically a very small portion of employee costs.

This is less true in some parts of the world. The author was teaching in Asia several years ago when there was an economic crisis. The students, who were employees of organizations there, disclosed that their organizations would reduce costs by reducing incentive awards, rather than reduce headcount. Since reducing headcount is generally less acceptable in many Asian countries, the governments are often willing to suspend employer and employee contributions to the retirement systems, in order to avoid downsizing. In addition, most organizations had direct compensation packages with a much more significant component in the form of performance-sharing plans than U.S. firms, thereby making their compensation costs more flexible. These realities made it much more possible for these organizations to offer relatively secure employment.

Intrinsic rewards can be made possible by well-designed organizations and employee roles. The Job Characteristics Index, created by Hackman and Oldham,[11] provides a model that can be used to design jobs that produce greater satisfaction. There has been extensive research that supports the propositions put forth, and the model is illustrated in Figure 3.4.

It is likely that motivation, performance, employee satisfaction and low turnover are desired outcomes for most organizations. The model posits that in order for the desired outcomes to occur the job design must produce psychological states that include a sense that one's work is meaningful, an assumption of responsibility for outcomes and knowledge of the results of one's work. The five core dimensions of a job that contribute to these psychological states are: 1) the job enables the employee to utilize the variety of skills possessed; 2) the employee understands how his or her work relates to an end result; 3) the result is significant in some way; 4) the employee is given appropriate autonomy to perform the job well; and 5) the employee receives feedback that communicates the level

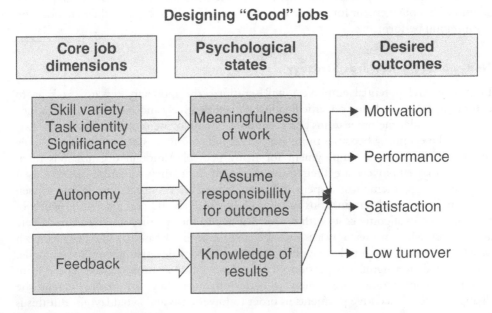

Figure 3.4 Designing "good" jobs

of performance and how it might be improved. Jobs containing appropriate amounts of these dimensions are likely to be more valued than jobs that do not, making it possible for the employee to experience intrinsic benefits from doing the job. The appropriate amount of any dimension can vary significantly across cultures and types of jobs. Autonomy is sought by most professionals in cultures where personal initiative is desired and rewarded, but may be found to be inappropriate in a culture where top-down control is the accepted way of managing.

The context within which the job is performed can be viewed positively or negatively and will in some fashion be factored into the employer value proposition when employees or potential employees make decisions about employment, engagement and performance. Jobs that involve hazards or adverse working conditions will be considered less desirable than jobs with a better environment. Although it is not possible to monetize job context, many organizations are willing to compensate people for working long hours, different shifts and in hazardous or unpleasant conditions. This can be done through differentials that are provided as a separate component of the compensation package. These realities may also be built into the job definition and reflected in the job evaluation process, by including factors such as hazards and adverse working conditions in the job evaluation plan. In the U.S., the Equal Pay Act mandates that employers consider working conditions when setting pay, in addition to skill, effort and responsibility. Other countries also have laws and regulations governing how these factors are considered.

Evidence-based Rewards Management

It has been commonly believed that the people in the Human Resources field who have well-developed quantitative skills belong in the Compensation function. Since workforce analytics have become widely used in staffing, human resource development and employee relations in recent years, the value of an analytical perspective has increased across HR functions. Compensation certainly does deal heavily in numbers. Yet it also involves the need for understanding human nature.

There is a tendency today to extol the use of data analytics, adopting the philosophy that if something cannot be measured numerically, it cannot be important. "Quant jocks" can dazzle with multiple regression models but it is also necessary to judge whether that is the right statistical tool and to know what independent variables to use in the analysis. The latter requires business acumen and an understanding of behavioral science principles. Much of the quantitative analysis used in rewards management is relatively basic. But the basics are still important. An understanding of the principles discussed in this book's Appendix 1 is required at the minimum.

One of the claims appearing in the literature has been the contention that paying above market average compensation to executives has a positive impact on organizational performance. This is a claim that is often supported by finding correlations between executive pay and organizational performance. But correlation is only a relationship and does not in itself establish causation. It might be that organizations that perform well have the financial resources to pay more . . . and boards are more apt to be generous when setting executive pay if things are going well. The direction of the causal arrow is as important as establishing correlation. Certainly, without correlation there can be no causation but correlation is only a necessary, but not sufficient, pre-requisite for causation.

The selection of "evidence" is critical when evaluating the effectiveness of rewards strategies and programs. But what constitutes evidence is a debate. Do opinions based on experience deserve consideration? Is intuition ever useful when deciding on how to interpret data? The answer is, "it depends." Those responsible for gathering and evaluating evidence are responsible for ensuring their findings and recommendations are sound and unbiased. If the analyst wants to find data that supports what (s)he believes or wants to be so a prolonged search will be likely to find some supporting evidence. This is so because cognitive bias causes us to more readily accept evidence that is consistent with current beliefs/preferences than evidence that refutes the desired outcome. The validity of a research study is threatened if the researcher does not state the hypothesis in advance of evaluating data. An extended "fishing expedition" in a large data set can usually discover relationships and these can be used to then formulate the preferred hypothesis.

One of the most common forms of evidence in rewards management is compensation surveys. When an organization wants to determine the pay levels among organizations that compete for similar knowledge and skills a survey is the most common technique used to gather that information. But selecting competitive organizations can be a biased process. There are large differences in pay levels across geographic areas . . . San Francisco and New York pay levels for jobs will almost certainly be significantly higher than those in the Midwest or less urban areas. Although it can be argued that pay levels for executives and senior level professionals should be measured based on national data, there are still differences in some large urban areas for a number of reasons. So the selection of data that will enter any analysis should be based on objective measures rather than the preferences of someone trying to prove a point.

For decades researchers attempted to find support for the hypothesis that increasing employee satisfaction would increase productivity. But although there generally was found to be a small positive impact, it was not statistically significant and thereby lent weak support. When the impact of increased satisfaction on attendance and turnover was researched, a strong positive correlation was found. This was certainly an indication that the level of satisfaction was important, albeit for different reasons. Yet increased productivity is a much more compelling result and often those who strongly supported focusing on improving satisfaction continued to promise a result not supported by evidence, at least when it was interpreted in a bias-free manner. This can present a dilemma . . . good things (attendance; turnover) happened when satisfaction increased, but not what was promised. Should those making the recommendation be rewarded for the good things or punished for the failed promise?

When formulating the rewards strategy, organizations must decide if they will use the same strategy and the same programs for all employees. It has been argued in Chapters 2 and 3 that there are common principles that may be applied to the rewards programs for all employees. But in order to design and administer programs that fit the varying contexts within which employees work it may be advisable to customize the strategies to fit different employee categories. Differences may be created by occupation, by geographic location or by business.

As with performance management rewards management has been evolving and workforce analytics, artificial intelligence and machine learning tools are increasingly being utilized to make better decisions. Since rewards management involves the extensive use of quantitative measures, it is understandable that the increased application of scientific methods has been occurring. The two areas where quantitative methods have been used are determining internal equity and external competitiveness. Job evaluation techniques of varying types are used to develop a relative internal value hierarchy, enabling organizations to classify jobs into grades. Analysis of market surveys has been used to measure prevailing market rates so that pay ranges can be attached to the grades in a manner that is consistent with the competitive posture the organization wishes to utilize.

The use of ranking, classification and point-factor job evaluation methods enable relative values to be assigned to jobs. Although quantitative models are widely used, the determination of relative internal value still remains a subjective decision. Point-factor plans utilize factor weights and scales to develop valuation models, giving the impression that users are being "scientific" in their scoring. However, determining whether a job requires a high school education and three years' experience is a judgment. Another user of the valuing model may feel the job requires an AA degree and four years of experience. It is common for organizations to use committees to reconcile different subjective judgments, hopefully producing the best consensus. During the 1970s, consulting firms attempted to promote the use of multiple regression models that were developed by replicating market values for jobs. By building the statistical model in this way the plans were intended to enable an evaluator to determine what the market would have paid a job even though there was no market data to apply. This was a way to value jobs that were unique to an organization in their design, a common occurrence. But in effect this approach makes the market the ultimate arbiter of value, rather than the organization's valuing system. For example, an organization may value specific work experience very highly and weight that factor more heavily than formal education, while the model had incorporated the market's higher valuation of education. An unfortunate reality is that if pay discrimination exists in the market it will be replicated in the evaluation method. Using a method that employs a gender/age/race neutral approach that is focused on the skill, effort, responsibility and working conditions associated with jobs can avoid importing past discrimination.

The difficulty associated with defending relative internal valuations based on subjective decisions caused many organizations to decide to let the market directly determine value. Underlying this approach was the assumption that the organization had to meet market rates anyway and that attempting to apply internal values was futile. Although this numerically derived approach seems more scientific and objective, two problems exist. It is unusual for an organization to price all of its jobs using market data. Due to the reality that an organization's structure and the actual responsibilities assigned jobs frequently creates unique jobs the match to survey jobs is problematic. For example, a research-based organization might use a five-level career management structure to classify scientists into grades while published surveys use three or four levels in their matching model. This results in the pricing process becoming more subjective, even though the model used is objective.

The second issue is that the data in surveys is based on a sample of participating organizations. If that sample does not contain the organization's major competitors for talent, the market values reported are not an appropriate basis for the creation of a pay structure that will position the organization in its desired position to market. Sample stability from one year to the next can also be a challenge, particularly in turbulent economic conditions.

Beginning in 2008, a major shift in samples occurred in most of the respected surveys. Because many organizations faced a severe economic downturn during that time, they ceased participation in surveys. If the organization is freezing or even reducing pay, there is little reason to expend the staff effort to participate in the surveys and to pay the required fees. The result was the creation of statistical artifacts due to sample changes. Calculating the percentage change in average pay from the prior year to the current year is the standard approach to determining the rate of market movement. But since a disproportionate percentage of organizations who would have reported zero or negative change dropped out of the surveys, the result was an overstatement of market movement. The author tracked the impact of this problem in several major surveys and found that the overstatement of market movement was 1–2%. This overstatement resulted in some federal contractors who are contractually mandated to "meet the market" to move their structures and set their budgets at rates that resulted in above market rates after two or three years.

When using a "pure market-based system" to value an organization's jobs, changes in market values reported in surveys creates a problem. The relative internal values of jobs tend to be relatively stable, and if erratic market data cause the valuing model to suggest significant variations year to year, a dilemma is created. Employees make internal comparisons based on established relative values and find it difficult to accept that the value of some jobs went up, others stayed the same and others went down. Although they might accept that current market averages vary, the jobs have not changed and trying to import market data to drive an internal valuing model can result in confusion or a lack of acceptance of the approach as sound.

The application of sound statistical methods to compensation data is necessary if the data is driving critical decisions. Yet the market data does not provide a clear answer as to what the value of a job is. There has been a debate about whether the median or the mean is used as "the market rate." Some argue that the median is more appropriate since extreme outlier values do not impact the measure as much as they do the man. Others believe the outliers represent reality and must be considered. If the median and the mean are relatively close, the choice is less critical, although in large samples the mean will generally exceed the median by about 3–4%, based on extensive analysis of several major surveys. The reasons for this are discussed in the Appendix 1 on Quantitative Methods at the end of this book.

When selecting a competitive posture relative to prevailing market rates many organizations attempting to adopt a premium pay position have stated they "pay at the 75th percentile." Yet percentiles are distribution measures, not central tendency measures, and two jobs with the same average market rate can have widely differing 75th percentile rates due to the degree of dispersion of rates in the sample. For example, if there is a very wide spread in the rates in a sample the 25th and 75th percentiles will be further away from the average than they are in samples with less dispersion. Trying to explain to the incumbents why two jobs with the same value will have different target rates is probably futile. This is an example of using the wrong statistic to drive policy.

Part II of this book will analyze the characteristics of different employee types and discuss performance and rewards management strategies that would be the best fit to each. Part III will address how to align strategies and programs in a manner that produces organizational effectiveness.

Application of Principles: Chapter 3

A health care chain consisting of hospitals and clinics has been experiencing difficulties with retaining Information Technology staff. The turnover has resulted in increased system outages and a delay in replacing one of the major modules to increase the capacity for storing and processing patient records and lab tests.

The HR department analyzed two salary surveys that included data from principal competitors for IT staff and found that the IT salary ranges are about 15% lower than the market averages. Since there is an integrated salary structure including all jobs there are two possible approaches to making IT ranges more competitive: 1) move the IT jobs up a grade in the structure, or 2) create a separate IT structure that would have competitive ranges. A consultant had recently suggested that the organization could create multiple structures, which would allow each major occupational group to have ranges closely tied to the labor market for jobs in the occupational family. By creating a separate IT structure the HR head felt that there would be no internal equity issues raised when IT ranges were increased. However, the CEO felt that having all jobs in a single structure was consistent with their "family" culture and that the other option, raising the grade levels for IT jobs, was preferable.

A preliminary decision was made to reclassify the IT jobs in the current structure. But the head of nursing abruptly showed up at the HR director's office and angrily suggested that the reclassification was absurd. Her contention was that the central and critical function of the organization was to provide patients with the best health care possible. The physicians, nurses and medical technologists were the people who provided the medical care and these jobs were central to mission fulfilment, and the IT people were peripheral to the critical functions. After all, the entire department could be outsourced without affecting the effectiveness of patient care. The HR director agreed that RNs were a critical occupation and that they went through extensive education and specialized training but countered that unless they offered competitive pay to IT specialists there would be more turnover and that would impact timeliness of lab results and patient records. The head nurse pointed out that the lack of internal fairness would promote a sense of not being valued on the part of the nurses and since there were plenty of jobs in the field this discontent could lead to nursing turnover, which would make IT turnover seem like a walk in the park.

You have been asked for a separate opinion. Make a list of the advantages and disadvantages of each option and prepare a recommendation. Provide a justification for your recommendation.

Notes

1 Dabos, G. & Rousseau, M., "Mutuality and Reciprocity in the Psychological Contracts of Employee and Employer," *Journal of Applied Psychology*, 84 (1999).
2 Rynes, S., Gerhart, B. & Parks, L., "Performance Evaluation and Pay for Performance," *Journal of Applied Psychology*, 56 (2005), 571–600.
3 Thaler, R. & Sunstein, C., *Nudge* (New Haven, CT, Yale University Press, 2008).
4 Mahoney, T., "Employment, Compensation Planning and Strategy," in *Compensation and Benefits*, Gomez-Mejia, L., Ed., ASPA-BNA Series, vol. 3 (Washington, DC, Bureau of National Affairs, 1989).

5 Lawler, E., *Pay and Organization Effectiveness* (New York, McGraw-Hill, 1971).
6 Henderson, Richard I., *Compensation Management*, 10th ed. (Upper Saddle River, NJ, Prentice-Hall, 2005); Milkovitch, G. & Newman, J., *Compensation*, 9th ed. (Boston, MA, McGraw-Hill Irwin, 2007).
7 Doeringer, P. & Piore, M., *Internal Labor Markets and Manpower Analysis* (Armonk, NY, M. E. Sharpe, 1971).
8 Lawler, E., *From the Ground Up* (San Francisco, Jossey-Bass, 1996).
9 Lawler, E., *Pay and Organization Development* (Reading, MA, Addison-Wesley, 1981).
10 Lawler, E., *Pay and Organization Development* (Reading, MA, Addison-Wesley, 1981).
11 Hackman, J. & Oldham, G., *Job Redesign* (Reading, MA, Addison-Wesley, 1980).

Part II

Custom Strategies

Strategies for defining, measuring, managing and rewarding performance must fit the nature of the work performed, the contexts within which the work is done and the people who do it in order to be effective. Common principles should guide performance and rewards management strategy, but localized customization is often necessary, in order to provide a good fit to local contexts. Good fit increases the chance that the strategy will work and that it will be viewed as equitable, competitive, appropriate and acceptable to the employees impacted by the strategy and the supporting programs.

It is critical that the criteria used to identify where differentiating locally will increase workforce effectiveness and acceptance be the right ones. Criteria can be based on occupational differences, location differences or the nature of the work performed within specific functions or units.

Part II examines different contexts that might warrant local customization. Figure P2.1 suggests two alternative approaches to developing strategies. The first, a "topdown" approach, is to use guiding principles to identify strategies that are common throughout the organization, and then to develop one set of programs for executing the strategy. The second, a "bottom-up" approach, is to analyze each local context and determine best-fit strategies for each. Once that is done, the organization can decide the degree to which they are combined for purposes of consistency. The material in Part 2 is based on the assumption that a detailed analysis of each context is necessary, whether the objective is to have one strategy if at all possible or to fit strategies to each local context to maximize their fit. Part 3 examines how to integrate the common principles and the custom strategies.

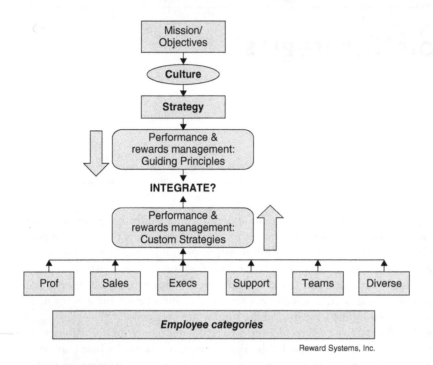

Figure P2.1 Integrating global principles with custom strategies

Chapter 4

Rewarding Performance
Executives and Managers

There are characteristics of executive and manager roles that should be considered when developing strategies for defining, measuring and rewarding performance. Executives (senior management personnel) are usually the highest paid 1–2% of employees in large organizations. Another way to identify executive roles is to identify top decision makers that set the strategic direction of the organization, or a significant part of the organization, whether that part be a strategic business unit or a corporate function. The performance of executives is generally measured in terms of overall organization or business unit performance, and the measurement periods used tend to be longer. The mix of their total compensation package is typically different than the package for other employees, consisting of more variable compensation and more long-term incentive programs, at least in the private sector. The impact of tax laws and regulatory agency rules is much more significant when dealing with executive compensation, and specific knowledge of legal, tax and regulatory impact of programs is required. Executives will be discussed in the first part of this chapter and other levels of management thereafter.

Given the unique characteristics just described, it is not surprising that "executive compensation" is often treated as a separate discipline within compensation management. In some organizations executive compensation is managed outside of the human resources function, either by the board of directors or by the executives themselves.

Since executives are responsible for the strategic direction of an organization, as well as formulating policies, it is reasonable to define their performance in organization-wide terms. Certainly, the CEO and COO can legitimately be measured solely on overall results. Top functional or business unit executives, the second tier of executive management, also tend to have their performance evaluation based at least partially on organizational performance, although functional or business unit performance is usually considered as well. Performance metrics such as profit, return on investment, return on equity, revenue growth, market share, economic value added and total shareholder return are commonly used in performance models used to evaluate and reward executives. These organization-wide measures are tangible and are routinely computed via the accounting systems. Although the emergence of the balanced scorecard concept[1] has promoted the addition of non-financial criteria to the factors considered in evaluating executive performance, in most organizations financial measures dominate performance measurement, at least for the top tier of executives.

In corporations and in most other private sector organizations the board of directors is directly responsible for establishing the criteria and standards used to measure and reward executive performance. But often the board merely approves plans that are designed by the executives themselves, utilizing experts on their staffs or consultants. The board is accountable principally to the shareholders and as a result is charged with determining what is reasonable from the perspective of the investors and the investment community. In the case of not-for-profit and public sector organizations, the board represents the constituencies (e.g., the public, contributors and the government).

Since key executive positions usually have only one incumbent the issue of performance and rewards management can become, or at least appear to be, personal. For that reason it is common for emotions to play a role in the governance process and for personalities and relationships to make the process contentious. Board members fear being criticized for being too generous by stakeholders but at the same time want to attract and retain the best available talent for the key positions. The human resource function, which is generally charged with designing and administering performance and rewards management, is often less involved in executive compensation than it is with compensation programs for other employees. When it is involved there is always a concern about neutrality, since the HR executive is accountable to top management.

In the book *Good To Great*, Collins reports on the extensive research into the impact of leadership on organizational effectiveness: "great organizations have level 5 leaders—individuals who have extreme personal humility, modesty and a ferocious hope and resolve to do whatever it takes to make a great company."[2] In order for an organization to effectively use its intellectual capital, it must have adequate social capital. Since social capital is built on trust and requires that all constituencies believe there is equity in the organization it can be assumed that how and how much executives are compensated will significantly impact social capital.

The 1990s and the first two decades of the twenty-first century have been a tumultuous time for executive compensation in the U.S. The media reports of accounting irregularities and executive compensation arrangements that seem out of touch with reality have created widespread public anger aimed at how executives comport themselves. Believing they were performing well and that they should be richly rewarded was easy for many executives throughout the ten years of uninterrupted prosperity the U.S. enjoyed during the 1990s. It was much like the post-WWII era (1945–70), when American managers convinced themselves of their brilliance, forgetting that it is easy to compete when everyone else's factories have been destroyed and when demand is far in excess of supply. But the arrogance of the 1990s tied to the economic boom has regrettably resulted in the compensation gap between top management and the rest of the organization widening at an increasing rate. As reported in *The New American Workplace*, CEOs of Fortune 100 companies earned about 39 times what the average worker in their organizations earned in the 1970s.[3] In 2000 the multiple had grown to about 400 times. The multiples existing today seem absurd to many when they are compared to any standard of fairness or to the typical gap existing in other countries. The 2008 financial system crisis caused a public outcry over the earnings of Wall Street managers and bankers, the very people who seemed to have created the crisis. Many of the financial institutions shown to be in poor condition had been rewarding executives handsomely, raising doubts about the system governing executive compensation.

As more and more employees view the widening gap between executives and themselves as unwarranted the social tension has escalated. Employees through the 1990s wondered "If I do not benefit now, with all of this sustained prosperity, then when?"

The most destructive fallout has been the erosion of trust and the increase in cynicism on the part of the parties with a stake in the well-being of organizations: employees, shareholders, customers, suppliers and the general public. In their view, employees of many organizations believe the governance structure has failed. The recent passage of legislation in the U.S. aimed at questionable accounting practices might help reassure investors somewhat but there are fundamental issues about how much and how executives should be compensated that must be addressed before the level of trust necessary for organizational effectiveness can be reestablished.

Who Should Determine How Much and How Executives Are Paid?

How much the CEO and other management personnel should be paid is an issue upon which different constituencies are apt to differ, given their different perspectives. It is important to understand the perspective of each party and how they are likely to answer this difficult question. It should be recognized that each party will view theirs as the "right" perspective. It is therefore useful to understand what those differing perspectives are and why they are held. The issue of perception is most pronounced with executives, since they have the most authority to influence their own compensation.

The Executives Themselves

Executives compare their earnings primarily to those of other executives with similar roles in similar organizations. Some have put forth the argument that they make less than star athletes, considering their endorsements, but few take this comparison model seriously. Others view their compensation in light of how much shareholder value has increased during their tenure, but, since they do not typically risk their own funds in the way that investors do, this argument does not hold up well under scrutiny. The basis most often accepted is how much other executives make. Graef Crystal, one of the most prominent executive compensation experts, has long suggested that these comparisons serve to escalate average levels if not carefully done and if not related to performance.[4]

Prevailing executive compensation levels can be determined using a number of sources: proxy information, surveys, board members (who are usually executives themselves), analysis done by HR and/or outside consultants and even newspaper and magazine reporting. Executives have technical specialists available to them who can accumulate and analyze competitive data, either in the HR function or from the outside. When surveys are utilized, specific comparator samples are chosen, most often based on organization size, industry or similar levels of performance.

Other Employees

It has become apparent that other employees have a different perspective when it comes to evaluating the executive pay levels of late. They often compare executive pay with their pay. It could be argued that this is a poor metric for determining equity, but emotion enters into these comparisons and both unions and the press have made the multiple of their pay the metric that is talked about.

Employees typically do not have direct access to professionally managed compensation surveys, but an enormous amount of data is readily available in magazines and in newspapers. The union websites are also very helpful, taking the trouble to calculate for an employee how many minutes or hours the CEO has to work to earn the employee's annual salary. The articles in the press have their own bias (the bigger the numbers the greater the reader interest) but employees typically are not making detailed comparisons. The degree of resentment among employees is greatly impacted by how they feel about their treatment by the organization. If they enjoy relatively competitive pay and benefit levels and have a reasonable amount of employment security, the amount of angst they might feel when they see comparative data is apt to be lessened. When their organization is facing a crisis the executives are typically blamed for the situation, and as the confidence that their employment is secure wanes the employees become even more critical. Like coaches of sports teams, executives tend to get too much credit for success and too much blame for poor performance.

Government and Society

There has been a flurry of activity in Congress in response to the public outcry over executive compensation abuses. In 2008 the government began bailing out agencies such as Fannie Mae and Freddie Mac, as well as financial institutions, causing the public to focus on executive pay. Although the economic system in the U.S. does not encourage governmental control of what a corporation pays its employees, elected officials do respond to complaints from the citizenry. The legislative responses up to 2008 had been focused on disclosure and exposure, as well as provisions for holding the governance structure and the auditors accountable. Many legislators know little about the technical aspects of executive compensation and they struggle to decide how much is too much and what the permissible techniques are for determining executive compensation levels. The financial crisis of 2008 triggered activity by Congress to ensure public funds were not being used for excessive compensation levels for executives. And the president in early 2009 stated, there should be a cap on cash compensation for those organizations receiving government assistance.

Beginning in 2016, the regulators in England began to talk about capping executive pay, primarily in response to complaints from the public. In 2018 both England and the EU are struggling with regulatory actions that could impose limits, or at least review processes that will increase governmental intervention in private sector executive compensation. Whether this will increase the pressure on the U.S. government to consider regulations is not known but if that were to happen it would represent the most aggressive governmental posture in modern times. In theory, publicly traded for-profit organizations are regulated by their investors. "Say for pay" and other shareholder mandates are also increasingly aggressive and may be joined with government regulations to exercise control over executive compensation. Given the nature of the U.S. system it can be argued that even when share ownership is widely dispersed or in the hands of large managed funds, pressure can be exercised without formal governmental actions. But pressure by the public can cause legislatures and regulatory agencies to believe they have to take some action.

Board of Directors

The board is charged with evaluating executive compensation levels in comparison to other similar organizations and for ensuring they are "reasonable" according to whatever philosophy they adopt. Board compensation committees are required to develop and articulate a compensation philosophy and to demonstrate that the programs they approved were consistent with that philosophy. And the committee members must be "outsiders," rather than company executives. But the executive compensation philosophy sections in proxy statements bear striking resemblances to each other and are stated in such general terms that they do not overly limit the discretion of the board. Giving organizations great flexibility is consistent with the economic system and political environment that has prevailed in the U.S. And since most compensation committees are composed of outside directors who have knowledge of compensation principles, there is some basis for confidence that this board responsibility is in capable, or at least knowledgeable, hands. The board also utilizes the HR function within the organization, to provide them with the competitive information needed, often supplemented by the use of outside professionals. Board compensation committees in the U.S. have been impacted by disclosure requirements imposed by the Securities and Exchange Commission and by regulatory action such as the Sarbanes–Oxley Act, which addresses governance.

Shareholders

The people who provide the capital for publicly traded organizations are very diverse and are huge in number if vested stakeholders in pension funds are included. As a result, their interests are varied and their perspectives relative to executive compensation are hard to characterize. Since most are not involved in the management of the organizations they own the prevailing viewpoint is typically focused on total shareholder return (dividends plus stock price appreciation). If the return is better than they believe they can get anywhere else at an equivalent level of risk, they will tend to hold the stock. And since they are also free to divest themselves if they believe otherwise, there is less pressure for them to complain about pay levels.

Most investor interests are represented by a professionally managed fund, and individuals may not even know which companies they own stock in. Some institutional investors have holdings that are so large that they prefer to take concerted action rather than sell stock. They press on issues relating to corporate governance and "suggest" guidelines to be followed if an organization wants them to purchase and hold their stock. Those guidelines are dominated by the theme of paying only for performance and limiting the conditions under which stock programs operate.

Which of These Perspectives Is "Correct" and Who Decides?

It is predictable that each constituency believes the perspective it holds is correct. Given the multiple parties at interest and the diversity in their perspectives about executive compensation, it is difficult to decide who reconciles them and how. This must be the responsibility of the compensation committee of the board, according to legal or regulatory mandates. On the other hand, the members of these committees are typically conversant in the issues but not highly skilled in the technical aspects of executive compensation. Many boards retain outside advisors to provide that expertise, but any such consultant will lack the benefit of working within the organization and knowing its context intimately. HR may be viewed as biased, given that the CEO and other senior executives outrank the top HR executive and make decisions impacting the employment and compensation of that executive. Still, it is critical that HR demonstrates its ability to consider all perspectives and to advise the board on how the differences can be reconciled.

Effective and Defensible Executive Compensation Programs

The characteristics of executive compensation programs that will stand up under scrutiny by the various constituencies are:

- *Relationship to the organizational strategy is clear.* Executive compensation levels should be based on performance criteria and standards that are related to the organization's strategy. For example, if the firm needs to increase market share while retaining existing customers, it is reasonable to expect customer measures to impact incentive awards to some extent. If there is a need is to grow through acquisition then both success in making acquisitions and the success of the acquisitions should appear on the list of performance criteria. And since there are almost always multiple objectives in today's complex world, a "balanced scorecard" approach should be used. Perhaps the most common mistake made by organizations that depend on the quality of their intellectual capital is avoiding people measures just because they are difficult to score in a quantitative manner. It can be argued that many executives are rewarded by incentive plans based on profits when these profits are created by firing the very people whose skill and knowledge will be needed to make the organization viable in the future. It is therefore critical that financial, operational, customer and workforce effectiveness measures are all considered in proportion to their true importance.
- *Shareholders are paid a fair return on their investment before programs reward executives.* Incentive thresholds that ensure shareholders receive a fair return before any award pool is generated are very effective in convincing parties at interest that executives must "earn their salary" before cashing in on additional incentives. The same principle holds true for stock-based programs. If executive options increase in value even when the organization's stock price appreciates at a slower rate than the average of its competitors, the shareholders are justified in viewing this as a sort of giveaway program. More organizations are building in a feature that increases the exercise price of options in concert with the average price appreciation within the industry or selected group of competitors. This ensures that shareholders are realizing a total return equivalent to investors in other organizations.

In addition to receiving a fair return, shareholders should understand the potential costs of all programs in advance of approving them. In order for them to make an informed judgment, they should know what the costs will be under multiple scenarios, ranging from optimistic to pessimistic projections of results. This enables shareholders to decide if there is an appropriate amount of downside given bad performance, in addition to knowing what executives will be paid if things go very well.

Finally, the board and shareholders should know how the executive total compensation package compares to that of a sample of relevant competitive organizations. It is critical that all parties agree on what constitutes a fair and relevant competitor comparison group, as well as what the organization's competitive posture will be. Research has shown that many organizations (typically one-quarter to one-third) target the 75th percentile as their desired competitive position and that virtually no organizations choose to fall below the average.[5] This obviously inflates compensation levels within any comparison group, since basic mathematical laws dictate that effect. It is therefore critical to gain concurrence on the competitive posture, through dialogue among HR, the executives, the board and in some cases the shareholders. But it is also important to ensure the comparison group is selected using credible criteria. For example, if revenue is used as the metric for selecting other organizations within the industry this may be unfair to a smaller but rapidly growing and/or very profitable organization. On the other hand, a lumbering giant may be compared to large organizations that are performing very well. There is no "correct" model for selecting competitors; the best answer must be the consensus of the parties at interest and will typically incorporate multiple criteria.

- *Eligibility for program is inclusive, not exclusive.* Many incentive programs include only a small group of senior executives. Behavioral scientists have posited the notion that people who are rewarded for performance are more apt to perform well. Adam Smith long ago contended that "hired agents" would never have the drive and focused priorities necessary to succeed if they were not in some way aligned economically with the owners. His views have evolved into agency theory, which is widely used to examine governance systems. Although the sharp downturn in equity prices from 2000 to 2002 lessened the enthusiasm for having most or all employees participate in ownership programs there remained a strong psychological argument for doing so. The change to accounting rules in 2006 that required organizations to inflate the "value" of stock option programs reduced the number of organizations using them for a broad group of employees, since the new rules made doing so more expensive. But people tend not to wash (or maintain) rental cars. By creating a shared economic destiny through incentive programs with broad eligibility, an organization can more easily achieve the alignment and the motivation required to succeed in a difficult economy. It may therefore be prudent to still include the remainder of the workforce in programs that have traditionally been reserved for executives.
- *Program design is economically efficient.* Programs should be designed to efficiently deliver after-tax income to recipients relative to the after-tax cost to the organization. The use of devices such as incentive stock options can be questioned because their tax treatment is very costly to the organization and the other shareholders. The argument for them is that executives find them attractive, but the cost of focusing on recipient after-tax income is that the inefficiency of the instrument penalizes everyone but the executives. There should also be attention paid to the accounting impact of programs, since when and how much of an earnings charge must be taken may significantly impact the desirability of any program. In the U.S. any direct compensation program that results in earnings over $1 million in a year for an individual must be tied in some way to organization performance or the excess amounts will not be

deductible for the corporation as a business expense. This makes individual salaries over that amount a highly questionable practice, or at least a very inefficient way to compensate executives.

- *There is early and continuous communication about objectives, strategy, what is earned and why.* The story in the paper about an executive who earned $20 million recently, while closing plants and laying off thousands of employees, is not the dream of an organization's public relations department. Even though $19.5 million of this amount was attributable to gains on stock held for ten years this detail is not apt to be in the lead part of the story, and the assumption will be that this is another example of self-serving greed. If this same program had been approved by shareholders and if there had been annual communication of the current value of the options and how much income was attributable to each year, the reception might have been different.

Explaining to all parties why a particular program was adopted and how it will work is the first step in ensuring that people understand why income is or is not realized from the program. The next step is to continuously communicate interim results and their impact on the value of the program to participants. For example, restricted stock grants are a form of equity incentives that have some very attractive features. But restricted stock is often viewed as a giveaway program, since the executive does not have to buy the stock. Restricted stock has retention power, since the stock cannot be sold, traded or encumbered while the restrictions are in effect. It also enables holders to vote the stock and collect dividends in a tax-effective manner. But unless this type of program is designed well and tied to performance requirements, it is likely to be viewed as irresponsible and inappropriate. Effective communication is also critical.

- *There is a credible system for oversight and governance.* The quality of board oversight believed to exist will impact investor confidence. Board composition is changing, with the trend being towards a higher percentage of outside and independent directors. But boards meet perhaps four times a year and they frequently know only what they are told. There must be provisions made for auditing practices to ensure they conform to policy and, of course, the law. But boards must demonstrate that they are capable of recognizing transgressions and that they are willing to deal with them. If the governance system is not appropriate and acceptable to all parties at interest, there will be suspicion that executives are excessively or inappropriately compensated.

Executive Compensation Programs That Should Be Avoided

There are programs that do not stand up under scrutiny and that will breed suspicion that the playing field has been tilted in favor of executives. These "third rail" programs should be avoided. Their characteristics include:

- *High upside potential; no downside risk*: Adverse reaction is inevitable when certain types of programs are used. High base salaries, incentive programs with low thresholds, stock plans that do not require sustained ownership and repricing stock options to a lower exercise price are sure to attract criticism. High base salaries enable recipients to live well even when everyone else suffers. Base salaries over $1 million are not tax deductible to the organization, since they are not performance dependent, and it is difficult to understand why they exist at all. Cash or stock-based incentive plans that begin paying out at very low levels of performance are also subject to challenge. The defensible principle is to pay for *good* performance. The ultimate abuse is to guarantee some portion of an incentive reward, which removes the performance threshold altogether. But the two ultimate high-risk practices are repricing stock options and lowering incentive plan performance requirements during the year to ensure a plan pays out when it otherwise would not have.

Repricing stock options sends the message to shareholders that options are a way to ensure executives prosper, rather than a way to align their economic destiny with that of the shareholders. Those who *bought* their stock will surely ask if they can have the same deal. Those responsible for repricing no doubt believe that executives will not be motivated if their stock options are priced at what the market value used to be, rather than today's much lower price. But the protests by investors became so intense that the government has mandated unfavorable accounting treatment when repricing occurs.

There has always been a debate about the wisdom of changing incentive plan performance standards during the plan year. Changing standards during the year can be a reasonable practice if the standards can be *either* lowered or increased. If unanticipated and uncontrollable external conditions turn out to be favorable, raising standards should be possible. If they are unfavorable, lowering standards should be equally possible. Each organization must decide if it responds by modifying the standards so that the plan is still viable. Some do, while others accept the reality that forecasts do not always work out. If such occurrences happen frequently it is time to reevaluate the plan design, which may be inappropriate for the context within which it operates.

One of the reasons for using stock-based plans for executives is that it aligns their economic interests with those of the shareholders. If executives receiving stock options sell their stock shortly after exercising, there is no sustained ownership and the interests of shareholders and employees are not aligned going forward. Since inspiring employees to share interests with shareholders is one of the key reasons for offering options, this is a problem. Programs that require sustained ownership requirements for executives can help to make stock programs more acceptable to shareholders. For example, each "tier" within the organization may have a different targeted ownership (e.g., ten times annual salary for top executives, five times for functional executives and three times for other participants). Failure to maintain the targeted level may result in cash incentives being diverted to stock purchase and/or denial of future option issues.

- *"Elitist" programs*: Perquisites that are not business related are anathema to the shareholders and to other employees. If they discover that a CEO purchased an $8,000 shower curtain with company funds they should insist that person be prosecuted and terminated. But they should also investigate the governance structure to find out why well-compensated executives felt they could obtain reimbursement for personal expenses. Personal and family use of planes, expense accounts and other company resources should also be carefully examined, since abuse can lead to the erosion of trust on the part of those who must contribute in order for the organization to succeed. To preserve his image the renowned Jack Welch gave back some of his retirement privileges when they became public and were subjected to criticism. Even when perquisites are technically legal and within established policy they send a message that there are different rules and principles for different people, which can erode the social capital within the organization and impact employee motivation.

- *Programs that reward something other than performance*: "Golden parachutes" programs that protect executives in the case of a change in control have their place. But excessive termination or severance arrangements that pay out no matter what the circumstances can easily increase the cynicism of the public about executive compensation. Disney paid a newly hired number two executive huge sums to leave shortly after joining the organization, due to conflicts with the CEO. Shareholders have a right to question why the selection process did not function better and why they should have to sacrifice their capital to rectify the mistake. If a total failure on the part of senior executives is rewarded, with the shareholders providing the funding, there is apt to be severe criticism of management.
- *Poorly communicated programs*: Bypassing shareholder approval, even if approval is technically not mandated by law, is common. Many of the egregious violations occurring within organizations today might have been avoided if shareholders had been able to review and approve the specific programs being adopted. When executive compensation is managed out of the sight of shareholders and of other employees, it becomes easy to slide down the slippery slope towards excess. Even when stockholders must be consulted, too many organizations use "legalese" that obfuscates the intent of programs and/or their potential cost.

Establishing an Acceptable Executive Compensation Strategy

Given the potential pitfalls associated with executive compensation, how can a strategy be formulated that both protects the organization's interests and is accepted by executives as fair and appropriate? The board must listen to, understand and consider the perspectives of all constituencies and reconcile them by ensuring compensation programs are reasonable, competitive and effective. The programs that have been described as "high-risk" must be avoided. And the programs that are utilized must be communicated to all parties at interest, when they are adopted and on an ongoing basis. The impact of strategies and programs on the social capital of the organization must be considered, while utilizing professional expertise to ensure the executive compensation package still attracts and retains high-quality executives.

Some of the steps that can be taken are:

1   Develop a clear compensation strategy in conjunction with the board, providing the function's technical expertise to those charged with developing a strategy.
2   Embrace "defensible" and avoid "high-risk" programs, as described earlier in this chapter. The fact that other organizations are using programs that attract shareholder criticism does not justify their use. If there is some doubt, shareholder approval should be sought even if it is not legally required.

3   Communicate freely and continuously to all parties, even going beyond legal and regulatory requirements when it is information that is relevant to shareholders and the investment industry. If participation in some programs is limited there should be an acceptable explanation for this decision.

4   Monitor adherence to policies and have the board deal with infractions. If the board does not address illegal acts, others have an obligation to report them to the SEC and other regulatory bodies. If someone loses a job by adhering to ethical principles the chance of getting another job is many times greater than if that executive went along with actions that violate policy, ethics or the law. The person who stood up and reported the abuse will still have his or her reputation.

5   Programs should be supported by empirical evidence, such as market data and competitive practice benchmarking results. If outside consulting assistance is used by executive management the same support should be provided to the compensation committee of the board. It has been argued that the board should have a separate consultant, but this often leads to "My consultant can beat up your consultant" confrontations that accomplish nothing except to positively impact the revenue of the consulting firms.

Strategies for defining, measuring and rewarding performance for management personnel other than executives should certainly conform to many of the principles just stated.

Technical Program Design Issues

The discussion thus far has addressed characteristics of strategies and programs that will be acceptable to constituencies: the political considerations. There are also technical design issues that should be addressed to ensure performance and rewards management is effective and appropriate.

The Level at Which Performance Is Defined, Measured and Rewarded

Identifying the appropriate organizational level at which to define, measure and reward executive or manager performance is critical if programs are to be viewed as fair and appropriate. Since the CEO and COO are responsible for producing the overall result, it is typically accepted that organization-wide performance is the appropriate metric. This is not to say that performance appraisals cannot consider personal performance factors based on judgments by the board on how well the incumbent did given the circumstances. Caution must be exercised, however, since giving an executive a large salary increase or a discretionary variable compensation award when the organization has performed poorly can result in questioning by other parties at interest. And when the organization loses money, but less than would have been expected given the realities, this may still constitute good performance. But without predetermined performance criteria and standards such an action may produce considerable backlash.

Many organizations design CEO or COO compensation packages that consist of more variable compensation than base salary—often by multiples of 3–5:1. By making total direct compensation contingent on results an organization can align costs and revenues and can ensure compensation costs are warranted by realized performance. This approach also focuses the executives on the specific results deemed important. Finally, it minimizes the chances of criticism by shareholders and the public that executives are appropriating undeserved sums by using their power to ensure their salaries are set at high levels.

Functional and business unit executives who make up the next one or two tiers of the reporting structure may be measured at least in part on how well their area of responsibility performs or a personal evaluation of how well they performed as individuals. Top staff function executives (finance, HR, legal, etc.) in many organizations have 100% of their variable compensation awards based on organization-wide performance. The philosophy underlying this approach is that they should be motivated to allocate staff resources optimally to produce the best overall result. On the other hand, some organizational cultures would cause this approach to be viewed as prone to underachievers being carried along by the efforts of others. What works best is what fits the culture of each organization. This also holds true for line executives. Top business unit executives in organizations where the businesses are viewed as independent may be measured and rewarded based on their results, with little or no contingency tied to overall organization performance. In organizations concerned with horizontal integration (e.g., sharing of best practices, coordination of operations, global branding) performance measures and rewards may be tied much more to overall results.

How Performance Criteria and Standards Are Selected and Weighted for Relative Importance

The increasing popularity of the balanced scorecard approach to defining and measuring organization performance has served to clarify expectations in advance and to define "performance" more broadly than has historically been the case. Historically, annual financial performance has dominated the definition. Given the increasing volatility of markets and national economies, profits can vary significantly from year to year (and certainly from quarter to quarter), making it difficult to truly measure an organization's health and continued viability with this single measure. The practice of including customer, operational and learning/growth (people) measures in the definition of organizational performance has given the board the opportunity to focus senior management on building sustainable success. This approach also recognizes the necessity of investing in "intangibles" (e.g., through R&D, employee development, etc.) even though these investments are expensed and reduce short-term profitability. But it also mandates the use of subjective evaluations of performance rather than "hard" metrics, thereby putting the board in the position of defending their judgment to parties with different views as to how well the organization is performing. The use of functional or business unit scorecards that are derived from the organizational scorecard is also increasing in popularity. Middle management personnel may be evaluated and rewarded based on measures that are tied to organizational performance, unit performance and individual performance, with the relative mix varying based on the nature of their responsibilities.

The Timeframe Used for Defining, Measuring and Rewarding Performance

One of the criticisms of executives is that they make decisions that are dominated by short-term considerations. CEO tenure has become relatively short. Behavioral theories would predict that individuals would focus on results that will be used to judge them and that determine how they are rewarded. An executive three years from retirement could be expected to think twice about building new capacity that will result in huge costs for three to four years, with the benefits forthcoming further in the future and in unknown amounts. Although it can be argued that appropriate governance and good planning systems can produce rational and prudent decisions, this issue should not be overlooked. Although there has been much discussion about making post-retirement income contingent on pre-retirement actions by using long-term incentive plans, this is rarely done. Even mid-career CEOs rarely face significant variations in their rewards after leaving an organization, since the "unvested" incentives are often bought out by the organization hiring them and/or the executive can cash out a substantial portion of their compensation (e.g., exercising stock options and then selling the stock). Vehicles such as restricted stock can be used to penalize defectors, but unless they are viewed as having enormous value their existence will probably have a limited impact on the decision to leave.

Reconciling the Interests of the Organization and of Executives or Managers

Although the most obvious conflict of interest is that executives want or expect high pay and organizations want or expect low costs, this dilemma exists with all employees. The use of a model that compares alternative compensation programs based on the extent to which they best satisfy both executive and company needs can be used to structure an optimal rewards package. The model should be constructed in a manner that first captures the objectives or priorities of both parties, such as those listed in Table 4.1.

The second step is to weight the relative importance of each of the objectives, both to the company and to the executives. The final step is to "score" alternative compensation plans against the objectives and relative importance weights, producing a measure of plan attractiveness to both parties. There will obviously be plans that score high on attractiveness to one party and low to the other, given the differences in perspective. But using an approach like this has the intrinsic benefit that is gained by identifying the wants and needs of each party, setting the stage for a reasonable analysis of which plans provide the optimal benefits overall.

Table 4.1 Balancing Company and Executive Objectives

Company Objectives	Executive Objectives
Tax-efficiency/favorable tax treatment	Favorable tax treatment
Control of long-term liability	Long-term guarantees
Retention power (risk of forfeiture)	No risk of forfeiture
Minimal charge to earnings	Ease of liquidating equity
Minimal shareholder dilution	No personal investment of capital
Positive cash flow for company	Positive cash flow for self
Shareholder acceptance as appropriate	Acceptable as fair to executive
Alignment of executive financial well-being with that of shareholders	Maximize financial well-being with minimum amount of risk
Justifiable based on competitive practice	Fully competitive with "peers"

Defining, measuring and rewarding the performance of executives can be contentious because of the differing perceptions by different parties at interest as to what is fair, competitive and appropriate. By recognizing and respecting these differences they can often be reconciled by adopting strategies that provide an optimum balance of the multiple interests.

The extent to which executives are treated differently than the rest of the organization should be decided based on the economics, the politics and the specific context within which they will operate. Organizational culture, internal and external realities and strategy should all be considered when developing strategies and designing programs.

Performance and Rewards Management for Other Management Personnel

The strategies for rewarding performance for other management personnel should be appropriately integrated with the strategies used for executives. Since directors, managers and supervisors make up the cohort that may produce the future executives, organizations should ensure that career management structures and the rewards associated with each level are in a proper relationship to each other. Designing the management pay structure is a critical step in making effective performance and rewards management possible. If there are too many levels in the reporting structure, defining responsibilities for purposes of measuring performance becomes difficult. In addition, compensation levels will be compressed relative to each other, diminishing the attractiveness of assuming higher levels of responsibility. If there are too few levels, the compensation potential may be adequate but the jump from one level to another may be too large, resulting in under-qualified personnel filling key slots. Another issue is the span of control associated with any structure. The author worked with a national research laboratory that had "flattened" its structure, leaving vice presidents with 15 or more directors reporting to them, making it difficult for those directing major programs to see the VP within a reasonable time. This created practical difficulties related to communication, but also made it difficult for a VP to do a credible performance appraisal on that many people—and, in fact, even know how well each of them was doing. "Flat is better" as a concept has its limits, although the management literature has been dominated by recommendations to move in this direction.

The major issue is defining performance at each management level. As mentioned earlier, senior executives are typically measured based on overall organization performance, although functional and business unit heads may be measured based on a mixture of organizational and business or function performance. Table 4.2 is an illustration of how performance could be defined at the various levels.

A model like this can be used to drive incentive plans, which compensate management personnel based on the appropriate performance level(s). At the lower levels of management, employees may feel they have less control over organizational performance and more over their unit's performance, as well as their individual performance. In some cases management incentive plans do not incorporate individual performance at all, leaving that to the merit pay system.

The mix of the total compensation package typically varies as the level of the organization changes. For example, senior executives often expect to see 50–75% of their total

Table 4.2 Defining Levels at which Performance is Measured

Level	Organization-wide Performance	Unit Performance	Individual Performance
Senior executives	100%	0%	0%
Business/function heads	50%	50%	0%
Directors	40%	40%	20%
Managers	30%	30%	40%
Supervisors	20%	20%	60%

compensation come from long-term cash or equity-based incentive programs, with salary and annual cash incentive plans making up the rest. Middle management personnel usually see a larger percentage of their package attributable to annual incentives, with less coming from long-term incentives. Lower-level management personnel often do not participate in long-term incentive programs and have a significant percentage of their package in the form of salary.

How performance is defined can of course vary across individuals at the same level. For example, a business unit that operates independently may compensate managers based largely or totally on unit performance, while another that is highly interdependent with other parts of the overall organization may base a significant amount of the performance rating on overall organization performance. Too many organizations fail to create an overall performance model and define in advance the level(s) at which performance will be measured and rewarded for all types of managers.

A necessary prerequisite for deciding on what constitutes performance is the clear definition of the responsibilities of managers. Table 4.3 illustrates a management level chart that can be used to define the responsibilities at each level and to indicate the impact of people at each level on other parts of the organization and on the overall organization.

Having management levels defined is useful for defining performance expectations and communicating to managers the changing role requirements as one advances through the levels. There is a need to define levels in such a way that they fit the individual organization and emulating other organizations should be done carefully, since the nature of the organization, its culture and its strategy will determine what kind of structure is ideal for it. An organization whose prime concern is reliability and safety, such as a utility, may justifiably have more levels of management, to ensure all decisions are subject to adequate review. A software design firm might have very few reporting levels, using multiple project teams extensively. What works is what fits. The structure certainly should also impact how performance at each level is defined and measured. The structure should impact how performance is rewarded.

Culture also has a major role in defining responsibilities for all types and levels of management personnel. In a national laboratory, managers may be expected to be thought leaders, operating at the leading edge of technical competence. In a utility, managers may be expected to manage the work processes and the people, ensuring they operate within established policy. A software design firm may have varying expectations, depending on what a manager is expected to manage (e.g., creating new technology or keeping the books).

Table 4.3 Management Level Definitions

	Operating Responsibility	Functional Responsibility	Organizational Relationships	Potential Impact on Organization
	Responsibility for decisions affecting operations and impacting success in meeting mission/objectives.	*Responsibility for creating and managing the organization's infrastructure, i.e., people, functional processes and systems.*	*Responsibility for integrating work of organizational units and for managing interfaces with entities outside the organization.*	*The scope and magnitude of impact of decisions on the performance of organization and its constituent units.*
Vice president/ top functional executive: provides leadership and direction to a division or major function	Responsible for developing a mission and long-range objectives for a major division/function that are aligned with and support meeting the organization's objectives. Scan the environment and ensure trends that may impact the organization and the division are identified and that scenarios are developed to respond to change. Create strategies and structures that facilitate meeting objectives and changing environmental conditions. Accountable for ensuring that the core capabilities of the division remain viable and that the performance of the division/function contributes to the success of the organization.	Responsible for organizing, selecting, developing and directing division/ function staff. Ensure division/function and constituent units integrate their strategies, tactical plans and policies. Ensure the human resource management philosophy is adhered to and develop divisional/ functional policies to ensure employees are fairly treated and effectively utilized. Monitor adherence to core organizational values and direct the continuous evaluation and refinement of these values and of the organization's culture. Anticipate future staffing/ functional process needs.	Represent the division/function and the organization to outside entities. Coordinate division/function activities with the rest of the organization to ensure integration. Oversee the development of programs, manage the interface with existing sponsors/stakeholders and represent the division and the organization to potential customers, sponsors and stakeholders. Direct negotiation with customers and stakeholders to produce agreements that fit the organization's mission and meet customer/stakeholder objectives. Develop new sources of revenue as appropriate. Serve on internal and external advisory groups that may impact the future of the organization.	Has a direct and significant impact on the short- and long-range performance of the division and direct and significant impact on the organization's reputation among customers, sponsors and stakeholders.

Director: provides leadership and direction to a significant part of a division	Develop strategy, structure and operating plans for a center that significantly impacts divisional performance. Responsible for the long-term performance of the center and for integrating its operations with the rest of the division.	Responsible for organizing, staffing and directing the staff of the unit. Ensure the center's human resource management philosophy and divisional policies are adhered to and directly manage performance of the management team. Anticipate future staffing/functional process needs.	Represent unit to outside entities as appropriate. Coordinate unit activities with the rest of the division/organization and ensure their integration. Oversee the development of programs and manage the interface with customers, sponsors and stakeholders. Develop new sources of revenue as appropriate. Participate in negotiating agreements with customers and stakeholders in establishing mutual goals. Responsible for ensuring customer and stakeholder needs are met. May serve on internal and external advisory groups that may impact the future of the organization.	Center performance has a direct and significant impact on organization's reputation among customers, sponsors and stakeholders, as well as significantly impacting the performance of the division/organization.
General manager: provides leadership and direction to several departments	Manage multiple departments encompassing a broad scope and significant variety/complexity or direct major programs/projects. Ensure department operating plans are integrated with function/center/division operating and strategic plans. Participate in formulating function/center/division policies and strategy.	Responsible for organizing, selecting, developing and directing subordinate staff, or directing program/project staff. Assist subordinate managers with development of their subordinates. Work with direct reports to project future staffing and functional process needs.	Represent departments with outside entities as appropriate. Ensure the integration of departments managed with those of the division and organization. Lead and/or participate in cross-functional teams to facilitate integration. Participate in negotiations with customers and stakeholders in establishing mutual goals. Accountable for meeting customer and stakeholder needs.	Performance of departments managed has direct and significant impact on the unit's reputation among customers, sponsors and other stakeholders, as well as impacting the financial and operational performance of the division and organization.

(continued)

Table 4.3 (continued)

	Operating Responsibility	Functional Responsibility	Organizational Relationships	Potential Impact on Organization
Department manager: provides leadership and direction to a department	Develop operating plans and strategies for organizational unit managed that integrate into an overall divisional operating plan. Organize to effectively and efficiently utilize department/division resources to optimize performance goals. Manage the operations of assigned unit.	Responsible for organizing, selecting, developing, leading, identifying, coaching, mentoring and directing subordinate staff and managing their performance through a variety of mechanisms. Project future staffing needs for a viable workforce. Project future functional process needs.	Represent department to outside entities as appropriate. Ensure that organization activities are integrated with those of other departments and that customer and stakeholder needs are met. Manage customer and stakeholder relationships, and resolve conflicts by optimally allocating available resources.	Department/unit performance has direct and significant impact on department's reputation among customers, sponsors and other stakeholders, as well as impacting the financial and operational performance of the division and organization.
Supervisor: provides leadership and direction to a unit	Organize section and manage day-to-day operations. Monitor performance against established goals, taking corrective action as needed. Responsible for meeting established unit budgets and plans.	Responsible for organizing, selecting, developing and directing subordinate staff (typically exempt and non-exempt) and managing their performance. Perform human resource activities for staff (e.g., appraisal, discipline, career planning, etc.).	Represent section on routine matters or specific program/ project phases to outside entities as required. Coordinate unit activities with those of the rest of the organization.	Section performance is measured in terms of meeting schedules, operating within budget and meeting established goals. Section performance significantly impacts the performance of the department and may impact other departments and the division.
Team leader/ supervisor: provides leadership and direction to a team of employees	Organize section and supervise daily activities. Perform tasks related to unit work as required or in training staff.	Provide direct supervision to primarily non-exempt staff. Perform human resource management activities for staff (e.g., appraisal, discipline, career planning, etc.).	Coordinate section activities with those of the rest of the organization.	Section performance is measured in terms of meeting schedules, operating within budget and meeting established goals. Unit performance impacts the performance of the department and may impact other departments.

There are significant differences across national cultures, relative to the role of managers. These differences have had a major impact on organizations operating globally, as discussed in Chapter 10. In some cultures the manager is expected to know the answer to any question asked by a subordinate, while in others it is permissible for the manager to admit they need to find the answer, or even to ask the subordinate to research the issue and make recommendations.

Leadership is a topic with a huge literature and is generally accepted to be a part of a manager's responsibility. Every year brings numerous offerings that suggest the ideal style is X (e.g., emulate Attila the Hun), accompanied on the bookstore shelves by other works suggesting it is Y (e.g., become more like St. Anthony). The concept that the best leadership style depends on the organizational and environmental context is widely accepted. Globalization has complicated the search for the appropriate leadership styles. Trompenaars, in *Twenty One Leaders for the Twenty First Century*, presented structured analyses of CEOs who succeeded in very different operational, economic and cultural contexts.[6] Rather than merely telling stories he used a cross-cultural framework developed in earlier research, which provided insights into why a particular style worked well in a specific context. Although difficult to do, each organization must decide how much and what kind of leadership its managers should exhibit and how this aspect of their role will be evaluated when judging their performance.

The GLOBE project is a very large research project examining which leadership styles seem to best fit specific types of cultures.[7] The national and regional cultures defined in the GLOBE study are matched to leadership styles that work well or poorly in each. Research such as this must be used cautiously, however, because national and regional cultures are difficult to define in global organizations where expatriates, inpatriates, local nationals and third-country nationals are mixed into their managerial cadres in all of their locations. But the research at least alerts organizations to the issues raised by cultural diversity. Trompenaars has put forth his "3 Rs" to address culture: *recognize* when cultural differences exist, respect people's rights to hold different beliefs and to have different values and reconcile the issues that are raised by the cultural differences.[8]

Leadership will almost certainly be a part of the definition of managerial performance. But it is much more challenging to measure objectively than hard financial metrics, so organizations struggle with using leadership effectiveness as a driver of rewards.

Management personnel are a critical part of any organization's workforce. The effectiveness of management personnel will almost certainly have a major impact on organizational performance in the short run and its viability in the long run.

Rewarding performance equitably, competitively and acceptably is critical.

Evidence-based Management of Executive Performance and Rewards

Throughout this chapter, emphasis has been placed on the need to develop a performance and rewards strategy for executives and managers that is acceptable to all constituents. Given the emotion that is elicited when how and how much executives should be paid it is important not to rely on subjective opinions when making strategy decisions. The use of relevant evidence to support recommendations and to make decisions is critical.

How executive performance is defined and measured has a profound impact on whether rewards will motivate executives to act in the best interests of the organization and all constituents. This is an issue that requires the use of subjective opinions to guide decisions. How much and how to reward executives is in some respects an easier issue to support with tangible evidence, since what competitors for talent do is widely accepted as a legitimate basis for developing a strategy. And what competitors do can be measured in quantitative terms. The average base pay, total direct compensation, long-term incentive awards, equity participation, benefits and perquisites offered by competitors can be computed in most cases using required disclosures (i.e., proxy statements, 401Ks and other reports legally mandated for publicly traded organizations). And there are numerous sources of surveys conducted by consulting firms and by organizations themselves that collect information on compensation. As a result, it is often straightforward to establish compensation levels being offered by competitors.

But once the "going market rate" is known the organization still has to decide what its competitive posture will be relative to that rate. Surveys can ask about competitive posture and an organization may find that 80% of competitors pay "at average." Yet that still leaves decision makers to adopt a posture that will get, keep and motivate the talent it requires. How to appropriately combine objective and subjective evidence has always been an issue. There is a tendency to favor objective (numeric) evidence over subjective evidence, since the latter is after all just someone's opinion. Yet just something can be expressed numerically does not make it more important or relevant than a personal judgment. Despite the increased use of workforce analytics to augment selection models the choice between candidates for an executive position will be impacted by opinions about whether a candidate's personality will fit in well with the culture and the personalities of other management personnel.

Research methodology has been broadened by the recognition that "systematic reviews" can be used to gather all evidence relevant to a decision. Research studies have historically been quantitative but systematic review methods have been developed that incorporate all types of evidence. As a result the quality of evidence-based decisions about performance and rewards management for executives can be improved.

There has been considerable research done on the question "does executive compensation impact organization performance?" Most people would assume that organizations that pay more would be able to get a higher quality of executive talent. Correlation studies have shown that higher paying organizations tend to be more financially successful. But as discussed in this book's Appendix 1 on quantitative analysis correlation does not establish causation. It is equally reasonable to believe that the correlation can be the result of financially successful organizations being able to pay more. Success generally improves the mood in the boardroom so high profits and growth may convince the board to be generous when setting executive pay levels. It is therefore prudent for those who recommend strategies and for those who approve them to be cautious in relying on evidence that does not in reality support the hypothesis that paying executives more will lead to improved future performance.

A final consideration when using evidence to influence decisions is whether the results realized by competitors when they adopt a particular strategy could reasonably be expected to the same for the organization. Benchmarking is only valid when the context within which competitors operate is substantially similar to the organization's context. Microsoft's successful incentive program may turn out differently if it were to be implemented by Walmart . . . or even Google or Amazon. Contextual determinants include things like culture, operational capabilities, customer bases and demands for innovation and given the relative uniqueness of many of these things makes emulation a risky proposition. If a board assumes that the organization must adopt a restricted stock plan to increase executive retention, based on the evidence that most of the direct competitors for talent use these plans it may fail to realize that emulation limits you to matching competitors and that by offering different inducements a competitive edge may be gained. It is, of course, necessary to be different when it is appropriate, rather than just to stand out. It all will depend on the subjective judgments of candidates whether your unique value proposition is a plus or a minus.

In summary, executive compensation has been largely about the numbers. And being different from the norm leaves an organization with no evidence about how a unique strategy will impact the attraction and retention of talent. But often having tangible evidence about competitive practice does not necessarily provide guidance that will lead to success.

Application of Principles: Chapter 4

A U.S.-based organization has begun expanding its operations globally, to Asia, Europe and the Middle East. The CEO has adopted a policy of selecting country and regional executives who will operate out of the U.S. in a manner that promotes diversity. Her belief is that executives who are from a region are more apt to understand the context. She also has mandated that the compensation philosophy and programs for executives be the same globally, to encourage them to align their ways of doing business and to socialize them into the culture of the organization. The current executive compensation package includes a very significant restricted stock program. The CFO and CHRO have appealed to the CEO to consider the differences in contextual factors, and to adjust performance and rewards strategies to reflect the cultural, legal, taxation, logistical and economic conditions in differing locations.

The CEO has asked for a briefing on the advantages and disadvantages of the two options: a homogenous philosophy or localized strategies. Develop a briefing that includes all relevant considerations without biasing the report to influence the CEO.

Notes

1 Kaplan, R. & Norton, D., *The Balanced Scorecard* (Boston, MA, Harvard Business Press, 1996).
2 Collins, J., *Good to Great* (New York, Harper Business, 2001).
3 Lawler, E. & O'Toole, J., *The New American Workplace* (New York, Palgrave Macmillan, 2006).
4 Crystal, G., *In Search of Excess* (New York, W. W. Norton, 1991).
5 Ellig, B., *The Complete Guide to Executive Compensation* (New York, McGraw-Hill, 2000).
6 Trompenaars, F. & Hampden-Turner, C., *Twenty One Leaders for the Twenty First Century* (Oxford, UK, Capstone, 2001).
7 House, R., Ed., *Culture, Leadership and Organizations* (Thousand Oaks, CA, Sage, 2004); Chhokar, J., Brodbeck, F. & House, R., Eds., *Culture and Leadership across the World* (Mahwah, NJ, Lawrence Erlbaum, 2008).
8 Trompenaars, F., *Riding the Waves of Culture* (Burr Ridge, IL, Irwin, 1994).

Chapter 5

Rewarding Performance
Professionals

There has been a rapid increase in the number of employees who are called "professionals" over the last several decades, owing in large part to the transition to a knowledge-based society. Included in this category are scientists and engineers and a broad range of formally trained specialists in finance, information systems, marketing and human resources. If one were to believe the hype in the literature in 2018, the only way to ensure employment is to become a data scientist or coder. But the emergence of these occupations is due to a backlog in data analytics and software design. Once organizations realized that the huge data bases already in existence could have real value if mined effectively, the race was on to see how much gold there was in those hills. This evolution raises questions about the continued appropriateness and effectiveness of the performance and reward management strategies most commonly used in an industrial era. If the typical employee of today has different characteristics than the employee of a few decades ago, it is likely their perspectives, needs and priorities are different as well. Since human resource management strategies must fit the nature of the workforce in order to be effective, their continuing effectiveness should be evaluated against current realities.

What Is Different about Professional Personnel?

Professionals rely on their mastery of a defined body of knowledge in a particular field and require extensive formal education and/or training in that field. There are a number of characteristics of professional personnel that may warrant different human resource management strategies than those used for other personnel:

1   *They perform knowledge-intensive work.* Because of the technical nature of the work it is necessary for incumbents to have deep levels of understanding of concepts, theories and principles, rather than relying on general knowledge. Few would retain a surgeon not possessing board certification, and most construction firms would be reluctant to have a bridge designed by a self-taught person lacking the necessary education and required licensing in civil engineering. The formal education and training required often mean these people do not enter their field until they have demonstrated their mastery of the fundamental theories and concepts underlying practice.

2   *They typically work interdependently.* Since professionals often have highly specialized knowledge, they often need practitioners from related fields to support them when facing complex, interdisciplinary challenges. For example, if designing a new ethical drug requires an advanced level of knowledge in chemistry, biology, statistics, IT,

pharmacology and patent law, no one is likely to possess all of the necessary knowledge to independently produce the desired result. Consequently, cross-disciplinary project teams are the accepted way to organize work involving these requirements. Technical failures are often caused by people with a specialized discipline who act as if they were islands unto themselves and who operate under their own set of rules, without regard to the impact on others and/or without counseling others with knowledge that is needed.

3   *Their work is predominantly project oriented.* Engineers and systems analysts rarely have traditional "jobs," consisting of a stable set of specific tasks. Rather, they move from project to project, changing roles frequently. This reality often results in them being classified through the use of occupational career ladders, rather than being assigned a job title and a job description. Their work is also performed on cycles that often do not coincide with the administrative schedules that are used for appraising performance and determining pay actions.

4   *Their orientation tends to be towards producing the very best, rather than what is good enough.* Any organization employing scientists will be familiar with the tendency of their people to want to achieve the very best (drug, system, idea), irrespective of developmental costs and the actual requirements. This largely results from the nature of their education and their professional pride. It also is the product of the need to work with the newest and best technology, in order to keep their knowledge and skills current and marketable. This tendency is often in conflict with the organizational standard, which is "good enough." The different perspectives make it difficult to keep the very best professionals satisfied with the way they are expected to function, how their performance is measured and how they are rewarded, particularly when resources are scarce.

5   *Their orientation is to progress within their field.* When someone has invested 16–20 years in formal education to learn the body of knowledge in their field, it is natural that they will be focused on that field, rather than on their current employer. This is particularly true in today's "free agent" market, where professionals are expected to be mobile. Professionals also rely on others in their field to keep them up to date, and therefore their networks often extend outside their employing organization. This may result in a focus on becoming a better professional, rather than rising through the ranks in the organization currently employing them. Professionals also tend to recognize authority based on expertise, rather than who has the highest position in the management hierarchy, which presents challenges relative to organizing and managing units consisting of professional personnel. With the increased use of freelancers, contractors and people screened through talent platforms, their options for making a living have broadened outside traditional employment with a single employer. This means the organization must recognize the ability of those with scarce talent to augment their job with outside work or to request an alteration to their current status with the organization.

What Impact Do These Characteristics Have on Managing Performance and Rewards?

The issues related to role definition, career management, performance management and rewards management for professional personnel will be discussed further, since they present the greatest challenges.

Role Definition and Career Management

The first step towards deciding how an organization defines, measures and rewards performance is to define the roles played by incumbents of a particular occupation or function and to value them from the organization's perspective. Engineering personnel are a good example for illustrating the decision process. The role of engineers is most often that of working on projects, usually as a member of a team. They enter their field after an extended period of formal education and they tend to remain oriented to their profession, since it is more likely they will work for other organizations as engineers rather than working for their current organization outside of their field. Given the long duration of study required to become an engineer, they may not aspire to retrain or to go into general management roles, although they certainly might choose to pursue engineering management roles.

Since most engineers are project oriented, rather than having a specific set of duties, they are often classified into occupational ladders, such as the example shown in Table 5.1. Given the competitiveness in the labor markets for many professional disciplines, organizations are forced to classify them and to pay incumbents based on their attained level of expertise, rather than what they happen to be doing at a given point in time. As a result, using a job-based classification system may be inappropriate. Professionals are progressed through the levels in the ladder as they grow in knowledge, skill and the ability to take on more responsibility for producing results. Their classification should be based on what they are capable of, rather than what they are currently doing. Movement from one level to another within the ladder is viewed by professionals as being just as much a promotion as it would be if they were to become a supervisor, and for many a preferred form of progress.

The process used to regulate the movement of professionals through a technical ladder is critical in determining how appropriately people are advanced. Although level criteria help to classify individuals, the process used must be viewed as appropriate and equitable by incumbents. If each of the direct supervisors makes decisions about progressions for their people there is a danger of uneven application of the standards. Some managers may be more aggressive in moving their people up than others, either because they interpret the standards differently or because they feel they must be advocates for their subordinates. On the other hand, it can be argued that attempting to control progressions on a centralized basis may result in decisions being made by people not intimately familiar with the qualifications of individuals.

A balance must be struck, and most organizations do so by having the supervisor make the original recommendation, supported by formal documentation, and then having a higher-level review of the nominations for consistency across supervisors. As the number of people in the function becomes large this balancing act becomes very difficult and often requires review by a panel of professionals representing a cross-section of the population. Progression into the highest levels in the ladder may also require the participation of experts from outside the organization, particularly if the candidate possesses knowledge that is beyond that possessed by anyone else in the organization. Senior members of university faculties and experts from other organizations or professional associations often are used as resources when a person's work involves discovery of new knowledge.

Table 5.1 Engineering Classification Standards

Job Criteria	Associate Engineer	Engineer	Senior Engineer	Consulting Engineer
Nature of work (type; complexity; variety; difficulty)	Performs engineering work in support of engineering staff. Applies knowledge in professional field/discipline. Utilizes knowledge of principles, concepts and theory in field to guide approach to assigned work.	Performs assigned engineering work. Applies technical expertise and knowledge of company processes to complete projects of limited scope and to assist more senior personnel on more complex projects.	Performs engineering work of significant complexity and requiring advanced technical knowledge. Works on projects of broad scope that may require developing new approaches to produce solutions.	Performs engineering work of very broad scope and requiring the application of the most complex techniques. Monitors developments in the field and may create new knowledge and approaches. Recognized as being an expert in the field.
Latitude/direction received (authority; creativity; nature of supervision received)	Works under direct supervision, applying established principles and theories.	Works under general supervision, applying established principles and theories and exercising independent judgment.	Works under general direction, applying advanced knowledge. May determine the approach taken to enable the project team to achieve the established objectives.	Works under general direction, determining how projects will be structured and what technology will be used. May take technical direction from experts outside the organization.
Responsibility for interpersonal contacts (type; level; frequency)	Exchanges information with peers, both within and outside unit, and with customers as directed.	Exchanges information with peers, suppliers and customers as required to perform work.	Develops professional network, utilizing outside sources to acquire necessary knowledge. Works with other units to resolve conflicts about approach.	Maintains a professional network encompassing experts in the entire field. Acts as an advisor on technical issues to management, customers and suppliers.
Responsibility for work of others	Provides guidance and training to technicians as required to complete assignments.	Provides guidance and training to technicians and inexperienced engineers to complete assignments.	Responsible for guiding the work of less experienced engineers and may supervise their work on assigned projects.	Determines how projects will be staffed and directs how resources will be utilized. Serves as role model and expert advisor to other engineers.
Potential impact on unit (quality; cost; effect on customer; responsiveness)	Quality of work will impact project costs and results, as well as impacting effectiveness of unit.	Quality of work will have a significant impact on project costs and results and on the unit's effectiveness.	Quality of work and direction provided to others will determine success of projects and/or significantly impact costs.	Technical leadership will significantly impact the quality of engineering and the performance of the function.

	Internal Progression	External Hire of Inexperienced College	Experienced Engineer Graduate Hire
Consulting engineer	– Meets level criteria – Must have *sustained* high performance/value of contribution for the past three years within the organization as a senior engineer – Is nominated and appointed through formal process – Percentage restrictions	N/A	N/A
Senior engineer	– Meets level criteria – Director approval	– Meets level criteria – Director approval – BS and 5–8 years of relevant professional-level experience or MS and 3–5 years of relevant experience	N/A
Engineer	– Meets level criteria – Director approval	– Meets level criteria – BS and 3–5 years of relevant professional-level administrative experience or MS and 1–2 years of relevant experience	– MS in relevant field
Associate Engineer	– Meets level criteria – Manager approval	– Meets level criteria – BS plus some relevant experience.	– BS in relevant field

A similar approach is increasingly being used for administrative professionals. Table 5.2 is an example of a career ladder for administrative disciplines. It shares similarities with the technical ladder, in that the criteria for defining the levels are the same. Ladders such as this are often used to career-progress people. They are often supplemented by occupational definitions that define the specific fields in which incumbents are trained. For example, there might be separate occupational ladders for finance, legal, HR, procurement, logistics management and so on. An advantage of having a common method for defining levels within ladders is that it sends the message of equivalent treatment, since progression is related to common standards. An advantage of having customized ladders is that each occupation can be separately measured against compensation levels prevailing in the relevant labor markets and pay ranges can be set at competitive levels, differing across occupations as appropriate.

It is critical to recognize that the career ladder serves as a way for organizations to administratively celebrate the growth of professionals in their field. By providing standards that act as score-keeping metrics the organization conveys the criteria and standards that will be used to recognize career progression. When an associate engineer is "promoted" to engineer it does not mean the person was radically transformed on the effective date of the progression. The reclassification is an administrative acknowledgement that the person

Table 5.2 Administrative Classification Standards

Job Criteria	Associate	Staff	Senior	Principal
Nature of work performed (type; complexity; variety; difficulty)	Performs administrative activities of broad scope, related to business and technical operations, processes, programs and projects. Conducts analyses to determine how well administrative processes are functioning and contributes ideas for solving problems/ addressing issues and for improving unit effectiveness.	Performs a wide variety of administrative activities of broad scope, related to key business and technical operations, processes, programs and projects. Evaluates administrative effectiveness for programs and processes and formulates recommendations for solving problems/ addressing issues and for improving unit effectiveness.	Performs the full range of administrative activities required to support large and complex projects and programs. Participates in formulating policies and develops methods for effectively managing business and technical operations, processes, programs and projects. Evaluates major programs, processes and operations and formulates recommendations for improving administrative effectiveness.	Performs the full range of administrative activities required to support large and complex projects and programs. Participates in formulating policies and develops methods for effectively managing business and technical operations, processes, programs and projects. Evaluates major programs, processes and operations and works with executive management to formulate strategies for improving overall administrative effectiveness.
Skill/knowledge required	Applies knowledge of principles, concepts and theory related to a professional administrative discipline/ field and employs a systems approach to address issues and to define and resolve problems.	Applies knowledge of principles, concepts and theory related to a professional administrative discipline/field and employs a systems approach to address issues and to define and resolve problems. Uses experience with administering projects and programs to apply knowledge.	Applies expert knowledge of advanced principles, concepts and theory related to professional administrative discipline(s)/field(s) and employs a systems approach to address issues and to define and resolve the most difficult and challenging problems. Utilizes broad scope of understanding about organizational processes and operations.	Applies expert knowledge of advanced principles, concepts and theory related to professional administrative discipline(s)/field(s) and employs a systems approach to address issues and to define and resolve the most difficult and challenging problems. Utilizes understanding of organization-wide operations and its objectives to act as an authority on key administrative matters.
Latitude exercised/ direction received (authority; creativity; autonomy; nature and frequency of supervision received)	Works independently, with general direction, receiving more specific direction on issues new to incumbent or on more complex assignments.	Works independently, receiving direction as required to ensure project/program objectives are met and that administrative policies and strategies are appropriate.	Works independently, receiving direction on project/program objectives and strategies. Makes decisions on how to perform own work and formulates strategies for improving operations/processes.	Work is guided by consultation with management, based on project/program objectives and strategies. Makes decisions on behalf of management, within prescribed scope of authority.

(continued)

Table 5.2 (continued)

Job Criteria	Associate	Staff	Senior	Principal
	Exercises discretion and judgment in performing work and contributes recommendations for improving operations/processes. Assists in implementing improvements to existing processes as appropriate.	Exercises considerable discretion and judgment in performing work and conducting evaluations of operation/process effectiveness. Initiates changes required to implement improvements.	Directs initiatives to implement improvement strategies.	Utilizes organization-wide perspective to identify possible improvements to key business processes.
Responsibility for interpersonal contacts (type; level; frequency; expected results; potential impact)	Exchanges information and works with peers, both within unit and from other units. Works with outside agencies, customers/sponsors and suppliers as assigned and coordinates work of own unit with that of others.	Works with other units and outside agencies, customers/sponsors and suppliers as required to effectively administer projects and programs. Develops relationships as needed to perform work effectively.	Develops and maintains relationships with customers/sponsors, suppliers, outside agencies and other units within the organization as needed to facilitate meeting project/program and unit objectives. May act as principal representative of the organization.	Responsible for creating and developing relationships with key parties at interest relative to long-term issues and initiatives. Acts as principal representative of the organization and assists in negotiating the terms of critical administrative relationships.
Responsibility for work of others (mentoring, assigning/directing work, providing technical direction)	May provide guidance and training to administrative support personnel, students, interns, contractors and other support personnel as required to complete assignments.	Provides guidance to administrative support personnel, students, interns, contractors and other support personnel, as a mentor or as a team/project leader.	Directs the work of administrative support personnel, students, interns, contractors and other less experienced personnel, either as a mentor or as a team/project leader. Serves as a role model and source of expert knowledge.	Provides overall administrative direction on long-term and critical programs and projects. Establishes organization-wide standards and participates in developing/applying new technologies to administrative management.
Potential impact (cost; customer/supplier relations; unit performance)	Quality of work can have a significant impact on project quality, costs and overall results and impact the effectiveness of the unit.	Quality of work can have a major impact on project/program results and substantially impact the effectiveness of the unit.	Quality of work directly and significantly impacts the quality of project, program and/or unit administration.	Quality of work directly and significantly impacts the performance of major projects and programs.

better fits the standards for the higher level—a reality that emerged gradually over time. It is important for the organization always to remember that career progressions are for many professionals the only tangible evidence that they have grown in their field. Many professionals start their careers classified as accountants or systems analysts or engineers and end their careers in the same category, albeit more capable than when they started.

A confidential benchmark study conducted by a U.S. national research laboratory found that premier research organizations typically used formal ladders that had from three to six levels of expertise defined. Many of these organizations considered it acceptable to have professionals peak at levels one to two levels below the top level. In other words, ending one's 30-year career as a senior engineer did not constitute a failure, even though there were levels above senior in the ladder. In fact, moving someone to the highest levels based only on longevity is often considered an administrative failure, since it dilutes the meaning of the achievement to those who warranted the classification based on their capabilities and their contributions.

The flurry of articles in HR publications and speeches at conferences in the late 1990s heralding the "new breakthrough" concept of "broadbanding" prompted many organizations to forget what career management structures meant to professionals. The broadbanding approach usually mandates collapsing five- or six-level professional ladders into two to three (in some radical cases even one) levels and to assign salary ranges to each "band" that were 100–200% wide, instead of the traditional 50%. This approach was promoted as a technique that enabled organizations to operate flexibly. Adopting broadbanding caused some organizations to collapse or abandon the ladders that had operated as the professional career metric for decades. In many cases this created an enormous backlash of dissatisfaction in the ranks. Senior-level people found themselves classified in the same band as associates (rookies) and thereby viewed the change as diminishing the value of what they had achieved through personal development. And even the associates were sometimes upset, when they compared their salaries to the top of their range (where every professional believes they belong). The author has counseled numerous organizations on undoing the negative impact of adopting broadbanding, by reinstituting the ladders, but the confusion and angst created by the adoption of bands had impacted employee satisfaction and made the professionals suspicious about the competence of the HR function.

Another consideration in defining the roles of professionals is whether "competencies" will be used for purposes of selection, classification and career progression. Table 5.3 is an example of an occupational family definition for human resource generalists. It defines the levels by specifying the "technical (HR)," "business" and "personal" characteristics required at each of the proficiency levels. This approach is less specific than the engineering ladder in Table 5.1 for defining the nature of the work performed. But it additionally defines personal characteristics required for success, and therefore is a "competency model" as well. Competencies were dominating the HR literature in the mid- and late 1990s, and the notion of "competency-based pay" was proposed by many of the consultancies, particularly for professionals whose roles did not consist of well-defined duties and responsibilities. These models are more useful for selection and career management than for performance and rewards management, since defining potential as performance and paying for it may leave the organization without the results that would warrant rewards. What the resurgence of competency-based strategies did accomplish is that it recognized behaviors as being important things to define and measure. As many professionals operate in a service capacity, responding to customer or user needs, *how* they performed their

Table 5.3 Human Resource Generalist

	Emerging Practitioner	Accomplished Practitioner	Senior/Lead Practitioner
Business Competencies *Strategic perspective:* analyzes trends and synthesizes information from all relevant sources; sells vision to others; has long-term perspective	Knows mission and strategy of organization; looks for ways to meet objectives; understands the need to frame decisions and actions in broad context.	Understands how HR strategy and programs fit into organization strategy; designs HR programs to support strategy; evaluates effectiveness of programs in facilitating success.	Assists in formulating HR strategy and plans; projects future objectives for programs and plans to replace or revise them so they will fit the objectives as they change.
Organizational knowledge: knows the organization; (context, products, customers and financials); has understanding of functional roles; selects strategies/plans based on clear objectives and their expected impact on organizational results	Knows about organizational context, its culture and how it is organized; works to understand roles of functions and business units and their needs; learns about internal and external customers and suppliers and how HR strategies and programs impact them.	Understands how the structure functions; knows the culture and its implications; applies knowledge to design and administer HR programs in a manner that fits the specific context of the organization.	Assists in assessing the culture and the organization structure and in reshaping them to fit organizational needs and realities; evaluates the extent to which HR programs support the HR strategy and assists in modifying the strategy to be effective Biven external and internal realities.
Business knowledge: knows about industry and related industries; understands economic/competitive forces; knows what is required for success; knows what knowledge/skins are critical and labor market realities for them	Knows about the economics of the organization and its businesses; works to understand the human capital needs of the organization and the realities of the external environment/labor markets.	Understands how economic realities impact performance of the businesses and the overall organization; designs and administers HR programs in a manner that contributes to business success.	Assists in evaluating HR strategies and programs to determine their business impact; ensures programs are cost-effective and based on sound business principles; evaluates strategy and programs continually to anticipate the need for change.
Customer/supplier knowledge: knows key customers (internal and external) and suppliers and understands their needs/priorities; adopts strategies to meet their needs and uses programs and processes to meet them	Knows about the needs of internal and external customers and how HR programs impact them; develops relationships with customers and works to understand how HR can make them more effective.	Understands what HR strategies/ programs can do to satisfy customers and make them effective; designs and administers HR programs that satisfy customer needs while ensuring they are cost-effective.	Assists in developing an HR service model that identifies needs of customers, suppliers and venture partners and that utilizes cost-effective processes; monitors HR's performance; adjusts programs as required; recommends modifications to improve service.

Technological knowledge/skill: knows about what is available and adopts appropriate tools; searches for new applications of technology based on their probable fit to context and their cost–benefit balance	Understands the commonly used tools and is proficient in using them; works to develop knowledge of emerging technologies and how they can be applied in HR.	Understands how technology impacts HR service levels and cost-effectiveness; assists in recommending technology to improve service and/or lower costs.	Assists in planning the acquisition/ application of technology to increase HR effectiveness; directs implementation and evaluates the impact on service levels and costs.
Technical Competencies *Staffing:* recruiting; selection; placement; workplace/role design; workforce planning	Understands staffing concepts, techniques and processes and develops competence in applying them in program design/administration.	Administers staffing programs; makes recommendations on program revisions to improve effectiveness.	Evaluates effectiveness of staffing strategies/programs; refines existing programs and develops new ones; directs implementation, communication/training.
Development human capital assessment; career planning/ management; training; education	Understands HRD concepts, techniques and processes and develops competence in applying them in program design/administration.	Administers HRD programs; makes recommendations on program revisions to improve effectiveness.	Evaluates effectiveness of HRD strategies/programs; refines existing programs and develops new ones; directs implementation, communication and training.
Performance management performance models at all levels; performance planning, measurement, feedback, development and appraisal	Understands concepts, techniques and processes and develops competence in applying them in performance management program design and administration.	Administers performance management programs; makes recommendations on program revisions to improve effectiveness.	Evaluates effectiveness of performance management strategies/programs; refines existing programs and develops new ones; directs implementation, communication/training.
Rewards management direct compensation; employee benefits; recognition/non-financial rewards; employee ownership	Understands rewards concepts, techniques and processes and develops competence in applying them in program design/administration.	Administers rewards programs; makes recommendations on program revisions to improve effectiveness.	Evaluates effectiveness of rewards strategies/programs; refines existing programs and develops new ones; directs implementation, communication/training.
Employee/labor relations (E/LR): employment policies; health, safety and security; ethics; communication; leadership; legal/regulatory compliance	Understands E/LR concepts, techniques and processes and develops competence in applying them in HR program design and administration.	Administers E/LR programs; makes recommendations on program revisions to improve effectiveness.	Evaluates effectiveness of E/LR strategies/programs; refines existing programs and develops new ones; directs implementation, communication/training.

(continued)

Table 5.3 (continued)

	Emerging Practitioner	Accomplished Practitioner	Senior/Lead Practitioner
Personal Competencies			
Learning agility/creativity: open to new concepts; observes, listen and absorbs new ideas; creates new approaches; adapts to new conditions	Develops knowledge of ideas and concepts to create varied repertoire; is flexible in realizing, accepting and adapting to change.	Actively seeks new ideas and techniques; tries new approaches; accepts contextual change and attempts to adapt to new requirements.	Scans varied external sources for new ideas; leads others in search for better ways to design and administer programs.
Cultural understanding: understands the similarities/ differences between values and beliefs; open to different approaches; leverages benefits of diversity	Develops knowledge of the perspectives of others; actively works to accommodate and respect differences when performing job.	Evaluates policies and programs to ensure they respect cultural differences; makes recommendations for changes.	Takes initiative to find approaches to work that will fit the beliefs and styles of others; evaluates policies to ensure they appropriately consider the impact on different cultures.
Flexibility/adaptability: willing to consider new/conflicting ideas; adjusts to different contexts and requirements; does not resist needed change	Open to new ideas; adapts behavior to fit changes.	Open to new models; searches for behaviors and approaches that will better fit changes in context.	Open to new paradigms; anticipates need for change and proactively initiates actions to make necessary changes.
Integrity/honesty: represents beliefs, values and ideas candidly; shapes actions based on laws and principles rather than on expediency.	Adheres to legal and regulatory requirements and to values/ policies; reports violations of organizational values and laws.	Ensures programs are administered by means compatible with organizational values; identifies violations and takes appropriate action.	Acts as role model; helps others develop behaviors that enable them to maintain integrity; ensures violations of laws, values and ethics are appropriately dealt with.
Communication effectiveness/ability to influence others: able to convey information in manner fitting audience; able to influence others to consider alternatives and to accept recommendations	Effectively expresses self in manner understandable to target audience; receptive to views of others and exerts appropriate influence.	Evaluates how well programs have been communicated and recommends how employee acceptance and understanding can be improved.	Effectively dialogues with all internal and external parties; exerts influence on policies and strategies; develops communication strategies for new programs.

Interpersonal skills: able to work with others to make them effective and achieve aggregate results; builds needed relationships	Interacts with others as required to share knowledge and exchange information; builds network of contacts.	Interacts with others to coordinate activities with parties at interest; creates effective relationships with others.	Motivates others to create effective working relations; facilitates sharing of ideas and knowledge across organizational units.
Planning/organizing skills: scans environment for emerging trends and plans for needed responses; organizes people and manages resources to produce needed results	Plans and organizes work to meet priorities/deadlines; allocates time and resources to meet established objectives.	Structures project management plans for assigned areas; evaluates results vs. plan and redirects resources as appropriate.	Identifies long-term trends and requirements; develops robust alternative scenarios to deal with requirements imposed by the context.
Analytical/synthesis skills: able to analyze situations using quantitative and qualitative methods; able to integrate information to understand what responses are required	Develops analytical skills through study of concepts and methods; translates data into usable information.	Analyzes effectiveness of processes and programs; determines what changes are required to increase effectiveness and efficiency.	Diagnoses context and identifies factors that impact results; integrates information in order to develop strategies for dealing with issues.
Change management skills: recognizes/accepts need for change; defines requirements and develops plans, involving appropriate parties; directs process to produce needed results	Develops skills required to implement modifications to programs.	Leads change initiatives and takes responsibility for motivating others.	Identifies need for changes to culture, strategy or policy; develops change plans and directs their execution; acts as role model for desired behavior.
Leadership skills: able to create vision others can understand; motivates and aligns efforts towards objectives; adapts approach to those being led	Directs aspects of assigned projects as appropriate; provides guidance to involved parties.	Provides direction for projects; defines roles for others and motivates them to achieve objectives.	Develops vision of successful organization and communicates it to others in a manner that guides effective action and that produces the desired results.

work is important. The focus on behaviors also acknowledged that professionals often cannot control outcomes and therefore their performance should be measured using criteria that they can control: how appropriately they behaved, given the circumstances.

There is a tendency on the part of many managers of professional or technical work to employ the very best people available, even though their qualifications may exceed the nature of the work. This temptation becomes great during economic slowdowns, when the supply of people exceeds the demand. But people overqualified for their roles will become bored and anxious that their knowledge is not keeping up with the state of the art. Throughout the 1990s, IT personnel were very focused on keeping their skills marketable, since the movement from mainframe systems to network-based technology was rapid, partly owing to the pressure put on by the impending requirement for Y2K compatibility. Those asked to keep the legacy systems running felt left out of the mainstream and were concerned that they would be less valuable when the new technology was in place. And it was also expensive to maintain a highly qualified workforce, particularly since they were mobile and oriented to their field. The organizations found that they had to pay them their market worth, in order to keep them, and the high costs often impacted the competitiveness of the business. One of the challenges then is to develop qualification standards based on the nature of the work performed and to staff the technical functions with the appropriate mix of expertise.

A critical issue related to both role definition and career management is the definition of managerial roles within professional and technical functions and how managers are compensated relative to the people they manage. From a career management perspective the best tool for providing opportunity is a "dual ladder." The objective of a dual ladder is to provide a choice to incumbents of technical positions as to whether their career growth should be through technical progression or through the assumption of managerial responsibility. The best path will depend on the individual in each case, since eventual satisfaction will depend on whether the role the person plays is consistent with their competencies and with their preferences.

Figure 5.1 is a graphic portrayal of the traditional dual ladder. Again using engineers as an example, the new entrant to the field would typically start as an individual contributor at the associate level. That person would then progress through the engineer and senior engineer levels, typically being classified using a ladder similar to the one in Table 5.1. At some point, in this case at the senior engineer level, the person faces a fork in the road: continue to specialize in the technical aspects of the work or begin to assume managerial responsibility. This decision should not be final and irrevocable. And Yogi Berra's advice ("When you come to a fork in the road, take it") might not be nonsense. An incumbent who decides to pursue management roles does not stop learning or stop being an engineer. Effectively managing professional or technical personnel requires substantial expertise in the field. To repeat an earlier point, real authority often follows expertise, rather than formal rank. So those aspiring to managerial roles find themselves with a wide variety of competencies to develop. And those making a choice of direction might also consider retaining the skills necessary to change paths if circumstances or preferences change in the future.

Not all professional or technical personnel are well suited to management. Promoting the best systems analyst to supervisor based on their technical performance can result in the wrong person managing projects or units. Some of the competencies differ between

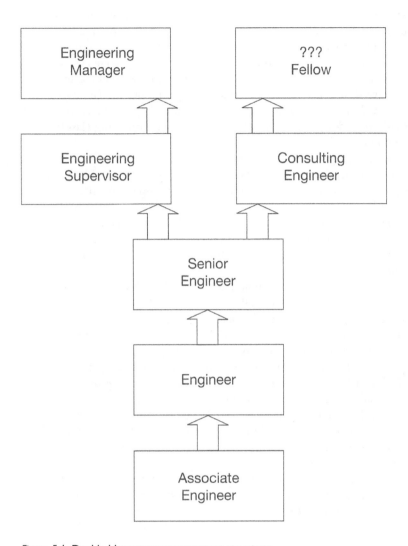

Figure 5.1 Dual ladder career management structure

the two orientations, and a professional who both likes and is good at working alone to develop ideas and solve problems is a questionable candidate for management. It may also be a waste to put a brilliant technical person into a managerial role, particularly if the administrative work takes them away from what they do best. And the standards that a Nobel Prize candidate would use to judge subordinates might be totally unrealistic, thereby making them a questionable choice to do performance appraisals.

The career management strategy should incorporate principles relating to movement between the technical and managerial branches of the ladder, to ensure that choices are not irrevocable. People change their aspirations over time and sometimes discover they are limiting themselves by sticking to an earlier choice. A financial analyst may realize that they will never be able to operate effectively at the highest level of technical expertise and that management is not as bad as it seemed earlier. By providing reasonable flexibility relative to horizontal movement the organization can maximize the effectiveness and satisfaction of a valued employee. On the other hand, the ability to change classifications should be limited by the person's ability to operate effectively in the other capacity. Too many organizations have disillusioned senior technical people by placing failed managers in a technical level they do not warrant just so their pay can be kept at the current level. As mentioned earlier, professionals view the prestige associated with being classified in a level based on who populates that level.

The levels above senior in Figure 5.1 are shown to be different but equivalent-equivalent in status and often in compensation potential. The consulting engineer would typically be in the same grade with the same salary range as the engineering supervisor. It is important that the career potential associated with both managerial and advanced technical positions be determined and clearly communicated to candidates, so they can make informed career decisions. Ensuring there is equivalence in the pay potential associated with both options helps people not to select the higher paid option when their heart and their qualifications better suit them to the other.

There are question marks shown on the technical side above the fellow level in Figure 5.1, suggesting there might be another level equivalent to director on the management side. This will depend on how sophisticated the technical work can be and how much expertise the organization can effectively utilize. For example, if an organization contracts out very complex work or major projects there may be no need for someone who is capable of operating at the "fellow" level. If an unnecessary level is added to the top of the technical branch of the dual ladder it will be filled, warranted or not. Resisting the temptation to use a promotion as a substitute for money is difficult when a valued employee is topped out in the range for their level but does not warrant progression to the next level. On the other hand, if the technical branch is overly limited, people who are best suited to technical work may feel they have to go into management for the opportunity, whether or not they want to manage or will be good at it.

Research-focused organizations employ significant numbers of people expected to create new knowledge and to generate technical innovations, who are therefore candidates for an extended technical ladder. It is not unusual for a technical level to be accorded similar status to a vice president or director, to whom they report administratively. This would mean that veteran technical personnel could be paid more than the person they report to, which in some corporate cultures would be heresy. However, the direct report manager may be incapable of supervising the actual work of a person at that level of technical expertise. The reality is that the manager is responsible for the person only administratively.

As more work is done in the form of projects, yet a third occupational branch is being added to the career structure. Project planning and administration has emerged as a technical discipline and when projects are long and complex keeping track of progress against project plan has become more critical. Stories abound about projects with cost and time overruns that seem to make original projections by planners laughable. Developing a project plan requires a deep understanding of the technology, materials and human effort involved, as well as how the segments of the project are to be executed and how they can be integrated with each other into the overall project. Those who call the shots on how things are to be done are usually considered project management personnel, while those who keep track of what is done are more appropriately considered project planning and administration personnel. The Project Management Institute (pmi.org) has a series of certifications for people involved in all aspects of projects and many organizations have added that third branch to their career management ladders.

Performance Management

Defining and evaluating performance is often a challenge when professional personnel are concerned. The metrics that are appropriate to use to define performance may be qualitative in nature, and evaluating performance often requires a subjective judgment by another technical person. A quip about doing performance appraisals for scientists performing pure research in a leading R&D institution was heard recently: "What do we measure—ergs of original thought?" Another familiar refrain is "My people do creative work and you cannot measure that." A manager of technical personnel may dread making performance judgments based solely on how intently their people stare into space for extended periods when they are attacking problems that may be insoluble. But such instances are the exception. Subjective assessments can be acceptable criteria for appraising performance, as long as the method and process used are appropriate and all parties understand and accept the basis for appraisal and who does the appraisal.

Performance is defined by establishing criteria and standards, as discussed in detail in Chapter 2. The criteria that will be relevant to the professional tend to include the standard productivity, quality and dependability dimensions, but since so many incumbents work on projects rather than performing recurring duties the definition of performance needs to be tailored to their work. Cross-functional work teams are being used increasingly to develop new products and to create new technologies.

An example would be a software design firm, where software engineers contribute by providing the design expertise, finance professionals by providing economic analysis and marketing professionals by creating the strategy for going to market. This type of design process presents two challenges relative to appraising performance at the individual level. Since it takes everyone involved to produce the result it makes better sense to measure performance at the team level, since relative contribution by individuals is hard to measure. The second challenge is that project work may be tied to project milestones, and the timeframes will almost certainly not coincide with the annual administrative cycle prevalent in most organizations. It is difficult for a manager to evaluate the performance of a systems engineer who is five months into a 14-month project segment. This raises the question of whether it is better to do the best appraisal possible at the end of the year or to appraise when results are clear, whenever that falls relative to the annual cycle.

It is, of course, possible to prorate the salary adjustment for someone who has to wait for more than 12 months until a project milestone is reached. There is no natural law that says everyone must have a performance appraisal and a salary adjustment every 12 months. Yet if performance appraisal is a continuous process, rather than a once-a-year event, appraising a professional at year-end should not be that difficult. Most organizations appraise performance and determine pay actions on a single (focal) date, and they tend to do this for all personnel. If this approach is used for professionals focused on project work, it is critical that some provision for periodic, if not continuous, performance measurement and feedback be built into the performance management system. Some organizations have separated personal performance from project performance and tie salary actions to the former and project incentives to the latter, which helps to reconcile the timing dilemma.

Another consideration relative to the performance of a professional is who should have input into the appraisal process. The professional's manager may have a narrow view of that person's performance, since it is not unusual for work to be performed for several project managers, out of sight of the manager. Strategies for employees whose work is project oriented and who work in teams are discussed further in Chapter 8. This type of working arrangement argues for multi-party input to the appraisal, which can provide the manager ultimately responsible for doing the appraisal with a broader perspective. Project managers, peers, support staff and even customers may have differing perspectives about a professional's performance. But it is the responsibility of the appraising manager to decide whose views should legitimately be considered and to take them into account when doing the appraisal. It is advisable to ensure project managers are responsible for providing formal written feedback on the performance of each of the staff members to the direct report manager when the staff members' work is complete. Otherwise, it may be difficult for the direct report manager to get reliable input at a later date, since the passage of time blurs memory. The direct report manager can then create a performance "diary" that can be used when the formal administrative appraisal is conducted.

In summary, it is conceivable that professionals will be appraised on both their individual performance and their contribution to a team or unit. It is also possible that they will be appraised on a timetable that fits the cycle of their work, as opposed to an annual administrative cycle. And although the direct supervisor will be responsible for the performance appraisal it may be based on multiple perspectives to appropriately reflect the consensus of relevant parties about the person's performance.

With more work being performed by people who are not employees the challenge of defining and measuring the performance of non-employees must be addressed. It is possible to use the career ladders to identify the level of work being done by an outsider and to evaluate performance against the expectations established for an employee at that level. Doing so enables the organization to demonstrate to employees that others ae held to the same standards.

Rewards Management

Although professionals are oriented to their profession and place high value on both interesting, challenging work and career progression they will almost certainly want some money as well. Although there are those who argue that extrinsic rewards might destroy intrinsic motivation, there is no credible research evidence to support this contention.[1] Few professionals are independently wealthy, so compensation is a necessity. Since professionals are inclined to keep score, using their grade level and their salary as metrics for determining how they are doing and how the organization values them, it is prudent to pay attention that the human resource management programs are appropriate.

It is important that the salary potential (salary range) for a professional be both internally equitable and externally competitive. The career ladders discussed earlier can be used to establish and maintain internal equity. Job evaluation plans can also be used to evaluate the levels, enabling the organization to incorporate professional ladders into the job grade structures used for other employees. External competitiveness is achieved utilizing data on prevailing compensation levels in the appropriate labor market(s). For example, market data on engineers is most often accumulated and reported using surveys that employ ladders much like the one in Table 5.1, although the definitions of the nature of the work are often less detailed. The survey ladder acts as a "Rosetta Stone," enabling organizations to match their people to survey levels, thereby enabling sound comparisons to be made by the survey participants, even though their ladders are constructed somewhat differently. The market data can then be used to develop ranges of pay opportunity that are appropriately competitive for people with specific levels of expertise.

Although a generic classification matrix such as the one in Table 5.1 may be used for all professional personnel, an organization can differentiate between specific disciplines when creating pay structures. Using engineering as an example again, there can be significant differences between market pay levels for the various disciplines within engineering (e.g., mechanical, electrical, nuclear, chemical, civil, facility and software). Organizations with large and diverse populations will often have different salary ranges for different disciplines, or at least different targets within a range. This enables them to be competitive with market levels but yet at the same time maintain internal equity by having grade levels decided on that basis. The worst approach is to let temporary market variations trigger changes to grade levels. This will erode internal equity over time, since the disciplines tend to take turns being "hot" and then cooling down. Frequent grade changes are also difficult to explain to incumbents, particularly when they are in a downward direction.

Assuming the performance appraisal challenges described earlier are overcome, the prevailing approach to salary administration for professional or technical personnel is merit pay. Table 5.4 illustrates a salary structure for an engineering family. The numbers are established on a relative relationship to each other and are not intended to reflect actual market rates. Given the width of the ranges (50%) and the differences between the range midpoints (25%), there is overlap provided to allow salaries to grow in a manner consistent with the rate of progression within and between levels. Those who perform at high levels will receive larger increases, meaning they will progress within their range more rapidly than those performing at a "meets expectations" level (see Chapter 3). They will also be allowed to penetrate into higher portions of the range. It is increasingly common for organizations to limit progression into the top portion of the salary range to those with full mastery and who have sustained high levels of performance over extended periods.

Many organizations treat professionals somewhat differently within their merit pay systems. It can be argued that performance should be the sole driver of pay. But pay adjustments based on the degree to which someone has mastered the knowledge and skills critical to their work also are an appropriate basis for evaluating the position of a

Table 5.4 Engineering Salary Structure

Level	Salary Range (Based on Grade)		
	Minimum	Midpoint	Maximum
Associate	36,000	45,000	54,000
Engineer	45,000	56,000	67,000
Senior engineer	56,000	70,000	84,000
Consulting engineer	70,000	88,000	106,000
Engineering fellow	88,000	110,000	132,000

Note: figures are relative and for illustration only. Organizations doing advanced work and pure research may have ranges that are considerably higher.

pay rate within a pay range. A systems analyst newly promoted from associate to analyst is typically paid in the lower part of the range for the new classification, while a seasoned analyst (assuming acceptable performance) would tend to be paid in the middle part of the range. A concern is that this pattern could be interpreted as paying for seniority rather than strictly for performance.

But it must be recognized that increasing knowledge and skill in their field makes an employee more valuable, particularly when there are long learning curves in the path to expertise. Therefore, the base pay rate must reflect both performance and competence for professionals, with more emphasis on the latter than is usually the case for other types of employees. And since performance of professionals is often difficult to measure objectively in concrete terms, as pointed out earlier, considering the rate at which employees increase their level of expertise when evaluating performance and adjusting pay makes a great deal of sense. It is prudent to ensure pay rates remain competitive, considering the mobility of professionals and their weak attachment to the organization.

When considering the use of variable compensation for professional personnel it is important to determine both what the organization intends to accomplish and what impact the use of incentives will be likely to have on the behavior of employees. It is also important to take into account the manner in which base pay is administered, so that the direct compensation package provides motivation to exert the required effort and to focus that effort on organizational objectives. Individual incentives may not be appropriate for professionals in some contexts. The contribution of any individual is very difficult to measure where the work is highly interdependent with that of others. Therefore, the use of individual measures may discourage cooperative and supportive behavior, even though it is critical to success at the aggregate level. However, professionals who operate in a relatively independent manner could certainly be candidates for individual incentives. This would typically be done by utilizing an approach based on individual performance against predetermined objectives. Incentive awards can also be determined using the performance appraisal system, which, if properly designed, measures individual performance.

Organizations providing variable compensation opportunity for professionals increasingly define, measure and reward performance at a group level. This acknowledges the nature of the work environment, and when used in conjunction with a merit pay system it enables the organization to reward both individual performance and contribution to group performance. Professionals whose work is project oriented are good candidates for project or team incentives. As mentioned earlier, the nature of the contribution made by project team members and the timeframes of projects argue in favor of measuring and rewarding performance at the aggregated levels and for doing so at project milestones. In addition, when projects produce new products it is not uncommon to create long-term incentives tied to market success of the product, either in the form of equity or simulated equity or as a cash award tied to sales or return on investment.

Yet another approach to providing incentives is to use the distribution of stock, in the form of options, restricted grants or bonuses. If it is believed that the success of the products developed will positively impact the market value of the organization then stock-based programs can provide a shared destiny and can also let the market "write the checks" to cover the wealth distributed among the participants. Another advantage of using stock is that it enables the organization to include those in a support capacity. Their contributions may be less directly measurable, so stock awards can provide them with both the incentive to perform well and the recognition that their work really counted.

A major equity issue is raised when some professionals in a unit participate in projects while others do not. For example, many organizations transitioned from legacy IT mainframe systems to distributed network systems in order to become Y2K compliant. In order to do so, they split their staff into those who worked on the new systems and those who maintained the existing systems and kept the business running. In cases where project incentives were offered to those working on the new systems but not to those doing maintenance, significant equity issues were raised. The portion of the staff expected to do all the maintenance work previously done by the full staff usually felt they were working just as hard as those working on the new systems. They also were concerned that they were restricted to using skills that were unlikely to be valued in the future, putting them behind the other group. In fact, many organizations had to enter training contracts with this group, promising to provide them with the new skills shortly after conversion. In addition, the wise organizations offered equivalent incentives to motivate this group to keep the existing systems operating effectively—and to preserve internal fairness.

Technicians: A Special Case?

The discussion to this point has been focused primarily on employees with university-level education in a field, who are often paid as much as or more than employees in management capacities. In many organizations there are technical people who learn their skills on the job and/or through trades programs. For example, a manufacturer of semiconductors will typically have highly skilled technicians who perform electrical and mechanical work critical to the functioning of the production process, as well as lab people who contribute to the quality control and research functions. Some of these technical employees are skilled tradespeople and may belong to unions that train them, place them and even provide them with their benefits. Other technicians will have learned their craft through extensive work experience. For example, the IT department may utilize people who are experts in creating and servicing networks. Although these employees are typically not classified as "professionals" their skill levels may warrant very high pay and their performance may be critical. This broad category of personnel will be discussed in Chapter 6.

Strategies across National Borders

The labor markets for professional employees vary widely depending on the level of competence and the occupation of the person. National and even international labor markets exist for highly respected scientists and engineers, as well as for individuals with very scarce skills in technologies that are employed globally, such as supply chain or logistics management. The labor supply for highly educated professionals has also become global, particularly with the appearance of technology that enables organizations to run 24×7 "global relay races." U.S. employees pass the baton to Asian employees at the end of their day, who subsequently pass the baton to the next way station, where employees will pass it back to the U.S. people to complete the cycle at the end of their day. The more standardized the work and the processes used the more possible this strategy becomes. And even for those organizations choosing to keep their work in one location it is increasingly likely that their workforces will be diverse in their national or ethnic background. Skilled personnel shortages among U.S. employers have created pressure for more work visas, and this has resulted in increased diversity.

Certainly scientists, engineers and other knowledge workers are not paid the same way or at the same level across the globe. The impact of cultural differences was discussed in Chapter 1 and will be discussed in more detail in Chapter 10. There are a few additional concerns where senior-level professionals are involved. First, when people raised in individualistic cultures (e.g., the U.S.) are mixed with people from collectivist cultures (e.g., Japan) there are going to be different views as to who really determines performance and how individual contributions should be rewarded. Since many professionals work in cross-functional teams or with people from different disciplines there will tend to be a higher degree of interdependence, as mentioned earlier in the chapter. When different cultural perspectives are present within a group there will be different views as to what constitutes fair and appropriate treatment. An example of potential differences is illustrated in Table 5.5.

These differences have a major impact on professional personnel, because of the unique characteristics mentioned at the beginning of this chapter. Professionals are typically focused on progression within the field, they have ease of mobility and they experience a lesser attachment to a single organization. If employees view the manner in which an organization defines, measures and rewards performance and how it recognizes or rewards career progression as being inappropriate they are more apt to depart or to become dissatisfied. As already discussed, professionals gauge their career progress by evaluating the people who populate the levels in the career ladders and by determining if they are being classified correctly relative to others. Therefore, if it becomes apparent that people "age" through the levels in the ladder, the fastest developers and the best performers with individualistic perspectives will leave early in their tenure, going to organizations that will recognize and reward their abilities and contributions. On the other hand, those with a different cultural perspective might view this basis for advancement to be appropriate.

This poses a true dilemma. If the organization's global population of professionals in a particular field is one-third American, one-third Indian and one-third Chinese, what is the best career, performance and rewards management strategy? The common guiding principles/custom local strategies approach could be applied here. The organization can adopt the principle that those who bring more expertise to their work, perform at higher levels and contribute the most to the organization will receive the largest rewards. But some of the rewards on offer could come in the form of recognition as a mentor and someone who shares their wisdom accumulated over time. If recipients value this form of reward as much as or more than a larger salary increase or a larger incentive award, why should the organization demand that there be no differences in local strategies? After all, the organization is attempting to maximize the perceived value to the employee.

Table 5.5 Potential Cultural Differences

Issue	Eastern/Southern View	Western/Northern View
Basis for promotion/ advancement	Age and seniority	Accumulation of skills and knowledge; expertise
Differentiation in performance ratings	Little differentiation; based on contribution to group/unit	Greater differentiation; based on individual results
Differentiation in reward allocation	Egalitarian distribution; based on group results	Greater differentiation; based on individual results

Rewarding Professionals Who Are Not Employees

The increased use of outsiders is particularly pronounced for professional personnel. And since organizations may have no good options to using outsiders they must decide on how rewards are determined for them. If a unit of work is to be performed by outsiders the nature of the work must be defined. The nature of the work and the qualifications required can be used to match it to the career ladder used by the organization, if it uses that approach. For example, if the work requires someone who can operate at the principal level (as defined by the organization's career ladder for that discipline) the rewards offered to outsiders can be made equivalent to what an employee would be compensated, assuming the person is a freelancer being dealt with directly. If a contractor is used the organization providing the talent will need to mark up the cost, to provide a profit and to cover administrative costs. The cost of using outsiders should be compared to what the cost will be if the work is done by an employee. Since using a contractor saves the cost of recruitment and of providing benefits a higher hourly or project rate may be found to be acceptable from a financial perspective.

Evidence-based Rewards Management for Professionals

An organization that has adopted a policy to compensate employees at the average pay levels prevailing in the relevant labor market must determine what the prevailing rates are for each professional discipline. Compensation surveys are widely available through third parties and organizations can conduct their own surveys. Most surveys use job-based approaches for matching survey jobs to participant jobs, but they also usually use the job family approach for professional roles. The job family definitions provide descriptions for each level within the family, although in much more general terms than the kind of career ladders used by organizations and illustrated in this chapter. Matching an organization's levels to survey definitions can pose a challenge in that the number of levels may differ. If an organization defines five levels of engineer and a survey includes four levels, it is necessary for someone to match to the survey. The survey results will be reported for four levels so the organization is going to have to figure out how to interpret survey data in a manner that relates to its five levels. When reporting pay rates into the survey the organization must figure out how to do so using four levels as well. It is important when presenting the evidence supporting the analysis of the organization's competitiveness that decision makers are informed of this "translation" process so they fully understand that there is some subjectivity involved. Chris Argyris has identified the responsibility of analysts as providing full, clear, unbiased information to decision makers.

When developing career ladders it is important to support them with evidence that they are appropriate for the organization and competitive with sound prevailing practice. I consulted with a research laboratory that was using ten levels in their scientist and their engineer ladders and used prevailing practice to argue for reducing the number of levels to four to six. The problems the lab had experienced with their system is that it was virtually impossible to match to surveys and the differences between the ten pay ranges were too small to be viewed as adequate by employees. Of course, managers could "promote" employees at a fairly brisk rate, since the differences in qualifications across levels were so small. The problem this produced was that much of the pay increase budget was consumed by the excessing number of promotions. Even though it would have been possible to collapse ten levels into five by just grouping two of their ranges into one (the resulting pay ranges would have aligned with survey data) this would have looked like a conspiracy between the consultant and the organization to rob them of half of their promotions. Instead we created design teams to develop the new ladders from scratch. This forced all parties to evaluate the proposed ladders to ensure there were adequate but not excessive differences between levels. This also enabled them to define the levels in terms that fit the organization and the work.

Application of Principles: Chapter 5

A research-intensive organization has in the past staffed only key management roles with employees and used contractors and freelancers to perform the work required. Since the organization performs research studies for others it responds to requests for proposals and provides a project management plan for each study to accompany their fee estimate. Using outsiders has enabled the organization to be cost-competitive and to align its staffing levels with the current workload.

A career ladder exists for both researchers and project management roles and an hourly pay rate is set for each level within the ladders. The pay rate is adjusted to provide a margin that covers administrative expenses and provides a reasonable profit. When a bid is won for a study the organization uses the established level definitions to project how many people at each level are needed and for how many hours to perform the required work.

Recently the availability of freelancers has been limited and the organization has found it difficult to staff projects that have been awarded to them. There is also a growing recognition that staffing each project with a unique group of people limits the organization's ability to create a knowledge base from its experience with past studies. Although it has attempted to do "lessons learned" follow-up sessions, it has been difficult to engage the freelancers involved, since they are looking for and/or performing work for other organizations.

Consideration has been given to build a core workforce of employees that would provide some continuity across projects. The staffing level would be kept at a level adequate to fit conservative estimates of a workload likely to exist at any time.

Identify the advantages and disadvantages of hiring full-time employees and having them work with outsiders who are retained to meet workloads exceeding the capacity of the staff. Describe scenarios that would favor each of the existing strategies.

Note

1 Rynes, S., Gerhart, B. & Parks, L., "Performance Evaluation and Pay for Performance," *Journal of Applied Psychology*, 56 (2005), 571–600.

Chapter 6

Rewarding Performance
Operating and Administrative Support Personnel

Virtually all organizations have employees who perform or support operating and administrative work. This category of employee works in the skilled trades, clerical and administrative roles, production/logistics roles and technical support. The work is not managerial or professional in nature. In some types of organizations there may be very few support personnel, such as software design firms. In others these people make up the vast majority of the workforce headcount, such as durable goods manufacturers or retail organizations. Because of the nature of the work performed and the type of direction received, this category of employee may call for different performance and rewards management strategies than are used for the other categories of employee.

There are several reasons for considering different strategies for support personnel. First, their work is typically performed under direct supervision, and what is to be done is largely prescribed by others. Although *how* the work is performed may be at least somewhat at the discretion of the support employees, overall direction is the responsibility of managerial or professional staff.

Second, their expertise is typically gained through work experience, rather than formal education at the university level. Skilled trades personnel often go through apprenticeships that include formal training, but this training is typically focused on building one's skills and knowledge, rather than on theory and principles that would be obtained through advanced education. Although technology utilized by tradespersons often involves formal training, the "master–apprentice" approach is still very widespread. This method of training requires that more experienced people convey the tacit knowledge that cannot be made explicit in procedures in a person-to-person process.

Third, support personnel most often are focused on prescribed duties that are performed according to established policies and procedures, rather than working more autonomously to meet assigned objectives.

Fourth, of all the employee categories, incumbents are the category most likely to be represented by a union and have their conditions of employment controlled by a collective bargaining agreement. And laws often determine how they must be paid if they exceed a specified number of hours.

Finally, the labor markets for operating/support jobs tend to be local.

There are often widely understood hierarchies of skill and associated pay relationships that shape employee expectations about rewards. There may also be a single prevailing wage that is paid to all incumbents of a particular classification in a labor market (e.g., journeyman electrician). Organizations may also create "internal labor markets,"[1] which establish "ports of entry" through which recruits are hired, and specific lines of progression through which employees progress internally. An envelope manufacturer the author consulted with used such a labor market, since all of the production equipment had been modified substantially, in order to obtain a level of productivity that gave it an advantage in a price-competitive market. New production employees were brought in as entry-level laborers and trained to move up into machine operation and maintenance. This was necessary, since even the manufacturers of the equipment were not able to maintain these dramatically altered machines. Another example would be a water utility starting road crew members as laborers, until they learned "where the pipes were buried" and until they obtained the necessary state licenses and developed specific skills to perform the more skilled work.

The above-listed characteristics should be taken into account when developing performance and rewards management systems to be applied to support personnel.

Performance Management

Since many operating/support employees have their roles defined by job descriptions, it is common practice to appraise performance based on how well each person did their job. Governmental regulations dealing with fair treatment, hours of work and other conditions of employment often restrict the employer relative to how personnel decisions are made. The job description becomes a critical component of performance and pay management programs, as well as specifying conditions of employment. The federal Uniform Guidelines for Employee Selection mandate that job analysis be used to clearly define duties and responsibilities, as well as performance criteria and standards.[2] This results in performance being defined as doing the job well in most organizations. Selecting individuals for hiring or promotion is also typically tied to the job, as defined in the description, and the qualifications, as defined in the job specifications.

There is a trend towards defining the roles of some types of support personnel using occupational ladders similar to those for professionals, as described in Chapter 5. The ladders may replace job descriptions that specify activities performed, or job descriptions may be used for selection and development, while the ladders are used for career progression and compensation. Table 6.1 is an example of a ladder for administrative support personnel. For those who belong to collective bargaining units the use of ladders will be a less frequent practice, since bargaining unit members will almost invariably want to have their work described very formally, in a job description and in work rules. Skilled trades personnel also typically operate under specific job descriptions. The use of ladders is more prevalent for white-collar clerical and support people, who may move across specific functions but are classified according to a more generic ladder. They are increasingly being used for technicians and technical support personnel.

Support personnel being classified using occupational ladders are often appraised, developed and promoted based on both their level of expertise and their current level of performance. As it becomes harder to define in advance specifically what people working in many capacities will be doing in today's lean and changing organizations, the occupational ladder approach enables the workforce to be deployed more flexibly. Since incumbents are being measured against and paid for their capabilities, irrespective of what they are doing at a particular point in time, it minimizes resistance to performing a wide variety of tasks because "they are not in the job description." For example, the typical office today has fewer personal secretaries, and less specifically defined clerical/administrative support "jobs." This is because there is an increased focus on skill or knowledge development and career progression. In this type of environment, using an administrative support ladder to classify employees seems appropriate. This approach avoids the need to evaluate a large number of specifically defined jobs and it is also more consistent with the way market data is being presented in surveys. When ladders are used for some support personnel they are often graded into a pay structure with others who have specifically defined jobs, using some type of job evaluation methodology.

The simplest format for a performance appraisal instrument used for operating/support personnel who hold specific jobs consists of three columns: 1) the duties and responsibilities; 2) the performance standards and expectations; and 3) how results compared to standards. This approach is consistent with motivational theory, since it provides for expectations being defined in advance and for continuous feedback on performance. The first two columns are filled in at the beginning of the performance period and are updated if necessary during that period. "Diary" entries can be made in the third column during the period, to serve as feedback and to ensure significant information is captured. The use of electronic media has made this process much less burdensome.

An alternative approach is to use factors based on job-related results. In Chapter 2, which introduced performance management principles, the use of performance criteria and standards was discussed. The criteria set most often used for support personnel includes four factors: 1) productivity; 2) quality of work; 3) dependability and adherence to values; and 4) contribution to the effectiveness of others and the unit. Figure 6.1 is a format for appraising performance based on these factors. The first three of these criteria have stood the test of time, as well as holding up under research scrutiny. The "contribution to others" factor has increased in usage over the last few decades, to reflect the increased interdependence of work and to lessen the extent to which appraisal puts employees in competition with each other.

In spite of the potential that goal setting has for increasing motivation and positively impacting performance,[3] the use of objectives against which results are measured is a practice that should be carefully considered before using it for support personnel. A person's role and the methods or processes used may be very specifically defined (e.g., a person doing the final setup of a blasting operation at a construction site). The organization has in mind only one objective: do your job well and exactly in the way procedures call for. The application of innovation would be discouraged in this situation. The management-by-objectives (MBO) approach is more often used for personnel having broad discretion. Defining and measuring performance based on results attained compared to predetermined objectives may not fit the context within which many operating/support personnel perform their work. On the other hand, there are instances where objectives outside of the normal job description are important, and a section for defining expectations and evaluating results can be added to the appraisal form when appropriate. George Odiorne, who along with Peter Drucker defined the modern MBO approach, told the author that organizations too often assumed the use of objectives was the right approach for everyone, rather than considering whether they might distract employees from the most important measure: doing their job well. But there is an opportunity to apply the principles of goal setting and feedback to performance management. Performance standards for ongoing task performance can be used to "stretch" employees and to communicate how well their jobs need to be performed.

Table 6.1 Administrative Support Staff Classifications

Job Criteria	Associate	Senior Associate	Specialist	Senior Specialist
Nature of work (type; complexity; variety; difficulty)	Performs routine administrative support to unit as assigned.	Performs varied administrative duties. Collects and organizes information required to perform assigned work.	Performs varied and complex administrative duties. Assists in coordinating unit activities with those of other units. May lead activities of others on projects or assignments of extended duration.	Directs varied and complex administrative tasks with broad scope. Coordinates unit activities with those of other units. Leads activities of extended duration.
Latitude/direction received (authority; creativity; nature and frequency of supervision received)	Exercises limited judgment in doing work, consistent with prescribed routines. Receives close supervision for more complex work. Manager sets priorities for performing work.	Exercises judgment in performing work. Works under general supervision. Sets priorities in doing work and manages time to ensure that deadlines and objectives are met. Seeks guidance for more complex work.	Works under general direction, reporting upon completion of assigned duties/projects. Guidance is typically in terms of results expected. Demonstrates creativity in work and may revise processes.	Works independently, reporting on results of assigned duties/projects. Guidance is in terms of overall objectives. Expected to recommend creative solutions to complex problems.
Responsibility for interpersonal contacts (type; level; frequency)	Exchanges information with others, typically within own group/unit.	Exchanges information with other units and outside entities as required to perform work.	Exchanges information with other units and outside entities and may be responsible for integrating the activities of own unit with those of others.	Exchanges information with other units and outside entities and takes responsibility for integrating the activities of own unit with those of others.
Responsibility for work of others	None.	May help new employees learn to perform basic work.	May provide guidance and training to other administrative support personnel as needed.	Provides guidance and training to other administrative support personnel.
Potential impact on unit (quality; customer satisfaction; cost; responsiveness)	Quality of work impacts unit's costs/efficiency.	Quality of work impacts unit performance and may significantly impact costs, efficiency or customer satisfaction.	Quality of work impacts unit performance, customer satisfaction and the degree to which unit objectives are met.	Quality of work has a significant impact on unit performance and on meeting unit objectives.
Education/training	High school.	High school.	High school, with course work in analytical techniques preferred.	High school, with equivalent of associate's degree preferred.
Experience and special skills	None required. Able to use basic office software.	1–2 years. Command of full range of office software.	3–5 years. Command of full range of office software.	5 or more years. Command of full range of office software.

ANYTOWN NEWS
Performance Appraisal
Employee Information

Name:_____   Job Title: Reporter

Dept.:_____   Supervisor Title:

Performance Period: from _____ to _____

Employee Job Summary

Researches and writes news, features, analyses, human interest stories. Develops and cultivates news sources and contacts. Completes assignments by deadlines, ensuring accuracy by verifying sources. Attends newsworthy events and interviews key sources. Respects confidentiality as appropriate.

Performance of Job

Productivity: Production is high relative to time and resources consumed. Develops expected number of stories and covers beat adequately to ensure stories are detected as they break. Stories are developed within timeframe that enables deadlines to be met and appropriate reviews are performed as they are refined.

Comments:

_____

_____

_____

_____

_____

_____

_____

Rating: ❏ Outstanding ❏ Significantly exceeds standards ❏ Fully meets standards
❏ Does not fully meet standards ❏ Unacceptable

Quality of work: Work meets quality standards and established editorial standards. Stories are written in clear and appropriate manner, are consistent with editorial policy and are fair and balanced. Research is thorough and encompasses all relevant sources, which are verified to ensure accuracy. Works with editors to revise and improve content. Develops and maintains network of contacts who can provide early notification of breaking stories.

Comments:

_____

_____

_____

Figure 6.1 (continued)

_____
_____
_____
_____

Rating: ❏ Outstanding ❏ Significantly exceeds standards ❏ Fully meets standards
❏ Does not fully meet standards ❏ Unacceptable

Dependability and adherence to company values and policies: Consistently meets deadlines; conforms to attendance policies; adapts to work demands; conforms to established values and policies; adheres to ethical standards of the paper and the profession; respects confidentiality as appropriate; behaves in manner that enhances the image of the paper.

Comments:

_____
_____
_____
_____
_____
_____
_____

Rating: ❏ Outstanding ❏ Significantly exceeds standards ❏ Fully meets standards
❏ Does not fully meet standards ❏ Unacceptable

Contribution to effectiveness of others/unit: Works with others within and outside the unit in a manner that improves their effectiveness; shares information and resources; develops effective working relationships; builds consensus; constructively manages conflict; contributes to the effectiveness of own unit/group and the paper.

Comments:

_____
_____
_____
_____
_____
_____

Rating: ❏ Outstanding ❏ Significantly exceeds standards ❏ Fully meets standards
❏ Does not fully meet standards ❏ Unacceptable

Performance vs. Objectives

Objective   Results vs. Expectations

1.

2.

3.

Rating: ❏ Outstanding   ❏ Significantly exceeds standards   ❏ Fully meets standards
         ❏ Does not fully meet standards   ❏ Unacceptable

Note: when rating performance against objectives weight objectives for relative importance to arrive at overall rating

Overall Performance Rating

Consider the ratings on each factor, the relative importance of each, performance against established objectives and the relative importance of the objectives.

Comments:

_____

_____

_____

_____

_____

_____

_____

_____

_____

_____

Rating: ❏ Outstanding   ❏ Significantly exceeds standards   ❏ Fully meets standards
         ❏ Does not fully meet standards   ❏ Unacceptable

Figure 6.1 (continued)

(continued)

Signatures

Appraiser:_____ Date:_____

Employee:_____ Date:_____

Note: employee signature does not mean agreement with the rating, only that it has been reviewed and discussed in person.

Employee Comments:

_____
_____
_____
_____
_____

Development Plans/Future Objectives

Development needed (training, special assignments) :

_____
_____
_____
_____
_____

Performance standards and objectives for next performance period:

_____
_____
_____
_____
_____

Revisions required to current job description:

_____
_____
_____
_____
_____

Performance Appraisal Instructions

Evaluate the employee's performance during the last performance period by completing the following steps:

1. Review the job summary to ensure it is accurate and current. Make any changes necessary.

2. Comment on performance relative to each of the evaluation factors. Relate results and behaviors to the job responsibilities as outlined in the job summary, using specific examples to support ratings.

3. Rate performance on each of the four factors, using one of the following ratings:
   a. *Outstanding:* Individual regularly made exceptional contributions that had a significant and positive impact on the performance of the unit/organization. Results consistently exceeded performance standards/objectives significantly over a sustained period. Employee has mastered all job-related skills and possesses a broad range of capabilities. Provides a model for excellence and helps others to do their jobs better.
   b. *Significantly exceeded standards:* Employee frequently exceeded all performance expectations/objectives significantly. Employee is highly skilled in all aspects of the job.
   c. *Fully met standards:* Employee consistently met all expectations/objectives and occasionally exceeded some. Is fully qualified in all aspects of the job.
   d. *Did not fully meet standards:* Employee has not consistently met all job requirements and/or met expectations and occasionally demonstrated unacceptable behaviors/results. May have the ability to perform most aspects of the job but may lack some knowledge/skills to perform others.
   e. *Unacceptable:* Employee frequently performs in an unacceptable manner and requires a performance improvement plan.

4. Evaluate the overall performance of the employee during the performance period. Consider the performance rating on each of the factors, weighting the factors for their relative importance in the specific job. If objectives are used for the employee compare results to expectations and weight the relative importance of each of the objectives when arriving at the summary rating. Provide supporting commentary that will enable the employee to understand why the overall performance was rated as it was.

5. Review the appraisal with your manager to ensure there is mutual agreement.

6. Review the appraisal with the employee and discuss any differences in views about performance or about specific events. Attempt to determine the reasons for different views and resolve them in a manner producing mutual acceptance. Discuss the impact of the appraisal on pay actions, promotions, reassignments or other personnel actions.

7. Allow the employee to comment on the appraisal in written form and have them sign the review form. By signing, the employee is not indicating full agreement, but only that the appraisal was reviewed with them and that an opportunity to comment was provided.

8. Agree on performance expectations for the next performance period. Discuss developmental actions that are appropriate.

9. Review the current job description and indicate what revisions (if any) are required to make the description current and accurate.

Figure 6.1 Format for appraising performance based on the criteria set most often used for support personnel

The job-based and the factor-based approaches can both be used for appraising the performance of operating/support personnel. If the job description is the standard against which performance is measured, standards should be developed to clarify expectations for the employee and to provide a more objective basis for rating. For those classified into ladders it may be necessary to develop more generic standards. As long as the global principle mandating that performance be measured in terms of job-related results and behaviors is adhered to, the format of individual appraisals can take many forms and still be accepted as fair and relevant.

If operating/support work is performed in groups, with high interdependence between employees, it may be advisable to develop a performance scorecard at the group level. This scorecard can be used to evaluate performance in situations where all members of a team or group perform whatever task needs to be done at the time, thereby making it difficult to differentiate between individuals relative to their contribution. This is discussed in more detail in Chapter 8, which deals with teams. Many organizations elect to evaluate individual performance and to use appraisal ratings to administer individual pay rates, using group/team incentive plans to reward aggregated results.

Deming and other quality management gurus have claimed that 70% or more of operating difficulties are caused by the system (context), rather than by individuals.[4] It is important not to hold employees accountable for factors outside their control. If the direction given is inappropriate or unclear, or if external issues not under their control have a negative impact on results, the employee should not be rewarded or punished for these externalities. It is also important to recognize when highly skilled employees actually determine how and how well their work is done. In this case it is reasonable to tie performance ratings to results more closely, since there is a greater degree of individual control in these situations. Wholesale abandonment of performance appraisal is not a good solution even when the context has a significant impact on results. Too many simplistic summaries of the work of Deming call for the outright discontinuance of performance appraisal, but to date none of the authors has volunteered to represent organizations in court when they are accused of basing pay actions on personal factors, rather than performance. If a job requires responding to uncertain events, performance can be defined as responding appropriately to whatever materializes. An example of this is customer service jobs, where an irate customer may remain dissatisfied, even though the employee gathered all the facts, treated the customer respectfully and correctly applied established policy to arrive at a decision as to how to deal with the complaint.

Rewards Management

The total direct pay package for operating and support personnel very often consists solely of base pay, whether it be in the form of a salary or an hourly wage. Base pay administration typically utilizes a pay structure, consisting of grades that reflect the relative internal value of jobs and pay ranges that reflect market pay levels and that define the range of pay opportunity for jobs in each grade. If roles are defined as specific jobs, some form of job evaluation is used to place jobs into levels. Point factor job evaluation and classification are the two most commonly used approaches to establishing the relative internal value of jobs. Although there is a great deal written about using "market-based systems," the failure to establish relative job values that employees accept as internally equitable has caused many of these systems to be ineffective. Given the increased variety of roles played by support personnel it is more difficult to make market surveys using "standard benchmark" jobs relevant to a wide variety of organizations. This is particularly true when organizations shift to occupational ladders and away from specific jobs. In spite of the rhetoric about making the market the ultimate arbiter of value, most organizations find the use of internal value determinations to grade jobs useful, particularly when they are unique and no viable sources of market data are available.

Organizations with relatively stable workforces and job definitions (e.g., utilities) can see that employees are very concerned about where their jobs fall in the grade structure relative to other jobs. This interest in relative internal values is most pronounced among those who work together or in close proximity, but conflict over the relationship of pay between production/field and office workers can be intense. The "market made me do it" plea in defense of job grade assignments does not alleviate the concerns of employees about fairness across jobs.

When occupations are dominated by one gender there has also been intense scrutiny of the values assigned to jobs across genders, particularly in the U.S., where laws such as the Equal Pay Act and Title VII of the Civil Rights Act prohibit gender-based discrimination. When gender concentrations exist in occupations, care should be taken when assigning jobs to grades and establishing ranges of pay opportunity to ensure the criteria used are gender neutral. As women and minorities are given freer access to jobs that traditionally have been dominated by white male incumbents, gender/race concentrations have lessened, but it is still incumbent on organizations to evaluate their grade assignments and pay actions.

Even when the focus is on relative internal value of jobs, the pay structure must reconcile those values with prevailing market rates if the system is to be viewed as both fair and competitive. In some cases it is necessary to target different rates for jobs in the same grades. For example, if accounting clerks, PC installers and warehouse workers are all placed into the same grade, but the average market rates for the three jobs are significantly different, it may be necessary to control pay rates in different sectors of the pay range, at least for as long as market rate differences persist. Tensions can run high when jobs that are critical to the organization have lower market rates than jobs that could easily be outsourced. An example is the disparity between health care personnel and IT support technicians in hospitals. Market pressures have sometimes forced them to pay less to the health care jobs than to the IT jobs, even though the health care jobs are more critical to their primary business than the IT jobs. These same tensions exist among professional personnel across occupations, but it is often less of an issue, owing to the higher turnover among professionals and the fact that they worry more about what is happening within their occupation rather than across occupations.

Prevailing local market rates for skilled trades personnel are typically the basis for determining competitive pay opportunity. There is often a single "prevailing market rate" for a classification (e.g., journeyman electricians in Chicago) and many organizations, unionized or not, elect to pay all incumbents that established rate. An organization may gain a competitive advantage in attracting the most skilled and highest-performing people by offering a pay package that allows employees to earn more by performing better. But that organization runs the risk of violating tenets of "fairness" and the practice may be rejected as inappropriate. It must be remembered that gaining employee acceptance of pay for performance systems mandates that they believe performance will be fairly and appropriately evaluated.

The majority of organizations utilize the same "pay for performance" principle (a.k.a. merit pay) to administer pay actions for operating/support personnel as they do for professional and managerial personnel, although skilled trades employees may be treated differently because of union membership or prevailing local practice. Although the practice of time-based progression of pay rates for operating/support personnel has had a long history and is still common in some industries (e.g., health care, education and the public sector) there has been a trend away from automatic pay rate increases. Given the rapidly changing technologies and the restructuring of how work is performed, many organizations have realized that longevity may not correlate well with current competence. And since base pay rates are a fixed cost, time-based pay progression increases the cost of labor, irrespective of productivity or revenue levels. This reality has made time-based pay progression unsustainable in many industries, particularly when the ability to deal with foreign competition is based on labor costs. Another drawback to basing pay on longevity is that this approach does not motivate high levels of performance and may lessen the willingness of employees to take risks in pursuit of needed results. Longevity pay appeals least to high performers, who could do better elsewhere, which may mean an organization is able to retain only the people they are least concerned about retaining.

However, the use of single rate and time-based systems is still used for support personnel in some industries, and in some cultures merit pay may be difficult to administer well. It is therefore advisable at least to evaluate which approach fits this category of employee.

The full range of alternative pay systems was described in summary fashion in Chapter 3. How they might apply to support personnel will now be discussed.

Single Rate Base Pay Systems

Single rates are most often used for employees belonging to collective bargaining units. They are also used in organizations that bill employees to customers at a fixed hourly rate. When single rates are used there is typically a progression of jobs that employees move through as they gain expertise and experience. The single rate for a job is usually derived from a prevailing local labor market rate and in some cases the rate is specified by laws or regulations. In unionized organizations the pay rates are bargained over, so there is little the organization can do to administer them differently for different people, no matter what their expertise or performance might be. For that reason organizations often treat these systems as a reality they must live with.

Time-based Base Pay Systems

There has been a long-standing tradition of time-based pay for support personnel in the public sector and many private sector organizations that benefit from workforce stability. This practice has often been adopted because of union pressure, because of the biases of regulatory agencies or because such plans are prevalent in the industry. The use of time-based plans in the public sector is addressed in more detail in Chapter 9.

The disadvantages of the time-based step rate system are too serious to ignore, as discussed in Chapter 3. To repeat, time-based pay works best when: 1) many jobs are repetitive and routine, with small variation in performance possible; 2) a collective bargaining relationship exists and there is not a high level of trust between the union leadership and management; 3) employees do not believe managers are able or willing to fairly administer a merit program; 4) budgetary limitations and/or customer rate pressures limit resources and require predictable costs; and 5) there is concern about potential litigation and/or employee disagreement relative to performance appraisal ratings and the size of pay increases. These conditions are most apt to exist with support personnel, and this category of employee is probably the most likely to be considered for time-based step progression.

Performance-based Pay Systems

Variable Timing Step Rate Programs

Many support jobs have limited performance variability. Yet there may be opportunities for exceeding performance standards in a way that positively impacts unit performance. The variable timing step rate approach incorporates a provision that allows managers to recommend double step increases or early step increases for those whose performance significantly exceeds standards. It also enables the manager to deny or delay the step increase for those whose performance does not meet expectations. Although this system provides a limited number of choices relative to the size and frequency of increases, it can help organizations acknowledge significant performance differences. Critics point out that someone may race through the steps by having a few good years and then enjoy a high rate of pay irrespective of ongoing performance. That should be considered.

If a performance appraisal system like the one illustrated in Figure 6.1 is used for support personnel the ratings can be used to regulate step progression. An outstanding performance rating may result in a double step progression, while a rating below "fully meets standards" may result in the step progression being withheld. Organizations wishing to adopt this approach must ensure that the performance appraisal system is well administered and that employees accept that it operates fairly and appropriately.

Combination Step Rate/Merit Pay Programs

Organizations with large numbers of employees working in jobs that have fairly standard learning times but in which incumbents can vary performance significantly once the job skills are learned, may wish to consider an approach that combines time-based and performance-based pay. For example, if control room operators in a utility must hold certain licenses and the license requirements mandate a minimum amount of relevant experience, the organization may allow step progressions based on time up to but not exceeding the job rate. Further increases may be subject to a performance test, based on the appraisal rating.

There is much to argue for this approach, particularly if the organization finds it difficult to discriminate between employees based on performance while they are learning the job. However, the organization should ensure that employees whose performance declines below the level that justifies the job rate would receive no further increases. This is consistent with the philosophy of *paying* for performance, rather than *giving increases* for performance; that is, if an employee is already paid significantly above the level justified by performance, no further increase may be warranted.

Merit Pay Programs

A third option is to make the transition to a full merit pay program. This is happening more and more often for support personnel, owing to the changes in the nature of their work, as discussed earlier. But a sound performance appraisal system is critical if merit pay programs are to be successful. This point cannot be made too often or too emphatically. Since support jobs may not lend themselves to making dramatic distinctions when appraising performance, it may be prudent to consider using fewer rating levels than are used for professional or managerial personnel. This should be influenced by the nature of the work and the workforce, as well as the culture and other contextual considerations.

Person-based Base Pay Systems

As discussed in Chapter 3 person-based pay programs pay employees for what they *can do* rather than what they *are doing*. The best applications of the various types of person-based pay are in units where the work is highly interdependent, cooperation/supportive behavior is required, flexibility of work assignment is needed and the skill or knowledge utilized is reasonably stable. A person-based pay system may work for some types of support personnel but not for others. In a plant where employees move from task to task based on the requirements of the current job flow a skill- or knowledge-based pay system may motivate them to learn how to do many different jobs. In an environment where employees must hold certain credentials to perform specific types of work the pay rate may be impacted by the credentials obtained.

Incentive (Variable Pay) Systems

Support work is often closely supervised, thereby limiting the amount of discretion incumbents can exercise. The types of incentive programs that are most frequently used for support personnel are:

1   *Lump-sum bonuses*, used to reward performance rather than using increases to base pay. For individuals who reach the top step in time-based programs, an organization can still offer annual awards to exceptional performers and those who must be retained. This approach can also be used when base pay rates have gotten too high relative to some standard (i.e., market average) and must be controlled to prevent further escalation.
2   *Cash incentive awards*, used to supplement base pay increases for outstanding performers. No matter how base pay rates are administered, it is sometimes desirable to have tangible, short-term reinforcement of outstanding behavior or results. Using cash awards enables the organization to bypass the established annual cycle of reward allocation and to make payouts close in time to the behavior or results being rewarded. For example, awards may be paid to a project team or task force when performance is known and deemed to be deserving of something beyond what the base pay administration program can provide (e.g., at the end of the project).

3   *Output-based awards*: If employees work in jobs that lend themselves to defining tangible output metrics an incentive plan can be developed that rewards productivity (often called "piece rate" plans). An assembler who produces 100 units per hour could be paid more than one producing 50 units per hour of the same quality, which provides the motivation to perform at high levels. The extra compensation cost is justified by more output, thereby creating a win–win situation.

There are also a number of *group incentive* approaches:

1   *Gainsharing*: Formula-based incentive programs that use measures such as productivity or cost and which share gains with employees.
2   *Cash profit sharing*: Formula-based incentive plans based on profitability and which share a percentage of profits with employees. Public sector organizations and not-for-profits could use a proxy for profit, such as performance relative to operating budget.
3   *Group/unit objectives*: Objective-based incentive plans that identify criteria (objectives), set standards and measure results against standards.

Gainsharing and performance-sharing plans often suit support personnel, since they promote a sense of shared destiny and may help to align the efforts of individuals towards established unit or organizational objectives. Gainsharing can be effective in giving support employees an economic stake in how well the unit performs (department, plant, etc.). Profit-sharing and organization-wide performance-sharing programs can also align their interests by basing rewards on how well the organization does. Some behavioral scientists argue that the motivational impact of rewards based on performance at levels far removed from the influence sphere of support personnel lack "line of sight" (ability to see the results of one's own efforts). But if the objective is to create alignment and shared destiny it is possible to sell the idea that if everyone does their part well the organization will do well, which results in rewards for all.

A last type of incentive compensation is the use of equity-based plans. Since the 1990s there has been considerable attention given to the possibility of using stock plans for all employees. The question is whether employee ownership programs encourage people in support roles to perform better and to be more satisfied with their jobs. The argument in favor of including support personnel in stock-based rewards plans has been that owners will think like owners, thereby aligning the interests of investors and employees. Further, since price appreciation in the investment markets generates the value, the use of these programs seems like a free lunch, which could be used to attract, retain and motivate without incurring the expenses associated with higher pay levels.

The "adjustments" in the U.S. equity markets in 2000 and 2008 put the debate on hold in most organizations, since support employees holding options saw their potential value go to zero. The loss in faith that stock could work well for support employees was exacerbated by the announcement that the accounting standards had changed and there would now be an expense to issuing options. But the question about involving support employees in equity programs still needs to be addressed. Enormous wealth has historically been created in equity markets and there is a compelling belief that if all employees benefit on an equivalent basis some of the animosity created by equity-based executive compensation programs might be lessened. Inclusive programs that align everyone's economic destiny may help to diminish the feeling that wealth is distributed differentially between the "aristocracy" and the "peasantry."

The most popular equity programs for operating/support employees have traditionally been stock purchase plans. Purchase plans were by far the most widely used path to stock ownership for all employees participating in stock plans until the 1980s. But any investment advisor worth their salt would caution against putting all of one's holdings in one basket and that is what stock purchase plans often result in for people at lower income levels. Besides, those with less discretionary income may be forced to make choices between purchasing stock and paying the mortgage or buying school supplies, which hardly seems a basis for happy employees. This is a particularly difficult position for lower-paid individuals if their lack of participation in purchase plans causes the organization to question their loyalty and commitment to the organization.

As more organizations believe that incentive compensation does motivate employees at all levels there is an alternative approach to enabling most or all employees to become owners. If performance-sharing plans generate awards these awards could be paid partially in cash and partially in stock, with the tax on the award being taken out of the cash portion. This enables the employee to immediately have tax-paid ownership of the stock, and to begin voting shares, receiving dividends and enjoying price appreciation. If the stock goes down in value it may have a negative impact on morale, but proper communication can get the message across that this is a long-term arrangement. Options become virtually without value if the price goes below the options' exercise price, but owned stock still has value as long as the organization remains viable.

Each organization must weigh the nature of its workforce, its culture and the relationship between organizational performance and the stock price before it plunges into broad-based employee ownership. Wildly volatile stocks can generate anxiety attacks among employees, as well as making the proposition seem like a trip to a casino. The "rich" 20-somethings of Silicon Valley in the late 1990s often lived as if their wealth was permanent, and when that turned out not to be true, through no fault of theirs, it is apparent who got the blame.

Rewarding Performance: Part-Time/Temporary Employees

There has been an increase in the use of part-time and temporary employees over the last few decades. A major 2006 study of the American workplace reported that 13% of the total workforce worked on a part-time basis and many others as seasonal workers, contractors and consultants.[5] Much of the upward trend in using other than full-time permanent workers is a result of cost pressures, particularly in industries such as retail sales. Walmart, one of the largest employers in the world, employs a huge number of part-time store employees, as do many of its competitors. Some of the preference by employers for part-time and temporary employees is due to seasonality, different work volumes during specific times of the day or variations in staffing needs for projects. Another major reason is the ability to offer only base pay and to avoid extending eligibility for benefits. Certainly some part-time or temporary employees prefer this type of scheduling, especially second-income earners, those retired from full-time employment and students. But a significant percentage of people who are working less than full-time would prefer to convert to full-time.

The manner in which an organization defines, measures and rewards performance for part-time and temporary employees is apt to differ from that for full-time employees. Eligibility for benefits is one major difference, since it would be impractical continuously to start and stop benefits for temporary employees. However, part-time employees are sometimes included in a select group of benefit programs, typically on a reduced, pro rata basis. This is most often the case when employees work half-time or more and/or when they serve a critical need for the organization. Peak-time tellers can help banks deal with surges in customer volume, although the expansion of online banking and auto-mated teller capabilities has lessened the criticality of these people. Distribution centers for newspapers are often staffed by people who also have split shifts, making recruitment and retention very difficult. Costco has a much larger percentage of its part-time employees eligible for benefits than does Sam's Club.[6] Each defends its practice as fitting its human resource management strategy.

Whether the base pay rates for part-time employees are the same, lower or higher than those for full-time employees also depends on the specific situation. Labor supply and demand will dictate the rates that must be paid to part-timers in many situations. But until recently it has been rare for part-timers to be included in incentive plans, whether the plans are organization-wide (profit sharing or performance sharing), unit plans (team incentives or business unit incentives) or individual plans (merit pay or performance bonuses). The author has asked why in several cases, pointing out that the performance of part-time employees is apt to be better if there is a financial incentive for performing well. When this logic has been accepted the organization will typically include permanent part-time employees in the plans on a pro rata basis. Although the same logic might hold for temporary employees it is even rarer for them to be included in incentive plans. The one exception is when seasonal employees work at a full-time level while they are employed. In this case it is more common to include them in incentive plans, which may treat the season as a project.

Contractors and consultants are increasingly being used to do work that had been per-formed by employees. This enables organizations to balance their staffing levels with work volume and deal with one-time projects better. Managing performance and rewards for all types of outsiders is covered in Chapter 11.

Application of Principles: Chapter 6

A county in a Western U.S. state has since its formation been emulating the U.S. govern-ment's GS system for its support personnel, both trades/crafts and office administrative personnel. The system has steps established within the pay ranges assigned each of the job grades. Progression through the steps has been tied directly to time on the job and all new hires must be brought in at the first step. The system forced the organization to increase every employee's pay rate during the 2008–2014 period by 3% annually, even though there was a hiring freeze in place and there was no real increase in prevailing pay rates in relevant markets for these jobs. Since tax revenues had declined precipitously other expenditures had to be cut and painful staff reductions were mandated. The county real-ized the potential downside of being locked into automatic pay rate progression and felt the need to consider alternatives.

You have been retained as a consultant to advise the county on how to deal with these challenges. Your mandate is to suggest alternative pay plans that would be accepted by employees. The county manager wants to add an element of pay for performance and does not want to be obligated to increasing every employee's pay every year. She also does not want everyone to get the same pay increase, no matter what their performance or how well they are currently paid relative to market average. Some of the department heads (police, fire and parks/recreation) feel there would be strong opposition by employees to changing the automatic increases. But the CFO will not accept increases to costs that are not offset by adequate revenues.

The ICO has lost some of his more senior people to organizations that offered more money and has had difficulty hiring replacements because the first steps of the pay ranges are below average market rates. Being short staffed has resulted in delaying important projects.

You have been given permission to have focus groups with employees and to meet with management and professional employees. How would you handle these focus groups? What facts would you relay to employees and what questions would you ask them? What factors would you consider when doing your analysis and formulating recommendations?

How might the county change its pay system to best meet the needs and preferences of all constituencies?

Notes

1 Doeringer, P. & Piore, M., *Internal Labor Markets and Manpower Analysis* (Armonk, NY, M. E. Sharpe, 1971).
2 Cascio, W., *Managing Human Resources*, 7th ed. (New York, McGraw-Hill Irwin, 2006).
3 Latham, G., *Work Motivation* (Thousand Oaks, CA, Sage, 2007).
4 Deming, W., *Out of Crises* (Cambridge, MA, MIT Press, 2000).
5 O'Toole, J. & Lawler, E., *The New American Workplace* (New York, Palgrave Macmillan, 2006).
6 Cascio, W., "Decency Means More than Always Low Prices," *Academy of Management Perspectives* (August, 2006).

Chapter 7

Rewarding Performance
Sales Personnel

Sales personnel and the work they do are "unique," according to most members of sales management. And that, they would tell you, is why they often do not want the human resource management policies that govern performance and rewards management for other employees to be imposed on the sales function. This view presents difficulties. The organization has an interest in ensuring that significant differences in the types of programs and how they are administered do not cause other employees to believe they are being unfairly treated and do not cause sales personnel to behave like free agents.

The belief that sales work differs substantially in many respects is valid. And in order for someone to be able to design performance and reward systems that fit the specific context within which they must operate the designer must intimately understand: 1) the products (goods and/or services) offered; 2) the customers they are offered to; 3) the sales processes utilized; 4) what role each sales job plays; and 5) what and how competitor organizations pay their sales people. That is a great deal to ask of any "outsider," and indeed most HR people do not have that kind of detailed knowledge. On the other hand, how much and how sales people are paid has an impact on the rest of the workforce: people do talk and they love to talk about how others are paid. The relationship between sales and non-sales personnel becomes even more intertwined at the management levels, and it is therefore in the best interests of management to be concerned about what the sales function does.

Those who design performance and rewards management programs should employ the same guiding principles that are used for non-sales personnel. This bold statement will be supported in subsequent commentary. But it will also be argued that sales programs should and do differ dramatically across industries and even across companies within the same industry, because the specific contexts within which the programs operate differ. That is, companies selling software packages may have very different approaches, owing to differences in market share, brand prominence, marketing niches, nature and diversity of products, customers served and the role of the sales representative in making a sale.

Because the performance metrics associated with direct sales are often quantitative and easily agreed to (e.g., more sales = good performance) one would think rewarding performance would be relatively straightforward. Yet sales compensation programs are often diabolically complex. One reason is that those designing them want to be sure every detail is considered and to ensure that no one can "beat the system." There seems to be a suspicion that people who perform sales work have but one mission in life: to get money they did not earn. And then there is the associated belief that the only thing sales people care about is money. None of this is completely true, of course, but these suspicions cause sales compensation programs to be in a continual state of revision.

The author has consulted with a manufacturing firm in the Midwestern U.S. that serves as an illustration of how seemingly straightforward metrics can cause sales programs to unintentionally misdirect sales personnel. The firm manufactures very high-quality machinery, which sells at a large premium over its global competitors. The quality of its products is evidenced by the fact that it receives replacement parts sales for machines sold decades ago. Customers who were tempted by low-price alternatives often find that the economics do not work over the long run, when one considers the productive life of the respective machines, the downtime endured and the maintenance required. These realities make parts sales for the Midwestern firm highly profitable and a stable source of revenue even in economic downturns. But therein was the problem with its sales compensation plans. Sales representatives were assigned territories, both domestically and globally, and all revenue from those territories was given sales credit for purposes of determining the compensation of the reps. A thorough analysis of the earnings of representatives showed that some were earning very high incomes due mostly to parts sales, rather than new machine sales. Management realized that this gave them an unearned annuity, since parts sales often came directly from the customer to the plant, without any intervention by the sales representative. Theoretically, this could discourage efforts to sell new machines, since the income was adequate for most reps and the effort required to find new customers was significant. On top of this, the sale of a new machine might produce a one-time commission but would be likely to result in lower parts sales for some time, making it almost a wash. To repeat a commonly stated principle: "What you measure and reward you most surely will get more of." And what the firm wanted was new machine sales: the parts sales would almost automatically materialize in the future.

Developing a Performance and Rewards Management Strategy for Sales Personnel

The first step in creating effective performance/rewards management programs for sales personnel is to develop a strategy that is derived from the objectives and strategy of the organization and that is a good fit to the context within which the organization operates. The context is a function of the external environment and the organization's internal realities, which include its culture, its resources and its structure. Prior chapters have emphasized the criticality of good fit to context for all human resource management programs.

Often, the requirements for organizational success dictate the importance of sales. A monopoly with no substitutes for its products may view sales as automatic and requiring no special effort. An organization selling a product that is a commodity, with many competitors, may view sales as its primary focus—its ticket to survival. How important sales are to an organization will determine the resources committed to generating sales and the amount of attention paid to how sales performance is to be measured and how much and how sales people are compensated.

Given these realities it is necessary to define the context within which sales activities are performed and to formulate a "good fit" sales strategy. The context is defined by a number of considerations:

1   *The nature of the product(s)*: the economics associated with it; its competitiveness with others providing it; the existence of substitutes; brand recognition and strength; current market share;

2   *The nature of the customers*: the needs and priorities of potential buyers; the image of the product with prospects; economic ability of prospects to afford it; value of the product to customers; existing customer loyalty; significance of the purchases of the product relative to customers' total purchases;

3   *The nature of the sales process*: typical timeframe; sales channels; role of various sales and support personnel in making the sale; points of contact in customer organization;

4   *The nature of the labor market for sales personnel*: how much and how competitive organizations pay; the supply of the needed knowledge or skills; the demand for critical knowledge or skills; current and evolving competitive conditions in the industry; and

5   *How performance is defined for the sales function*: what needs to be sold, to whom and under what terms; how the sales function should integrate with the other functions in the organization; what other key activities (e.g., market analysis) the organization needs for the sales personnel to perform.

While all of these are important considerations, understanding the role of sales personnel is perhaps the most critical. In some instances, the "sales representatives" serve as relationship builders and conveyors of product information (e.g., pharmaceutical reps calling on doctors). In other situations the representative *makes* the sale (e.g., telemarketers or face-to-face merchandise sales personnel). With the advent of new technology many sales personnel never see the customer (e.g., outbound telemarketing reps), while others practically live with the customer over extended periods (e.g., reps selling enterprise-wide IT systems).

Given the wide range of variability in the role played by sales personnel, it is typically folly to attempt to mimic what other organizations are doing with the sales plans. Certainly, a program designer must be aware of the compensation levels offered by competitive organizations, to ensure the program will attract and retain the quality of personnel required for success. But 95% of getting it right is understanding the role played by sales personnel and the significance of that role. Only then can it be determined if motivating sales personnel to achieve specific goals will benefit the organization, how much and how. Once that is understood the organization can determine what would constitute the ideal package of behaviors and results expected of the sales personnel. And that is the true key to the design of effective sales compensation strategies and programs.

Typical activities of sales personnel normally fall into the following two categories:

- *Direct selling activities*:

  - identifying/qualifying prospects;
  - building relationships/contact networks;
  - making sales calls;
  - developing and presenting proposals;
  - taking orders;

- *Support activities*:

  - researching market demand;
  - working conventions/trade shows;

 – handling inquiries and expediting orders;
 – resolving customer complaints;
 – presenting new products and promotions;
 – training customer personnel in the use of the product.

Once the role of sales personnel is fully understood it is also critical that the staffing and development strategies are appropriate, since compensation is not the sole determinant of success. If the wrong people are hired and/or if they are not developed well the best compensation program will not produce the desired results. Therefore, once the role of the sales staff is defined it is critical to identify what they do and the knowledge, skills and abilities required to do it well.

The model utilized in previous chapters to incorporate the major theories about motivation and satisfaction proposed that there are four prerequisites for performance. They, of course, apply both to individuals and to groups, and to both sales and non-selling personnel. The model specifies the requirements for success, and the relative importance of these activities should be a key factor in what the sales compensation strategy will be. The degree to which the sales representative is in control of results should be the principal determinant of the mix between base pay and variable pay. The criticality of the sales force in generating the required revenues will have a major impact on how competitive the compensation package will be. The degree to which a group effort is required will influence the level at which performance is measured (individual versus group). Finally, the economics of the sale will dictate how much of total sales can be paid out in the form of sales compensation.

Defining the Roles within the Sales Function

The compensation strategy must fit the design of the sales function and the roles within it. For example, if all sales reps do all of the aforementioned activities, one mix of base and variable may be prescribed. If the roles are split and sales reps do only direct selling activities, while others do the sales support work, a very different mix of base and variable may be prescribed, and the mix will probably differ between those doing direct sales and the support people. In many organizations the increasing complexity of products has resulted in the creation of sales teams, with direct sales, sales support and technical personnel populating them. This structure may result in yet another type of mix, and a need for rewarding group as well as individual results may arise.

Another key issue is whether there is a career path for sales reps, consisting of skill and knowledge levels. For example, professionals are typically classified into occupational ladders, with levels from "rookie" to "expert" being used to administratively acknowledge growth in individual competence. Some organizations use the same methodology to classify sales representatives, based on the principle that more experienced and accomplished reps are capable of contributing more and therefore command higher salary levels. The most common manifestation is a sales ladder, which consists of an associate (trainee) level, a representative (accomplished) level and a senior level. Each level is in a different grade (if the sales people are integrated into the organization's salary structure) or at least have a different salary range.

When this approach is used, salary administration can be a traditional pay-for-performance system, with promotional progression handled much as it is in the rest of the organization. However, the sales reps in most organizations are volume producers and they use variable pay potential to encourage people to develop and to perform at high levels. This latter approach is more reasonable when the sales rep has very substantial control over sales results, while the former would better fit the previously mentioned pharmaceutical sales reps, who are primarily disseminating product information and communicating research findings on new products.

It is very possible that both of these approaches would work in an organization where some of the sales personnel are focused on direct sales while others are focused on support work and market development. It should be noted that sales management will often question the need for multiple systems and may be reluctant to implement performance appraisal programs, salary administration guidelines and the like. But if this is the right strategy then the human resource function can play a significant role in defusing the tension about the feasibility of such programs and can help sales management in the training, communication and administration associated with this approach.

Mix of Base and Variable Compensation

Tables 7.1, 7.2 and 7.3 describe three mix profiles for the total sales personnel direct compensation package. Table 7.1 is an all-base-pay strategy, which is best suited for a sales role that is primarily made up of activities that fall under the heading of sales support. Table 7.2 is the other extreme, consisting totally of variable pay, and logically is most suitable for sales personnel who have total control over the amount of sales generated. Table 7.3 is

Table 7.1 "Base Pay Only" Package

Characteristics	Representatives are paid salaries, administered in the same manner as for other personnel.
	Sales results are considered by using them as a factor in appraising the performance of representatives.
Advantages	Employees are paid on the same basis as all others, precluding the feeling of "special treatment" or separatism often experienced.
	Income is reliable and predictable and costs are known in advance.
	Different types of sales representatives (technical assistants, account servicers, etc.) can be utilized without producing large income differences or "What's in it for me?" reactions.
	Promotes identification with the company and simplifies reassignment to different territories and product lines.
	Makes it easy to assign non-selling/missionary work.
Disadvantages	Income is not tied to sales results, lessening the motivation to sell.
	Encourages overemphasis on the products that are easiest to sell.
	The best performers are undercompensated relative to reps performing at lower levels.
	Compensation costs are fixed and do not vary with revenues.
Best applications	When the selling process is long and involves multiple contributors.
	When support/missionary activity is a significant portion of the job.
	When personnel are rotated in and out of the selling force.
	When product features or other factors are responsible for sales (only product available, market position dominant, stable customer base, high barriers to market entry, etc.).
	Predominance of house accounts; other accounts are "nice to have."
	When it is desirable to have costs fixed and known.

Table 7.2 "Variable Pay Only" Package

Characteristics	No salary; may be a "draw" against future commissions. Commission computed as percentages of sales, gross profits, number of units, etc., according to a formula.
Advantages	Easy to communicate and administer. Requires no forecasting. Commission can be varied by territory, product sold, new vs. existing customer, etc. Expense control; compensation level tied to results. Can be paid on any schedule (monthly, quarterly, annually).
Disadvantages	No protection against excessive payments unless a "cap" is used to limit earnings. No protection against loss of income during slow sales ("draw" may provide short-term income continuity). Rewards only sales; no credit for support activity or "investing in the future." Creates a different set of pay practices and raises equity questions by other personnel.
Best applications	The company feels no obligation to provide a guaranteed annual wage (may be seasonal product, part-time personnel, etc.). "Reps" or other non-employees are used as a sales force. High variability in income is acceptable (no concern about supervisor/subordinate earnings relationships). There is no mobility between direct selling jobs and other jobs in the organization. There is a high variable market demand and/or customer base.

Table 7.3 "Combination Base Pay Plus Variable Pay" Package

Characteristics	Salary only is paid until some quota or target sales figure is reached. Beyond the target, total direct earnings increase, according to a predetermined formula.
Advantages	Requires a certain level of performance (to earn a salary) before income begins to vary and costs increase. Quotas/targets can be set at different levels by territory and can be individual or group targets. Can be integrated with sales management and support compensation programs to produce equitable pay relationships.
Disadvantages	Good forecasting is necessary (must determine what level of sales "earns" salary). Salary portion of compensation is a fixed cost; if set too high, it rewards below-standard performance. Fixed costs (salaries) reduce funds available to discriminate between high and low levels of performance.
Best applications	Relationship of compensation with other personnel is important (considerable mobility in and out of sales jobs). A significant portion of the job is sales support (need to elicit multiple behaviors). A substantial amount of income must be guaranteed in order to attract and retain personnel.

everything else in between the first two approaches. The variable portion of the third option can be in the form of commissions, which are incentives directly tied to sales volume. They can also be incentives that are tied to predetermined criteria and standards.

There are few organizations that use an all-salary approach for true direct sales person-nel. Some retail establishments pay floor personnel on an hourly or salaried basis, but it is difficult to call what they do direct sales work, since the term "sales" implies persuasion and influence being applied to achieve an end result. Although pharmaceutical firms often pay newer "sales representatives" on a salary-only basis their work would typically be termed sales support. This is not to rule out an all base pay package as being viable, but direct selling activities typically warrant some form of financial incentive. If a role involves no direct selling activities it may be wise to call it something other than "sales" (e.g., customer service), since the sales label may encourage employees to make comparisons to market or to others within the organization that are not appropriate.

Correspondingly, there are few organizations that pay sales personnel totally in the form of variable compensation if they are full-time regular employees. Even if it is called a "draw" there is usually some weekly or monthly payment made on a regular basis and this payment is often the safety net sales personnel rely on when economic conditions are poor or when they are ill or taking time off. Again, this is not to rule out an all-variable-pay package, but only to suggest that the specific context should argue strongly for this approach before it is used.

The base–variable combination approach can come in an enormous variety of flavors. As already mentioned, the variable component can take the form of commissions, which vary income in direct relationship to sales volume. Typically, a formula is used, which most often calculates earnings as a percentage of sales, a percentage of sales over a specified threshold amount, or any number of different percentages that apply to sales in specified volume brackets (e.g., 2% of the first $200,000 of sales, plus 3% of the next $200,000 and 5% of all sales over $400,000). An increasing percentage is a recognition that as sales volume grows each incremental sale becomes more difficult. It may also be that additional sales are more profitable, since the employee has already covered their fixed expenses and therefore the net realized is greater for additional dollars of sales.

It is very common to set a "breakeven threshold" figure below which no commission is paid. If a territory is expected to produce $2 million in sales the threshold may be set at $1.5 million, indicating that this is the absolute minimum expected and that below this level the rep has not even earned the salary paid and/or covered the expense of maintain-ing a rep in the territory. Once the threshold is exceeded commissions begin to accrue.

Commission rates may also vary based on the product sold and/or the customer the product was sold to. If a new product is a difficult sale, owing to a lack of brand recogni-tion, it may be necessary to offer a higher commission rate so that sales reps will devote an adequate amount of time and attention to get it off the ground. If new customers are harder to sell to but are needed for future success it may be prudent to offer a higher commission rate than what is paid for sales to existing customers. Finally, if some prod-ucts are more profitable than others the economics may both allow and warrant a higher commission rate.

Incentives or bonuses can be used in lieu of or in addition to commissions. Incentives are rewards based on predetermined criteria and standards, while bonuses are determined after the fact, often on a discretionary basis or for specific activities. Bonuses may be paid for actions that may or may not generate immediate sales, such as making new prod-uct presentations or achieving a high customer satisfaction rating. Sales functions also run contests that are aimed at producing a specific result in a specific time period (e.g., generating the most new customers for a new product in a 60-day period). Particularly in competitive situations sales personnel encounter considerable rejection and it is often prudent to use contests and specific incentives to get their adrenalin levels back up or to focus them on doing something that might not produce sales in the short term. Contests can offer a quick dosage of energy and can provide a very specific focus.

It is often preferable to base rewards on more than one performance measure. Table 7.4 illustrates three options. The first two identify volume and productivity as the two critical measures and put the rewards schedule in the form of a matrix. The first matrix has the two factors weighted equally, while the second weights volume more heavily. The third adds sales to new customers as a third factor and rewards volume with additional earnings. Since there seems to be an endless variety of results that an organization might want to reward it is helpful to identify the tools that are available and to list those that might motivate specific results. Table 7.5 gives examples of rewards that can be used to address specific objectives.

Unfortunately, many sales functions enter a state of turmoil each year when setting sales quotas, determining commission schedules and devising bonus and incentive schemes. Even more regrettably some never come out of that state. Each sales person is concerned about the relative difficulty of the quota, the fairness or competitiveness of the commission rates or incentive/bonus formulas and the amount of support (product quality/diversity, advertising, sales materials, expense budgets, etc.) that will be forthcoming. This is natural, and concern about equity and competitiveness is common to all employees. However, owing to the numerical metrics used in sales compensation, everything seems very specific—and specific measures beg debate. There are debates about the relative attractiveness of territories or product lines, and sales reps are very focused on comparing their "deal" to that of the others within the function. But the sales reps are also in constant contact with their counterparts from other companies, and hearsay (e.g., about what others make) is inevitably exchanged. This is not unique to sales personnel but it is usually much more pronounced than for other occupations.

Table 7.4 Alternative Strategies for Using Multiple Performance Measures

Alternative 1: Two performance factors; equally weighted
Net profit after selling expenses

Sales Volume	Threshold	Target	Bull's-Eye
Threshold	100% of target	150%	200%
Target	50%	100%	150%
Bull's-eye	0	50%	100%

Alternative 2: Two factors; volume = 75%; profit = 25%
Net profit after selling expenses

Sales Volume	Threshold	Target	Bull's-Eye
Threshold	150% of target	175%	200%
Target	75%	100%	125%
Bull's-eye	0	25%	50%

Alternative 3: Bonus for sales to new customers

Sales (Quarter)	Bonus
up to $50,000	2% of sales
$50,000–100,000	3% of sales over $50,000
over $100,000	4% of sales over $100,000

Table 7.5 Fitting Sales Compensation Plan Design to Organizational Objectives

Objectives	Possible Plan Design Features
Emphasize specific products	A Higher sales credit per dollar of sales.
	B Higher incentive on products/services.
	C Contest focused on products/services.
Encourage sales	A Higher sales credit per dollar of sales to new customers.
	B Higher incentive on new accounts.
	C Separate bonus for each new account.
	D Bonus for presentations to prospects.
	E Contest focused on new accounts.
Control sales	A Base incentive on "net" expense (sales less expense).
	B Deduct expenses over allotted level.
	C Do not reimburse expenses.
Promote cross-selling and other joint efforts	A Add sales credit for group sales.
	B Split sales credit between reps.
	C Credit sales to all contributors.
	D Award "referral" bonuses.
	E Separate group incentive plan.
Develop skills and effectiveness of sales force	A Provide training.
	B Give "promotions" to more skilled.
	C Reimburse/reward added education.
	D Provide recognition awards.
	E Make management available for joint sales calls and field support.

Determining Competitive Position Relative to the Market

If an organization is to be able to attract and retain high-caliber sales personnel it must provide a competitive compensation package. Depending on the nature of the labor market other items such as employee benefits may also be critical, as might the availability of a company car and the policies governing sales expense. It is important to consider cars and expenses, since they can represent remuneration in a tax-effective (or tax-free) form, increasing their perceived value. Sales expenses are often a significant factor in determining the profitability of a sale—fancy dinners and golf outings at a private club can quickly dissolve the benefits of the resulting sales. There are many approaches to controlling expenses, the easiest of which is not to reimburse them. This may not be appealing to the sales person, however, and by not incurring any expenses they may lose sales that might otherwise be had. Real estate brokerages typically forgive a given percentage of commissions to cover advertising a property, meaning that a rep who sells a lot per dollar of advertising is compensated better than one who beefs up the revenue of advertising channels without generating enough revenue to support it.

Attempting to determine how competitive the sales compensation package is through the use of market surveys can be devilishly difficult. Surveying salary and variable compensation levels separately brings into question what a salary is. For example, if a competitor cuts a check for all sales reps for $3,000 every month as if it were a salary, but requires that this amount be covered by a given level of sales, should this be reported into the survey as a salary or as a draw? Because of this imprecision in measurement, many surveys do not even attempt to make the distinction and report only direct compensation earnings. This creates its own problem, since it still begs the question as to what a competitive base and variable mix is. Obviously, most sales personnel would welcome a very high base salary as long as there is still a large upside opportunity achievable through variable compensation, since they are protected against the downside associated with economic downturns and yet prosper in the good times.

Surveys that measure only total direct compensation without attempting to differentiate between base and variable portions will often add a section on program design that gets at what is earned under multiple outcome scenarios. For example, the author conducted a software industry sales compensation survey for several years. The survey asked what the threshold volume was (the point at which the employee had earned the salary/draw) for each product type and then asked what earnings would be at a number of higher sales volumes. Needless to say, this not only requires a great deal of effort on the part of the surveyor but requires that the participants know the compensation plans in detail. Often, the HR function provides data for surveys but it is sales management that knows the details of the sales plan, which may result in estimated data being reported owing to the lack of specific information.

Critical Administrative Issues

No matter how well an organization formulates the sales compensation strategy and designs the programs, success will be dependent on effective implementation, sound administration and continuous evaluation of the results they produce.

Implementation

Effectively communicating the objectives the organization wishes to achieve, the methods and processes to be used and the role of each of the involved parties is critical to success. Training people to discharge their roles allows the communicated intent to be translated into a reality. If sales managers will be doing performance appraisals on sales personnel for the first time, the training challenge will be significant, since a new dimension will have been added to the manager's role. Management must ensure that the training is appropriate and adequate. Evaluating current managers against any new role requirements may indicate some of the incumbents will not make it in the new context, or that they will make it only with the help of extensive training. If the strategy or programs are new or substantially modified it may be wise to pilot them, or at least use historical data to ensure they will produce the desired result under conditions the organization experiences. Sales personnel do not like their compensation package to be subject to frequent and major overhauls any more than other employees, so it is prudent to take every step to ensure the new approach will be successful.

Administration

How well the day-to-day details of administering sales compensation programs are handled will go a long way to determining their impact. Sales compensation suits are among the most numerous types of civil legal actions in the U.S. Since sales compensation plans are often very contractual in nature, how well they are administered can have a significant impact on an organization's exposure to legal liability. And the degree to which they produce satisfaction among sales personnel will also impact the organization's ability to retain good performers, which impacts the expense associated with unwanted turnover.

Defining when a sale is a sale and whether returns or accounts that are not collectible are charged to a representative's earnings are administrative issues that are the source of most of the conflict between the organization and the sales person. Often, the allure of making a sale results in a rep booking a transaction that "will not stick." Selling to an account that is unlikely to pay the bill is not productive and probably should be prevented by the organization's credit function, but decisions are rarely clear cut. And often the rep gathers the information on the account, opening the door to distortion of the facts, whether it is intended or not. And overloading an account in December in order to make the annual quota, even though a return is almost certain to occur, is an act that is difficult to detect in advance, and the rep may be the only one with all the facts. Therefore the administrative policy that determines whether a sale is compensated when the order is written, when the product is provided, when the order is invoiced or when the money is collected is a very key one and it should be consistent with the realities faced by each organization.

Another administrative issue is whether a rep is given any price discretion. Reps in the field with one chance to make the sale often feel that a less profitable sale is better than no sale at all. But the rep also typically lacks the broad perspective necessary to realize the impact of a single price reduction on the treatment of all other accounts and the behavior of all other sales reps. Often, a policy is formulated by sales management that establishes prices but that also allows consideration of the specific circumstances. With the proliferation of communication technology, the ability to get an instant answer on a potential concession has been greatly facilitated. And if some flexibility exists but there is a deduction in crediting the sale if the standard price is not met, this may balance the rep's judgment on what the price should be.

An associated issue is whether "supplemental payments" can be arranged for the party responsible for making the purchase. In some countries it is accepted practice to make payments to facilitate the transaction, while in the U.S. this is often illegal, or at least inconsistent with the organization's code of ethics. This issue has become difficult when reps find their competitors from other countries are not similarly restricted and when failure to engage in the practice will surely cost them the sale. The answer to this dilemma is dealing with it in advance, by establishing global principles that govern how the organization does business. It must be clear to sales personnel that the Foreign Corrupt Practices Act has extraterritorial jurisdiction and bribes are illegal everywhere.

How often incentive earnings are calculated and paid out is an issue important both to the organization and to sales personnel. Timing varies from monthly to annually, and the option used should fit the sales cycle. A shorter determination period is typical when the base pay levels are low, when the sales cycle is short and when significant earnings variation across payment periods is acceptable.

One of the most emotional issues is whether sales compensation is "capped." If a sales rep makes as much as the director (or even the CEO) it is certain that the event will prompt considerable discussion. The culture may accept this result, and even celebrate it, but it is very important to anticipate the reaction before the event is allowed to materialize. Behavioral scientists will argue against maximum earnings limits on motivational grounds, but they are rarely the ones who have to deal with the results when extreme variations occur. If uncontrollable windfalls or cave-ins can cause compensation levels to vary wildly, it may be prudent to anticipate this and to build parameters into the program design that enable the organization to adjust formulas to reflect unanticipated developments.

Evaluation

Sales compensation programs age and often do not do so gracefully. The rate of change in today's environment requires that organizations continuously evaluate effectiveness and whether their strategies and programs continue to be appropriate. The balance between sales volume and profitability is apt to change for a product throughout its life cycle, since market share is often a dominant consideration for a new product, while profitability may become the key measure when the product is established. The measures that drive sales compensation will decide which measures reps pay attention to, so continuous evaluation, adaptation and communication become prerequisites for continued effectiveness.

Compensating Sales Support Personnel

Given the increasing complexity of products and customer needs the direct sales representative may often lack the technical knowledge needed to close the sale singlehandedly. It is increasingly the case that engineers, system designers, IT analysts and others play a significant role in preparing sales proposals and even whether the organization can respond to a customer need. Often, these people spend long hours shoulder to shoulder with the sales representative making the sale possible and then see the rep off to the luxury car dealership to celebrate the financial benefits he or she will enjoy (alone). There may also be customer support or administrative support personnel in the regional sales office who make it possible for the rep to be effective, and it is increasingly common for these people to question why their economic fate is not in some way tied to the sales they contribute to. This is always a difficult issue to deal with, since once others start being rewarded it is difficult to decide where to stop. It is, however, a very important issue for an organization to think through and to deal with.

Compensating Sales Management

The manner in which sales management personnel are compensated is just as critical as how direct sales representatives and support personnel are compensated. Those from the simplicity school of design often suggest adding up the results of the subordinate personnel and having that drive the compensation of the manager. This may, in fact, work in situations where the manager's principal job is to make decisions on how to deploy the reps and allocate territories or customers and to monitor the activities of the reps. In situations where the dividing lines are clear relative to geographic territory or product lines the "add it up" approach probably is well suited to the first and perhaps second line of management (e.g., district and regional sales managers).

When developing a compensation strategy for senior sales management jobs it is often necessary to recognize that other responsibilities and objectives are an important part of the role. As a result, it often makes sense to treat these jobs more like the managerial jobs in other functions. The top sales executive in most organizations has at least a portion of their direct compensation contingent on the performance of the organization and/or the performance of the sales function defined by factors other than just volume or profit. When equity programs such as stock options are utilized, eligibility is often determined by organizational level, and sales management (at least at the senior levels) will typically participate, thereby broadening their focus.

Measuring and rewarding the performance of sales management personnel based solely on quantitative results does have significant limitations. There are many who argue for making the quality of management a significant factor in defining and rewarding performance. A more complete picture of performance may require using criteria such as the level of unwanted turnover among sales representatives, developing reps for assuming higher levels of responsibility and the contribution to the effectiveness of other functions and the overall organization. The sales personnel can impact production by not over-promising on the delivery schedule and by creating orders with adequate volume to enjoy economies of scale. They can also impact customer service by not overpromising. They can impact finance by selling the more profitable products. And they can contribute to the future viability of the organization by selling the new products that provide opportunities in the long run. All of these behaviors may detract from revenue volume but be critical to organization performance. If performance is defined as volume and rewarded on that basis alone it is unlikely that these other, more qualitative measures will be foremost in the minds of sales personnel as they do their work.

Compensating International Sales Personnel

When sales are made by employees who reside outside the headquarters country or sales personnel are from other countries, the impact of cultural differences should be considered when designing sales compensation programs. For example, the culture prevailing in the U.S. results in a propensity to focus on individual results and to apply one set of rules for everyone. Although few would change this culture, given the economic success it has produced, some would suggest moderating it or questioning the assumptions underlying it. If sales people are the free agents they are often thought to be, paying them based on what they sell makes a great deal of sense. The approach will probably be consistent with the way their role is defined and the way they work. However, if the organization sells its product in countries with very different cultures it is wise to consider how the sales compensation strategy works in those countries. Asian and Latin cultures tend to be more collectivist in nature, and people there may believe it takes everyone to make a sale, thereby rendering the "Reward only the hunter who fired the shot" strategy inconsistent with their beliefs.

Differences in personal views regarding what constitutes a valued reward often produce undesirable consequences. U.S. companies paying large bonuses to a top sales producer in Japan could result in personal embarrassment and discontent for the person being "rewarded." It is a mistake to stereotype a nationality, of course. But organizations need to recognize where values, beliefs and priorities differ, particularly in a sales force. Since the metrics used to measure performance in direct sales are typically quantitative, it is usually possible to determine the level of individual performance (defined in revenue terms). But it is more difficult to determine what that success will be attributed to. In some cultures success will be viewed as the collective efforts of all. In others, luck is given much of the credit. In others, the sale will be viewed as the result of the prestige of the organization and its sustained relationship with customers. Since the rewards tend to be quantified in monetary terms the way in which they are distributed leaves little doubt as to what the organization attributes success to, and if that conflicts with what employees view as appropriate the results may not be desirable.

Not only is it respectful to consider the culture of the employees, but also it may be economically prudent. If individually based incentives keep employees with great potential from performing as well as they could because they do not want to stand out from their peers, one has to question the wisdom of pushing a philosophy that produces the wrong result. It may come to abandoning the "one best way" approach and allowing for local customization, as long as it is consistent with global principles.

Application of Principles: Chapter 7

A software firm has had complaints from their design staff that they are the reason the products sell so well, yet the direct sales reps are the only ones rewarded for sales. The firm provides standard products but customizes each product to fit a customer. This requires extensive communication between the customer and the designers, since the sales personnel often lack the technical knowledge to even know what a customer wants and what level of effort will be necessary to provide it. Designers often accompany sales reps when the product is being pitched to a potential customer and they must "think on their feet" when a prospect asks if specific features can be incorporated and how much that will impact the price. The Compensation Manager has also had complaints from sales support staff who feel that they contribute greatly to the efficiency of the reps, by generating leads, scheduling presentations, preparing proposals and handling follow-up activity.

The Compensation Manager feels that there will be no end to the requests for being rewarded for sales if any staff members receive incentive awards or bonuses. Yet he realizes that they do have a point . . . the reps could not pull it off on their own. You have been retained as a consultant to counsel the firm on this issue. How would you go about formulating recommendations . . . what information would you need and who would you get input from?

Chapter 8

Rewarding Performance
Teams

The increased use of teams as a form of organizing work has called into question whether the same human resource management strategies work effectively for teams as they do for individual jobs. A critical first step in developing effective performance and rewards management strategies for a "team" is determining the *type* of team that the strategies are being developed for. There are three basic types of teams: work (process) teams, project teams and parallel teams.

- *Work (process) teams* are organizational units that perform work on an ongoing basis. Membership is relatively permanent and members work full time in the team—it is their organizational role. The team member role description is simple: do whatever needs to be done at the time. As a result, it is beneficial to have each member acquire and develop the full gamut of knowledge, skills and behaviors required by the work. An example would be a production team that builds a product or part of a product.
- *Project teams* consist of a group of people assigned to complete a one-time project. The members typically have well-defined roles and may work on specific phases of the project, either full time or in addition to their other responsibilities. They often work in different occupations and most often report to a project manager relative to their work on the project, rather than to their regular manager. An example would be a cross-functional team that is using concurrent engineering to develop a new product.
- *Parallel teams (a.k.a. task forces)* consist of people assigned to work on a specific task, typically in addition to their normal role. The term "parallel" suggests that task force work is carried on while the regular work continues, and members are almost always assigned to a task force on a part-time and temporary basis. Typically, members work in different occupations and different parts of the organization, although employees in the same occupation could evaluate ways of improving a current process or project in addition to their regularly assigned work.

The type of team is critical when considering how performance is defined, measured, managed and rewarded. Since the different types of teams require different types of members and ask for different commitments, as well as having different objectives, it is reasonable to assume that the type of performance and rewards strategies that will be effective will be different. Before deciding on performance and rewards management strategies for different types of teams it is prudent to consider whether a team is the right structure to perform the work. It is also necessary to ensure teams are effectively designed and managed, to ensure that performance is not impeded by the way the team is structured and how it is utilized.

The criteria for effective teams suggested by Katzenbach and Smith are: 1) the team has a purpose that is accepted by and meaningful to members; 2) the team is small enough to allow for internal coordination of work; 3) the membership possesses the required knowledge, skills, abilities and behaviors; 4) specific goals are defined and understood; 5) the methods and processes employed are appropriate and effective; and 6) there is an acceptance of mutual accountability.[1] If any of these characteristics are missing it is difficult to accept that members can be rightfully held accountable for the team performing well—and that they are fairly rewarded based on results.

The characteristics of effective teams and team leaders proposed by LaFasto and Larson are consistent with those just cited but are focused more on how a team is led and managed.[2] They are: 1) clear, stretch goals; 2) results-based work design; 3) competent members; 4) unified commitment; 5) collaborative climate; 6) explicit performance standards; 7) external support and recognition; and 8) directed by principled leadership. The two authors also describe the characteristics of effective leaders: 1) demonstrate commitment to team goals; 2) give members an appropriate amount of autonomy; 3) make explicit team goals and measures; and 4) reward group progress. They found that ineffective team leaders: 1) do not recognize and resolve performance problems; 2) mandate too many goals and/or change goals frequently; 3) do not prioritize goals; and 4) misrepresent expectations.

The rather unique issue associated with performance management in all types of teams is how leaders deal with individual performance problems and how they differentiate between members when appraising performance. Teams often require interdependent and supportive behavior, and differentiating between individual members when evaluating contribution or determining rewards can create divisiveness. However, there is a common misunderstanding about how team members generally want management to handle individual performance problems. Managers often feel they would be intruding to deal with these problems, while the research cited by LaFasto and Larson demonstrates that members do not want to carry people who cannot or will not contribute their share to the team. This same research demonstrates that the "Go forth and do good deeds—you figure out what and how" kind of direction does not resonate with team members and negatively impacts effectiveness. As discussed in Chapter 2, Locke and Latham's research has shown that goals need to be specific and clearly understood in order to motivate performance.[3]

Performance and Rewards Management for Work (Process) Teams

Work team members have as their primary role doing the work assigned to the team. Although "Do whatever needs to be done at the time" sounds like a strange role description, it actually fits many teams. If members are expected to acquire all the knowledge and skills required to perform all of the operations assigned to the team, and if their responsibilities include performing all of these operations, then the role of "team member" can be described in a manner similar to that of the traditional job description.

When the work performed by team members is complex and varied it is advisable to consider defining several levels of individual expertise. This can provide a basis for a career ladder for team members, into which individual employees can be classified. The ladder approach is discussed in Chapter 5 on professionals. For example, a member still learning to perform the duties is classified into a developing category (often called associate team member or trainee). Someone who has become competent in most or all operations is classified into a team member category. And someone who has developed mastery and who may assist less experienced others can be classified as a senior team member. Individuals are progressed through this ladder as they acquire the skills and knowledge associated with each classification level. Each of the levels can be assigned to a grade in the organization's pay structure, with a pay range determined by competitive market rates. This enables easy integration with the pay system for other employees.

Individual pay rates can be administered within those ranges, based on performance, progress in achieving competence at that level, or a combination of both. If the work of the team is relatively simple there may not be a need to create different levels of team member, since the knowledge and skills can be developed in a short time and base pay differences would not be warranted. It would also serve no purpose to create "promotions," which would require differentiating between members whose capabilities did not differ much.

Another approach is to define specific skills or skill sets associated with the work of the team and to establish a process for testing mastery of each of the skills. Skills related to each other can also be grouped into sets or blocks. Pay is progressed as individuals learn more skills, which is consistent with the philosophy that a multiskilled member of a work team is more valuable than someone with only a single skill. Termed "skill-based pay," this approach was discussed in Chapter 3. It is intended to motivate skill development and in a way it equates performance to becoming skilled more widely and/or deeply. In a "Do whatever needs to be done" environment, a multi-skilled workforce is able to shift resources to peaks in workloads and to minimize lost time due to temporary overloads on a limited number of people able to perform the specific work. Many organizations have found that although average pay rates are higher when skill-based pay is used, total payroll is similar, or even less, owing to their ability to staff at lower levels because of the reduction in lost time. But if these economies cannot be realized, owing to contextual limitations, skill-based pay can still benefit the organization by increased productivity of the team.

Using base pay as the only way to reward team members may limit effectiveness. This is often the case when pay level is based on individual performance, as focusing on individual rewards can promote the wrong mindset and behavior. Since performance may only be apparent at the team level, it is questionable practice to focus on individual performance. This practice may put individuals in competition with each other for limited pay increase funds, rather than encouraging cooperative and supportive behavior. An all-base-pay strategy is also questionable when skill-based pay systems are used, since people are being rewarded for learning skills, rather than meeting team goals. This may motivate them to become full-time students rather than producers.

For these reasons more organizations are using variable pay programs for work teams that provide the motivation to achieve team objectives. Used in conjunction with base pay programs the incentive programs can encourage members to align their efforts and to balance learning skills with getting the work done. Peer pressure will often keep the person who wants to learn skills full time from doing so, since the lack of productivity will impact the earnings of the entire team.

One of the most effective models for group/team incentives is "gainsharing." The philosophy underlying this approach is to encourage workers to do what needs to be done better, more cheaply and/or faster, by providing contingent awards that share the gains in productivity. The gain (stated in economic terms) is shared, often 50–50, between the organization and the employee. Perhaps a better term for this approach is "performance sharing," since in today's service-oriented environment performance factors such as customer satisfaction, innovation, quality and other less tangible measures have replaced the cost and output numbers associated with a manufacturing world. This has produced a trend towards using multiple criteria to define performance for use in group incentive plans, with standards and scales assigned to each criterion. Overall team performance is then used to determine the incentive funds available, and these funds are typically distributed in an egalitarian manner (equal percentage of base pay, equal dollars, equal dollars per hour worked, etc.). The use of team incentives in conjunction with a skill-based approach to administering base pay has been proven to be successful in balancing the focus on individual performance and team performance.

Managing performance in teams presents different challenges than those associated with hierarchical, job-based structures. Research on teams has repeatedly shown that team members want management to identify and deal with performance problems within the team, contrary to the widespread belief that management should leave this to the members. Management can choose to remove team members who fail to perform. Individual rewards can also be a device for encouraging poor performers to improve. If the organization uses merit pay, the performance rating can impact base pay adjustments, thereby sending the message that individuals must contribute. Another way is to institute a "world series team share" clause in team incentives, which makes receipt of an employee's share of team incentives a pass–fail proposition, with the rewards being contingent on their performance fully meeting expectations or standards. Although some organizations use the performance appraisal rating to calculate individual incentive awards, assigning different levels to different ratings, this in conjunction with merit pay can easily result in more competitive and less cooperative behavior in teams. One way to temper this is to add performance criteria to the appraisal that reward supportive behavior, such as "contribution to the effectiveness of others" and "contribution to the effectiveness of the team." The resulting appraisal measures both performance as an individual and performance as a team member, as described in Chapter 2.

The approach to defining, measuring and rewarding performance should fit the nature of the roles of team members and their interrelationships in performing their work. The method for determining base pay, the method for determining variable pay or both may vary in the same organization across work teams. What works is what fits the context, and this principle should guide program design based on the context.

Relative to the process used to measure and reward performance, there is an issue concerning who evaluates the performance of team members. If there is a manager or team leader who is designated as the first-line supervisor of team members, traditional practice would suggest that person appraise all members. However, since team results usually impact customers (which may be internal or external) it can be argued that these customers should have input into appraising performance. Also, since team members are highly interdependent it seems reasonable for peers also to have input into the appraisals of their co-workers. Whether or not multi-party input is appropriate will of course depend on the culture of the organization and the culture of the team. In fact, the author is familiar with organizations that have successfully used peer ratings to determine whether individuals get their "world series team share" of the reward pool generated by team performance, typically using a pass–fail rating and requiring that at least two-thirds of the team members concur if individual awards are to be denied.

Another issue related to work teams is how the role of the person responsible for managing the team is to be defined, how performance will be measured and how rewards will be determined. Variously titled "manager," "supervisor," "team leader" and even "coach" or "facilitator," this role can vary from traditional supervision of team activities to acting as a liaison to other units or entities. Based on the role definition, a set of performance criteria and standards can be developed that fit that role. Failure to effectively redefine the role of a foreman who becomes a team leader can cause confusion, as well as result in filling the role with someone lacking the skills to be effective. Traditional supervisors are expected to plan, organize, assign and direct work, and someone skilled at doing these things may not be effective attempting to coach team members and to enable them to self-direct their activities.

The role played by the person directing the team's activities should also determine how compensation is managed. Supervisors typically participate in pay programs for management personnel, while a team leader may appropriately be paid more like the team members.

Performance and Rewards Management for Project Teams

The life of many professionals consists of a series of overlapping projects, rather than a defined "job." Increasingly, other occupations are operating in a project-focused manner, owing to changes in organizational structures. In addition, project teams are being used to design and refine key business processes that extend laterally across the organization. Given the increasing prevalence of project work it is important to examine performance and rewards management strategies used for project staffs.

Projects are generally defined by their end results, timelines and specific milestones along the way to project completion. Because they are of limited duration and are "one time" in nature, projects lend themselves to being managed using a formal framework. Building a new plant or laboratory and installing an enterprise-wide IT system are endeavors with a definable end result. Figure 8.1 is an example of a project management plan. Given the magnitude and complexity of such projects, technology will inevitably be used to plan, execute and evaluate the work performed to produce the result. Keeping track of progress on the back of an envelope is hardly feasible. Software packages are readily available today that enable users to keep track of materials, people and capital at every step along the way. Project management itself has become an occupation, and the Project Management Institute has developed formal certifications for various levels and types of project and program management expertise.[4]

When projects demand staffs from different occupations and functions, it is often necessary to use different management structures. The IT network representative on a cross-functional design team may administratively report to an IT manager, but the person's work will be directed by someone designated as the project manager, thereby creating the dreaded "two boss" scenario. This scenario is dreaded because performance and rewards management systems are under the control of line direct reports, who may know little about how well an employee performed on the project. The other management challenge is that project staff members often work on the project part time, while they continue in their "regular jobs" concurrently. This raises the critical issue of how their performance is measured: based on project performance, performance in their "regular job" or a combination of the two. It is, admittedly, difficult to get direct report managers to do effective appraisals and do them on time, but attempting to get two or more managers to coordinate their efforts to do joint appraisals makes this look like child's play. For that reason it is prudent to ensure that project managers have a responsibility to do performance appraisals for each employee assigned to the project, either on an annual basis or when their involvement is over on the project or a segment of the project. The appraisal of performance on the portion of the project the employee was involved in may be briefer than a performance appraisal and may even be binary but having it done enables the line supervisor to refer to it when doing the annual appraisal.

Because project work can represent a significant portion of the time of employees, it is necessary to consider how that work will be factored into administering both base pay and incentive pay plans. When project milestones are relatively easy to define and performance criteria are clear and straightforward, incentive plans may be simple to design. For example, if a new system will be evaluated on the basis of cost versus budget, completion versus schedule and system performance versus standards, these measures can be used as performance criteria that will determine if incentives are paid to staff members who were directly involved in developing the system. This approach is illustrated in Figure 8.1.

But if project staff members are eligible for project incentives, while the rest of the employees in their home units stay behind and "run the ranch" without being eligible for incentives, a potentially contentious issue is raised. Assume two systems analysts are classified into the same grade, with the same pay range. One is assigned to the project and the other left to maintain the current operations. If both had been eligible for incentives, with the same target as a percentage of base pay, having different assignments does not present a big challenge. The person on the project has their performance evaluated for purposes of incentive awards based at least proportionately on project work, while the other analyst is evaluated based on maintaining the current system. If the project person spends only part of the year or works part time during the whole year on the project, then performance

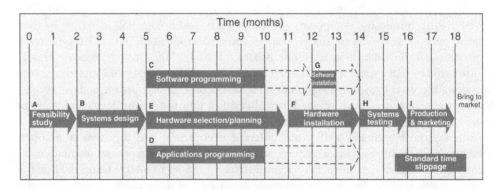

Figure 8.1 Project management plan

would be evaluated on two bases, proportioned based on relative time spent. It is possible that someone could be assigned to the project in addition to other responsibilities and be expected to work very long hours, and in this case it may be fair to reward them with incentives on top of base pay. But the instances of 100-hour weeks on IT projects seem to have become less frequent, since too many professionals have come to expect it is their right to have a life. And if part of a unit's staff is drawn off to work on projects it is likely that those remaining to do the ongoing work are experiencing heavier demands as well. It is therefore difficult to justify providing an incentive opportunity only to those working on the project.

When project incentives are used, the question arises as to whether overall results or individual contribution should determine awards. Much of this should depend on the degree of interdependence of the work. If someone contributes to a project by doing separate, stand-alone specialist work, it may be appropriate to reward him or her at least partially based on individual performance. On the other hand, measuring and rewarding performance at the team level may be advisable.

When project teams are developing new products, be they goods or services, the organization may wish to provide an incentive to contributors based on product success. Project staff can be given a "piece of the action" by allocating a percentage of first-year (or multi-year) sales to an incentive fund. The fund may also be based on how customers evaluate the product or on profits. This approach extends the perspective of project staff beyond the completion date and motivates them to develop a successful product. Once again, there should be consideration given to the impact of incentives on the total direct compensation of project staff compared to others in the same grades and even in the same jobs.

For organizations without formal incentive plans it may still be advisable to recognize contribution to projects with monetary rewards. If a "spot bonus" or "performance award" program is in place, project contribution can be recognized using existing mechanisms. If incentives and performance awards are not available, perhaps the organization should ask itself if this is a realistic and viable strategy in an era where project success often has a major impact on organizational success.

One of the current-day challenges relating to project teams is that members may not be collocated and may be occupationally and culturally diverse. Technology has made "global relay teams" possible, with work being passed around the globe, capitalizing on time differences. However, when occupation and culture cause communication issues, this approach can be very difficult to administer effectively. Even when translation software enables language differences to be addressed, not all work is formulaic in nature, requiring subjective interpretation of words and meanings. This is a truly daunting challenge if very dissimilar cultures are involved. For example, if Asian members of a team assume all decisions will be consensual, made only after considerable dialogue, while American members use a "Go forth bravely" individual decision-making approach, the probability of conflict or misunderstanding is great. And if substantial team incentive awards are at stake the intensity of the conflict can be so great as to erode the effectiveness of the team. Cultural issues are treated more fully in Chapter 10.

An even greater challenge is the cross-organizational team, which is becoming more common in this age of joint ventures and alliances. It is very difficult to bridge occupational or geographical differences within an organization. It becomes even more daunting when two or more organizations are involved, each with different cultures and different performance management and rewards management strategies. Since one of the most difficult issues associated with "sharing" employees is aligning their efforts and motivating them to work in a cooperative and supportive manner, it seems that performance and rewards management could act as a tool to achieve that result. On the other hand, choosing the approach used by one of the organizations to appraise performance and to reward employees is apt to be a difficult process. Perhaps a third approach could be formulated, but this means everyone will have to accept the change, rather than only the members of one of the organizations.

Employees who are a part of the joint venture or alliance on a full-time basis for an extended period can be considered to be employees of that entity, at least for the purposes of performance and rewards management. But it will be important to consider what happens to those employees in the future. If they are expected to return to their "home" organization the impact of the alliance or venture assignment on their careers and on their compensation levels over the long run should probably be limited. Also, equity issues will arise in the meantime, since there is almost certainly going to be communication with peers in the home organization and comparisons made relative to rewards and promotions. These employees are similar to expatriates, in that a repatriation plan needs to be formulated prior to the start of the assignment, so that employees understand that out of sight does not mean out of mind.

As will be discussed in Chapter 11 the increasingly common practice of using outsiders to do the work of the organization presents challenges as well. The use of consultants, contractors, freelancers and talent platforms to acquire the needed knowledge and skills can be particularly complex if employees and outsiders work jointly to produce results. If work is deconstructed into segments and they are assigned either to an employee and outsider, fewer issues may present themselves. However, the work must be integrated and the methods compatible so even the segmentation approach requires managing the interfaces.

Performance and Rewards Management for Parallel Teams

Task forces are the most common form of parallel team. Participation on a task force is rarely considered a substitute for the "day job," and membership is both temporary and part-time. Increasingly, task forces are being used to perform evaluations of existing systems and processes, selection of new technology, improvements of existing products, and the like. Too often, they are considered to be a free lunch by the organization, since it is rare for additional compensation to be expended on members. This belief that this work is free is delusional, since time, energy and resources expended on task force work are not available for the ongoing work of the organization.

Task forces are often not managed well, and may not be managed at all. An example is people being assigned to (or volunteering for) a task force and given a vague mandate such as "Take a look at on-site day care and see how much it would cost and if it would give us a competitive edge in attracting and retaining call center operators." Without a well-defined set of objectives, a timeline and an agreement on the financial and time resources available, the task force is apt to stumble forward and do the best job it can. Contributions to task force work are often ignored when performance is measured and rewards determined, thereby sending the message that doing this work well is nice but not critical. And very often members are selected (or volunteer) who have no experience working with each other and who may not have the interpersonal skills to work effectively. A questionable approach is to have people who are not fully occupied or who are not performing critical work named to participate, since they will not be missed on their regular job. Their skills may not fit the work of the task force.

Research has provided guidance on steps that can be taken to increase task force effectiveness. These are: 1) clearly define why the task force is being formed and why its work is needed, including the work to be done and the expectations (timelines, performance criteria and standards, etc.); 2) select competent members; 3) gain commitment to the objectives of the commissioning party; 4) define and commit resources (time, money, information, staff support, rewards available); and 5) provide an effective *modus operandi* (authority structure, training, relationships).[5] These steps are very consistent with the earlier-mentioned guidelines for managing other types of teams and make the point that resources are consumed by task forces and it is worth it to manage them well.

When task forces are assigned important work that requires considerable investment of time it becomes problematic that these contributions do not have any impact on performance evaluation or rewards. The author was interviewing a key executive in charge of the entire logistics chain of an organization, who pointed out that she was (rightfully) working on three major task forces involved with implementing new technology. She concurred that her participation was absolutely necessary but pointed out that the task force work was consuming 60% or more of her time—and yet her performance on her "full-time job" was the sole basis for determining her performance rating, salary action and incentive award. She made her point.

Task force work, when significant, can be folded into performance and rewards management in the same manner as in the example cited earlier of the systems analyst who worked part time on the project and part time in the regular capacity. It seems a mistake to ignore it, since this sends the message the work is not important or that it is not valued. On the other hand, occasional task force participation may be rewarded with recognition or non-monetary rewards, such as dinners or even afternoons at an event celebrating the contributions of those who have contributed. If the organization culture supports celebration of contribution and if the organization has developed the skills to do it well, appropriate recognition can be both motivating and rewarding. Communicating what has been done by the task force throughout the organization not only provides recognition but also can disseminate what has been learned.

It is also possible to use task force work as a career development tool. "Stretch" assignments can be made that can develop new skills, and "out of occupation" work can increase understanding of how different bodies of knowledge and occupational perspectives can be used to produce more robust solutions.

"Communities of practice" (COPs) are informal collectives that can under certain circumstances be considered a type of parallel team. They do, however, differ from task forces or even very short-term ad hoc groups. These COPs are "shadow" entities, in that they typically receive little or no formal sanction from the organization but may fill very important roles in learning, knowledge dissemination and individual development. The definition most commonly used is "groups of people who share a concern, a set of problems, or a passion about a topic, and who deepen their understanding and knowledge of this area by interacting on an ongoing basis."[6] The most frequently cited example was Xerox copy machine repairers who shared solutions to problems they commonly faced, through informal meetings, adding to the knowledge of peers. Others might be all actuaries or civil engineers spread throughout an organization, who find ways to help each other deal with their work and to grow within their field. In order for COPs to be considered teams, even informal ones, they probably need to be "shared purpose and practice communities," since it is possible that engineers could exchange information that was of value to individuals but did not facilitate the attainment of an organization's objectives or add to its pool of usable intellectual capital.

Since most of these communities are informal, it is easy to dismiss their value. However, an organization's ability to create new capabilities or sustain existing capabilities may be greatly enhanced by these communities. And significant amounts of employee time and energy may be consumed by community participation. For example, a group of software designers may work on a package with no apparent immediate commercial application and end up creating a new generation of technology that the organization turns into a core capability with great competitive advantage. The question then becomes: should the achievement be reflected in the performance appraisals of the designers? In their pay actions? In their incentive awards? If the group is rewarded for diverting part of their efforts into an unsanctioned project and they are rewarded, how does the organization prevent others from spending resources on other "pie in the sky" projects that end up only serving as personal amusement?

By formally sanctioning and supporting communities, an organization stands to gain benefits, albeit intangible initially and not directly measurable. These benefits include increases in the knowledge pool, learning that leads to increased innovation, improvements in the quality and speed of product development and better retention of talent.[7] It is difficult to acknowledge participation in these communities by considering their activities when defining performance criteria and standards that are used to appraise employees. It is equally difficult to fashion formal group incentives that have predetermined award criteria. In the event a community creates something of apparent value to the organization, it is possible to reward this with after-the-fact bonuses, stock awards or even career progressions. On the other hand, this should be imbedded in a process where impartial review panels representing all portions of the organization evaluate contributions and determine the appropriate rewards. This will promote equivalent treatment across the organization and provide a way to value results that cannot be counted in gross sales, profits or other quantitative measures.

Recognition can be used in lieu of financial awards, particularly since it could be argued that people used time that theoretically should have been spent on other organization business and that the salary provided compensation. 3M has had for decades a provision that anyone can spend 15% of their time pursuing something they believe will lead to a productive result. If this type of sanction is provided there may be no need to develop any other formal mechanisms into the performance or rewards management programs.

Application of Principles: Chapter 8

A retail organization has found that store volumes are diminishing, while online sales are increasing. Although the IT systems record either type of sale the online ordering process is cumbersome for customers and the decision has been made to completely redesign the online portion of the systems. It has been decided that the current staff has the knowledge and skill to handle the design and staffing levels are adequate since the project will be spread over two years. IT staff who will do the new system design work will be eligible to participate in an incentive plan that is tied to the project plan. The project plan has been segmented into modules, each of which has milestones defined. Performance criteria for each segment are cost vs. budget, completion date compared to due date and quality measures compared to standards. Each participant in each module is eligible to receive an incentive award if the criteria are met and if the employee's contribution is rated as meeting expectations.

As the project moved through its early stages there were complaints by IT staff members who were not slated to participate in the project work. Their argument was that they were only eligible to receive their salary, while "the chosen ones" could receive incentive awards. Management initially responded by pointing out that project participants were working long hours but when the other employees informed them that all of the ongoing work was being done by a smaller staff . . . and long hours were a reality for non-participants as well.

You have been asked to advise the Compensation Manager on this issue. What information would you need, what would your sources be and how would you go about getting it? Once you had the necessary information what factors would you consider when formulating your recommendations?

Notes

1 Katzenbach, J. & Smith, D., *The Wisdom of Teams* (Boston, MA, Harvard Business School Press, 1993).
2 LaFasto, F. & Larson, C., *Teamwork: What Must Go Right; What Can Go Wrong* (Newbury Park, CA, Sage, 1989).
3 Latham, G., *Work Motivation* (Thousand Oaks, CA, Sage, 2007).
4 Project Management Institute: pmi.org.
5 Ware, J., *Managing a Task Force*, Case 478002 (Boston, MA, Harvard Business School Press, 1992).
6 Wenger, E., *Communities of Practice* (Cambridge, Cambridge University Press, 1998) and Wenger, E., McDermott, R. & Snyder, W., *Cultivating Communities of Practice* (Boston, MA, Harvard Business School Press, 2002).
7 Saint-Onge, H. & Wallace, D., *Leveraging Communities of Practice for Strategic Advantage* (Amsterdam, Butterworth-Heinemann, 2003).

Chapter 9

Rewarding Performance
Public Sector and Not-for-Profit Organizations

Whether public sector and not-for-profit organizations should manage performance and rewards differently than private sector, for-profit organizations has always been the subject of considerable controversy. Should public and non-profit organizations emulate the strategies and programs used by the private sector or are there contextual differences that make it prudent for them to do things differently? It will be argued here that common principles apply across sectors but that custom strategies may need to be employed, owing to differences in the context within which both public sector and not-for-profit organizations must function.

Performance Management

The most apparent difference relative to performance management between the sectors is that performance in a private sector organization involves measuring things such as profit, cash flow and return on investment. Performance is most often defined in terms of profit if you are in management or as total shareholder return if you are an investor. But it can be argued that this has changed even in for-profit organizations. Many of them have begun to use the balanced scorecard and other approaches for defining performance using multiple factors.[1] The balanced scorecard uses four categories in measuring performance: 1) financial; 2) operational; 3) customer; and 4) learning and growth (workforce metrics). This "balanced" view of performance has not made financial results unimportant, but rather acknowledges that other dimensions should be included in the definition of performance when appropriate. Backward-looking measures have also in many organizations been replaced or augmented by measures that consider what will drive future performance and viability. As the environment has become much more dynamic, competitive and globalized, an increased need to ensure ongoing viability and flexibility has emerged, for both the private and the public sector.

So what about public and not-for-profit sector organizations? Profit is obviously not available as a metric for measuring performance, so what can be used? The simplest approach is to measure actual expenditures versus budget and to treat that as a profit surrogate. But this often leads to establishing inflated budgets, which are easy to conform to. It also may lead to the reduction of the quantity and/or quality of services to remain within an established budget. A public sector organization focusing only on staying within budget is as simplistic as using only last year's profit in a private sector organization. It is even less valid, since it does not reflect what has been accomplished with the resources consumed. As a result, more public and not-for-profit sector organizations are adopting multiple measures in a manner consistent with the balanced scorecard philosophy.[2] For example, citizen or constituent satisfaction can typically be used as customer measures. Productivity measures can be used at the organizational, group/unit and individual levels in many cases, in order to evaluate operational effectiveness. And if a viable process for establishing realistic operating budgets can be implemented, the "expenditure versus budget" measure can still be used as one of the key dimensions of performance, acting as a proxy for profit.

Learning and growth (workforce) measures present more of a challenge. Since there is not a profit and loss statement for public sector organizations it is difficult to evaluate whether too little or too much is being invested in the workforce. The Saratoga Institute in the U.S. has for years surveyed organizations on a wide variety of HR-related metrics so that participants can compare their numbers to "similar" competitors for people, which can be done for the public or the not-for-profit sectors just as it is done by the private sector.[3] But a metric like annual average hours of training per employee measures only activity and has no "return on investment" number to indicate if the expenditure was warranted and if it produced the results desired. Effectiveness and efficiency impacted by HR initiatives have been addressed to some extent in works such as *The Workforce Scorecard* and *Investing in People*.[4] But much more work needs to be done, and all types of organizations need to define and measure how effective the workforce is as a part of the definition of performance. One distortion in public sector organizations can be the level of benefits provided. Most public pension plans are unfunded, which means there is no current accountability for the liabilities that are being accumulated. This makes it easy for legislatures to give in to union and employee demands for enhanced benefits without having to provide a way to pay for them. Paid time off tends to be dramatically more generous in the public sector as well, often costing over 15% of payroll, and, once again, the liability this generates is just passed on to future generations to deal with.

There may be other differences even between public sector organizations and not-for-profits that are significant enough to warrant different strategies. For example, not-for-profits have to generate their revenue stream and do not have the option of raising taxes to generate it. It could therefore be argued that there is less difference between not-for-profits and private sector organizations than there is between not-for-profits and public sector organizations.

Below the organization-wide level in public sector organizations the major staff functions (e.g., finance, human resources and legal) tend to be measured in a manner that is similar to what is done in private sector organizations. These functions are increasingly assigned specific objectives, both quantitative and qualitative, and they are evaluated based on how well they attain them. They do not meet the test of being a profit center. "Line" functions in private sector organizations, such as manufacturing, sales, procurement and logistics, typically have quantitative measures that can be measured accurately. There are often no direct equivalents in governmental agencies or in not-for-profits providing services. However, public sector organizations also have to procure resources and charitable organizations must raise funds, both of which often entail marketing, if not a sales effort, and metrics are available in some staff functions.

The "bottom line" for both public sector and not-for-profit organizations is how their constituencies view their performance. Charitable organizations rely on contributors for resources and if those parties feel there is too much spent on administration or if the services are not delivered effectively, it will adversely impact revenues available.

The United Way in the U.S. suffered diminished resources in the mid-1990s when the CEO behaved in an arrogant manner and received what was widely viewed as excessive compensation. Governments that seem to consume more than is warranted by the value they deliver to the citizenry will be subjected to pressure, which is often political in form. The most direct form of accountability that citizens can muster is at the polling places, where they may act to remove policy-level officials. In countries where elections are not a viable vehicle for replacing ineffective or non-responsive governments, the most effective source of influence may be a reluctance to pay taxes and to support the government. In the case of United Way the contributors punished the organization by reducing their financial support.

Measuring and appraising individual performance in the public sector is often done differently than is common in the private sector. The Civil Service Reform Act and other civil service regulations generally require that governmental agencies evaluate performance and use those evaluations in making decisions relative to employment and career progression. The Uniform Guidelines for Employee Selection, which govern several aspects of federal human resource management in the U.S., specify "There shall be a job analysis which includes an analysis of the important work behaviors required for successful performance . . . Any job analysis should focus on work behavior(s) and the tasks associated with them" (s. 14.C.2). Further, the regulations require that the results of the job analysis need to be formulated into written statements that are communicated to the employee. Finally, appraisers must be trained or at least provided with written instructions about the use of appraisal instruments. In addition to the Uniform Guidelines, employees in governmental entities have property rights in their jobs, as well as due process rights. This mandates compliance with additional regulations if an employee is terminated for poor performance.

The use of formal performance management systems is less widespread in public sector organizations at the state, city and county level than it is at the federal level, and when such systems exist they may be used only for promotion and disciplinary actions. For example, approximately one-third of the public water utilities in the U.S. currently use step rate pay structures that progress pay rates based primarily on longevity.[5] Most utilities with step rate structures use a "pass–fail" scoring system in their appraisals, or do not do them at all, since they usually do not result in differences in the size of pay adjustments based on performance ratings. Getting appraisals done well and on a timely basis is difficult in all organizations, but when there is no differentiation between individuals relative to their pay adjustments, it is even harder to convince managers that this is a critical part of their management responsibility. However, as the move to merit pay from longevity pay has become more widespread in the public sector over the last decade, there seems to be an increased use of formal performance appraisal systems that do differentiate between individuals. This trend can also be seen in utilities, since a majority of them were using longevity pay ten years ago.

There is another fundamental difference between some public sector organizations and the private sector that has a major impact on defining and measuring performance: the manner in which they must be staffed. Fire stations and police stations must be staffed at a level that ensures there is a high probability they will have the resources to respond to the most critical event. The federal agency FEMA was incapable of appropriately responding to Hurricane Katrina, and its credibility suffered. It is therefore impractical to use conventional measures of productivity to evaluate the performance of an entity that responds to demand outside its control. This characteristic may make it impractical to measure productivity at the individual level. This type of staffing mandate applies to a significant portion of the public sector. Although the public are cost-conscious when evaluating public sector organizations, they are more concerned that their greatest needs are met—immediately. A library gets no credit for having the material a citizen wants on hand (it is expected), but it does incur criticism if it is not readily available. Hospitals are an even more dramatic illustration of the "staff at maximum potential demand" mandate. This presents a dilemma for the management of these entities, since they will invariably be evaluated by those making the demands. For-profit private sector organizations are left to figure out how to maximize shareholder return, while maintaining customer service and product quality at acceptable levels. During economic downturns public sector agencies are subject to increased scrutiny of any "excess capacity," and the judgments on budget allocations are often biased to cutting currently unused capacity. This further complicates the process of establishing and using reasonable performance criteria and standards.

There are two other differences that may exist between the public and private sector. One is the legal and regulatory scrutiny to which public sector organizations are subjected. Although discrimination laws also apply to the private sector, the public sector places much more emphasis on testing the statistical impact of personnel practices. The State of California has perhaps the most restrictive employment laws, causing some organizations to avoid employing people there. This scrutiny makes it more difficult for managers to differentiate significantly between employees when measuring performance, since differences can lead to challenges or employee appeals. Because of the due process regulations and open-ended appeals that often exist in the public sector, it is more difficult to punish poor performance by discharging employees. It is also more difficult to adequately reward outstanding performance, owing to the absence of merit pay programs and incentive plans that provide significant rewards on a differentiated basis. In most cases the amounts available for rewarding top performers are limited by the reality that legislatures regulate funding, based on what is available, rather than what is needed or warranted. The control of salary budgets by legislatures and councils also has a major impact on compensation planning. In the private sector the decision about how much to budget for pay adjustments is based solely on what management believes is needed to stay competitive and what the decision makers are willing to make available, while in the public sector the size of the fund available may be out of management's hands.

The second difference is the existence of unions in the public sector. While the private sector in the U.S. has experienced sharp declines in the percentage of employees who are covered by collective bargaining units, the public sector has seen increases. Unions representing public sector employees tend to apply pressure to treat everyone similarly and to make it difficult to do otherwise. Since performance appraisals will typically have limited or no consequences, many public sector organizations having unions do not do them at all. There are, of course, some unions that have consented to adopting personnel practices that are more like those used in the private sector, but they are in the minority.

Rewards Management

One of the principal differences between the private and public sectors is the variety of rewards that can be utilized. Private sector organizations that are publicly held have tools such as stock options, stock grants and other programs that facilitate employee ownership available. Even privately held for-profits can use simulated ownership devices (e.g., phantom stock) to motivate employees to behave like owners and to increase their earnings by making the organization successful. Public sector organizations lack the ability to use employee ownership, although some would argue that psychological "ownership" has as much motivational power as equity. Employees who feel they are a part of something good and necessary can become more engaged in the organization's mission, which typically results in increased employee satisfaction. This has a positive effect, even though it does not impact the employee's standard of living.

Most of the other compensation tools are available to public sector and not-for-profit organizations. Base pay, variable pay, employee benefits, perquisites and recognition can be used. There have traditionally been significant differences in the way these tools are used, however. For example, merit pay and variable compensation are much more widely used in the private sector than in the public sector.[6] Part of the reason for this is traditional. As previously mentioned, the public sector has a long history of progressing base pay by using time in position as the driver. The U.S. federal government and the majority of state and local governments have used step rate systems to administer wages and salaries for several decades. Although the trend is to replace this time-based approach with pay-for-performance systems, in some sectors it is very difficult to make the transition with in-place workforces, which will resist any effort that is viewed as a "take-away." Additionally, managers are often not trained in making refined performance distinctions and defending them to the satisfaction of employees. And since employees in many public sector organizations have seemingly endless avenues of appeal to use in contending judgments that impact their pay, managers may be reluctant to begin these endurance contests. It is also common for managers to be measured more on the level of industrial peace they maintain than on how well they tie rewards to performance.

Each of the alternative approaches to administering base pay rates within a public sector or not-for-profit organization should be considered. The choice of an alternative should be based on what fits the context of each individual organization, just as it should in a private sector organization. For example, a NASA center responsible for space missions might have a very different type of workforce than a water utility servicing a city, and both of them would differ from a charitable organization.

Time-based Pay

Public sector and not-for-profit organizations often assume that time-based "step rate" base pay programs are their only feasible option. This point of view is frequently the by-product of hearing horror stories about sophisticated for-profit organizations failing with merit pay and/or incentive compensation programs. In addition, there has been a long-standing tradition of time-based pay in the public and non-profit sectors. Private sector organizations managing outsourced municipal services under contract may also often use time-based pay plans, because of union preferences, because of the biases of regulatory agencies or because such plans are prevalent in the industry. There certainly are obstacles to making performance-dependent pay systems effective. On the other hand, each organization should consider alternatives to paying based solely on time spent in a job. The disadvantages of the time-based step rate system are too serious to ignore.

Also, the pressures to deliver high-quality service at a "reasonable" cost are too great in today's environment to afford the luxury of assuming people will be productive when performance does not impact pay.

Disadvantages of Time-based Pay

When an employee's rate of pay is based solely on how long he or she has held a job, the employing organization will typically have difficulty controlling payroll costs and motivating employees to perform well. Under a time-based system, an employee must only survive on the job for a sufficiently long period of time in order to be paid substantially above the average market rate for the job. As a result, time-based pay raises costs without making cost increases contingent on the organization receiving the benefits derived from high levels of performance or productivity. It also sends a strong signal to employees that performance does not matter, which will typically send better performers elsewhere (where they will be paid for their contribution) and encourage those who are left to play it safe and to maintain their membership in the organization above all else.

A common dilemma for an organization that has used time-based pay for a number of years is to have a significant percentage of its employees at the top pay rate in the schedule, which is a high-cost workforce, and yet face complaints by these very well-paid people that they receive only pay schedule adjustments. This situation is even more troublesome if a significant number of these employees are not performing well in their jobs.

Why Do So Many Public Sector Organizations Use Time-based Pay?

Time-based pay allows an organization to predict costs with more certainty than does merit pay. It also avoids the challenges associated with performance evaluation. Time-based pay works best when jobs are repetitive and routine, with small variation in performance possible, or when a collective bargaining relationship exists and there is not a high level of trust between the union leadership and management. It can also lessen discrimination suits filed because of employee disagreement relative to performance appraisal ratings and the size of pay increases.

On the other hand, the nature of many public sector and not-for-profit organizations is not that different from that of most private sector firms. There are routine and repetitive jobs, but they are often no more numerous than they would be in private sector organizations. And both union leaders and employee groups may be willing in today's environment to accept alternatives to time-based step rate pay systems if management includes them in developing the systems and respects their need to believe they will be equitably and competitively compensated.

What Are the Alternatives to Time-based Pay?

A number of viable alternatives to time-based pay exist. They were discussed in general terms in Chapter 3, and more detail about managing these programs will be discussed in Chapter 12. Organizations using step rate systems should be aware that changing the method of administering pay *does* involve disruption and requires that all parties learn to think differently about what should determine one's pay level. There need not be major confrontations or wholesale revisions to existing pay levels, however, and in many cases the change can provide a foundation for a pay administration system which is seen as more equitable and acceptable.

An organization having jobs with short learning times and which involve limited performance variability may find the time-based pay approach fits those jobs. But there are still options for recognizing very good or very poor performance. The variable timing step rate approach is one such system. It incorporates a provision that allows managers to recommend double step increases or early step increases for those whose performance significantly exceeds standards; it also enables the manager to deny or delay the step increase for those whose performance does not meet expectations. Although this system provides a limited number of choices relative to the size and frequency of increases, it can help organizations acknowledge significant performance differences. However, this system mandates that performance criteria and performance standards be established and that individual performance be credibly measured using those standards. If a formal performance appraisal system does not exist, there is a danger that the option to vary the size of increases will be used incorrectly or in a discriminatory fashion. The lack of sound measurement also leaves the organization open to challenge and even litigation.

Organizations with large numbers of employees working in jobs that have fairly standard learning times but in which incumbents can vary performance significantly once the job skills are learned, may wish to consider an approach that combines time-based and performance-based pay. This combination program provides step increases to the range midpoint based on time. Once the employee is being paid at this "control point" for the job, which is typically considered the going market rate, further increases may be subject to a performance test. The employee who is paid at the control point and who performs at a "fully meets standards" level will have his or her pay rate adjusted when and by the amount the pay range is adjusted. Employees will remain at the control point as long as performance remains at that level. An employee who "exceeds standards" or is "outstanding" may move above the control point. There is much to argue for this approach, particularly if the organization finds it difficult to discriminate between employees based on performance while they are learning the job. Once an employee is paid at the control point, it can be argued that "fully meets standards" performance does not warrant increases above that level. It is assumed, of course, that the control point is set at a level consistent with pay levels prevailing in the relevant labor markets and consistent with the organization's competitive posture relative to the market. A disadvantage of this approach is that it places considerable pressure on the performance appraisal system of the organization. Since something significant is now at stake, employees will subject the performance appraisal methodology and the process to greater scrutiny. It could be argued that the variable step rate option also requires sound performance appraisal, but the approach emphasizing merit requires even more refined performance distinctions.

A third option is to make the transition to a full merit pay program. There are reasons why a public sector organization may be reluctant to adopt merit programs; on the other hand, the benefits of performance-based pay programs can be enormous. A sound performance appraisal system is a key to successful merit pay programs. Another key is ensuring managers have the skills and knowledge required to appraise performance effectively. Much of the difficulty experienced in making performance appraisal effective is, in the experience of the author, a result of under-investment in managerial training and employee communication. The lack of attention to developing a credible process and convincing employees that it is equitable also contributes substantially to failure. It is also a failure on the part of top management if managers are not made aware of the reality that performance management is a critical responsibility of anyone in a management role and that how well they discharge this responsibility will impact their performance evaluations.

Another approach to individual pay administration that differs significantly from the options already discussed is "person-based" pay. Person-based pay programs pay employees for what they *can do* rather than what they *are doing*. An engineer is typically paid for the relevant knowledge he or she commands, even though for extended periods the work performed does not require these qualifications. A mechanic may be paid for the number of job-related skills he or she has demonstrated mastery of. The best applications of the various types of person-based pay are in units where the work is highly interdependent, cooperation or supportive behavior is required, flexibility of work assignment is needed and the skill or knowledge utilized is reasonably stable. Organizations using work teams often find that employees tend to make greater contributions when they are motivated to increase their job knowledge and their skills. A person-based pay system may not work for all occupations within a public sector organization. A water utility may have occupations that are already paid differently, and the adoption of skill-based pay for some (e.g., maintenance mechanics), merit pay for some (e.g., managerial, professional and administrative employees) and time-based pay for the rest may be acceptable. On the other hand, many organizations find different pay systems for different groups to be politically contentious or administratively impractical.

Though not an alternative to base pay, cash incentive programs can be combined with various types of base pay programs to produce a total direct pay package that supports the organization's culture, structure and environment. The organizational level at which performance can be measured and should be rewarded will have an impact on the types of incentives considered.

The impetus for considering change will have a great deal to do with whether any of the alternatives discussed warrant evaluation. If an organization has a large percentage of its employees paid at the top step in the range, has limited promotional opportunity and expects to have these employees around for quite some time there will be pressure to use some type of monetary incentive to motivate continued performance or continued employment, as well as some mechanism for controlling further cost increases. Though it could be argued that highly paid employees cannot go anywhere else and do as well, it should be remembered that those who are capable of very high levels of performance and/or assuming much more responsibility do have other options. The big payoff from motivational pay programs will be realized where employees who are capable of and willing to perform are those who remain with the organization.

Another major factor in determining how rewards are managed in the public sector is the political and legalistic nature of the environment. Governments are highly restricted by laws, regulations, codes and personnel policies that are arrived at through a lengthy political process. Legislatures are typically fragmented bodies, with members acting on behalf of their local constituencies, and as a result laws are often compromises that can attract a majority of votes. Regulations are formulated by agencies that are often bound by tradition and by the political climate. This results in less latitude for management when managing rewards, leading to egalitarian treatment. The executives of a private sector organization can approve the adoption of pay for performance systems or radical restructuring of rewards programs, while this is rarely feasible in a public or non-profit entity.

It is also much more common today for public sector employees to spend their entire career in a single organization than it is for private sector employees. Therefore, once in the system an employee is often a party to a fully prescribed, rigid system that regulates pay progression and vesting in benefits. The longer the employee is in that system the more difficult it is to change the conditions of employment, unless it is clearly to the advantage of the employee.

Given the resistance that may occur when management attempts to reward performance in a public sector entity there must be compelling benefits if the costs are to be incurred. One of the obstacles to creating a sense of urgency to change is that most public and quasi-public entities are monopolies, lacking viable competition. For example, when utilities supplying water, gas and other necessities consider incurring the disruption associated with moving from a time-based to a performance-based pay system they must believe that it is a necessity and that it will have a positive impact on organizational performance. Governments are more frequently considering privatization of some of these services in order to reduce their costs and/or improve the services. So if a utility faces competition there may be some pressure to consider changes that would enable it to perform better. But the utility will face uncertainty about the ability of the individual managers to effectively manage new programs. If a time-based pay system has been in place there will be no experience with doing performance appraisals that have consequences, and it is much more difficult to do sound appraisals when they impact employees. So management will have to learn new ways of doing things and to sell the new program to the employees it will impact.

Another significant difference between the public and private sectors is in the type and level of employee benefits provided. The private sector in the U.S. is rapidly moving away from defined benefit retirement programs and adopting defined contribution plans in their place. The enormous liabilities that have built up when defined benefit plans are utilized by a private sector employer have made it difficult for some industries in the U.S. to be competitive globally, since their competitors are less often impacted by voluntary pension programs. General Motors had more retiree health care costs in a vehicle than their costs of steel. In most foreign countries the retirement liabilities are incurred by the government, so individual organizations are not forced to carry them on their books or to recover the costs out of revenues. This gives Toyota and other foreign car producers a cost advantage over GM and Ford.

There has not been a similar change in the prevalence of defined benefit plans in the public sector. Governments look at potential liabilities very differently than do private sector organizations. Although in theory they must consider these liabilities, they are most often considered the problem of future administrations, making it easy to continue to use generous retirement, health and time-off benefits as an inducement for people to seek government employment. It also provides rewards for staying in the sector once employed, at virtually no immediate cost to the employing agency. The use of defined benefit plans also encourages longer service, owing to the lack of portability when a person changes employers. A worker who changes jobs every three or four years may never be vested in a retirement benefit from a pension plan, unless they are a participant in a union plan or a plan that moves credit across employers (e.g., the system used for most teachers). Although it is unlikely that individuals in their 20s or 30s will feel they must stay in the same organization for their whole career because of the retirement benefits, those who are closer to retirement may be more apt to adopt that view.

Health care benefits have become an economic as well as a political issue for U.S. organizations. Increasingly, private sector organizations are reducing health care benefits or requiring that employees contribute a larger share of the costs. Coverage that is provided free to employees or that requires only a small contribution is becoming increasingly rare in the private sector. The standard in the early twenty-first century is that employees should contribute 25–30% of the cost of health care coverage. And because of a change in accounting regulations in the 1990s, which mandated recognition of liabilities associated with retiree health benefits, their usage has declined dramatically in the private sector. This has created a wider gap between the private and public sector relative to prevalence of usage, since public sector employers have more often continued their provision of retiree health benefits and health care coverage that is free or very inexpensive for the employee. Also, the public sector workforce in the U.S. has a higher average age than does the private sector workforce, and generous retirement and retiree health benefits may motivate employees to retire at an earlier age, creating a critical skills shortage that need not have occurred.

It is difficult for organizations to measure the relative attractiveness of base pay, incentives and benefits to people making decisions about accepting employment. There was speculation in 2009 that the financial crisis would provide employers who offered low-cost comprehensive health care and defined benefit retirement plans an advantage in attracting and retaining critical skills. But the relative attraction and retention power of different forms of rewards are impacted by who is making the judgments. People in their mid-40s and later may place a much higher value on the type of total compensation package common in public sector organizations, while younger people will prefer organizations offering more current cash. But public sector organizations have traditionally used more generous paid time off programs than the private sector, and generational research shows a preference among younger employees for more time off and work–life balance.[7] Public sector organizations must also consider what will motivate people to perform well. The total value proposition offered as an employer will be the key to success in talent competition, and it is incumbent on organizations to decide which mix of rewards will best serve their purposes, whether they are in the public or private sector.

If a public sector organization has the freedom to adopt systems that more effectively reward performance there are a number of challenges they face in determining how much and how they reward employees. One of the principles underlying effective base pay systems is that pay ranges and pay levels are competitive in the relevant labor markets. Given the unique nature of many public sector jobs, it is difficult to define the competitive arena and to compare their jobs to jobs appearing in market surveys. There are surveys that focus on public sector organizations, but for occupations with skills that are mobile across all types of organizations the alternative sources of employment include the private sector. Accountants, programmers and electricians have skills that are applicable across a broad range of organizations, making it necessary for the public sector organization to look at the full range of potential competitors for people. But a degreed accountant in a water utility might be a specialist in rate setting and administration, making that person worth more to a utility than to other types of organizations. And a purchasing agent in a governmental agency might have a very different skill set than someone with the same title in a manufacturing firm. The uniformed services are relatively unique to the public sector and are more highly skilled than security guards in a private sector organization. These differences do not prevent public sector firms from comparing to the market but the comparisons are in most cases much more difficult. Readers wanting more details on rewarding performance in public sector organizations are encouraged to consult *Human Resource Management in Local Government*, by Buford and Lindner.[8]

Most of the discussion of organizations that do not operate in the private, for-profit sector has to this point focused on public sector organizations. There is a significant not-for-profit sector in the U.S. and most other developed countries, and it is important to compare and contrast these organizations to the other two sectors. As mentioned earlier, some would argue that the not-for-profit sector is much like the private sector, except that profit is not the primary performance metric. However, when one considers the number of health care and educational institutions and the number of people employed in these organizations, it seems advisable not to overlook contextual differences that might impact how performance is rewarded.

Many not-for-profit health care organizations would contend that their sole purpose is the health of the populations they serve. However, they would also recognize that they compete with for-profit organizations when they staff their organizations and not being competitive would result in an inability to get and keep qualified personnel. Educational institutions also must be competitive, particularly for employees who are not faculty. One of the challenges faced by both types of not-for-profits is that they must ensure they appropriately define, measure and reward performance for the occupational groups that are central to their primary mission and critical to their performance. This often leaves too few financial resources to pay other occupations at competitive levels. Additionally, the focus of attention on defining and measuring performance is on the central and critical occupations, and this can result in limited efforts to manage other personnel in a way that makes them productive and effective.

As mentioned earlier, a not-for-profit can create a balanced scorecard that represents a complete definition of performance. This makes it possible to use a wide range of rewards for employees, even though the metrics may differ from both the private sector and the public sector. For example, most health care organizations pay considerable attention to patient satisfaction and educational institutions to "customer" (student) satisfaction. However, both have multiple constituencies, and it is necessary to consider the perceptions of all of these. Hospitals and universities spend considerable effort on achieving high relative rankings by "neutral" third-party evaluation sources. This is not illogical, since reputation impacts the fees that can be charged and the resources that will be made available, through grants, contributions and public support.

Using performance-based incentives at the individual level can encounter resistance by constituencies. There is often a perception that employees are not focused on the mission of the organization if they care about their earning level, and there is a fear that paying incentives will focus people on the wrong outcomes. This is shortsighted. If it is true that what you measure and reward you most surely will get more of, then the key to success is to measure and reward the right things. Yet the hospital administrator or university president who considers the use of financial incentives must be sure to make this approach acceptable to the key constituencies and be sure that what is rewarded is what is desired.

It is possible that performing meaningful work that benefits others may have a psychological payback that trumps less-than-competitive pay packages. Most private sector employees are asked to "make those shareholders wealthy." Since most employees are not shareholders and may not even know any, that is not a particularly motivating objective. But it is dangerous for a not-for-profit to assume that its employees or candidates for employment will focus on the importance of its work and disregard non-competitive rewards packages. Substituting "psychic income" derived from meaningful work for monetary rewards may produce positive feelings but will not pay the bills. The resources available to the not-for-profit may preclude aggressive pay levels, and the culture may work against differentiating significantly between employees relative to pay decisions. But the employees still face the same living costs as those in the private sector and will more than likely incorporate that reality in their employment decisions.

Application of Principles: Chapter 9

The new City Manager of a large Western city has a background in the private sector and wants to apply the best practices used by for-profit organizations if they fit the context. One of his first initiatives is to replace the time-based step progression system that has been used to administer wages and salaries. He also plans to approach the City Council with a recommendation to create an outstanding performer award. During the initial presentation a Council member adamantly opposed implementing several radical changes and challenged the City Manager to produce evidence that the change would not escalate costs dramatically while producing no tangible positive results. The City Manager conceded the changes would require considerable managerial training and communication with employees. He further stated that whatever change you make someone is going to resist it.

Develop a presentation that would support the proposed changes, utilizing motivation theory and research findings. Provide a rationale for tying pay increases and incentives to performance and for developing a sound performance management system. Consider the differences between the public and private sectors and how they might impact the effectiveness of performance and rewards management systems.

Notes

1 Kaplan, R. & Norton, D., *The Balanced Scorecard* (Boston, MA, Harvard Business Press, 1996).
2 Leavitt, W. & Greene, R., "Reward Strategies for Re-invented Public Sector Organizations," *ACA Journal* (Summer, 1996).
3 Fitz-enz, J., *The ROI of Human Capital* (New York, AMACOM, 2000).
4 Huselid, M., Becker, B. & Beatty, J., *The Workforce Scorecard* (Boston, MA, Harvard Business Press, 2005); Cascio, W. & Boudreau, J., *Investing in People* (Upper Saddle River, NJ, FT Press, 2008).
5 Water Industry Compensation Survey, American Water Works Association, Denver, CO.
6 Leavitt, W. & Greene, R., "Rewards Strategies for Re-invented Government Organizations," *ACA Journal* (Summer, 1996).
7 Greene, R. & Tulgan, B., "Gen X Compatible Rewards Strategies," *ACA Journal*, 1st Quarter (1999).
8 Buford, J. & Lindner, J., *Human Resource Management in Local Government* (Cincinnati, OH, South-Western, 2002).

Chapter 10

Rewarding Performance
Global Workforces

Today's increasingly globalized organizations are employing workforces that are more diverse with respect to their national and ethnic origins. Whether these employees come to the headquarters location from other countries or are employed in their home countries by an organization headquartered in another country, the result is a culturally diverse workforce. Effectively and appropriately defining, measuring and rewarding performance is a difficult and complex challenge for any organization. Operating globally dramatically increases the challenges for management. Cultural, legal, logistical, economic and social differences encountered when operating across borders add to complexity. Cultural differences between individuals present yet more complexity.

For those readers who are deeply involved in managing culturally diverse global workforces, the book *Rewarding Performance Globally: Reconciling The Global – Local Dilemma* is recommended.[1]

Organizations wishing to effectively attract, retain, motivate and satisfy a high-quality diverse workforce must *recognize* cultural differences, *respect* them and *reconcile* them.[2] Those who argue that there is a convergence of cultures underway and that eventually everyone will be content to spend their Sundays (or Saturdays or Fridays) in a mall populated by Starbucks, McDonald's and Armani could be correct. But those who actually do research, rather than merely speculate based on surface indicators, are not so sure. Many studies suggest that national and ethnic cultures are very resilient, and eminent scholars such as Huntington reject homogenization as being likely, even in the long run.[3] There is also practical evidence of cultural resilience: many immigrants to the U.S. seem to be disinterested in being absorbed into a "melting pot" and retain much of their heritage in their values, beliefs and behaviors. European countries that are experiencing an increased influx of people from other countries and continents are faced with the same reluctance to leave one's socialization behind.

Malcolm Gladwell describes the potential impact of cultural influences when reporting on research into the causes of numerous airplane crashes by Korean Air.[4] The socialization of crew members taught them deference to authority, and this characteristic precluded the other crew members from correcting the captain, even when they were sure he was making a fatal error. By identifying the problem, the airline was able to train Korean crew members to act as equals in a unified team, thereby correcting the problem.

Cultural differences within the workforce raise critical issues for human resource management practitioners. Concepts such as formal appraisals and rewards based on individual performance have proven devilishly difficult to implement and to make work effectively in some parts of the world. Some of the reasons for the difficulty are relatively obvious.

For example, the notion of differentiating at the individual level for purposes of pay administration is not universally accepted. But even where pay differences based on individual performance are acceptable, the *manner* in which performance is defined, appraised and communicated will have a significant impact on motivation level and on attitudes about appropriateness. Principles such as making rewards contingent on individual contribution may be increasingly adopted on a global basis, but local strategies may shape the way the principles are applied.

The behavioral theories that have withstood research scrutiny in the U.S. and the "Western world" (e.g., expectancy, equity and reinforcement theories) suggest that if there is a tight linkage between employee competence, performance and outcomes this should produce positive motivation. But perhaps it is difficult to make pay for performance work well in some countries and cultures in Asia, Latin Europe and the Middle East/North Africa (MENA) region because these theories do not apply in the same way in all cultures. Virtually all of the research supporting theories relating to culture has been conducted on Western/Northern employees in Western/Northern organizations and done by Western/Northern researchers. One could therefore ask the question: "Will the findings hold up in other parts of the world?"

Although there are not discrete categories into which country cultures can be categorized, it is useful to develop models that can be used for comparing and contrasting cultural tendencies. Table 10.1 creates two conceptually polar profiles to use as a framework for this purpose. Even though no single culture exactly fits either the "Western/Northern" or the "Eastern/Southern" cultural profile, positioning cultures on the continuum between these poles will help in understanding how to deal with the effect of culture on workers and their employers.

The characteristics used in Table 10.1 are based on cultural research by Trompenaars and Hofstede, who identified cultural differences between countries by measuring the extent to which the characteristics existed in samples of the national populations.[5] Both researchers used cultural "dimensions" to describe contrasts across national borders. The characteristics used in Table 10.1 are based on the following contrasts:

- *communitarian* (group or society oriented) versus *individualistic* (self-oriented);
- *particularistic* (circumstances or who is involved causes the actions to change) versus universalistic (one set of rules to be applied to everyone in all situations);
- *ascriptive/ascribed status* (how people are treated depends on who they are) versus *achieved status* (all status is earned through achievements);

Table 10.1 Contrasting Cultural Profiles

Eastern/Southern Cultures	Western/Northern Cultures
Characteristics of cultures: communitarian; hierarchical; particularistic; ascribed status; person focused; external control; intuitive/holistic; high power difference	*Characteristics of cultures:* individualistic; egalitarian; universalistic; achieved status; task focused; internal control; analytical/reductionist; low power difference
Countries with cultures that favor this profile: Japan; China; Egypt; Indonesia; Turkey; Brazil; Venezuela; South Korea; France; Greece; Italy; Spain	*Countries with cultures that favor this profile:* United States; United Kingdom; Canada; Australia

- *outer directed* (person not in control; external forces impact outcomes) versus *inner directed* ("can do" attitude caused by belief that people control results);
- *high power difference* (hierarchy and authority are prominent) versus *low power difference* (less differentiation by level and more democratic processes).

No country's culture exactly matches either of the two admittedly exaggerated profiles in Table 10.1. But the research and practical experience indicate that there are significant differences between national cultures. And these differences have been shown to have a material impact on the success of HR strategies and programs. Yet, when attempting to recognize and respect the cultural orientations of individual employees, models such as the one in Table 10.1 can lead to stereotyping and overgeneralization. For example, if an employee comes from India there is a tendency to assume that the employee will hold "Indian" beliefs and values. But a group of employees from India may not share the same religion, socio-economic status or geographic region and may exhibit a wide variety of perspectives.[6] It is therefore dangerous to use national identity to predict cultural orientation. Yet it is helpful to examine research and to understand that differences do occur and that ethnic and national heritage can suggest a tendency to hold specific beliefs and values, at least as they apply to the work context.

This chapter will focus on the impact of national and ethnic culture on the effectiveness of performance and rewards management methods and processes. It is important first to identify differences between contrasting cultures, so that organizations can anticipate the impact of these differences and search for ways of reconciling the resulting conflicts. This can be done by defining opposites, recognizing the values associated with each and determining how the differences can be reconciled. Thought processes suitable for dealing with paradox must be utilized, e.g., "How can we ensure recognition of the group's performance through identifying individual contributions, and then how can we recognize individual contributions through the group and the group's performance?" This type of circular logic is anathema to some cultures, but it can be used to ensure that basic assumptions of one culture (e.g., the Anglo-Saxon viewpoint) are not accepted without considering the assumptions prevailing in other cultures.

There are principles underlying performance and rewards management systems that have proven to be effective in "Western/Northern"-type cultures. These will be discussed first. Whether these principles are likely to be valid in other types of cultures (e.g., those decidedly more Eastern/Southern in nature) will be examined next. Hypotheses will be presented that can be used to anticipate how effective various methods and processes might be. Finally, implications for managing performance and rewards effectively in global organizations will be examined.

In order for performance appraisal to be effective in a task-focused, individualistic, universalistic (Western/Northern) culture a number of prerequisites must be in place. First, performance must be defined and measured in a way that is compatible with the organization's objectives and that is acceptable to employees. The criteria used to define performance, the level at which performance is measured and the nature of the appraisal process are all critical issues. The "Western" approach focuses on defining and measuring performance at the individual level, although performance models at the unit or process and organization-wide levels typically exist as well. The "Western" approach also emphasizes clarity of objectives and standards, open communication and a supervisor-controlled appraisal.

The characteristics of a sound appraisal process (Western/Northern style) include:

1   clear individual performance criteria and standards, which are related to the job/role and communicated clearly at the start of the period;
2   adequate training and communication for all parties;
3   continuous measurement and feedback;
4   developmental activities occurring throughout the period, to remedy poor performance and to build on good performance;
5   performance appraised based on job-related results and behaviors, rather than personal characteristics;
6   attribution of good or poor performance to correct causes, with clear and direct two-way communication regarding good and poor aspects of performance; and
7   formulation of plans to correct poor performance and to build on good performance in the future.

It should be noted that there may be multiple subcultures in any organization, some of which may vary from the Western/Northern profile, despite being in a country with that type of culture. For example, there are organizational cultures in start-up high-tech U.S. companies that revere creativity and innovation and that are very person focused rather than task focused (e.g., the "Silicon Valley" kind of culture). The reaction of employees to a particular performance appraisal methodology or process may in these organizations take on many of the characteristics of the Eastern/Southern cultural profile. Further complicating the anticipation of culture's impact is the reality that there may even be units or occupational clusters within a "Western" corporate culture that have their own subculture. For example, the R&D function may be more "Eastern," as a by-product of the type of work being done, the processes utilized and how individuals are educated. As a result, it is perilous to assume a particular approach will be acceptable to all employees even when the organization's overall culture fits the Western/Northern profile well.

The highly individualistic cultures fitting the Western/Northern profile favor doing individual appraisals that involve direct and specific feedback. "Telling it like it is" is a cornerstone of these cultures, although it is more the case in Western countries such as the U.S. and the Netherlands than it is in the U.K., according to research by Trompenaars.[7] Clearly demonstrating where an employee failed and doing it in quantitative terms is not only acceptable but expected of managers. But this is not as acceptable in more collectivist and person-focused cultures, since it will cause the employee to "lose face." Other more effective and appropriate methods of demonstrating the need for improvement may be needed. The anthropologist Hall differentiates between "high-context" cultures (such as Japan) where intensive socialization makes the restatement of values and expectations largely unnecessary and "low-context" cultures (such as the U.S.) where explicit communication is needed to define what is expected, since the context does not provide the required clues.[8]

The practice of appraising performance at an individual level may also be questioned in the more Eastern/Southern cultures. When the prevailing view is that it takes everyone to achieve continuous improvement (e.g., Japan and several Asian countries) the act of singling out one employee's contributions or lack thereof may not be accepted, or at the very least may be emphasized much less. When work is assigned to teams, rather than individual jobs, it may be difficult to convince employees that accurately measuring the relative contribution of each person is possible. When everyone does whatever needs to be done at the time, the concept of measuring individuals against specific objectives or performance standards is difficult to defend. A way to address this is to empower teams to establish their own criteria for differentiating individual contributions. After all, if they choose to "carry" a noncontributing member, for whatever reason, how can management intervene without threatening the cooperative fabric of the team? And if they as a group choose to recognize and reward differential contributions is it not reasonable for management to allow them to allocate the rewards the team earned as they see fit? It serves management well to understand that those more collectivist in their views are apt to organize work in a manner that is focused on overall results as opposed to individual contributions.

The universalistic character of Western/Northern cultures favors the same set of rules for everyone, with performance measured against established expectations. But close personal relationships may cause poor results to be overlooked in particularistic cultures, since the relationship must be preserved. It is hard for Western managers to accept this particularistic point of view, as evidenced by the negative reaction to "nepotism" experienced in the U.S. However, in many parts of the world it may be reasonable to give preference to a family member, since there is an established trust and a belief that the person would not do anything to damage the family reputation or his or her standing within the family, making him or her a better risk than a stranger. Those who manage a workforce thus inclined should be prepared to recognize that social sanction may be more effective than top-down attempts at controlling behavior.

Many Eastern/Southern cultures believe that who is being evaluated should be a consideration. For example, if a recent graduate of a highly respected university is contributing little to organization performance it might be assumed that circumstances have caused the poor performance. This is especially true when the culture is "ascriptive" as opposed to "achievement" oriented, since ascriptive cultures focus on who the person is and his or her status. Because the person's quality has already been ascribed to him or her because of the status of that school's graduates it is difficult for evaluators to attribute poor performance to the person in the ascriptive culture. Many schooled in the "Protestant ethic" view ascriptive cultures as elitist and indifferent to actual achievement. But those who would be effective in leading workforces made up of those holding diverse views must be able to see the legitimacy of both perspectives and attempt a balanced view that reconciles the conflict.

Another dominant belief in Western/Northern cultures is that people are typically in control of their destiny and should be held accountable for results—the "can do" mindset. However, a significant portion of the world's population believes that fortune and external forces will determine outcomes as much as or more than will individual effort. For people holding that belief it is difficult to accept that tying rewards to a measure of individual contribution is fair or appropriate. This is particularly true when employees feel they expended their best efforts and the desired results were not forthcoming. For such people a logical conclusion would be that poor results were not their fault and that external forces were indeed in control of outcomes. Once again, it is necessary for those leading a culturally diverse workforce to recognize that both individual effort and external causes impacted results to some degree. By not holding individuals accountable for things that were indeed out of their control, the manager can assess performance fairly and not blindly adhere to an outcome measurement, as often happens in individualistic cultures with those subscribing to internal control.

Self-appraisal is a technique used in many Western/Northern organizations, since it is believed to promote employee engagement and facilitate acceptance of performance appraisals. This practice might be a disaster in cultures where disagreeing with the superior is viewed as being inappropriate and/or ill advised. It would be difficult to implement in high-context cultures, where everyone should be aware of the source of difficulties, obviating the need for spelling it out. If it is also important not to place the employee and the supervisor in a position where they must confront performance issues head on and if "saving face" is necessary to preserving the relationship, other approaches might be necessary.

Hypotheses about the Impact of Culture on Performance Management

The aforementioned contrasts between polar cultures can be compressed into testable hypotheses that can be used to anticipate conflicts and plan for approaches to reconciling them:

- *Hypothesis 1*: Measuring individual performance and tying consequences to the appraisal will be more acceptable in cultures that are *individualistic* than in cultures that are *communitarian*. Employees from countries such as the U.S., the U.K., Canada, Denmark, the Netherlands and Australia tend to be individualistic in their orientation and accepting of this approach. Employees from Egypt, Mexico, India, Japan, France and Venezuela will be more likely to prefer performance to be measured at an aggregated level, since they believe results require collective effort. This is not to suggest that individualistic cultures are blind to the importance of group results, or that collectivist cultures ignore individual performance and its relationship to group results. Reconciling different perspectives will require the recognition that both individual and collective results are critical to success.
- *Hypothesis 2*: Holding the individual totally accountable for meeting performance standards will be more acceptable in cultures that believe in *internal control* than in cultures that believe in *external control*. Employees from countries such as the U.S., the U.K., France and the Netherlands will generally accept personal responsibility for results. Employees from countries such as Venezuela, China, Russia, Kuwait, Egypt, Saudi Arabia and India will be more likely to believe outcomes are due to forces at least partially outside their control. Reconciling differing perspectives requires recognition that both internal and external factors impacted results and that both must be considered in appraisal.
- *Hypothesis 3*: Evaluating individuals based on what they accomplish rather than who they are will be more acceptable in cultures that are *achievement oriented* than in cultures that are *ascription oriented*. Employees from countries such as the U.S., Australia, Canada, the U.K. and the Netherlands will tend to accept evaluation based on what people have accomplished. Employees from countries such as Egypt, Japan, China, Russia, Mexico and France will be more likely to believe the status or qualifications of the individual should be a consideration in evaluating performance. Reconciling differing perspectives requires recognition that performance must be defined in terms that reflect all types of contribution. A well-connected person who is the key to disseminating needed knowledge through his or her network may be recognized for that contribution, while the person who succeeded individually as a result of

applying that knowledge should be credited for his or her contribution. A performance appraisal process that allows for excellence in different types of contributions can help to resolve this dilemma.

- *Hypothesis 4*: Employees from *universalistic* cultures will believe that the same policies, methods, processes and standards should apply to appraising all employees, as opposed to those from *particularistic* cultures. Employees from countries such as Canada, the U.S., Sweden, the U.K., Australia, the Netherlands and Germany will tend to believe in one set of rules that apply to everyone under all circumstances. Employees from Venezuela, Russia, China, India, Japan and France will be more inclined to accept that the identity of the person and the circumstances should be considered. Reconciling different views requires that those who adapt policies or processes to make the best of unanticipated circumstances should be credited for their initiative and good judgment, even in a control-based culture. Those who ignore policies and favor friends to the detriment of the organization should be admonished, even in a particularistic culture.

- *Hypothesis 5*: Employees from countries with *low power difference* cultures will expect to participate in setting performance standards and debating ratings with the supervisor more than will those from *high power difference* cultures. Employees from the Netherlands, the U.K., Australia, Canada and the U.S. will tend to be more active in the process and challenge the supervisor when there is disagreement on performance level. This would be less likely to occur among employees from countries such as Mexico, Venezuela, France and China.

These hypotheses, supported by a substantial amount of research, should be a consideration for human resource practitioners when designing performance appraisal systems. Knowing what to expect relative to employee reactions to an appraisal system based on their culture is valuable and enables HR to consider what to do about differences.

As discussed in Chapter 2, there are several motivational theories that address the preconditions for performance. They can be summarized into a model that cites four prerequisites: 1) employees must *want* to do what is required; 2) they must *be able* to do what is required; 3) they must *be allowed* to do what is required; and 4) they must *know* what is required.

In any culture, performance appraisals should share some common characteristics. Even when employees know what is expected and feel they are fairly and appropriately appraised, there are other prerequisites for performance. An employee who does not have the skill or knowledge to do what is expected must be given the necessary tools or the expectations must be changed. Someone without permission to do what is required must be given the appropriate autonomy and support. Someone who does not believe good performance will be rewarded is not going to be adequately motivated to succeed. These prerequisites for an employee to be motivated to perform must be considered if focused motivation is to occur.

A critical principle underlying effective performance management already mentioned but worth stressing is that employees should be held accountable only for things they can control. However, this view is much more easily accepted in Western/Northern cultures. If a person in a service capacity can control only behaviors and not results it may be appropriate to consider *how* the employee behaved as constituting performance. If service providers cannot directly control customer satisfaction they should be motivated to behave in the desired manner and should be appraised on that basis.

Even in the most Western culture with strong belief in internal control it must be recognized that a "can do" assumption works only if what is being attempted is achievable. It is also important that appraisers accurately determine what the cause of poor performance is so that corrective action can be taken. One cause may be poor *placement*, which resulted in the wrong person being in the job. Another cause may be inadequate *development*, which left the incumbent without the knowledge, skills and abilities necessary to perform well. Finally, the cause is often poor *job/role design*, which makes it difficult for anyone to succeed in the job. The solutions to these causes are often to modify components of HR strategy other than the performance management strategy.

Evaluating Performance Appraisal System Effectiveness

Any performance appraisal system needs to be continuously evaluated, to determine if it is effective and to identify opportunities for improving it. The mix of cultural orientations within an organization will be likely to change in today's dynamic environment. Viewpoints should be gathered from all levels and from all parts of the organization, including different geographic locations. Perception is reality when it comes to system acceptance, and employees will act on what they believe to be true. By carefully assessing the views employees and managers hold on how appraisal is supposed to work and how it is working, it is often possible to discover that there is misunderstanding, and this recognition can provide the basis for further communication or for system refinement. The type of communication and how it is done will vary across cultures, but understanding is a prerequisite if managers and employees are to behave in the appropriate manner.

The existence of a viable and accessible appeal system can take a great deal of pressure off managers, without undermining their authority. It is not uncommon for a manager and an employee to have difficulty communicating effectively, owing to personality differences, and when employees see no feasible solution to disagreements on a one-to-one basis frustration and anger can build up. Some way of breaking these interpersonal logjams should be found, and the approach should be consistent with the culture of each organization or unit. But great caution must be taken when providing an appeal process. In some cultures an employee would not dream of telling someone else they cannot communicate with their manager or that they believe they have been unfairly treated. In fact, much empirical data on employee attitude surveys indicates that in some cultures employees will rate all items high because to do anything else would reflect badly on the manager and on the unit or the company. It is also dangerous to assume that one who appeals through "approved" formal channels and who is "in the right" will not suffer consequences, particularly with respect to their standing among peers. The social fabric of the group or community may be much more important to people in some contexts than insisting that each individual gets his or her due in each instance.

A common challenge is aligning the perceptions of the appraiser and those being appraised. Research has shown that the median Western/Northern employee will typically estimate that his or her performance is at the 75th or 80th percentile within a comparison group, which means there will always be some degree of dissatisfaction with ratings that are honest and accurate, at least by those who fall below where they believe they belong. One U.S. organization that is consistently rated as one of the best managed has made its middle (third of five) rating "Fully meets high XYZ standards," sending the message that this rating is a perfectly acceptable one—and that the person might be a top performer in other organizations with less lofty standards. This organization is able to rate 70% of its employees at that level without a revolution breaking out. The middle rating does not have to be the equivalent of getting a "C" in graduate school if the organization makes it something else. There is regrettably no available research that tells us if this "overrating" issue exists in non-Western cultures.

Hypotheses about the Impact of Culture on Rewards Management

The aforementioned contrasts between polar cultures can also be applied to create testable hypotheses about reward system effectiveness:

- *Hypothesis 1*: Measuring individual performance and basing rewards on the appraisal will be more acceptable in cultures that are *individualistic* than in cultures that are *collectivist*. Employees from countries such as the U.S., the U.K., Canada, Denmark, the Netherlands and Australia will tend to be individualistic in their orientation. Employees from Egypt, Mexico, India, Japan, France and Venezuela will be more likely to prefer performance to be measured and rewarded at an aggregated level, since they believe results require collective effort.
- *Hypothesis 2*: Rewarding the individual for meeting performance standards will be more acceptable in cultures that believe in *internal control* than in cultures that believe in *external control*. Employees from countries with "can do" mindsets, such as the U.S., the U.K., France and the Netherlands will be likely to accept personal responsibility for results. Employees from countries such as Venezuela, China, Russia, Kuwait, Egypt, Saudi Arabia and India will be more likely to believe outcomes are due to forces at least partially outside their control.
- *Hypothesis 3*: Rewarding individuals based on what they accomplish rather than who they are will be more acceptable in cultures that are *achievement oriented* than in cultures that are *ascription oriented*. Employees from countries such as the U.S., Australia, Canada, the U.K. and the Netherlands will tend to accept rewards based on what people have accomplished. Employees from countries such as Egypt, Japan, China, Russia, Mexico and France will be more likely to believe the status or qualifications of the individual should be considered.
- *Hypothesis 4*: Employees from *universalistic* cultures will believe that the same policies, methods, processes and standards should apply to rewarding all employees, as opposed to those from *particularistic* cultures. Employees from countries such as Canada, the U.S., Sweden, the U.K., Australia, the Netherlands and Germany will tend to believe in one set of rules that apply to everyone under all circumstances. Employees from Venezuela, Russia, China, India, Japan and France will tend to consider the identity of the person and the circumstances.
- *Hypothesis 5*: Employees from countries with *low power difference* cultures will expect to participate in setting performance standards, determining results achieved and arriving at an appropriate reward with the supervisor more than will those from *high power difference* cultures. Employees from Germany, the Netherlands, the U.K., Australia, Canada and the U.S. will be active in the process and challenge the supervisor when there is disagreement on performance or rewards. Employees from countries such as Mexico, Venezuela, France and China will be less inclined to do so.

These hypotheses, supported by a large body of research, should be a consideration for human resource practitioners when designing rewards management systems. Knowing what to expect relative to employee reactions to how they are evaluated and rewarded based on their culture is valuable and enables HR to consider what to do about differences.

A global organization can adopt one global rewards strategy and set of programs, utilize different strategies or programs for each locale, country or region or agree on a set of global guiding principles and then allow some latitude for local customization as long as the principles are adhered to. Certainly, an organization employing software design engineers in Boston, Bangalore, Beirut and Buenos Aires may pay incumbents at different levels or in different forms. What is meant by a single global strategy here is that the basis for defining, measuring and rewarding performance is relatively consistent and how people are paid does not vary significantly.

The decision about one rewards strategy versus multiple strategies is a "yin–yang" balancing act. The more universal the strategy the easier it is to align all employees and units with organizational values and objectives. The more locally specific the strategies the easier it is to conform to local laws, culture and competitive practices. DuPont decided to give a set number of share options to all employees globally, in order to celebrate an event, only to find that many obstacles were presented by local realities: laws prohibiting ownership in foreign corporations, dramatically different pay levels that made the value of the options enormous or minuscule, data privacy laws that blocked access to the information necessary to administer the program, established practices that caused employees to view the options very differently, and more.

The nature of the competitive labor markets within which employees work will have a major impact on how different the amount and mix of direct compensation should be in various locations. For example, in Asia large chaebols dominate the Korean market, while smaller, family or family-like organizations may be the competitive concern in Taiwan and some parts of China. In the Netherlands and Sweden multinational enterprises (MNEs) may dominate, while domestic firms may do so in Japan. Concentrations of very large organizations in a labor market will create a different competitive environment than typically exists where small independent firms provide the employment opportunities. This is particularly true when the large organizations are part of MNEs, since corporate values and priorities (if not corporate policies) often impact the type of rewards strategy they utilize.

Another factor that will impact whether an organization adopts one or multiple rewards strategies is the diversity of reasons for locating operations in the different countries. For example, if an MNE has natural resource extraction operations in some countries, sales and marketing operations in others, manufacturing plants in others and R&D centers in others, this diversity will impact the type of workforces that will be employed and the competitive realities faced in each country. Employing a large percentage of local workers in a developing country where an excess supply of labor exists may prompt a rewards strategy that involves paying locally competitive wages, providing only those benefits that are legally required or competitively mandated and avoiding programs that create long-term liabilities. On the other hand, employing world-class R&D personnel in a developed country with a highly competitive labor market for skilled people may mandate an entirely different rewards strategy.

Legal or regulatory and social constraints may also operate to prescribe the type of rewards strategy utilized. If offering stock to local nationals is illegal it is probably not wise to attempt it. If traditional practices dictate egalitarian distribution of rewards then differentiating between individuals may not be accepted as fair or appropriate. If giving a one-time award for an achievement triggers acquired rights, requiring the amounts to become a permanent part of pay, then the use of certain types of incentive plans will logically be avoided.

The culture of a global organization may be very strong and executive management may wish to adhere to the values and principles that guide behavior for *all* employees. However, the factors just discussed can weigh in heavily to force some relaxation of consistency, in order to make local accommodations. The organization can certainly rely more heavily on expatriates to fill critical slots throughout all operations globally if it wishes to ensure things are done according to corporate policy. The use of a global cadre that is fully socialized can set the tone for operations everywhere, even when they occupy only key management roles and work with workforces dominated by local nationals. Although this practice has been used by MNEs headquartered in developed countries, particularly the U.S., the U.K. and Japan, more developing countries are adopting legal limitations on the use of "foreigners" and/or are applying considerable social pressure to fill key slots with local nationals more quickly. This has an impact on rewards strategy, since expatriate remuneration packages can be largely homogeneous, with focused variations relating to different living costs and tax structures to keep expatriates "whole" wherever they are assigned. The homogenization becomes more difficult when local nationals and third-country nationals replace expatriates.

For global organizations concerned about the high cost of using expatriates and/or the negative reaction this practice generates in some countries, there are options. Research shows that the use of expatriates is generally declining, replaced by more short-term project assignments and extended business commuting. There is also growth in the use of inpatriate assignments, which allows local nationals to be brought into headquarters for extended periods. The purpose of these inpatriate assignments may be to socialize future managers to the organization's culture, provide them with management training and/or have them educate corporate personnel about their home countries and how to successfully do business there. This enables the MNE to maintain the local remuneration packages of inpatriates, supplemented by temporary allowances. Infosys, a large Indian organization, won an award given by the Society for Human Resource Management for creative programs: they brought graduates of U.S. universities to India for six months to be trained in the way the organization does business and then sent them back to work in the U.S.

No matter which approach is used it is inevitable that the global organization will face the realities associated with treating people working together somewhat differently with respect to their remuneration. How dramatic the differences are and how long they will persist will impact the reactions of incumbents. Everyone is subject to the "grass is greener" syndrome when someone else is treated differently. However, by understanding the potential legal, economic and cultural conflicts that may occur an organization can craft rewards strategies that minimize negative reactions or uneconomic practices. When the plant manager in one country wants to distribute an incentive pool in an egalitarian fashion and the plant manager in a neighboring country chooses to differentiate between individuals or units it is wise to understand why they would choose to do this differently before mandating consistency. There may be much more gained in the form of employee acceptance and motivational impact by allowing differences than by insisting on similarity.

The increased use of global teams, consisting of members from different occupations or functions, different countries and different organizational levels, raises a number of issues relating to rewards strategy. Some of these teams will be co-located while others are disbursed across borders and time zones, causing them to interact asynchronously. Although it would seem those working "shoulder to shoulder" would be more concerned about rewards consistency than those who are separated, any differences in how and how much members are rewarded can be divisive. If a Chinese engineer receives a $1,000 cash incentive award while an American colleague receives $4,000 for a similar contribution it may make little difference that the award is the same percentage of base salary for both. If they both shop together in San Francisco to celebrate their success, the difference in award size will be very apparent. And if the team leader awards some individuals more because their contribution is thought to be greater, the cooperative fabric of the team could unravel. Such differentiation is most apt to be viewed as inappropriate by members from collectivist cultures, even though they acknowledge the value of the contributions of those rewarded more richly.

Evaluating the Effectiveness of Rewards Strategies

Rewards strategies and programs need to be continuously evaluated, to determine if they are effective and to identify opportunities for improvement. The mix of cultural orientations within an organization will be likely to change in today's dynamic environment. Viewpoints should be gathered from all levels and from all parts of the organization, including different geographic locations. Perception is reality when it comes to system acceptance, and employees will act on what they believe to be true.

By carefully assessing the views employees and managers hold on how employees should be rewarded and how well programs are being administered, it is often possible to discover that there is misunderstanding about how things are supposed to work. This recognition can provide the basis for further communication or for system refinement. The type of communication and how it is done will vary across cultures, but understanding is a prerequisite if managers and employees are to behave in the appropriate manner.

Evaluation of strategies and programs is typically done as an "after the fact" exercise, and often only when things have deteriorated to an intolerable level. This is unfortunate, since it is often too late to do anything but damage control. It is possible to perform evaluations of why strategies and programs seem to work in some contexts and whether other contexts are sufficiently similar to project success in those locations. This enables the organization to anticipate problems in transferring practices across locations and cultures before they become a reality. For example, Lincoln Electric had prospered for decades in the U.S. with a rewards strategy that consisted of "output-based" rewards (a.k.a. piecework) for individuals and a gainsharing plan that rewarded everyone for overall success. This highly successful strategy worked reasonably well when it was implemented in the company's new operations in the U.K. and Mexico, but failed to gain acceptance in parts of Europe and in Japan. The failure was largely due to cultural conflicts, which seemingly could have been anticipated if in-depth research on the characteristics of each of the cultures had been done before attempting implementation.

No matter what types of reward strategies and programs are used, there should be a periodic independent audit of the way in which they are impacting various groups of employees and different locations. Adverse impact on a protected class raises legal concerns in countries with extensive laws governing this (e.g., the U.S.), but adverse impact not attributable to a valid cause should raise equity or ethical concerns. Whether or not the HR function takes the responsibility of monitoring the system outcomes or the responsibility is given to an independent audit function, there should be some verification that everyone is being treated in a consistent and fair manner and that their values and beliefs are respected.

The HR Function's Role in Performance and Rewards Management

Since the HR function has so many tools available to facilitate motivation to perform it could be assumed that it will play an active role in applying the tools effectively. In some parts of the world (e.g., Japan) the executive in charge of HR is often second to the CEO in rank, which sets the stage for active involvement. However, in many countries HR plays a much more modest role in selection, placement, development and performance management, and responsibility is often shifted to line management. Even in countries like the U.S., where HR has become more like a profession, there are very successful companies that do not have a formal HR function (e.g., Container Store).

The HR function is typically accountable for formulating strategies that get, keep and appropriately motivate a workforce capable of helping the organization succeed. Therefore, it is important that a framework is created that ensures programs support the HR strategy, are well integrated with each other and fit the beliefs, values and needs of the workforce. Diverse workforces make motivating employees more challenging. It is therefore critical that HR should do the following:

1   Identify the cultural composition of the workforce. Without stereotyping people based on their national or ethnic origin, a concerted effort to understand their views about performance and rewards management should be undertaken. This may take the form of a survey, focus groups or another data-gathering method.
2   Determine the degree of "fit" between the current performance management strategy and methodology and the views of the workforce as to what is appropriate.
3   Decide how much accommodation will be made to people holding different views. Certainly, this will be more clear cut when the organization has a unit in China with all Chinese employees, a unit in France with all French employees and the bulk of the workforce, predominately of third-generation Western European derivation, in headquarters in Chicago. The local customization of methods and processes to fit the cultural profile of employees can in this case be done without raising equity issues within each unit. If the local workforces are diverse culturally it becomes a more difficult proposition. Although there can be some variation in how a supervisor conducts a performance appraisal with each of his or her people, it is unlikely that variation in performance criteria or standards and the format of the appraisal will be permitted, especially in organizations with Western/Northern cultures. It is also likely that there will be specified methods for determining rewards in any culture.
4   Develop cross-cultural training initiatives for those managing diverse people to ensure they appreciate that not everyone thinks the way that they do. Diversity training is already in place in many organizations, although national and ethnic culture is often

not addressed. What managers must understand is that it is important for them to recognize cultural differences, respect that they are legitimate and attempt to find a way to reconcile conflicts between what employees feel is appropriate and what the organization does.

5   Monitor employee reactions to how performance is appraised and rewarded and inform management as to how effective and how well accepted the processes are.

Application of Principles: Chapter 10

A durable goods manufacturer has U.S. plants in El Paso, TX, Seattle, WA and Chicago, IL. The workforces in the plants are predominantly Mexican–American, Asian–American and Western European respectively. The organization has implemented a plant incentive program that measures costs, quality and productivity. If the quarterly results for a plant meet the established "meets expectations" standard no incentive pool is created. However, when results exceed expectations, formulas are used to calculate the fund. All three plants have exceeded standard and incentive pools of between one and two million dollars have been created. Although the plan provided that the distribution of the fund would result in awards that were the same percentage of salary for all participants, a meeting of the plant managers disclosed different opinions about the appropriate distribution.

The managers agreed that the purpose of incentives was to motivate employees to perform at high levels but they differed in how much weight should be given to the preferences of the employees. Based on what you know about the cultural predispositions of the dominant national cultures present in the plants what do you think employees would prefer if they were able to vote? If you believe their preferences would differ what are the advantages of accommodating culture? The disadvantages? You are a consultant used by the multinational frequently and they asked you one question: what should they do and why?

Notes

1 Trompenaars, F. & Greene, R., *Rewarding Performance Globally: Reconciling the Global – Local Dilemma* (New York, Routledge, 2017).
2 Trompenaars, F., *Managing People across Cultures* (Chichester, UK, John Wiley & Sons, 2004).
3 Huntington, S., *The Clash of Civilizations and the Remaking of World Order* (New York, Touchstone, 1998).
4 Gladwell, M., *Outliers* (New York, Little, Brown, 2008).
5 Trompenaars, F., *Managing People across Cultures* (Chichester, UK, John Wiley & Sons, 2004); Hofstede, G., *Culture and Organizations* (Thousand Oaks, CA, Sage, 1991).
6 Cohen, A., "Many Forms of Culture," *American Psychologist* (April, 2009).
7 Trompenaars, F., *Riding the Waves of Culture* (Burr Ridge, IL, Irwin, 1994).
8 Hall, E., *Beyond Culture* (New York, Anchor-Doubleday, 1976).

Chapter 11

Rewarding Performance
Contractors, Consultants and Freelancers

Organizations are increasingly using people who are not employees to perform the work required . . . producing things, providing services and creating new products/services. The practitioner literature has heralded this trend as the arrival of the "gig economy." Numerous estimates suggest that 40–50% of work in the U.S. will be performed by people who are not employees by 2020. This dramatic change raises workforce management issues. The utilization of contractors and consultants has been common in organizations that do major projects requiring skills and knowledge not available in their workforces for a long time. Entire functions have been outsourced. And volunteers have been widely used by non-profit and charitable organizations. So work being performed by outsiders is not new. But the nature of work is changing rapidly, with more being done in the form of large and complex projects. This magnitude of change raises questions about the approaches that have been used to do workforce planning, staffing, development, performance management and rewards management.

Organizations using contractors and consultants to provide solutions to challenges they face in product design or technical issues that exceed the capabilities of their core workforce realize many benefits. They are able to temporarily increase staffing levels to meet the increased demand and then to reduce staffing without facing the painful and expensive process of terminating employees. The most common approach for utilizing outsiders is for the organization to develop a request for proposal that specifies what is needed. Contractors, consulting firms and individual freelancers are then solicited to submit proposals, which are used to select a provider. Talent platforms such as UpWork and TopCoder may also be utilized to source the needed talent. They have been created to operate as clearing houses between organizations and freelancers, similar to how employment agencies have operated for a long time. In some cases "crowdsourcing" is used to cast a wide net, seeking people willing to provide their expertise for specific blocks of work. This creates a direct connection between individuals and the organization and makes it possible for individuals to remain in employment elsewhere and to treat the block of work as a part-time job, rather than relying totally on "gigs" to provide them with income. There is evidence that increasing numbers of people are leaving full-time employment in one organization and becoming freelancers. The pure crowdsourcing approach is based on an agreement that if the organization uses what is done by the freelancer an agreed-to amount of compensation is paid to the contributor. Contests are sometimes run that put individuals into competition, with them doing the work and the requesting organization selecting one or more of the entries to use. If the work is not used there is no compensation. This provides organizations with two benefits: 1) costs are aligned with the value provided, and 2) additions to fixed cost payroll are not required.

Some work is difficult to outsource, often due to concerns about security. Having worked in top secret organizations, it has become apparent to me that protecting confidentiality sometimes trumps cost and efficiency considerations. That does not mean that work outside the security fence cannot be outsourced, but if it is connected to the secret work there is often great danger in leakage via accidental disclosure. In other organizations the primary concern is that specific knowledge and the capacity for effectively using it may be the sole source of competitive advantage. If intellectual capital cannot be turned into legal property via patent protection then disclosure can result in the loss of that advantage. U.S. organizations are very wary about partnering with foreign firms when it is clear that the partner will require full disclosure, opening the door to the emergence of a new competitor. When employees work side by side with outsiders, either co-located or virtually, there is danger of transfer.

Another obstacle to using outside sources may be the degree to which the work requires organization-specific knowledge and skill. The author consulted with an envelope manufacturer that had so customized the production equipment that the original manufacturer could not work on it. Organizations develop unique processes that require a high level of familiarity with how things are done and it is therefore unlikely that the use of outsiders would produce benefits.

In addition to operational issues, there has been a recent history of litigation in the U.S. involving organizations using contractors. Clear criteria exist in the law regarding the determination of whether someone doing work for an organization must be treated as an employee. Microsoft and other technology firms have lived through major lawsuits regarding classification. But the emergence of organizations like Uber has increased the regulatory focus. Uber has contended that it is an IT platform only, acting as an intermediary between drivers, who use their own vehicles whenever they choose to do so, and riders needing specific service. The regulations specify that contractors must be free to do the work in a manner dictated by their discretion and that they must supply their own equipment. If their work is directed by an organization's manager, it brings into question whether it is legitimate to treat them as contractors, not provide benefits or pay certain taxes. Much has yet to be resolved and the stakes are high for organizations using outsiders.

Each organization must make a strategic decision about what constitutes the knowledge, skills and capabilities required to perform work. Human Resources is a critical function and organizations should consider workforce management as a core competence, with HR providing oversight. Certainly, organizations have outsourced transactional work to contractors and done so successfully. Anything that can be directed using a fully specified methodology can probably be outsourced if there is a cost advantage and if quality can be maintained. But talent management strategy is at the heart of any organization's business strategy and must be carefully formulated and executed.

The increased use of outsiders should prompt organizations to carefully evaluate the effect of using outsiders on the current employees. The Human Resources function is a natural partner for the internal unit using outsiders, to ensure the value proposition offered potential contributors is viewed as equitable, competitive and appropriate. Outsiders with needed knowledge and skills must be motivated to make the effort to respond to the organization's requirements, either on a one-time basis or as an ongoing resource. The objectives for the value proposition are conceptually similar to those used by the organization for employees . . . to attract, retain and motivate. But the issue of employee–outsider equity may become important.

The common practice when using outsiders is for the unit within the organization that needs the contribution of outsiders to manage the process, often without input from the Human Resources function. But a case can be made that any activity requiring the use of outsiders be vetted through Legal and Human Resources. It is certain that employees will begin to make equity comparisons with the outsiders. They might feel all the "cool new stuff" is turned over to others, depriving them of the opportunity to keep their skills updated. It could also make them feel the organization does not have faith in their capabilities. And they might feel inequitably paid relative to outsiders. Perhaps the most unsettling possibility is that they may feel threatened with the loss of their jobs.

Many examples of poor outsourcing management occurred during the Y2K crisis. The IT functions that outsourced the development of network-based systems to replace the legacy systems found that they created angst among their employees. The inside staff members were often asked to keep the rickety old systems running while the outsiders developed the new systems. This led employees to view outsourcing as a practice that deprived them of the opportunity to acquire the new skills that would be in demand in the future. When incumbents asked to be trained in the new skills so they could do some of the design work, organizations frequently viewed this as an unnecessary cost, due to a duplication of effort. The resistance to making the investment in the employees was also fueled by the belief that it increased the attractiveness of their current employees to competitors . . . especially when the demand for the new skills far exceeded the current supply as it did in the late 1990s. Regrettably, many organizations did not consider the perspective of employees.

When I was consulting with an investment management firm during the Y2K era enraged employees accosted the HR Director because they discovered what the hourly rate being paid to the outsiders was. The employees multiplied that by 2,080 and concluded the annual pay of an outsider was many times what employee annual salaries were. In addition, the employees had to train the outsiders on the requirements and functional of the organization's systems. Pointing out that the contractors did not have job security was a weak selling point in the eyes of people feeling threatened, since they had little faith in their own security. When the HR Director noted that contractors did not get benefits, an offer to forego their benefits was made . . . if the organization would increase their salaries by the difference between their annualized salary and that of the contractors computed using their formula (their hourly rate times 2,080, clearly an inappropriate calculation).

The potential for increased use of outsiders is magnified during a time when technology is being developed at a rapid rate. Those coming out of school know "the new stuff" while employees who have been in the field for some time may lack that knowledge. And training employees is often viewed by Finance as a certain cost with no guaranteed measurable future benefit, making it a struggle to get the training and development resources required to maintain the viability of the workforce. Employee satisfaction and engagement are hard to measure, so they are rarely used in making investment decisions. Therefore, the potential impact of changing out the staff on a regular basis seems to have limited downside to those making purely economic calculations. But there are costs associated with downsizing that often escape analysis. In "Costing HR" Cascio provides an analysis of all considerations that should be included when an organization enters the world of serial upsizing and downsizing.[1] This will be a critical issue if the economic cycle will become more volatile, as predicted by most Economists.

There needs to be someone responsible for making an assessment of using outsiders that considers the bigger picture. Loyalty to the organization may impact an employee's long-term decision to stay and to contribute their maximum effort, especially during difficult times. Those arguing for widespread employee ownership often believe the maxim "people don't wash rental cars." So someone needs to factor in all considerations and ensure operating management does not simplistically focus on the benefits of using outsiders to augment the existing workforce. Ensuring that this is done well has gained in importance. For employees to be engaged and satisfied, they have to feel a sense of ownership, emotional if not legal. Involvement by the Human Resources function in ensuring the use of two different sources of worker is done in a manner that is equitable and that the impact on employees is considered.

It is surprising that there has not been more recognition of the fact that there may be a tradeoff between work completion targets and the resources that will be made necessary by the imposition of a deadline. In the Y2K instance there was a deadline for system conversion and that was not going to change. The most critical problems faced by organizations were attributable to the lack of time to develop systems. The failure to begin planning earlier for meeting an inflexible deadline was a major oversight. If there had been more time for development other options would have been feasible, such as retraining employees. So chalk that debacle up to a lack of respect for workforce planning and how critical timing may be.

But many projects can be completed a number of different ways. If NASA is planning an unmanned space mission to another planet, the relative position of Earth to the planet may have an impact on things like flight time, fuel consumption and other operating costs. The explosion of a space shuttle was mostly due to the rush to launch, in addition to human communication problems. One wonders just how much damage waiting another day, week or month would really have done. A parallel would be an organization attempting to leapfrog competitors into the market with a new software product. The early provider may indeed have an advantage, in that premium pricing can be levied, but if being first means that outsiders must be brought in to do the development someone should examine the costs vs. benefits of any schedule. Marketing and R&D will no doubt be for ASAP, yet HR might suggest that problems will arise if outsiders are mixed in with employees or outsiders are to do all the work.

Defining and measuring the performance of outsiders can be similar to doing it for employees. But there are other types of contributions that are often required of employees that generally are not required of outsiders, such as doing things that contribute to the effectiveness of their unit and the organization but are not tied to a current project. In contrast, outsiders who are contracted to do defined segments of work are appropriately focused on doing what the project specifications define as performance. Rarely are outsiders asked to or expected to keep a parental type of eye on newer employees or those requiring guidance. And they won't be expected to be a cheerleader for the organization or be involved in recruiting efforts. Finally, they are unlikely to be concerned with the long-range impact of the work on customer satisfaction, which a long-term employee may view as important.

One of the most critical requirements for project planners is deconstructing the work into segments and developing performance criteria for them, typically using criteria such as cost, timeliness and quality. In Chapter 5, which focuses on professional employees, a model for project management was used as an example of defining segments, assigning performance criteria and standards and integrating segments to ensure that they were compatible. A major unmanned space mission run by NASA encountered major issues when using sub-contractors . . . some used the metric system and others did not. And when Boeing developed the Dreamliner, parts of the plane were designed in places across the globe. One of the biggest concerns was the compatibility of the parts when it was time to assemble the aircraft.

When discussing project management in Chapter 5, it was suggested that the skill set required was unique enough to warrant considering it a separate occupational specialization. In organizations that are experienced in doing large and complex projects, there will probably be people skilled in project management, so developing a project plan that deconstructs the work into segments and ensures the segments will be compatible may not pose a major challenge. But organizations facing the need to do a major project without adequate experience may flounder. As previously noted, this occurred in many organizations during the Y2K transition. Organizations that had relatively basic IT systems that were peripheral to their core competencies faced the challenge of modifying or replacing their systems without deep project management skills. Their IT staff was often capable of keeping the system current and functioning, but not of designing a new system. This in some cases led to wholesale outsourcing of the work, leaving current IT employees holding the old system together until it was replaced. This scenario caused organizations to think of the new system design and the current system maintenance as totally separate. And that led to believing there was no need to compare performance and rewards management for outsiders to current employees.

When employees work side by side with contractors, opportunities and challenges present themselves. There is an opportunity for employees to learn new skills from contractors, which serves the organization well after project completion. There is also an opportunity for employees to make contractors aware of how the outputs of the system are used in the organization and also to identify the ongoing need to train system users in doing their work using system output. But what may seem like an efficient way to structure output to a contractor may result in internal users being challenged to understand how to use the output. Anticipating the needs of internal users for training is something that often does not occur to anyone and when untrained people attempt to use the new system productivity might fall rather than rise. The antidote is to be sure someone is focused on user training needs and is responsible for ensuring they are addressed.

Adopting a long-term view in doing project planning will help to ensure that after the project is completed the ongoing operational needs are considered. Things like user training may be incorporated into the project plan. If this is done contractors may be charged with responsibilities like training employees if they are best suited to do it. And a separate maintenance agreement may be appended to the project plan, which assigns responsibilities after project completion to a designated party. Contractors will be expected to be paid for assuming ongoing responsibilities and this needs to be incorporated into the definition of performance that is used to manage and reward them. It should be remembered that what is rewarded is most likely to be done. When contractors are paid based on hours worked they may be motivated to work as many hours as possible, never finish and avoid training client staff. This is hardly the type of motivation an organization wants to deal with. Yet in some cases it is very difficult to forecast the number of hours a unit of work will require, particularly if the same activity has not been done before. If the experts are asked to estimate the effort required and they are the ones that will perform the work, one must wonder about the neutrality of their perspective when they develop time estimates. This is the reason that organizations attempt to get multiple bids on contractor work. But even if the expert views are not biased by self-interest, they may not have had experience with a similar project and estimates may become guesses, albeit educated ones.

Another performance management challenge is for the organization to set reasonable standards for both contractors and employees. Just because a contractor can code a unit of work in 30 hours does not mean a current employee can meet that standard. This is where cost–benefit analysis helps. Since it is likely that a contractor working for a consulting firm will be billed at three to four times their salary the contractor will be more expensive than a current employee. So if the contractor can generate twice the output an employee can but will cost three times as much what is the best way to allocate work? This, of course, assumes both are full-time on the project work. If employees have additional responsibilities and make unrelated contributions to organizational performance that should also be a part of the calculation. Expecting employees to stretch their reach to equal that of a contractor may be unreasonable, and this may result in overly harsh standards being applied to employees. And if employees are expected to educate contractors on integrating the project work with other systems and processes that should also be considered when setting performance expectations. Although company culture is often overlooked as something that impacts standards, it impacts how employees work and their expectations about things like their workload. If an organization's culture does not result in the realization that employees must renew their skills and knowledge as required as a pre-requisite for continued employment, it may be difficult to avoid an aversion to change. No contractor could be expected to anticipate that unless they are made aware of "softer" limitations as to what can be expected of users.

When a "gig" approach is utilized and numerous individual freelancers are assigned to a project, the issue of equity across outsiders should also be considered. Individuals who work independently focus on their worth, both absolutely and on a relative basis. Working recently with a national research laboratory, three IT career ladders were developed: one for professional level IT analysts, one for support people and another for cyber security specialists. This approach enabled the organization to identify different market rates where they existed and to adjust compensation accordingly. With the increased concern about information security comes the development of more and more sophisticated software to control access to data and systems. And the cyber specialization stood out. Numerous certifications in this area have recently developed and organizations are still trying to sort out their relative worth and to develop competence tests to determine who has a command of the required skills and knowledge. The compensation premium associated with holding those holding these certifications will be determined by the relative difficulty of obtaining certification and the supply of certified people compared to the demand. In some cases talent platforms can act as a source of guidance on how to determine if someone has the skill to do what is required and what the competitive rate of pay is for the qualifications required. Organizations must accept that different rates for different specialties may be necessary in order to maintain competitiveness across contractors/freelancers.

The form that rewards come in may differ between contractors and employees. Employees will certainly receive a salary and benefits and may be eligible for incentives of various types. They may also participate in stock-based programs. Contractors may be paid an hourly rate and may be eligible for incentive awards on top of the base rate for exceeding cost, timing and quality standards. Or they may not receive any reward based on time and have their compensation based solely on outcomes compared to performance standards defined in the contractual agreement. For extended timeframes it may be necessary to pay out interim awards, since they will have day-to-day living expenses just like everyone else. When deconstructing the project segments this should be considered. Milestones may be inserted where it is possible to approximate percentage of completion and these milestones may be tied to interim payouts.

Having received shocked responses to the suggestion that an organization consider using stock programs for contractors in a manner that would produce a shared destiny and a sense of ownership of the project, I am cautious in making such a recommendation. There are several approaches to using stock and some are more appropriate than others. Each approach can be more or less appropriate given the context. If an organization is creating a new product that will be spun off into a separate legal entity, offering the prospect of stock in the new entity may attract entrepreneurial types, since they are apt to believe the eventual payout will be greater than what can be earned on a project incentive basis. And it can provide an incentive to outsiders to ensure the product is successful. It may also help an organization function with a limited cash flow during the early days. The use of phantom stock can alleviate some of the complications associated with using actual company stock.

Offering stock in an ongoing company with operations other than the product produced may be viewed with less enthusiasm, since external factors might have more influence on stock price than the success of the project. And offering stock awards does not preclude the immediate sale of shares, unless vesting requirements are included, so the benefit of using stock will not be realized and additional administrative effort will be required. For this reason it may be prudent to attach a vesting clause to the awards granted during the project, as an added incentive for the outsiders to remain engaged for the duration of the time the organization needs them.

For some time companies have "rented" skilled people. An interim CEO or CFO can be brought in for a mid-range turnaround of an organization. Someone with no vested interest in long-term career growth may be able to operate free of politics and special interest influences. Typically, this initiative is taken by a board or by a group of investors who have an agenda they wish to have pursued. Although it might seem there is a big difference between a rented CFO with 30 years of experience and a 20-something freelancer, there are similarities. Each has a prescribed agenda with a known end date and is focused on specific work to be accomplished. As a result, the decision on how to reward performance may produce the same strategy that is used for contractors performing work on a shorter timetable.

Outsiders can become insiders when mergers, acquisitions or alliances occur. Research has shown that 70% or more of mergers and acquisitions fail because of people issues. The bringing together of two workforces that have dissimilar histories, cultures and expectations is similar to bringing in outsiders to work alongside employees. The acquired organization is apt to look at those from the acquirer as outsiders, who do not have the same understanding of how things should be done. Although technically both workforces are now employees of the same organization, it very often does not seem like it. If the two organizations to be joined are from different countries the issues associated with cross-cultural management become apparent. Chapter 10 addressed global workforces but some of the same challenges occur when crossing borders and when combining outsiders with employees.

Part-time and seasonal employees raise issues for some organizations. If someone works ten to 20 hours a week they most often are compensated differently from the package offered full-time employees. Management must decide if they are paid an hourly rate that is the same, higher or lower than employees doing the same or similar work. One approach is to pay somewhat more, to reflect the fact that benefits are generally offered to full-time employees and that the person will probably be busy most or all of the time. Banks have often paid part-time tellers more to reflect the intensity of the workload they face throughout the busy periods they are employed to deal with. It may also be that part-timers do the more routine work and would be paid less than full-timers, even though in theory they are all doing the same job. The organization must also consider that the supply in their labor market for part-timers is greater or less than the demand. Having an ample supply of eager candidates for part-time work may be a luxury enjoyed by an entity in a college town and bargaining power could be used in setting the hourly rate. But if most of the supply in a market consists of people who need or want full-time jobs this may mandate offsetting an undesirable employment condition with a higher wage. It may also be possible to offset the reluctance to take a part-time job by making it the pipeline to full-time employment.

Another category of employee that is critical for some industries is seasonal employees. Retailers and resorts make significant use of seasonal employees and if they are unable to get the talent they need it may severely impact their operations. Students flood the market at Christmas and summer holiday times and there may be a benefit to have them work more than one season if there is considerable training necessary to be effective in their roles. A ski resort would certainly not want to rely on a completely new cadre of instructors or snow machine operators each season, since they would lack the familiarity with the conditions and the customers. And it would be difficult to maintain brand integrity as a highly rated restaurant if a new chef and kitchen staff was used each season. If there is high value in having seasonal personnel return, an organization may increase the compensation based on "longevity" in order to make working for the organization more lucrative for the employees than starting over with another employer. It may be prudent for the employer to evaluate seasonal employees to see if they are a source for full-time employment. College students serve internships that enable each party to evaluate the other. Co-op programs enable organizations to prescribe a path to employment through several seasons, giving them the advantage when it comes time for the student to make a decision about employment.

In summary, the era of work being done by outsiders has arrived. Whether organizations will decide to increase the use of outsiders and to focus on how they might engage them most effectively is to be determined. Some organizations may reduce the "core" workforce and use outsiders for both short and long term periods. The challenges of integrating the work of non-employees and employees are largely known but the strategies for effectively managing and rewarding performance are still under debate. Different types of organizations will address the issues differently. Organizations will adapt their strategies to fit the nature of the work. Again, "what works is what fits."

Application of Principles: Chapter 11

An investment services organization has found it necessary to replace their aging computer and supporting systems in order to be able to process the growing volume of transactions and the complexity of the work. Current systems must be functioning while the transition takes place.

There are three alternatives. One is to design and implement the new system using current IT staff. The IT Director has developed a project plan that would require an increase in staff size of 15% and an investment of 100k in training current staff members in the new technology. This option would require stretching the timeline to 18 months. The second is to hire a contractor to design and implement the new system. This option will require the payment of 400k to the contractor and the conversion can be completed in 12 months. The third option is to have outsiders work on some portions of the project while current staff would do the remainder of the work. This option will require fees of about 200k to outsiders, who will be freelancers obtained through a talent platform, and the conversion can be completed in 15 months.

Specify what additional information you would require in order to make a recommendation. Make a list of the advantages and disadvantages of each option and then formulate your recommendation and provide a justification for the recommendation.

Note

1 Cascio, W., *Costing HR Resources*, 4th Ed. (Cincinnati, OH, South-Western, 2000).

Part III

Strategy Integration

Part I defined the process of developing human resource management strategies that are a good fit to the organizational context and that will contribute to organizational success. It then identified common principles that can be used to guide the formulation of effective performance and rewards management strategies.

Part II examined different categories of employee that might warrant customized performance and rewards management strategies, which will provide a good fit to the local contexts while remaining consistent with guiding principles.

Part III offers guidance that will enable custom strategies to be integrated effectively, resulting in successful execution and in workforce effectiveness. Options for deciding how many and what kinds of strategies should be employed and how those decisions should be made are explored here. Figure P3.1, which was introduced in Part II, illustrates that an

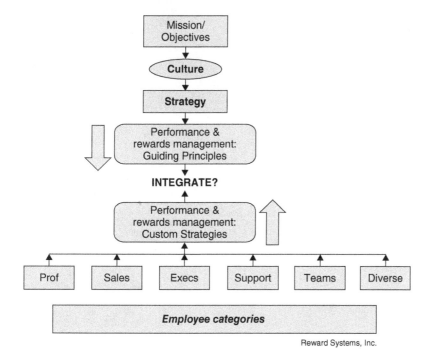

Reward Systems, Inc.

Figure P3.1 Integrating global principles with custom strategies organization has two options. It can start at the top (beginning with one global strategy) and work down to local strategies. Starting at the top can predispose the decision maker to try to find one strategy to fit all employees. The other approach begins by examining each local context, developing a custom strategy that fits the contexts, and then work up, attempting to integrate the custom strategies. Starting at the bottom will predispose the decision maker to fit each local context as closely as possible. The option chosen is largely a function of management's philosophy. The central question is how to integrate strategies that fit the context while adhering to the guiding principles defined by the organization. And it is critical to do so in a manner that results in workforce effectiveness and organizational performance.

Chapter 12

Managing Performance

What you *measure* and reward you most surely will get more of.

(Unknown)

If your people are headed in the wrong direction, don't motivate them.

(G. Odiorne)

The principles underlying sound performance management were discussed in Chapter 2. Whether to utilize one performance management strategy or many hinges on how diverse employees are and the role they play in making the organization successful. If a software design firm employs only software designers and outsources sales and administrative activities, it can adopt a single strategy that is custom designed to fit technical professionals. But if that same organization performs all functions in-house the strategies must fit its executives and managers, sales personnel, professionals, administrative personnel and support personnel. Given this degree of workforce diversity it is less likely that a single strategy can fit all employees well. At the organization-wide level the firm can create a balanced scorecard to define performance. It can then ensure that all performance management programs motivate employees to contribute to high levels of organizational performance, as defined in the scorecard. The programs utilized can differ for each group to produce a better local fit, as long as they are guided by common principles and integrated with each other in a synergistic manner.

In addition to defining performance appropriately another critical decision is how performance will be evaluated. In Chapter 2, defining performance at the organization, unit and individual levels was discussed conceptually, and the use of guiding principles explored. In Chapters 4 through 10 each major category of employee was analyzed, to determine how performance might be defined and measured in a manner that was a good fit to the nature of the work performed and to those who perform it. From a practical standpoint the critical decision is whether to appraise individual performance in the same way for everyone or to employ custom strategies that constitute the best fit to each category of employee.

Many employees view the performance management process as being that form that is filled out each year telling them how their supervisor rates their performance. But if the supervisor incorporates planning before the start of the performance period and utilizes continuous measurement and feedback this will increase the chances that the employee will recognize that appraisal is a continuous process. And if the method used to appraise individual performance seems relevant to the nature of the work performed, as well as acceptable to the employee, the process can be effective. The results of employee surveys over several decades demonstrate that both the employee and the rater are often dissatisfied with performance appraisal.[1] When HR professionals attempt to evaluate the source of the discontent their first stop is typically the form used to appraise performance.

As stated in Chapter 2, many think getting the form right is the key to success, whether it is one form for everyone or different forms for different groups. Over 30 years of experience says it is only one of the prerequisites for successful performance management. It is certainly important to get the form right, since it is the physical manifestation of the appraisal process, and it is what goes into the employee's personnel file. But the process must also be viewed as just and as appropriate, and the participating parties must be competent to execute the process. Having one form sends the message that appraisal is done consistently. Having many forms sends the message that appraisals are designed to fit the nature of the work and the local context within which it is performed. It is therefore critical to develop formats that produce a balance between good fit to context and equivalent (not necessarily identical) methods for everyone. Figures 12.1 and 12.2 are examples of two performance appraisal formats. These formats are meant to be electronic templates, which can be called up, modified and put back into a retrievable database.

Figure 12.1 is a format best suited for use with employees who do not manage and who are not professionals. The format best fits operating and administrative support personnel. This example describes the basis upon which a reporter working for a newspaper might be evaluated. The process for using this format would include the following steps:

1 Develop a job summary that includes the critical elements of the person's responsibilities. Although the same job description may be used for all incumbents of a job, some organizations find that customizing the job summary for each person is helpful in making each employee feel they are being evaluated on what they actually do, particularly if there are significant variations in the expectations across incumbents of a job. The amount of detail can vary, based on what the organization is trying to accomplish. It is even reasonable to consider having the first page of the appraisal form be the complete job description. Doing this makes it possible to review the descriptions at the start of every performance period and to modify them during the performance period when things change. This approach helps to keep job descriptions current, which is necessary but which often is considered something to do when there is nothing else to do.

2 Comment on performance relative to each of the four evaluation factors. The factors traditionally used in appraisals are productivity, quality of work and dependability. But in today's workplace there is an increased need for each employee to perform in a manner that makes others and the unit more effective, hence the addition of the fourth factor "contribution to the effectiveness of others/unit." This factor can be given considerable weight in contexts where employees are highly interdependent, such as in teams.

The comments must relate results and behaviors to the job responsibilities as outlined in the job summary. They should also contain specific metrics when they are available and relevant. For example, "output per hour" could be included as a specific metric under "Productivity," "defects per thousand" under "Quality," and "absences" under "Dependability." These examples are all quantitative and results can be expressed in numbers, which makes many managers more comfortable, since the arguments tend to be fewer when dealing with hard metrics. However, there is a danger that things easy to measure with numbers will be accorded importance, whether or not they really are, and that measures requiring qualitative judgments will be avoided. This is a serious problem, because employees are easily sent down the wrong path or led to establish priorities that are inconsistent with organizational needs. Judgments can be expressed in qualitative terms, such as "Assists others in overload situations." Another option is to weave the critical measures into the factor descriptions for each job or employee. For example, a reporter for a newspaper who covers City Hall may be appraised using different measures than one who does investigative research, so the definitions used for each factor would differ. No matter which approach is used, the factors should be focused on specific results and behaviors that are related to what the person is expected to do.

3   Rate performance on each of the factors, using one of the following ratings:

a   *Outstanding*: Individual regularly made exceptional contributions that had a significant and positive impact on the performance of the unit or organization. Results significantly exceeded performance standards or objectives consistently. Employee has mastered all job-related skills and possesses a broad range of capabilities. Behavior provides a model for excellence and helps others to do their jobs better. Anticipates potential difficulties and deals with them proactively. Work is of the highest quality, worthy of emulation by others.

b   *Significantly exceeded standards*: Employee frequently exceeded all or most performance expectations or objectives by a significant amount. Is highly skilled and knowledgeable in all aspects of the job. Responds promptly and effectively to workload peaks and to unexpected difficulties. Work is of very high quality.

c   *Fully met standards*: Employee fully meets all job requirements. Consistently meets all expectations and objectives and occasionally exceeds them. Is fully qualified in all aspects of the job.

d   *Did not fully meet standards*: Employee has not consistently met all job requirements and/or met expectations. Has the ability to perform most aspects of the job but may lack some knowledge or skills to perform others. May require assistance with more difficult and complex aspects of work. Sometimes does not meet productivity or quality standards.

e   *Unsatisfactory*: Employee frequently performs in an unsatisfactory manner. Productivity and quality of work are well below standards. Requires a performance improvement plan and performance must improve or consideration should be given to removal from the current job.

Note: Five rating levels are not always the ideal number, although research indicates that having three to five levels is most apt to be effective.[2] Some would argue that if a rating of "Unsatisfactory" is necessary for the entire period the manager has failed in addressing problems during the period and that the employee should have been placed on a performance plan during the year. However, since the form can and should be updated during the year this rating may be used to trigger a performance improvement program. Other organizations combine the "Outstanding" and "Significantly exceeds" ratings into "Significantly exceeds" and make all employees rated at this level eligible to be nominated for further recognition or reward. The number of rating levels should be decided based on the degree to which performance can vary for specific types of jobs. An inserter on a machine-paced assembly line may be judged on a "pass–fail" system, especially on factors such as attendance and safety. When rating an employee's performance it is important to consider their experience and longevity in the job. A relatively new incumbent cannot be expected to have mastered all aspects of the job fully, while a more experienced incumbent will be held to a higher standard. Although some employees might object to different expectations being used for incumbents of the same job, this is a realistic and fair practice.

4   Evaluate results compared to established objectives and goals, if they have been established for the employee. This dimension should be optional, as some jobs have only one objective—perform the job well. If this is the case, forcing the use of objectives and specific measurable goals becomes a frustrating exercise with no real purpose. On the other hand, many jobs consist of project work almost exclusively, thereby making them a good candidate for an objective-based evaluation. For example, a maintenance mechanic may be appraised based on machine downtime and other operational factors for which performance standards have been established. Those metrics can either be built into the rating factors or be defined as objectives. It is important that objectives be developed consistent with the SMART test—specific, measurable, achievable, realistic and time-bound. Vaguely defined objectives, such as "Improve customer service," will not provide the guidance needed and will probably result in year-end disagreements between rater and employee. Objectives such as these must be translated into goals, such as "Increase satisfactory customer ratings from 75% to 85%," which allows the rater to accurately measure results and gain employee acceptance.

5   Evaluate the overall performance of the employee during the performance period. Consider the performance rating on each of the factors, the relative importance of the factors, the rating of performance on objectives and the relative importance of the objectives (if objectives are used). Provide supporting commentary that enables the employee to understand why overall performance was rated as it was, including how the factors were weighted relative to each other. Commentary is critical and should be the basis upon which appraisal ratings are made. Without written support it is very difficult for the rating to be defended. Job-related results and behaviors should be the only considerations in arriving at ratings, and if supporting commentary is missing it is easy for an employee to dismiss the rating as a subjective guess.

6   Provide the employee with an opportunity to prepare a self-appraisal, using either a prescribed format or one of the employee's choosing. The culture of the organization and the management style of the evaluator should determine whether a self-appraisal is used, and it should be optional. Forcing an employee to do a self-appraisal could easily backfire if it does not fit the relationship between the evaluator and subordinates and if an employee is intimidated by the process. People from many cultures are very uncomfortable with providing their point of view, as discussed in Chapter 10.

7   Review the appraisal with the appraiser's manager to ensure there is mutual agreement prior to communicating the appraisal to the employee. This step also allows the second-level manager to ensure the standards being used are equivalent with those of other appraisers.

8   Review the appraisal with the employee and discuss any differences in views about performance or about specific events. Attempt to determine the reasons for different

views and resolve them in a manner producing mutual acceptance. Discuss the impact of the appraisal on pay actions, promotions, reassignments or other personnel actions.

9 Have the employee comment on the appraisal in writing and sign the review form. By signing, the employee is not indicating full agreement, but only that the appraisal was reviewed with them and that an opportunity to comment was provided.

10 Agree on performance expectations for the next performance period. Discuss developmental actions that are appropriate. It is at this point that an assessment of personal capabilities (a.k.a. competencies) may be appropriate. Although things like job knowledge will likely be addressed when attributing performance to causes, it is important to keep them separate from appraising performance. Job knowledge, creativity and analytical ability may all be competencies that enable an individual to perform at a given level but they constitute *potential*, which may or may not be realized. In order for ability to result in performance, effort is required, so considering potential when evaluating performance is unfair to people who are performing well in spite of limited capacity. It also sends the wrong message to those with great, albeit unrealized, potential.

Separate assessments of future potential and of promotional readiness can also be done when someone is performing in an outstanding fashion. This can help to determine if the employee should be considered for a broader or different role or if the person is performing well because they are doing what they are best suited for. Tying performance appraisal into the career management system is a very wise thing to do but it should focus on how well the person is doing in the current role. Appraising potential or determining readiness for promotion should be based on different measures. Just because a programmer performs at a high level as a programmer does not mean the person is the ideal candidate for the next programming manager opening. And the person may well be performing very well because they are very competent at what they are doing and are doing exactly what they want to be doing. But even though a high level of current performance does not signal potential for advancement it certainly is advisable to make the performance appraisal a part of career management.

Figure 12.2 is an appraisal format better suited to managerial and professional personnel. It evaluates both performance relative to the employee's ongoing job responsibilities and the employee's performance against predetermined objectives or goals. Objectives tend to be given a significant amount of weight when evaluating managers, but this will not always be the case. The example used here is for a top HR executive, and both ongoing responsibilities and objectives, expressed as specific goals, are evaluated. The process used is similar to that used for the Figure 12.1 format, except that standard factors are replaced by specific job responsibilities. The weights given to job responsibilities and to objectives can each vary from 0 to 100% in individual instances. Some employees may be focused on their ongoing job responsibilities, making that the focus of the appraisal. Others work on projects full time, and results compared to objectives may be given more weight than the ongoing responsibilities for these employees.

When objectives are used to measure performance a major challenge is to make them equally difficult across employees. For example, all engineers might have the same objective, such as "Redesign product A to be competitive," but have different goals related to that objective. It is important to have employees accept the different goals as fair. One approach is to use the scoring method employed in Olympic diving. The score is the

Employee Information

Name:_____   Job Title: Reporter

Dept.:_____   Supervisor Title:

Performance Period: from _____ to _____

Employee Job Summary

Researches and writes news, features, analyses, human interest stories. Develops and cultivates news sources and contacts. Completes assignments by deadlines, ensuring accuracy by verifying sources. Attends newsworthy events and interviews key sources. Respects confidentiality as appropriate.

Performance of Job

Productivity: Production is high relative to time and resources consumed. Develops expected number of stories and covers beat adequately to ensure stories are detected as they break. Stories are developed within timeframe that enables deadlines to be met and appropriate reviews are performed as they are refined.

Comments:

_____

_____

_____

_____

Rating: ❏ Outstanding ❏ Significantly exceeds standards ❏ Fully meets standards
❏ Does not fully meet standards ❏ Unacceptable

Quality of work: Work meets quality standards and established editorial standards. Stories are written in clear and appropriate manner, are consistent with editorial policy and are fair and balanced. Research is thorough and encompasses all relevant sources, which are verified to ensure accuracy. Works with editors to revise and improve content. Develops and maintains network of contacts who can provide early notification of breaking stories.

Comments:

_____

_____

_____

_____

Rating: ❏ Outstanding ❏ Significantly exceeds standards ❏ Fully meets standards
❏ Does not fully meet standards ❏ Unacceptable

Dependability and adherence to company values and policies: Consistently meets deadlines; conforms to attendance policies; adapts to work demands; conforms to established values and policies; adheres to ethical standards of the paper and the profession; respects confidentiality as appropriate; behaves in manner that enhances the image of the paper.

Comments:

_____

_____

_____

_____

Rating: ❏ Outstanding   ❏ Significantly exceeds standards   ❏ Fully meets standards
        ❏ Does not fully meet standards   ❏ Unacceptable

Contribution to effectiveness of others/unit: Works with others within and outside the unit in a manner that improves their effectiveness; shares information and resources; develops effective working relationships; builds consensus; constructively manages conflict; contributes to the effectiveness of own unit/group and the paper.

Comments:

_____

_____

_____

_____

Rating: ❏ Outstanding   ❏ Significantly exceeds standards   ❏ Fully meets standards
        ❏ Does not fully meet standards   ❏ Unacceptable

Performance vs. Objectives

Objective   Results vs. Expectations
1.
2.
3.

Rating: ❏ Outstanding   ❏ Significantly exceeds standards   ❏ Fully meets standards
        ❏ Does not fully meet standards   ❏ Unacceptable

Note: when rating performance against objectives weight objectives for relative importance to arrive at overall rating

Overall Performance Rating

Consider the ratings on each factor, the relative importance of each, performance against established objectives and the relative importance of the objectives.

Comments:

_____

_____

Figure 12.1 (continued)

(continued)

_____

_____

Rating: ❏ Outstanding ❏ Significantly exceeds standards ❏ Fully meets standards
       ❏ Does not fully meet standards ❏ Unacceptable

Appraiser: _____ Date: _____
Employee: _____ Date: _____

Note: employee signature does not mean agreement with the rating, only that it has been reviewed.

Employee Comments:

_____

_____

_____

_____

Development/Future Objectives

Development (training, special assignments) needed:

_____

_____

_____

_____

Objectives/priorities for next performance period:

_____

_____

_____

_____

Figure 12.1 Example of performance appraisal format for employees who do not manage and who are not professionals (continued overleaf)

product of the degree of difficulty and the quality of execution. Although this places a greater burden on the manager doing the appraisal, it does allow for considering differences in degree of difficulty, which can contribute to fair evaluations.

There can be flexibility that allows units to customize the rating format, but to do so while adhering to guiding principles. The key guiding principle is that performance be defined in terms of job- or role-related results and/or behaviors. The customization can be at the individual, job or occupation level, whichever best suits the nature of the work.

Variations can be built into the process as well, to include using multi-party input (by peers, customers and subordinates).

The frequency of appraisal can also vary across types of jobs. For example, IT and R&D personnel typically work in a project-centered environment, and the best time to evaluate performance is when projects are completed or major milestones are reached. Although this degree of flexibility in timing may be administratively inconvenient, the improved quality of the result may offset the extra effort. However, in organizational cultures that emphasize centralized control and standard application of policies, this may prove problematic. If an annual appraisal on a common date is mandated by policy it can be a summary of appraisals done for each project. It should be remembered that employees will be more apt to view the appraisal process as relevant and appropriate if it is designed to fit what is done and the specific context within which it is done.

When developing the methods and processes governing performance appraisals it should be remembered that if appraisal ratings are used in making pay, career progression and termination decisions they in effect become "tests" under the Uniform Selection Guidelines.[3] Since most organizations use appraisals for one or more of these HR decisions, it is best to be conservative and assume that some reasonable attempt should be made to ensure appraisals could be validated. As discussed in Chapter 9, public sector organizations are subjected to heavier scrutiny, from multiple parties at interest, with regard to performance management. There is also an extensive appeal process in place for most of these organizations. Therefore, it is prudent for them to make a greater effort to relate performance to the specific job-related results and behaviors that are required by the job definitions. In some cases this requires considerable detail at the task level, both in the job documentation and in the appraisal. Assuming performance is defined adequately and that the appraisal process includes procedural justice the quality of appraisers becomes critical.

There is considerable legal precedent for the notion that even the best-designed methods and processes in the hands of untrained appraisers will be misused. In fact, the requirement that appraisers be "trained" is codified into the law and must not be ignored. Unfortunately, the guidance as to what constitutes adequate training is far less clear, and each organization must decide what meets its needs. What is critical is that appraisers are trained before they assume the responsibility. Police departments do not give recruits badges and guns and send them on assignment without having them attend the academy first—because the departments know they will be held accountable for any mistakes the recruits make. Although the damage that can be done by an untrained supervisor is not that dramatic it certainly can be significant.

Having trained appraisers increases the likelihood that employees will view the appraisals as coming from a credible source, which is a critical prerequisite for acceptance. Also, trained appraisers are more apt to provide specific, fair and timely feedback, which will address performance problems to be dealt with more constructively and which will recognize and reinforce good performance. Too often, organizations skip training, assuming people will figure out how to carry out their roles. This is a perilous strategy, to say the least. The quality of the first line of supervision is critical in producing employee effectiveness. But at the same time span of control is widening in most organizations and less time is being allotted to do the "supervision stuff," owing to reduced staffing levels. So the price of not training becomes greater when finding the resources to do the training are scarce.

Performance Appraisal

Name: *Job Title: VP, Human Resources*

Supervisor: *Supervisor Title: EVP & COO*

Performance of Job

Major Job Responsibilities

1. Formulate HR strategy that enables organization to attract, retain and motivate critical knowledge and skills.
2. Develop programs in HR functional areas: staffing, HR development, performance management, compensation, benefits, employee and labor relations and occupational safety and health.
3. Staff, organize and manage the HR function.
4. Advise and assist management to ensure the workforce is effective and that HR programs are administered in a manner that complies with legal/regulatory requirements and organizational values and policies.
5. Participate in professional, industry and community organizations in order to monitor trends and ensure strategy/programs are appropriate for the context currently and into the future.

Comments:

_____

_____

_____

_____

❑ Outstanding   ❑ Significantly exceeds   ❑ Fully meets   ❑ Does not fully meet
❑ Unacceptable

Performance vs. Objectives

Objective   Results vs. Expectations
1. Implement HRMS system by xx/yy/zz
2. Implement new compensation system by aa/bb/cc
3. Implement new performance management system by dd/ee/ff

Comments:

_____

_____

_____

_____

❑ Outstanding   ❑ Significantly exceeds   ❑ Fully meets   ❑ Does not fully meet
❑ Unacceptable

Impact of Unanticipated Events/Conditions

Comment on impact of unanticipated factors on performance of job responsibilities or achievement of objectives:

Overall Rating

Comments:

_____

_____

_____

_____

❏ Outstanding   ❏ Significantly exceeds   ❏ Fully meets   ❏ Does not fully meet
❏ Unacceptable

Signatures

Appraiser:_____ Date:_____

Employee:_____ Date:_____

Note: employee signature does not mean agreement with the rating, only that it has been reviewed and discussed in person.

Employee Comments:

_____

_____

_____

_____

Development/Future Objectives

Development (training, special assignments) needed:

_____

_____

_____

_____

Objectives/priorities for next performance period:

_____

_____

_____

_____

Figure 12.2 Example of performance appraisal format for managerial and professional personnel

Figure 12.3 is a topic outline for a training program for both raters and employees. Effectively communicating these topics requires a substantial investment in focused training. The length of the instruction will depend on the amount of dialogue and whether case examples are used to allow for hands-on involvement. Having all management personnel attend the same training sends the message that this is important and sends the message that executive management is committed to doing it well. One of the benefits of having managers hear the same thing at the same time is that word-of-mouth communications do not distort the message. Having senior executives attend also helps to send the message that the organization is committed to appraisal. And training employees, rather than just communicating what is going to be done to them, helps them understand how the system should work and what impact it will have on their pay and careers. The author's strong preference is to have executives, managers and employees in the same sessions. That is, if a manager has employees in a session the manager should be there to. The objective is to make performance management a continuous dialogue and it is important for everyone to hear the same thing.

The most important belief to instill during training is that doing performance management well is one of the most productive and critical things managers can do with their time. Of course, this requires that executives set an example by doing appraisals well and on a regular basis. HR must assume the responsibility for pointing out to the CEO that if appraisals are not done for VPs it is hard to convince VPs to ensure they do them for their directors—and so on down through the organization.

Appraisal must be a continuous process, and doing it continuously actually saves time in the long run, as well as increasing its effectiveness. As the Generation X cohort began to flood into the workplace, it became clear this "constant feedback seeking" group did not accept waiting a year to find out what they had done wrong or not done at all. Playing Dungeons and Dragons on a computer gives you instant and unequivocal feedback on the effectiveness of both your strategies and the quality of your execution—and the D&D mindset did not equip these new labor force entrants to deal with the long periods of silence or the "You are doing fine" platitudes they were able to squeeze out of their supervisors.

Often appraisers dread doing appraisals because they know they do not remember clearly what happened more than a few weeks ago, except for the disasters they are still paying for. They also fear that when they do re-create the year the employee will remember it differently. With the advent of electronic databases it is now possible for supervisors to quickly make "diary" entries throughout the performance period and to provide feedback to an employee, electronically or personally. This facilitates concurrence between the evaluator and the employee as to what actually transpired. It also provides a sound basis for deciding what needs to be done, if anything, to increase effectiveness or to build on successes. The use of the diary approach is even more critical when objectives are used, since priorities often change and unanticipated events occur that are outside the control of the employee. The use of diary entries makes the period-end appraisal a review of events both parties had discussed during the period as they happened. But having the capability available does not guarantee supervisors will use these tools. And that is why it is critical to train appraisers and to instill in them the belief that this is a daily part of management.

One of the most important topics to cover in performance appraisal training is the accuracy of ratings. The quality of ratings is a product of rater motivation and rater ability.

Performance Management Training Program

1. Performance management and its components
   a. Planning
   b. Measurement and feedback
   c. Development
   d. Appraisal

2. Prerequisites for performance
   a. Knows what is required
   b. Able to do what is required
   c. Allowed to do what is required
   d. Wants to do what is required

3. Objectives for performance appraisal
   a. Define performance (criteria and standards)
   b. Communicate criteria, standards and measures
   c. Provide feedback to enable development
   d. Identify employee capabilities
   e. Develop employees to their capacity

4. Appraisal methodology to be used

5. Appraisal process to be used

6. Consequences of appraisal
   a. Pay
   b. Career progression
   c. Retention
   d. Development

7. Role of evaluators and challenges
   a. Legal compliance
   b. Employee acceptance
   c. Timely and consistent appraisal
   d. Rating validity and reliability
   e. Fair standards across individuals
   f. Correctly attributing results to causes (system; employee)
   g. Utilize employees optimally and develop them to potential

---

Figure 12.3 Topic outline for a training program

There is considerable evidence that the consequences of ratings will impact the level at which employees are rated. A combination of several research studies (a meta-analysis) showed that if ratings are used for administrative purposes the scores are one-third of a standard deviation higher than if the appraisal is done for developmental purposes.[4] Every rater is subject to making the common types of errors. Identifying each type of error and discussing how each can be avoided during training helps to minimize its occurrence. Some of the most common errors are:

- *Lack of differentiation*: Raters often lack confidence in defending different ratings between employees. If they know they will face resistance they may rate everyone pretty much the same. This may take the form of *leniency* (everyone gets high ratings), *severity* (everyone gets low ratings) or a lack of differentiation—everyone is just fine (everyone gets rated in the middle, which is termed *central tendency*). The reluctance to differentiate can often be attributed to poor training or the failure to make it clear that these judgments are a part of management's responsibility. If trait checklists are being used it creates the impression that the *person* is being judged, rather than job-related performance. This approach does not fare well when challenged in court, another reason this approach should be avoided. Creating distinctions where they do not exist is also a common mistake. This sometimes is the product of a system that mandates forced distributions (e.g., 10% must be rated "outstanding" and 10% must be rated "does not meet expectations." If the work performed is prescribed by specific rules, with little employee discretion or control, it is inappropriate to force such distinctions. And organizations that have "gone lean" may well have already removed those not meeting expectations. This would result in forced distributions that result in adequate performers being rated at artificially low levels.
- *Recency error*: When managers are not diligent in continuously measuring performance, providing feedback and documenting results, they often cannot remember the earlier part of the performance period. As a result they weight the most recent events too heavily. If they can be convinced that continuous measurement and feedback should be an integral part of their routine this kind of distortion can be minimized. Using the "diary" approach described earlier is the best cure.
- *Personal bias*: If job-related results and behaviors are not the focus of the appraisal it is easy for managers to allow their impression of the person or their feelings about them to dominate the rating. This can lead to adverse impact on a protected class and expose the organization to legal liability. Besides, it is just not fair or appropriate. A focus on the job and predetermined criteria and standards is the best tool for avoiding bias.
- *Inconsistent standards across raters*: Perhaps the rating problem that is hardest to correct is inconsistency *across* raters. Research has shown that merely making raters aware of the types of potential errors and how they might avoid them does not in itself do much to promote cross-rater reliability. In scientific terms, consistency is measured in terms of reliability. And the challenge of training managers to be consistent is one of the largest associated with performance management. Frame of reference (FOR) training addresses this issue.[5] Potential evaluators can have their standards better calibrated with each other by having them jointly arrive at ratings in training, using case studies, and subsequently discuss why they rated as they did. Another approach is to share their performance rating distributions compared to other raters. This is not to suggest that every rater should be forced into a bell-shaped distribution or that raters appraising different employee populations will correctly end up with the same distributions.

The best administrative tool for leveling ratings is a review of the ratings by the next level of management, with all the direct reports contributing face to face. This is unfortunately an infrequently used technique. Reluctance to perform this valuable review is partly due to the reality that it takes a strong manager to have subordinates jointly combine and calibrate their ratings. If this is not done, however, employees will sense the inequities, and research shows that a lack of consistency across the organizations is currently the source of much dissatisfaction. Management should ensure that ratings distributions are regularly analyzed, to determine if standards are uneven across the organization.

Although there might be concentrations of very good or poor performers in small units, causing unbalanced distributions, there should be a reasonable pattern exhibited in groups of 50 or more. Often, expected guidelines can be developed (i.e., 10–15% outstanding; 20% significantly exceeds; 60–65% fully meets; 5–10% does not fully meet or unacceptable). Each appraiser should be required to support and defend significant variations from those guidelines. Ratings would not be expected to conform to a normal distribution unless the organization uses a random number generator to hire and fire. But having an expected distribution can provide managers with common guidelines and make them aware that significantly varying from the expected distribution will require significant support.

The practice of involving employees through the use of self-appraisals is common, although the process takes many forms. Some organizations ask employees to do a self-appraisal in advance and then to submit it to the supervisor so it can be taken into consideration when appraisal is being done. Others ask employees to bring a self-appraisal to the discussion with the supervisor. Finally, many organizations make self-appraisal optional and leave the format and process to the participants. There is a good deal of research support for the involvement of the employee in the appraisal but there is no one approach that seems to stand out as being superior. Making self-appraisal optional is probably the best approach, given that some people will be intimidated by this practice and in some cases it may be inconsistent with the working relationship between the employee and the supervisor. The different categories of employee discussed in the Part 2 chapters certainly may require different approaches to self-evaluations. Sales and professional personnel often operate in a relatively autonomous manner and it is typically useful to have them provide their perspective on both their results and their behaviors. On the other hand, support personnel who are strictly regulated in what they do may feel this to be a useless exercise or even be intimidated by it.

Because of the increasing rate of globalization and the increased mobility of labor, organizations need to consider the cultural diversity in their workforces. Whether an organization employs people outside the home country or employs people from other countries the result is the same—employees with different beliefs, values and norms. As discussed in Chapter 10, the highly individualistic culture of the U.S. favors doing individual appraisals that involve direct and specific feedback. This is not as acceptable in more collectivist cultures, since they will cause the employee to "lose face." The universalistic character of U.S. culture favors the same set of rules for everyone, while other cultures believe the context or who is involved should cause the practices to vary. The dominant belief in the U.S. culture is that people are in control of their destiny and should be held accountable, while in many parts of the world this is not the prevailing belief. Self-appraisal is used in many U.S. organizations and is often believed to be a positive step towards employee engagement and acceptance, while this practice would be a disaster in cultures where usurping the superior is inappropriate and/or ill advised.[6]

Accommodating cultural differences by varying performance appraisal methods or processes may not fit the management philosophy, but there should at the very least be an understanding that cultural differences exist and they should be respectfully considered when doing appraisals. It is both high-handed and unrealistic to assume everyone views appraisal in the same way, and a diverse workforce can be made more effective by addressing the issue, at least through training.

It has been emphasized earlier that performance appraisal should be focused on *job-related results and behaviors*, rather than individual characteristics or "competencies." This does not mean that *how* someone achieved results is not important. If a manager always makes the numbers but does so by brutalizing subordinates, it is in the organization's best interests to make it clear that behavior fell outside acceptable parameters. And using personal competencies to evaluate potential is also a valid activity, particularly for developmental purposes. However, it should be remembered that performance appraisal is about what is realized, rather than what someone is capable of. Another critical principle that needs to be repeated is that employees should be held accountable only for things they can control. If a person in a service capacity can control only behaviors and not results it may be appropriate to consider how the employee behaved as being the result. Deming rightfully preached that employees should not be held responsible for things caused by "the system," and if service providers cannot directly control customer satisfaction they should be motivated to behave in the desired manner and should be appraised on that basis.[7]

It is also critical that appraisers accurately determine what the cause of poor performance appears to be, so that corrective action can be taken. One cause may be poor *placement*, which resulted in the wrong person being in the job. Another cause may be inadequate *development*, which left the incumbent without the knowledge, skills and abilities necessary to perform well. Finally, the cause is often poor *job or role design*, which makes it difficult for anyone to succeed in the job. The solutions to these causes are relatively clear cut once accurate attribution is made. When instances of poor performance form patterns it can alert HR that its staffing or development strategies and programs need examination or that the way in which a unit defines jobs or roles should be evaluated.

The appraisal system needs to be continuously evaluated, to determine if it is effective and to identify opportunities for improving it. Figure 12.4 provides a questionnaire that can be used to evaluate perceptions. It is most valuable when input is gathered from all levels and from all parts of the organization. Perception *is* reality when it comes to system acceptance, and employees will act on what they believe to be true. Finding out that there is misunderstanding on the part of employees or managers can provide the basis for further communication or for system refinement. The existence of a viable and accessible appeal system can take a great deal of pressure off managers, without undermining their authority. It is not uncommon for a manager and an employee to have difficulty communicating effectively (that "chemistry" thing). When employees see no feasible solution to disagreements on a one-to-one basis frustration and anger can build up. Some way of breaking these inter-personal logjams should be found and the approach should be consistent with the culture of each organization or unit.

As discussed earlier, research has shown that the median U.S. employee will typically view his or her performance at the 75th or 80th percentile within a comparator group, which means there will always be some degree of dissatisfaction with ratings.[8] One organization that is consistently rated as one of the best managed has made its middle (third of five) rating, "Fully meets high XYZ standards," a perfectly acceptable one. This organization is able to rate 70% of its employees at that level without a revolution breaking out. The middle rating does not have to be the equivalent of getting a "C" in graduate school if the organization makes it something else. Employees also give more weight to external factors (lack of resources, co-worker failures, unfavorable conditions) when attempting to explain less than desired results, while raters tend to attribute results more to internal factors (personality, motivation, ability). It is critical to gain some semblance of agreement between the rater and the rate, so these challenges must be met.

Evaluation Questionnaire

Performance Appraisal System

Evaluate the current performance appraisal system by scaling each of the items below from 1 to 7, based on the extent to which you agree with it. Scale value of 1 = not at all and scale value of 7 = completely; values in between should reflect varying degrees of agreement.

1. Managers are held accountable for doing effective appraisals.
2. Performance is defined and measured at all levels and communicated.
3. Individuals know how their performance impacts the performance of their work group and of the organization.
4. High levels of performance are valued, recognized and rewarded.
5. The system was designed with input from all levels.
6. The system measures the right things.
7. The system measures both results and how they were achieved.
8. The system is viewed as fair by employees.
9. The system is legally defensible and explainable to employees.
10. Employees understand how the system is supposed to work.
11. The appraisal process is simple and is not overly time-consuming.
12. Managers view appraisal as a valuable management tool.
13. The system impacts recognition and rewards appropriately.
14. The system impacts promotion and development appropriately.
15. Ratings are accurate and reflect actual performance.
16. Managers are timely in doing appraisals and always do them.
17. Poor performers are provided with developmental opportunities.
18. Performance problems are dealt with quickly and effectively.
19. Repeated poor performance results in appropriate consequences.
20. Managers treat appraisal as a continuous process, rather than a one-time event at the end of the performance period.
21. Feedback is adequate and employees know both what is expected and how they are doing at all times.
22. Managers are appraised on how well they do appraisals.
23. Performance standards are consistent across the organization.
24. Training in performance appraisal is provided for all appraisers.
25. Training in performance appraisal is provided for all employees.
26. Managers are skilled in doing appraisals.
27. Adequate job-related commentary is provided to support ratings.
28. Parties other than the direct supervisor have input into the appraisal process when they have relevant input.
29. There is an adequate appeals process in place.
30. Ratings are based on performance and not on the personal characteristics of the person being rated.

Figure 12.4 Questionnaire for evaluating perceptions

No matter what type of system is used, there should be a periodic independent audit of the way in which the appraisal system is impacting various groups of employees. Adverse impact on a protected class raises legal concerns, but adverse impact on anyone should raise equity or ethical concerns. Whether management takes on the responsibility for monitoring the system outcomes or the responsibility is given to an independent audit function there should be some verification that everyone is being treated in a consistent and fair manner.

According to a study by Lawler, the characteristics of an appraisal system found to have the most impact on its effectiveness were, in order of significance:[9]

1   ownership by line management;
2   appraisers are adequately trained;
3   how results were attained is included in the appraisal;
4   senior management actively provides leadership of performance management;
5   the system is periodically evaluated;
6   employees being rated are trained, not just notified;
7   performance goals are driven by business strategy;
8   ongoing feedback on performance is provided;
9   managers are appraised on how well they do appraisal;
10   jointly established goals are used;
11   performance planning and development are done;
12   competencies, when used, are based on business strategy;
13   pay actions are closely tied to appraisals;
14   competencies are considered in the appraisal process.

Performance appraisal at the individual level is a critical part of performance management. It is a necessary but not sufficient prerequisite for employee effectiveness. Planning, continuous measurement and effective development are also required if appraisal is to contribute significantly to employee effectiveness. It is critical that employees understand how and why performance is defined, measured and managed. They must also know if the same system is used for all employees, and if systems differ they should understand why. Explaining the rationale behind the organization's strategy or strategies can help employees understand that the strategies fit the local contexts while being consistent with guiding principles, whether that results in a single strategy or multiple strategies.

There is no right answer to the question "Should there be one performance management system for all employees or multiple systems, each customized to fit the context?" The balancing act between global and local should be influenced by the culture of the organization, its ability to manage multiple systems and the impact of the systems on the employees. If employees do not view the manner in which their performance is managed as equitable and appropriate, the organization will not be able to reward them appropriately, as discussed in Chapters 13 and 14.

Application of Principles: Chapter 12

You are considering a consulting partnership with two large consulting firms specializing in performance management. While discussing philosophy about how to manage performance, you find there are basic differences between the two firms. One has standardized systems that they use for all clients while the other develops custom systems for each client.

The one using one set of systems believes that employees want to believe that everyone is on a level playing field and that differentiation actuates the "grass is greener on the other side" mentality. They believe this raises suspicions that internal equity does not exist and that employees will not feel they are equally respected and valued.

The firm that customizes strategies and program design to fit different parts of the organization and different types of employees believes this approach recognizes that the variations in the role of employees, the nature of the work they do and their beliefs about how they should be measured and rewarded mandate differentiation.

List what you believe to be the advantages and disadvantages of each of the approaches and how different types of organizations might better fit each.

Notes

1 Aguinis, Herman, *Performance Management* (Upper Saddle River, NJ, Pearson Prentice-Hall, 2007); Lawler, Edward E., *Talent* (San Francisco, CA, Jossey-Bass, 2008).
2 Aguinis, Herman, *Performance Management* (Upper Saddle River, NJ, Pearson Prentice-Hall, 2007); Bernardin, H. & Beatty, R., *Performance Appraisal* (Boston, MA, Kent Publishing, 1984).
3 Cascio, W. & Aguinis, H., *Applied Psychology in Human Resource Management*, 6th ed. (Upper Saddle River, NJ, Pearson Prentice-Hall, 2005).
4 Cascio, W. & Aguinis, H., *Applied Psychology in Human Resource Management*, 6th ed. (Upper Saddle River, NJ, Pearson Prentice-Hall, 2005).
5 Hauenstein, N., "Training Raters to Increase the Accuracy of Appraisals and the Usefulness of Feedback," in *Performance Appraisal: State of the Art in Practice*, Smither, J., Ed. (San Francisco, CA, Jossey-Bass, 1998).
6 Trompenaars, F., *Riding the Waves of Culture* (Burr Ridge, IL, Irwin, 1994).
7 Deming, W., *Out of Crises* (Cambridge, MA, MIT Press, 2000).
8 Cascio, W. & Aguinis, H., *Applied Psychology in Human Resource Management*, 6th ed. (Upper Saddle River, NJ, Pearson Prentice-Hall, 2005).
9 Lawler, Edward E., *Talent* (San Francisco, CA, Jossey-Bass, 2008).

Chapter 13

Managing Rewards

Base Pay

What you measure *and reward* you most surely will get more of.

What works is what fits.

Performance should be rewarded in a way that fits each organization's context and that fits both the nature of the work and the nature of the workforce being rewarded. As with performance management, utilizing the same guiding principles when deciding on how to reward different types of employees does not necessarily mean that using the same strategies for everyone is mandated.

Whether to utilize one rewards management strategy and one set of programs or many hinges on how well the strategy and programs fit the various types of employees in the organization. If a firm employs a large sales staff it may use variable pay as the key driver of performance for those employees. The same firm may use merit pay to reward its professional employees, long-term incentives that involve equity ownership to reward its management personnel and hourly wage rates as the only form of direct compensation to its operational and administrative support personnel. Some organizations will reward performance only at the individual level, while others may choose to use unit and organization-wide incentives that reward performance measured at the aggregated level as well. Increasingly organizations are seeking ways to reward performance at all three of these levels.

The principles underlying sound rewards management were discussed in Chapter 3. Guiding principles, once defined, can be used to formulate custom rewards strategies that are tailored to various types of employees. Chapters 4 through 11 discussed alternative strategies for rewarding different types of employees. Although many organizations use the same strategies, and even the same programs, to reward all of their employees, this may or may not be optimal.

Once the "best fit" approach for each category of employees is found, it may then be possible to use the same strategies and programs for multiple categories, or even for all employees. Very small organizations may use one set of programs, since having multiple programs requires administrative resources and capabilities. Organizations with relatively homogeneous workforces may also find using one set of programs to be advisable. One strategy and one set of programs is less likely to be appropriate for large, complex organizations with very diverse workforces.

This chapter and Chapter 14 will analyze how direct compensation strategies and programs used for different categories of employees can be integrated to produce the desired level of overall performance. This chapter addresses base pay management, and the next addresses variable compensation management. The balancing act between consistency and local fit is a challenging one when rewards are involved. The author has worked with organizations that have a single base pay structure and a single incentive program based on organizational performance. At the other end of the spectrum was a financial organization that had over 100 variable pay programs in place, with multiple base pay structures. Many different approaches can work. What works is what fits the context.

Managing Base Pay

Base pay is the major component of direct compensation for most employees. Sales personnel working strictly on commission and production employees rewarded largely or only through output-based incentives are an exception. Executives may also receive the majority of their direct compensation in the form of variable compensation. But as discussed in Chapter 3, base pay is what establishes the standard of living for most employees. And the base pay rate is to many employees a reflection of how the organization values what they do and how well they do it. The trend is for variable compensation to be used more broadly and as a larger component of direct compensation, but it rarely equals base pay in amount, except for some executives and sales personnel. There are several types of base pay systems. How each can be designed, implemented and administered for different types of employees will be discussed here.

Merit (Job-based) Pay

The most widely used approach to managing base pay is merit pay. As discussed in Chapter 3, most organizations establish a budget for adjusting base pay rates annually. The budget is based on a number of factors: 1) the organization's economic ability to pay; 2) competitor actions; and 3) the relationship between current rates of pay and competitive market levels. Budgets have averaged from 1–3% since 2007 in the U.S., according to the annual salary budget surveys conducted by WorldatWork, a professional association (WorldatWork.org). With budgets being so limited, it is a challenge to allocate the available resources equitably, competitively and in a manner that is acceptable to employees. It is that last requirement that impacts the pay-for-performance philosophy. Should outstanding performers receive 5%, satisfactory employees 2% and those not fully meeting standards 0%? Or should everyone receive the same percentage?

The "two-dimensional guide chart" approach was introduced in Chapter 3. It bases individual base pay adjustments on both current performance and the relationship of the current pay rate to the pay range. As explained there, this approach supports paying more for better performance. It also supports the notion that someone being paid near the top of the range (10–20% above market average) has less of a need for an increase than someone near the bottom of the range. Simple arithmetic tells us that the same dollar increase to people at differing positions in the range will result in different percentage increases. But the two-dimensional guide chart is based on the belief that someone high in the range should be performing at a higher level, in order to earn the high rate of pay, and may not need a significant increase. It also supports the notion that employees who are performing well but being paid low in the range are very susceptible to being lured away by a competitor: they are good and they are inexpensive. As a result, they should receive adjustments that move their pay rates closer to market averages relatively quickly.

The culture of an organization certainly will impact what the budget allocation principles will be. Additionally, the nature of the work and the workforce will have an impact. For example, hourly paid production or office workers may have jobs with limited discretion, making it unlikely that very large performance differences will occur. This may result in a narrow range of increase amounts between people. On the other hand, Bill Gates of Microsoft contends that their top software programmer is worth ten or more times as much as the one who ranks second. In that environment very large differences in reward amounts will be likely.

At the executive level, base pay is a much smaller percentage of direct compensation than it is at lower levels in the organization, since incentive programs make up a larger part of executive pay. For this reason the variations in base pay adjustments may actually fall in a narrower range than they do for mid-level managers and professional employees. For professional employees base pay adjustments driven by a merit pay system may be the only way the organization differentiates between employees. In these cases the difficulties faced in adequately rewarding the top performers when budgets are limited are magnified.

The condition of the economy and how well the organization is performing should be a consideration in establishing base pay adjustment budgets and in allocating budgeted amounts. In the late 1990s, conditions were good and budgets were larger. There was also a shortage of talent in some occupations, particularly in IT. Many organizations with a critical need to retain their IT personnel and to attract people with specific critical skills diverted a significant portion of their base pay adjustment budgets to IT. This resulted in increased guidelines for IT personnel that differed from those for other occupational groups considered to be less critical and/or less difficult to attract and retain. The 2002–07 period was back to the "talent war" and pay levels loosened up, at least for critical skills that were in short supply, such as engineers. Then came the downturn in 2007–08 and cost control became the immediate concern. Since then, turbulence has been continuous. Whether the next decade will be as changeable is debatable, but it seems prudent to prepare for cyclicality by implementing strategies that are robust and that will work fairly well in a number of possible futures.

The culture of the organization is another consideration in creating guidelines. If an organization wishes to move from having pay adjustments tied to longevity to having them tied more closely to performance it might modify its guide charts to support this change. Table 13.1 reflects a low to moderate differentiation between outstanding performers and those who meet expectations given a 3% increase budget. Table 13.2 allocates the same 3% budget differently, with larger increases going to the better performers. The "Percentage Rated" column represents the distribution of performance appraisal ratings. . . what percentage rated at each level.

Table 13.1 Salary Increases: Low Differentiation Based on Performance

Performance Rating	Percentage Rated	Position in Range		
		Lower Third	Middle Third	Upper Third
Outstanding	10%	7%	5%	3%
Significantly exceeds standards	20%	6%	4%	2%
Fully meets standards	65%	3.5%	2.5%	1.5%
Does not fully meet standards	5%	0–2%	0–1%	0%

An approach being used more frequently involves using the budget to fund a combination of base pay adjustments and cash performance awards. Table 13.3 illustrates this approach. The amount in the top row of each cell represents the base pay adjustment. The pattern of increase amounts is similar to the one used in the two-dimensional guide chart. But in this case 1% of the budget has been reserved for cash performance awards, which are indicated on the second line in each cell.

Since only 10% of employees are expected to be rated "outstanding," the 5% cash awards for them will cost 0.5% of payroll. Approximately 20% of employees are expected to be rated "Significantly exceeds standards," so the 2.5% cash awards for them will cost 0.5% of payroll. Hence the 1% carved out of base pay adjustments is converted into cash awards, and the base payroll going forward will be 1% less than it would have been if all the budget had been used for base pay increases. The expenditure for adjustments and cash awards in that year will have been the same as it would have been if all of the money had gone into increases, but the cash portion of it will have to be re-earned in future years. In difficult times the amount diverted from base pay increases to cash awards could be increased, perhaps to 1.5–2%. If there is a concern about increasing the base payroll at all, the entire budget could be delivered in cash awards, as illustrated in Table 13.4.

If the cash award portion is large there is a danger that employees performing at adequate levels will rebel at the extreme distinctions being made based on performance. This approach might also result in increases that vary more than the differences in performance warrant. For example, support personnel in jobs with limited discretion and/or impact on unit results may view the difference in rewards to be inappropriate. Another concern with this approach is that over time base pay levels will fall behind prevailing market

Table 13.2 Salary Increases: Greater Differentiation Based on Performance

Performance Rating	Percentage Rated	Position in Range		
		Lower Third	Middle Third	Upper Third
Outstanding	10%	10%	8%	6%
Significantly exceeds standards	20%	7%	5%	3%
Fully meets standards	65%	4%	2%	0%
Does not fully meet standards	5%	0	0	0

Table 13.3 Combination Salary Increase/Cash Award Guidelines

Performance Rating	Percentage Rated	Lower Third	Middle Third	Upper Third
Outstanding	10%	10%	8%	6%
		5%	5%	5%
Significantly exceeds standards	20%	7%	5%	3%
		2.5%	2.5%	2.5%
Fully meets standards	65%	4%	2%	0%
		0	0	0
Does not fully meet standards	5%	0	0	0
		0	0	0

rates, particularly for employees whose direct compensation is all in the form of base pay. However, if the organization is attempting to reduce fixed costs or realign pay rates that are above market, this approach may enable it to do so without depriving employees of any reward.

The use of cash awards in conjunction with base pay increases is a powerful way to amplify the pay-for-performance message. But it also can be tantamount to running higher voltages through old wires. If the performance management system is not sound and well accepted this approach should be used with caution. Using cash awards highlights differences in amounts allocated to individuals and it will raise emotions. Of course, it is folly to attempt to administer any merit pay program with an inadequate performance management system. In many cases people have accepted the way things work, albeit imperfectly. But they might withdraw that acceptance when the stakes are raised. Notice how the good will and casual attitudes at family penny ante poker games change when they become dollar limit games.

In fact, there are many prerequisites for any merit pay program to work well. The first is that jobs are appropriately valued, both internally and with respect to prevailing market rates. If the salary range, which represents an employee's salary potential, is not both internally equitable and externally competitive then that will be the dominant issue. If the performance standards for the job are not clearly communicated in advance, this will reduce the perception that the employee is being given a fair shot at performing well. If managers are not well trained in continuously measuring performance and providing feedback, this will frustrate employees (remember that the number one factor impacting employee satisfaction and effectiveness in the Gallup poll was "Knowing what is expected"). If managers do not determine the causes of good and poor performance and do not invest in employee development there will be a perception that employees are disposable parts. If managers do not honestly appraise performance, based on job-related behaviors and results, the system will not be effective. Finally, if a strong budgetary discipline is not in place managers may "go to bat" for their employees and either break the bank or rob other managers of resources. Once the rewards are clearly specified for performing at a given level the temptation to consider all of one's subordinates as "outstanding" is very strong. Most have heard managers contending "If they were not outstanding they could not work for me" or "To be an executive in this organization you have to be outstanding."

Using merit pay is more appropriate for some occupations than for others. The vast majority of professional employees can be included in a merit pay plan, while including support employees whose performance cannot vary substantially is much more difficult. As discussed in the chapters in Part 2, how well this approach will fit the different types of employees varies dramatically. Team members may be included in merit pay plans but

Table 13.4 Guide chart Allocating the Entire Budget to Cash Awards

Performance Rating	Lower Third of Range	Middle Third of Range	Upper Third of Range
Outstanding	9% cash	7% cash	5% cash
Significantly exceeds standards	5% cash	4% cash	3% cash
Fully meets standards	3% cash	2% cash	1% cash
Does not fully meet standards	None–2%	None	None

will often have a smaller percentage of their rewards in the form of base pay increases tied to individual performance, with team incentives being added on. Merit pay can motivate competitive behavior, while cooperative behavior is typically needed in teams. Research and development personnel may work on very different types of challenges, some of which are insoluble. Trying to reliably differentiate between individuals based on their performance when they work full time on a multiple-year pure research project may be untenable. And attempting to base salary actions on individual performance differences may be unacceptable in some national cultures.

Given all of these obstacles, it is not surprising that some organizations have given up on their merit pay plans being effective. Unfortunately, they have no viable alternatives in most cases. The vast majority of organizations continue to use merit pay, with all of its imperfections, but they do other things as well. For example, they use person-based pay programs for those employees where it fits the nature of the work and of the workforce.

Person-based Pay

There are many different manifestations of the concept of paying the person for what they bring to the organization, rather than what they happen to be doing at a given point in time. In the late 1990s there was an outburst of claims that a "new" approach had been found and that it was "competency-based pay." The euphoria has since declined because many realized potential (competence) constitutes potential not performance. However, the enormous and disproportionate coverage in the literature that this "new" approach using competencies received did something that was needed. It increased awareness that behaviors are a legitimate basis for measuring performance. Unfortunately, paying people solely based on what they could do rather than on what they produce can bankrupt the organization. Unrealized potential is hard to turn into profits. And given the legal environment in the U.S., it is very risky to differentiate between people on any basis other than job-related results. Yet there are approaches to reconciling what seems to be a contradiction between paying for qualifications and paying for results.

Notwithstanding the claims of sure-cure discoveries, there are three sound approaches to tying base pay to what people have in the way of qualifications that have worked for decades: 1) skill-based; 2) knowledge-based; and 3) credential-based pay administration. These approaches were introduced in Chapter 3 but will be elaborated on here.

Skill-based Pay

Skill-based pay makes the base rate contingent on how many job-related skills the employee has learned, the level of skill mastery or a combination of both. For example, if a work unit requires that in aggregate the workforce must possess five skills (or skill sets), and management believes it is most effective to have most or all employees completely cross-skilled, then pay might be based on the number of skills a person has mastered. Someone entering the unit would start at the zero-skill rate and then progress to the five-skill rate when mastery had been demonstrated in all five skills.

Another type of system links together related roles into a career management system. Figure 13.1 illustrates the progression of an entry-level operating support employee through successively more skilled roles. Starting as an operator the employee can progress his or her pay rate as specific skills are mastered. Once all operator skills are acquired the person is at the top pay rate and can then move into other occupational classifications, where further pay progression is forthcoming once the requirements are met.

Experience has shown that average pay rates will usually go up under skill-based systems—good news for the employees. But if management utilizes the people well the staffing level can usually be reduced. There is less wasted time, owing to the flexibility of the workforce, which can shift tasks to fit the workflow. Therefore, total payroll may not increase, or may even go down—good news for the organization. So skill-based pay can stimulate productivity and help control costs. But it is critical to be sure the context fits skill-based pay.

Some cultures reward longevity rather than performance or job mastery, and this is often difficult to overcome. In such a culture skill-based pay is difficult to administer well, since the mindset of managers (pay for longevity) may create a reluctance to bypass individuals who do not master skills, particularly if this persists for an extended period. Moving relative "rookies" past "veterans," even for the right reasons, is difficult. It is also difficult to retrofit a skill-based plan into a unit where longevity pay has prevailed, since people may be paid at levels that are inconsistent with their skill mastery. For this reason many of the successful skill-based pay systems have been installed in start-up entities, such as new plants.

There are other obstacles as well. There must be some "test" that determines skill mastery and there must be someone willing to administer that test and to stand behind it. Many skills are difficult to test directly, particularly in white-collar and service-related jobs, and the test often boils down to someone's judgment. First-line supervisors are reluctant to do the testing, given that everyone they fail will be miserable to be around. But if they pass everyone the system will not be viewed as being credible.

Skill-based pay systems fit some employee categories better than others. This approach is most often used for operational and support jobs, since the work is more likely to be well defined and what incumbents need to do their jobs effectively is relatively stable. Production jobs lend themselves most readily to this approach, whether the employees work on sequential operations or in teams. Some applications are found in the office environment, particularly when the work involves producing a defined result using operating procedures.

Knowledge-based Pay

Knowledge-based pay systems are most often used for professional employees. These systems typically utilize career ladders, which identify expertise levels within the same occupation or discipline. For example, analysts at all levels of expertise perform work of the same nature, but do so at varying levels of knowledge, skill and responsibility (see Table 13.5).

An associate analyst may be defined as a person possessing a BS degree in a related field and having 0–2 years of systems experience, while a senior analyst is expected to have an MS or equivalent technical training and 5–8 years of relevant experience. There will be other differences as well, to include the complexity of work they are expected to deal with, the amount of latitude they are given and the impact of their work on the unit effectiveness. This occupational/job "family" represents a career progression through which employees move, based on their development. Progression through the levels happens at differing speeds, based on individual abilities and the manner in which they gain command of the knowledge in their field.

Timing	Pay Rate (relative to start rate)	Qualifications Required
	Operator	
Entry	1.00	Basic qualifications for entry
6 months	1.05 or termination/probation	Progress/performance OK
12 months	1.10 or termination	Basic operation skill set
18 months	1.15 or 6-month extension	Progress/performance OK
2 years	1.20 or termination	Advanced operation skill set
	Operator/set-up person (career branch A)	
2½ years	1.25 or stay at 1.20 (operator)	Progress/performance OK
3 years	1.35 or 6-month extension	Basic set-up skill set
4 years	1.50 or stay at basic level	Advanced set-up skill set
	Maintenance mechanic (career branch B)	
2½ years	1.25 or stay at 1.20 (operator)	Progress/performance OK
3 years	1.35 or 6-month extension	Basic maintenance skill set
4 years	1.50 or stay at basic level	Maintenance mechanic skills
5 years	1.70 or stay at 1.50	Progress/performance OK
6 years	2.00 or stay at 1.50	Master mechanic skills

Note: Those achieving advanced set-up who progress into the mechanic branch will receive an additional 0.25 increment for basic mechanic skills (to 1.75), a 0.50 increment for mechanic skills (to 2.00) and a 0.75 increment for master mechanic skills (to 2.25).

Policy provision: Entry into advanced set-up and master mechanic classifications requires the unit to demonstrate an operational need for the staffing mix resulting.

Figure 13.1 Example of a skill-based system for operational support personnel

If the organization uses a single salary structure the levels within each family can each be assigned to a job grade, based on relative internal equity and/or external market rates. The pay range for the grade assigned to each level becomes the range of pay opportunity for incumbents of that level, just as it does for other jobs. When an employee has developed to the extent that they more correctly belong in the next level, this can be treated as a promotion, since the grade will be higher. Some argue that this is so similar to a job-based system using merit pay that it should be treated as such. The key distinction, however, is that employees are classified and progress based on their level of expertise, rather than on their specific job assignment. In effect, their pay opportunity is based on what they are capable of doing, rather than what they happen to be doing at the moment. For example, a senior engineer may function as a support person on one project and then as the lead person on the next—but will always be a senior engineer. If the organization fails to pay incumbents based on their qualifications they may find another home.

The vast majority of scientific, engineering and professional occupations lend themselves to this approach. Accounting/finance, legal, information technology, purchasing and human resources are examples of disciplines with a defined body of knowledge that people formally train for and work within for most or all of their careers. As a result, their

Table 13.5 Analyst Career Ladder

Job Criteria	Associate Analyst	Analyst	Senior Analyst
Nature of work (type; complexity; variety; difficulty; scope)	Performs varied assignments involving routine analytical work.	Performs a wide variety of relatively complex analytical work, ensuring schedule, budget and performance requirements are met. Must be able to perform multiple assignments simultaneously. May direct phases of a single revenue-producing project. May prepare customer quotations on routine jobs with clearly defined protocols.	Performs the full range of analytical work in a given area, including the most complex tests, ensuring schedule, budget and performance requirements are met and that the technical quality meets standards. Evaluates customer requests, determines testing requirements and prepares project quotations.
Latitude exercised/ direction received (authority; nature and frequency of supervision received)	Under general supervision, works with established protocols, seeking assistance with unusual situations or when problems occur. Work is reviewed for technical soundness before it is sent to customer.	Under general direction, works with established protocols, seeking assistance with complex/difficult problems. Work may be sent to customer prior to its technical review.	Works independently with the full range of established protocols in a given area. Solves complex and difficult problems, assisting others as required. Work may be sent to customer prior to its technical review.
Creativity and ingenuity required	Exercises judgment in using defined procedures, in order to determine appropriate course of action.	Exercises discretion in selecting protocols to use. May recommend revisions to established protocols.	Develops improvements to established protocols and may create new methods and processes that improve productivity or expand capabilities.
Responsibility for interpersonal contacts (nature; level; frequency; impact)	Limited customer contact, involving the exchange of information and answering questions. Interacts with peers and internal support personnel to coordinate work.	Contacts customers to define scope of work, to clarify information and to resolve issues.	Develops customer relationships to expand range of services provided and to maintain high level of satisfaction.

Responsibility for assets and information	Protects confidential information and proprietary processes. Handles materials and company equipment in a responsible and efficient manner.	Protects confidential information and proprietary processes. Handles materials and company equipment in a responsible and efficient manner.	Protects confidential information and proprietary processes. Handles materials and company equipment in a responsible and efficient manner.
Responsibility for the work of others	May provide direction to support staff and technicians.	Provides technical direction to support staff and technicians; assists in training analysts.	Provides technical direction to less experienced analysts and assists in their training.
Potential impact (costs; quality; customer satisfaction; productivity)	Poor-quality work or failure to obtain results may cause delays to schedules and require the expenditure of additional resources.	Erroneous decisions may cause loss of revenue, excessive costs and/or customer dissatisfaction.	Erroneous decisions typically cause loss of revenue, excessive costs and/or customer dissatisfaction.
Education/formal training and work experience required (type; level; duration)	BS or MS in science/engineering or equivalent relevant experience.	BS in science/engineering plus 4–5 years of specifically related experience or MS plus 2–3 years of experience or PhD with no experience. Experience should be in performing analytical testing with sophisticated equipment. Material characterization experience highly desirable.	BS in science/engineering plus 8–10 years of specifically related experience or MS plus 5–8 years of experience or PhD plus 2–5 years of experience. Experience should be in performing analytical testing with sophisticated equipment. Material characterization experience highly desirable.

knowledge and expertise in their field grow over time and become the metric for shaping their roles in their organizations. What an engineer (or other professional) actually does over time typically varies. It is therefore difficult to use a "job-based" system to assign job grades and pay ranges and to make employees feel current duties are the appropriate metric for gauging their worth. In addition, professionals tend to be oriented more to their fields and their growth in those fields than to their employing organization. This argues strongly for the use of career metrics that are oriented to that field. The use of merit pay is still a viable approach for administering salaries within the pay ranges.

Credential-based Pay

A third person-based approach is typically not a stand-alone system, but rather recognizes formal credentials as a basis for impacting pay and career progression. Licenses, professional certifications, admission to the Bar and other such formal designations can act to do several things: 1) limit who can do certain kinds of work, thereby acting as a gate-keeping device to control occupational entry; 2) control who can be promoted to higher levels; and 3) act as the basis for paying differentials or lump sums that acknowledge the credential. An example of requiring credentials to perform work is attorneys, who must be members of the Bar if they are to represent the organization in court. Another is engineers, who must be licensed as professional engineers to sign off on structural designs.

How the acquisition of credentials impacts pay depends on the circumstances. As previously mentioned, the possession of the credential may result in a promotion. Or acquiring the credential may not result in a classification change, but instead trigger a base pay increase or a lump sum bonus. Some organizations require incumbents to use the credential (or the skills the credential recognizes) in order to maintain the additional pay. If that will be the policy it is advisable to treat the added reward as a contingent differential, which does not become a permanent part of base pay, to be earned only when appropriate.

Administering Base Pay Programs

Large organizations and those with occupationally diverse workforces may well choose several of the approaches to base pay rate determination already discussed. Although it could be argued that simplicity dictates using one approach for everyone, it may not be practical. It may be more effective to administer different programs for different groups, since programs that fit each of the groups can be adopted. Sales and executive personnel have traditionally been covered by different compensation programs. As already mentioned, many organizations use person-based approaches for professionals, even though they may use job-based systems for other employees. The differences will usually occur in the method used to define and value jobs or roles and to determine the range of pay opportunity. When it comes to administering individual pay rates, merit pay is the dominant choice, used for most or all employees.

There are a number of administrative issues that must be dealt with no matter which pay determination choice is used: 1) timing of pay actions; 2) administrative controls utilized; and 3) evaluating program effectiveness.

Timing of Pay Actions

Pay actions most often occur either on a single (focal) date or on anniversary dates throughout the year. Although there are arguments for both approaches the vast majority of organizations utilize the focal date approach. It enables managers to make pay action decisions at a time when they best know how well the organization or unit did, how well the employee did, how the performance of employees compared to that of others and what resources are available for pay actions. The biggest advantage of using a focal date is that all decisions are made at the same time, making it easier for a manager to compare across employees, relative to both performance appraisals and pay actions. The single best argument for anniversary dates is the workload that a manager may experience at one point in time. But this is a weak justification, since no manager can know the performance of more than a few employees well enough to do an accurate appraisal, and others will probably be involved, reducing the workload.

It is important that the timing of the performance appraisal and the timing of the salary action are coordinated. If an employee is to believe pay is tied to performance there must be a visible connection. Long periods of time between the performance review and the salary action diminish the connection. Lawler and others have used research to establish that employees view an appraisal as incomplete unless the consequences are made known as a part of the review process.[1] In a national research laboratory I found that they had separated performance appraisal (focal) and pay determination (anniversary). When I asked how they could assume that an employee who had been appraised in December would be performing that same way when their anniversary date came around in November, the response was that they expected managers to update their view of the employee's performance when making the pay recommendations. While doing a stealth survey I found managers looked at me as if I just got off a space ship from another planet . . . they wondered who would repeat the work involved in appraisals and believed that people's performance did not vary much. Making this point to executive management resulted in performance appraisals and pay actions being both shifted to a focal date.

Administrative Controls Utilized

Pay structures and pay increase budgets are the two most common control devices used for base pay administration. As described earlier when discussing merit pay, it is critical to evaluate where pay rates fall within the pay ranges, in order to determine if the organization is acting in a manner consistent with its pay policy. Of particular concern to an organization are pay rates that fall below or above the pay range minimums or maximums, respectively.

Pay structures are the framework within which base pay rates are administered. As discussed in Chapter 3, pay structures consist of *job grades* (levels), into which jobs are placed, based on internal equity, and *pay ranges*, which are based on prevailing market levels of pay. There is no one best answer to the question "How many structures?" Some organizations use a single pay structure that covers all employees (with a common exception being direct sales personnel and senior executives). Most organizations have two to five structures, depending on their size, their complexity and their management philosophy.

Those having two structures often group executives, managers and professionals in one structure and all other employees in a second structure. But there are some that separate administrative support (office) personnel from "blue-collar" (plant/field) jobs. And if an organization is geographically dispersed, there are often pay structures for each location, to reflect differences in prevailing market rates.

There are two principal design issues relating to pay structures: the number of grades and the width of the pay ranges. The author managed several large national compensation surveys, and the large databases (e.g., 500,000 rates from 2,000 organizations in an IT survey) provided the data for determining what the typical difference was between levels within a management structure, professional career ladder and support personnel job families. It was found that the range midpoint differences between grades including senior management levels tended to be 25–35%, between professional levels to be 12–20% and between levels in support job families to be 7–8%. There will be significant differences between organizations, depending on how many layers there are in management structures and job families. In relatively flat organizations the differences between management levels will be larger, while in hierarchical structures the differences will be smaller. As discussed in Chapter 5, it is typical for professional career ladders to have three to five levels defined, excluding supervisory and management jobs, but the author has worked with organizations having more levels of individual contributors in a career ladder. The number of levels in a support job family can also vary wildly. One state government had nine levels of clerk/secretary, and although it was very difficult to tell the difference between levels when reading the job descriptions they seemed to be able to function with this approach. The principal justification was that employees felt rewarded by being "promoted" frequently. In today's world of small budgets the cost of "promotions" would exceed the budget and certainly not leave any funds for moving people up through the ranges.

The width of pay ranges should also vary, depending at least in part on the number of grades an organization uses. In the state government with nine support levels people tend to be promoted every one to two years, making wide ranges unnecessary, since no one is in a grade for very long. At the other extreme, organizations that have "broadbanded" their structure can have ranges of 100–200%. Pay ranges are principally control parameters, and having ranges of much more than 50% seems to render them useless as a control device. In fact, many of the organizations adopting broadbanding created "zones" or "sectors" within each band, with control parameters set for each. How this differs from a traditional pay structure is unclear. The zeal for broadbanding has all but disappeared due to organization's discovering the problems associated with administering them.

The most common approach is to have narrower ranges (25–35%) for unskilled and semiskilled jobs, since there is typically only so much an organization is willing to pay for this type of work. And since performance is unlikely to vary significantly there is less of a need to differentiate between incumbents of jobs within a grade. In fact, single rate structures or two rate (probationary rate and job rate) structures may be used for these jobs. For management and professional jobs it is more typical to have ranges of about 50%, since people may stay within the same level for much longer periods and wide variations in job mastery and performance level are more likely in these roles. And such differences need to be adequately recognized with base pay level differences if employees are to accept the system.

It is necessary to ensure that the number of job grades and the width of pay ranges enable an organization to effectively administer base pay rates within the ranges. As previously mentioned, ranges can be somewhat narrower if a large number of grades are used, since the incumbents will move through them more rapidly. Flat organization structures with fewer grades may require the use of wider pay ranges.

Administering individual pay rates within the established pay ranges can be challenging. Employees will expect to be paid at least the minimum, and the organization will attempt to avoid paying above the range maximums. But circumstances often produce below-minimum and above-maximum instances. Pay rates below the range minimums have a relatively simple solution: raise them. However, the cost of this option is often outside the organization's ability to pay. During times of rapid market escalation much of the budget is used up just keeping people at their current position in the range, since the ranges must be adjusted significantly in order to keep them competitive.

The late 1990s saw average market rates for people with certain information technology skills escalate dramatically, often by more than budgetary constraints would allow organizations to increase their pay rates. The organizations that limited range adjustments so that actual rates would not fall below the minimum found during the next year that their pay structures had fallen even further behind market. This dilemma could have been resolved for many organizations through the use of outside contractors, to perform the "heavy lifting" associated with implementing new network systems that required short-supply and expensive skills. Since conversions to new systems are primarily a one-time effort, this approach could have limited the degree to which many organizations would have had to compete for these scarce skills, and this would have reduced the amount of temporary salary inflation. This experience has caused a lot of employers to question whether they must always pay fully at market rates, no matter the cost, and perhaps to look more favorably at developing current employees through training as an alternative to competing in unbalanced labor markets.

Pay rates that are above the range maximums are a much more difficult situation to correct than pay rates below minimums. Base pay is only flexible in an upward direction, since cutting someone's wage or salary is typically viewed as an extreme act of aggression. So rates that are significantly above a maximum are going to take time to fix, and the fix is often difficult. Freezing the base pay of an employee who has gotten increases every year for an extended period is a tough thing to do, particularly if the employee is performing at or above expectations. It makes things easier if the organization has had the "We pay for performance, not give increases for performance" discussion described earlier. But it still is a difficult situation when it occurs. An employee who knows their pay is frozen, perhaps for more than one year, has no economic incentive to perform at the highest level possible, and in fact may be motivated to behave in a manner that best protects the job and the income stream, rather than taking risks that might improve performance.

Increasingly organizations are adopting performance-based cash awards for people at or over their range maximum, to motivate them to sustain high levels of performance. An example might be: no award for someone who meets standards, a modest cash award for someone who significantly exceeds standards and a large cash award for outstanding performance. The base pay rate is not affected, and as the pay ranges are adjusted the maximum will catch the pay rate, assuming the person stays long enough. The author installed a new pay plan in an investment services firm. When the pay ranges were finalized the pay rate of a long-service employee was found to be 30% over the range maximum. Given that the employee was already middle-aged and that structures rarely move more than 4–5% even in the wildest times, it was unlikely the maximum would have caught during the employee's working lifetime. There is no easy way to deal with situations such as this. To prevent them organizations should consider the consequences of not taking action to adjust salaries when situations occur that would cause a pay rate to be substantially above the range maximum. Often, someone who fails in a management position is moved back in the ranks but no adjustment is made to the pay. Although this seems to be the humane approach it creates difficult situations and this should be anticipated.

Budgets are a useful way of controlling overall pay levels, since they limit the increase to the fixed payroll. Unfortunately, they raise significant administrative issues. The most common practice is to settle on an amount (e.g., 3% of payroll) that can be used for increases. This amount may or may not include promotional increases. One approach for allocating the budget is to give each unit the same percentage of its current payroll. But often there will be large differences across organizational units relative to where pay rates fall within the pay structure. A unit that has experienced considerable turnover may have a large percentage of its employees in the lower part of the range, given that they are still new and learning their jobs. But if that unit has only 3% of its relatively small payroll it will have a difficult time funding the larger percentage increases prescribed by merit increase guidelines such as those illustrated earlier. On the other hand, another unit with a mature workforce may have most of its employees in the middle or upper part of the range and need only a smaller percentage of current pay. But that unit will have a larger *dollar* pool, since 3% of its larger payroll produces a bigger fund. So management is faced with giving one unit inadequate funds relative to need while overfunding another. Expecting the overfunded unit to offer some of its budget to the ailing unit voluntarily is seriously delusional, so some type of correction is called for.

A compa-ratio is a measure that expresses current pay rates as a percentage of range midpoints. Individuals paid at the midpoint of their range have a compa-ratio is 1.0, while someone at the minimum of a 50% range would have a compa-ratio of 0.8 and someone at maximum a compa-ratio of 1.2. This measure is generated in most HR information system packages, since it is a handy way of monitoring actual pay rates against intent (range midpoints). It can be calculated at the unit level as well. This measure can be used to adjust the out-of-line budget allocations just discussed. If the allocated 3% fund for each unit were to be divided by the unit compa-ratio, this would result in an allocation better fitted to "need" and would avoid asking for voluntary give-ups of funds. Because units with compa-ratios of less than 1.0 will have their funds increased and those with compa-ratios greater than 1.0 will have theirs decreased a greater balance with need for increases can be achieved. Of course, the argument will be made that people in the unit with the high salaries are better performers and should get larger increases, and that needs to be considered and dealt with.

Budgets are certainly affected by the organization's ability to pay, and may conflict with what the organization feels it should spend on increases. But this does not diminish the usefulness of having policies and programs that incorporate sound principles, since they will result in the optimal allocation of what is available.

Another issue facing many organizations is that average base pay levels in the market move at different rates, making it difficult to maintain internal equity while responding to market levels. An example would be an organization employing large numbers of engineers who are in different engineering disciplines. Over the last three decades the relative averages for electrical, mechanical, nuclear, chemical and civil engineers have fluctuated relative to each other. One of the national research laboratories the author worked with had a single career ladder for engineers, and each level within the ladder was assigned to a grade and pay range. This was to preserve internal equity. However, the lab adjusted the *control points* for each discipline separately, based on movement in market averages. The control point within a pay range is the rate that a fully competent and fully satisfactory performer should be paid on average. The range midpoint is often the control point, at least in aggregate. However, an organization can set the control point above or below the range midpoint, in order to adjust pay targets to meet prevailing market conditions. The variable control points were used by the research laboratory to guide base pay actions each year, by basing each individual's increase on both their performance rating and the position of their current pay rate relative to their control point, rather than to the midpoint of the range for their grade. This enabled the organization to move salaries more aggressively for those disciplines with rapidly escalating market averages and to moderate increases for those disciplines experiencing slower growth on average.

Customized versus Consistent Base Pay Programs

There are organizations with a single base pay structure and common policies regulating how individual pay rates for all employees will be set and adjusted. Given the diversity of local contexts described in the chapters in Part 2, this would seem to limit the degree to which whatever system is used will be a good fit to the diverse occupations. Yet having a single system that is administered centrally can send the message that everyone is treated equivalently—not identically, but equivalently. In highly structured, centralized organizations that are focused on internal equity this approach would probably be more feasible than it would be in organizations that have very flat or more flexible structures and that move people in and out of the organization frequently. Hierarchical organizations typically move people vertically through established career ladders, making internal equity a major concern, and the base pay structure is a primary tool for ensuring internal equity is maintained. However, given the increased occupational diversity in workforces, local customization may be the better choice even for the most rigidly structured organizations. The best strategy is most often a mix of consistency and customization.

Application of Principles: Chapter 13

You are considering a consulting partnership with two large consulting firms specializing in rewards management. While discussing philosophy about how to manage rewards, you find there are basic differences between the two firms. One has standardized systems that they use for all clients while the other develops custom systems for each client.

The one using one set of systems believes that employees want to believe that everyone is on a level playing field and that differentiation actuates the "grass is greener on the other side" mentality. They believe this raises suspicions that internal equity does not exist and that employees will not feel they are equally respected and valued. They also contend that using one approach makes their work more efficient and their consultants only need to understand one kind of system.

The firm that customizes strategies and program design to fit different parts of the organization and different types of employees believes this approach recognizes that the variations in the role of employees, the nature of the work they do and their beliefs about how they should be measured and rewarded mandate differentiation. Because of the knowledge required to define an organization's context, consider a number of alternative systems and select the best one for that client. Consider that the firm only hires experienced people with a track record that confirms they are capable of using their methodology.

List what you believe to be the advantages and disadvantages of each of the approaches and how different types of organizations might better fit each. You should refer back to your response to the managing performance issue presented at the end of Chapter 12. Do you feel the same way for both performance management and rewards management? Why?

Note

1 Lawler, E., *Pay and Organization Development* (Reading, MA, Addison-Wesley, 1983).

Chapter 14

Managing Rewards
Variable Compensation

What you measure *and reward* you most surely will get more of.

What works is what fits.

Variable compensation was defined in Chapter 3 as direct compensation that does not become a permanent part of base pay and which may vary in amount from period to period. Other names for variable compensation include: variable pay, incentive compensation, incentives, bonuses, commissions, cash awards and lump sums. Variable compensation can be short-term (one year or less) or based on long-term performance (over one year). "Incentives" are plans that have predetermined criteria and standards, as well as understood policies for determining and allocating rewards. "Bonuses" are awards delivered at the end of the period, based on a subjective judgment as to the quality of performance and the rewards that are warranted.

Variable compensation is a significant element of the direct compensation package for a growing number of organizations. There is a pronounced trend towards more organizations using variable pay, for these organizations to expand eligibility, and for them to increase the prominence of variable pay in the total direct compensation package. Since 2007–8, the labor market in the U.S. has been turbulent, as have the economic realities faced by most organizations. Revenues provide the resources to increase pay and revenues have been erratic for many organizations. As has been discussed earlier, aligning revenues and costs is a critical element of prudent management and since base pay and benefits tend to be fixed costs the erratic revenue patterns have caused organizations to downsize, often losing talent that would be needed in the future. Given these realities it is surprising that there has not been a major shift in the balance between compensation elements that are fixed to elements that can vary as revenues vary. One of the advantages that organizations in many Asian countries have over U.S. organizations is that they have historically had significant profit/performance sharing programs in place, enabling them to hold the line on staffing levels during revenue downturns rather than losing valued talent through downsizing. But a significant shift between fixed cost and variable cost compensation programs has not shown up in surveys.

Characteristics of Variable Compensation

Variable compensation differs fundamentally in several ways from other forms of compensation, such as base pay and benefits. The advantages of variable over fixed cost forms of compensation include:

- *Economics*: The conversion of what have been fixed costs to variable costs can be very beneficial to an organization. Variable pay awards do not compound the way base pay adjustments do, thereby slowing the escalation of pay rates over time. Assuming variable pay is tied to performance, it both allocates awards more optimally and is contingent on the organization's economic ability to pay. Finally, variable pay plans can be customized to fit different business units, providing a localized customization to the unit's ability to pay and creating a focus on its specific objectives.

- *Competitive practice*: Variable pay programs can be an effective tool for attracting and retaining critical skills, as well as high performers. Since the existence of a variable pay component in the compensation package offers less of a guarantee, but more potential income opportunity, this type of package will attract those confident of their ability to perform well and willing to do so. Leveraging the organization's strengths via variable pay plans is another opportunity: an organization experiencing rapid stock price escalation can include a heavy dose of stock options or grants in its plans, thereby giving it a competitive advantage. The flexibility associated with variable pay plans can enable the organization to emulate the best in its industry in order to stay competitive, which is often not possible with base pay or benefits.

- *Motivation*: Variable compensation has more motivational potential than base pay adjustments. Defining objectives, criteria and standards enables the organization to provide a sharp focus on its priorities, and to do so at every level. Variable pay awards act as reinforcement for those succeeding and provide a scorecard to enable people to continuously evaluate results. To the extent that people are provided with a "shared destiny" using group incentives, there can be a strong motivation to support each other and to work cooperatively rather than competing in a dysfunctional manner. Variable pay plans can be a tool in organizational initiatives to promote high levels of performance at individual, group and organization-wide levels.

- *Communication*: Variable pay, particularly if designed as an incentive, is one of the strongest signals an organization can send to its people as to what is important. Through the continual measurement of results, high-quality feedback can be provided, enabling people to know how they are doing. By making employees eligible for variable pay awards, it sends the message that what they do counts and that the organization is willing to show its appreciation tangibly. Finally, the criteria used in variable pay plans can promote the importance of mission attainment and of doing so in a manner that is consistent with the organization's values.

- *Other*: There are other reasons for considering variable pay. The plans can be used to communicate and direct a change from an entitlement culture to a performance culture, as well as to promote employee engagement. Variable pay can also provide a sense of ownership, even for organizations not able or willing to use stock or share equity, since emotional ownership can produce results even though financial ownership is not possible. By balancing the definition of performance to include both the short-term and the long-term it is possible to elicit a balanced perspective. Short-term maximization at the expense of long-term optimization is a danger that is fueled by having all rewards tied to short-term performance, which many organizations do. Finally, the most compelling reason for using variable pay is that it works. Research has demonstrated that some human resource programs and initiatives produce a significant impact on performance in organizations (as measured by factors such as quality, productivity, speed, customer satisfaction and unwanted turnover). The two initiatives that are consistently shown to produce statistically significant positive results are linking pay to performance and using variable pay.[1]

There are potential difficulties associated with administering variable compensation. Budgeting for variable pay requires more planning and the use of scenarios to determine whether costs at every level of performance are acceptable. It is also much more difficult to measure the competitiveness of the total compensation package. Unlike base pay levels, variable compensation levels vary dramatically for some occupations and in some industries, transforming the "prevailing market average direct compensation" into a broad range that varies, rather than a fixed point. This makes it necessary to decide the mix between base and variable that both fits the organizations needs and is accepted by employees as being fair and appropriate.

And variable pay does not fit an entitlement culture, since it is not a career annuity like a base pay increase. It must be re-earned during each measurement period. For organizations that have used all base pay packages, it is difficult to get employees to accept that going forward they cannot consider the current year earnings as a stable base upon which to establish their standard of living. Contingent income presents real challenges in day-to-day living, particularly with processes such as applying for a home mortgage. For this reason it is often prudent to ensure that earnings do not vary excessively, particularly for lower-income people with less discretionary income.

Since variable compensation plans are usually based on defined measures there is a need to make all performance criteria, measures and standards clear and defensible to all parties at interest. But as more employees operate in a service capacity, with no physical product that can be counted or weighed, the task of getting everyone to agree about what really happened during a performance period is increasingly difficult. When there are significant cash awards at stake, the emotions run even higher.

Deciding to use variable compensation for the first time is a big step. Each organization must ensure it will fit the context within which it operates. The potential advantages of using variable pay can be attractive, but the potential disadvantages should promote caution. Culture is a major consideration when considering variable compensation, and a strong "one big happy family" philosophy can make it difficult to differentiate between individuals and groups when passing out rewards. It is also a challenge for managers to look employees in the eye and defend that the rewards were correctly based on current period performance. An effective variable pay plan has two characteristics: 1) it pays off when it should; and 2) it does not pay off when it should not. When either of these principles is violated the plan's effectiveness will atrophy rapidly. If the culture works against differentiating in this manner, caution is advisable.

The strategy of the organization and the resources it has available should also be carefully considered. For example, if short-term financial results are going to take a back seat to developing new products via investments in research the impact on an annual profit-sharing plan may be viewed as unfair by employees, even though this strategy will help to ensure they remain employed over the long run.

Finally, the fit between variable compensation strategy and the other components of total compensation strategy and of the human resource strategy should be considered. The type of person being recruited, how they will be developed, how their role in the organization will be defined and their performance in that role measured and the nature of the indirect compensation package must all be considered when deciding what role, if any, variable compensation should play.

Where Variable Compensation Plans Fit

The types of variable compensation plans can be categorized by the level at which performance is defined, measured and rewarded (individual, group or organization-wide). They can also be differentiated by the timeframe associated with measuring and rewarding performance (short term or long term). Finally, they can be classified according to the form of award (cash, equity or recognition). Not all plans fit all types of employees. It is therefore necessary to consider the nature of the work and the nature of the workforce when deciding whether to use variable compensation. The chapters in Part II addressed the application of variable pay to different categories of employees. This chapter will address the design, implementation and administration of variable pay plans.

Individual Plans

When individual performance is the focus there are several variable pay approaches that motivate and reward at the individual level. The oldest type of individual incentive plan is the output-based (piece rate) plan that rewards productivity. Another type of output plan is the sales commission, which ties pay to the volume of sales produced by an individual. Anyone who has seen the classic *I Love Lucy* episode with Lucy and Ethel on the candy assembly line or Charlie Chaplin in *Modern Times* may view piece rate systems as exploitative, but where output is under the control of the individual and where quality can be controlled this type of plan can be highly motivating and can produce a direct link between pay and performance. Although most frequently used in production environments, output plans are also found in white collar settings where the work is production-like, such as claims processing in insurance or proof operations in banking. The key to success is being able to measure output accurately and to ensure that the individual is able to control output. If material availability, machine downtime or dependence on others creates issues it complicates gaining acceptance that the plan is fair.

Most output-based plans call for the payment of a base rate, with incentive pay kicking in above some threshold level of production that represents a point at which the employee has earned the base rate. Very often, the incentive rate escalates as the output level rises, to reflect that further improvement becomes more difficult the better performance is. A major concern of organizations using this approach should be the impact on the quality of the work product. Typically, there are established quality standards, and failing to meet them can result in deductions from output credited. If quality defects are a major problem the failure to sustain the required quality level may result in the loss of variable pay awards altogether. Producing a high volume of junk does not serve and organization.

Basing variable pay on the attainment of specific objectives is a widely used approach. This is often termed the "management by objectives" approach. The objectives can be quantitative, qualitative or time-based, and multiple objectives can be used. The most difficult measurement challenges are encountered when attempting to set objectives at equivalent levels of difficulty across units and occupations, as well as identifying objectives that both are under the control of the individual and can be objectively evaluated. One approach to making the difficulty of goals across individuals and units relatively equivalent is to apply the scoring method used in Olympic diving. Competitors are scored by considering both the degree of difficulty and the quality of execution. There are Olympic standards for the difficulty of the dives attempted, and these often do not exist in organizations, but the concept can still be employed. Management judgment enters into all significant decisions about performance. By training managers to negotiate the standards for goal difficulty and goal execution with employees in advance of the performance period the "scores" given to employees can be made to be as fair as possible. This approach also gives the employees more latitude in deciding which goals they adopt, rather than grudgingly accepting (on the surface) the goals management dictates.

There also are challenges associated with assigning relative importance weights to goals, as well as keeping track of progress against expectations on an interim basis, so individuals can keep score and redirect when appropriate. There are significant benefits associated with weighting multiple goals. Employees can set their priorities with knowledge of which results are most critical, providing them with latitude, and at the same time communicating the consequences of success or failure relative to each goal.

Merit pay can be objective based and can result in cash awards, rather than exclusively determining base pay adjustments, as described in Chapter 13. The cash awards are determined based on the performance appraisal rating, while base pay adjustments are tied to both the performance rating and the relative position of the employee's base pay in the range for the job. This approach can introduce variable pay without necessitating the creation of a separate variable pay plan, although it puts more pressure on the quality of the appraisal, since cash is at stake. It also mandates that both base pay adjustments and variable awards are based on the same criteria and standards, which may not serve the needs of the organization. The primary purpose for wanting to use incentives may be that they can focus employees on specific short-term objectives, while base pay is focused on attaining competence in the job and/or performing ongoing responsibilities well. If that is the case this approach may not work well.

The use of recognition at the individual level can also provide employees with valued rewards, even though they are not financial. Technically, recognition is not "variable pay," but it can serve some of the same purposes. It is important to recognize that behavioral research has established that being recognized and appreciated can be as powerful as cash in motivating future performance.

Individual plans work best in contexts where individuals work relatively independently of each other and have large amounts of discretion about how they do their work. In some cases, the technology used dictates individual measurement (e.g., inbound or outbound voice center operators who handle discrete transactions with customers on their own). Also, in individualistic cultures such as the U.S., the organization risks disappointing employees if it does not recognize the contribution of the individual: "socialism" is not a popular concept. Individual plans also can be a bad fit in units where employees are highly interdependent or when a wide variety of knowledge and skill is required and no one individual has all it takes to produce the desired result. And in countries where the culture is oriented towards collectivistic thinking and behavior individual incentives may be viewed as inappropriate.

Group Plans

When the objective is to define, measure and reward performance at the group, unit or team level there are several types of variable compensation plans that can be utilized. As with individual plans, the best choice will be the type of plan that best fits the specific context.

Productivity- or cost-based plans are often called *gainsharing plans*.[2] The name fits the concept; if productivity is increased, the value of the gain will be shared between the employees and the organization. These plans are typically based on formulas that consider cost, resource use or productivity ratios to determine awards. Since they are most often used in stable environments and with non-management employees, the payout period is frequently quarterly or even monthly. There is usually an employee suggestion process in place as well, in order that employees can influence their destiny. When the measures are financial and a "profit center" is the level of measurement, these plans become much like profit-sharing plans. When multiple measures are used and they include qualitative criteria, they are called "performance-sharing" (a.k.a. goal-sharing) plans.

Increasingly the work of employees is project based. This has always been the case with professionals (e.g., engineers or IT personnel). Because of this trend, variable pay plans tied to projects have become more common, encouraged by the development of project management technology, and these plans can be tied to individual incentives as well as group incentives. Professionals who are project based most or all of their time are discussed in Chapter 5. For employees who typically work at their job but who might be assigned to projects periodically it is important to consider how their contribution to the projects will be recognized through the performance and reward management programs.

Group recognition is also a form of reward that can have positive motivational impact. Pitting groups against other groups may create a positive competition, assuming their work is not interdependent, and celebrating the results of a group can increase its cohesiveness. Team-based incentives are treated in depth in Chapter 8. But other units, such as plants, area offices or departments, can be defined as groups. A large company with voice centers throughout the U.S. has for several years used contests that encourage friendly competition between the centers to earn trophies, pizza parties and other celebrations. Those who track productivity find that during contest periods productivity improves substantially. After the contest ends productivity drops off somewhat, but remains higher than before the contest. Although this looks like a free lunch it is important not to run contests too frequently, since they lose their impact if they become routine. What is effective is to change the performance metrics over time, which focuses employee attention on specific operational needs. Speed may be the focus of one contest, while accuracy may be the metric for the next, followed by customer satisfaction in yet another. Group meetings to share ideas about how to be successful can reinforce the motivation and the focus of employees.

Organization-wide Plans

When performance at the organization-wide level is the focus of variable compensation there are two major types of plans—one that provides rewards in cash and a second that uses stock or other forms of equity or ownership.

Cash plans are typically based on annual results, although multi-year plans are often used for executives. From the beginning of the twentieth century until the last few decades, the most common type of organization-wide cash plan was the profit-sharing plan. These plans typically share a portion of profits over a threshold level that provides a fair return to shareholders. Distribution of a profit-sharing pool is almost always egalitarian, with employees sharing an equal percentage of their base pay, or even receiving the same dollar amounts. The primary purpose of profit-sharing plans has been to create a "shared destiny" among employees, thereby motivating them to align their efforts and to focus on organizational profitability. Organizations such as Sears became preferred employers because of these plans. Profit-sharing plans can be designed as qualified deferred plans, which provide retirement income and estate building.

It has become increasingly apparent to organizations that profits are not the entire picture when defining what constitutes performance. This view has been reinforced by the popularization of concepts such as the balanced scorecard. Many plans that had been focused on profits were converted to multi-factor plans that can best be termed "performance-sharing" plans. These plans use multiple measures, many of which may not be financial (e.g., customer measures, operational effectiveness measures and growth and learning measures).

Stock- or equity-based plans differ from cash-based plans in several ways. They usually involve longer performance measurement periods. And they are often heavily impacted by external factors, as well as by organizational performance. The equity markets create the wealth produced by stock, through price appreciation, so organizational performance may determine only how much stock is distributed and not what it is eventually worth to the holder.

Stock purchase plans give employees an opportunity to buy stock, often at a preferred price. Although popular in the past, organizations came to realize that it was difficult for low-paid employees, who had little discretionary income, to participate extensively and that the volatility in stock prices often produced a level of risk they could or would not take. For this reason, most broad eligibility stock plans are in the form of stock bonuses, stock grants or stock options. Some profit-sharing and performance-sharing plans pay out partially in cash and partially in stock, with the ownership of the stock being transmitted to the employee. This avoids the affordability problem for lower-paid employees associated with paying the tax upon receipt and/or exercising options through purchase, and makes them immediate owners, able to vote the stock and to enjoy dividends and price appreciation.

Stock options are tools for providing privileged access to stock ownership, by granting the right to purchase a specified amount of stock at a set price for some time into the future (most commonly ten years). If the stock does not perform well, employees can walk away from the option without losing money. If the stock does well they can exercise and realize the appreciation, with the stock markets paying for the reward, although it should be remembered that the organization incurs an opportunity cost. Unless the employee makes a bad early-exercise decision, this is a risk-free program. Stock option plans were the darling of the second half of the 1990s, until the equity markets turned down sharply in 2000. A similar pattern was repeated in the years prior to the 2008 downturn. These wake-up calls remind organizations that options are not without limitations. However, when organizations abruptly withdraw from using options because of downturns it suggests they have not viewed these programs as long-term. Had organizations used options more carefully and done a better job of communicating to employees that they are intended to be long-term equity-building devices and not short-term get-rich schemes, the shocks associated with price drops might not have created the backlashes they did.

A final type of organization-wide variable pay plan is a deferred compensation plan, most often a plan that enables participants to delay receipt of income and to enjoy a matching contribution from the organization. The conventional forms of these plans have typically matched employee contributions using a set formula (e.g., the first 6% of employee contribution will be matched 50% by the company). But a simple change in design can build an incentive element into these plans, making the matching percentage variable, based on company performance. For example, the company might match 50% on a guaranteed basis, but if the company meets its targets it would increase the match to 75%, and if it performs at a very high level the match would go to 100%. This could be an attractive way to encourage more retirement plan augmentation, as well as make the company contributions contingent on its performance. It also sends the "shared destiny" message to employees in yet another way.

In summary, the type of plan used should fit the context and facilitate the attainment of the organization's objectives. Plans intended to align people would tend to be group or organization-wide, while plans attempting to maximize individual performance would be designed to measure and reward performance at the individual level. As more organizations operate in multiple countries (cultures), they find that it may be necessary to use different types of plans in different regions or in different business units, owing to the differences in the contexts within which the plans will operate.

Variable Compensation Plan Design Issues

There are seven key design issues that relate to the design, implementation and administration of a variable compensation plan.

Plan Objectives

The first step in the design of a variable pay plan is the establishment of those objectives the plan is intended to achieve. By first establishing the objectives the search for the appropriate type of plan is made easier and the selection is focused on the needs and priorities of the organization. One of the most common objectives is to align reward costs with performance, whether it is at the organization-wide, group or individual level. As mentioned earlier, when discussing the advantages of variable pay it should be recognized that each year's cost is a one-time expenditure that is not compounded in future years. The costs of the plan can be controlled through an annual budgeting process. By tying variable pay funds to the ability to pay under multiple scenarios there can be close alignment between revenue/operating budget and costs. Another prevalent objective is to motivate performance at the individual, group and/or organizational level. Because variable pay plans can be tied to predetermined objectives, employees know what is at stake and what it takes to realize rewards, as well as being able to "keep score" during the year and to determine how well they are doing. By developing multiple plans or plans with performance measured at multiple levels, the business plan can be integrated across levels to be sure individual and unit performance delivers the desired results at the organizational level.

Sharing success with employees is a way of expressing the importance of everyone's contribution and of displaying willingness to reward effort and results. It can also facilitate the attraction and retention of critical skills. Individual variable pay plans can send the signal that the organization provides larger compensation potential for top performers. They can also brand the organization as one that recognizes and values employees who perform at high levels. There is widespread acceptance of the belief that what you offer will determine what you get—in the way of employee quality.

One of the most overlooked characteristics of variable pay is its ability to act as a powerful signaling device. Effective communication of what the organization needs and wants is best done in a free market culture like that prevailing in the U.S. by providing inducements. This is not to suggest that cash is the only inducement that will encourage people to help the organization succeed, but it is a tangible yard-stick of accomplishment and it fits the type of employment arrangement typical in the U.S.

Type of Plan

When the objectives for the plan are established the next step is to determine what type of plan will best fit the context and have the best chance of meeting the objectives. In the previous section the various types of plans were discussed. The decisions about the type of plan will hinge on:

1   whether performance will defined, measured and rewarded at the individual, group or organizational level;
2   the timeframe for measurement;
3   the role variable pay will play in the total compensation package;
4   the performance measures that will drive the plan; and
5   what the performance standards will be based on and the level at which they will be set.

Eligibility

One of the critical plan design issues is who to include. The objectives established for the plan and the type of plan provide considerable guidance as to who it makes sense to include. A commission plan aimed at increasing individual sales would certainly include eligibility for direct sales representatives and may include sales support personnel and sales management. A plan intended to provide a shared destiny throughout the organization may not leave out any employee.

The criteria that can be used to determine eligibility for plans are varied. Deciding to include all employees sends the message that the plan objectives need the contributions of everyone. Basing eligibility on title or status (e.g., officer, vice president) was more prevalent in the past, when organizations were more hierarchical than today. Organizations use titles for many purposes, and these designations still might be appropriate criteria for determining plan eligibility. It is more common to base eligibility on job grade or pay level, since there tends to be a correlation between the grade and the potential impact the job has on organizational results. Unfortunately, there never seems to be a cutoff point that does not start "border disputes." Everyone who is one level below any cutoff begins a lobbying campaign to have their job raised one grade. This has been the undoing of many job evaluation plans, because those guarding the borders always seem to be overwhelmed by the aspirants.

One of the most common cutoff tests is whether or not someone has a *direct* and *significant* impact on organization or business unit results. But it is easy to see how these words can mean different things to different people. The same is true of using a criticality-of-skills test. Many refrains of "If we are not critical let's see how you do without us" have been heard in response to this test. The discretion of management is sometimes used, and the quality of the selection will depend on the quality of the criteria used and how well decision makers apply the test. Finally, the longevity of the individual may be used. If longevity is valued, however, it is usually better to establish a separate service award program, in order to avoid disconnecting rewards from performance.

One option to using a single eligibility criterion is to have tiers of participants, with the target award levels varying by grade or pay level. This lessens the "us–them" effect, and most employees will accept that those at higher levels are appropriately put more at risk and that they have a more direct impact on performance. But create a border and you create a border dispute. So even the tiered approach does not avoid debates, but it does tend to lessen their intensity, since there will be less at stake by crossing one border.

Formula for Determining Award Funds

There should be a set of criteria that will be used to determine how much is available for variable pay awards. This determination is critical, since it will govern the relationship between performance and reward costs. Below some level of performance, it will probably not be possible to afford and/or justify the payment of any additional awards on top of base pay. Many a shareholder rebellion has been caused by variable pay plans with very low performance thresholds. A California utility paid out millions in "incentives" the day before it sought bankruptcy protection, justifying this by saying it was part of the employee pay package. Merrill Lynch paid out executive bonuses early at the end of 2008, just ahead of being acquired by Bank of America—and after performance being so bad that it required the takeover as a bailout. It seems to some that people were rewarded in these two cases for destroying the organization, and this is bad public relations.

Discretionary determinations are not always inappropriate, since many organizations find it difficult to forecast with any certainty. If there is an unstable and unpredictable environment, it may be more appropriate to evaluate what results were at the end of the period and how good they were, considering what happened. On the other hand, discretionary plans with no predetermined criteria provide little motivation or focus and can be viewed as "Santa Claus" plans by shareholders. One way to improve on discretionary plans is to identify the criteria that will be used to measure performance in advance and to keep score during the period, communicating interim results frequently. This can provide focus without the certainty of having standards tied to the performance criteria.

When setting performance standards one can "look back" (compare to historical results), "look around" (compare to peers) or "look ahead" (set future goals). Stable organizations in settled environments often use compounded improvement formulas to drive their standards. Rapidly changing organizations that are in volatile and highly competitive environments may compare to others, thinking that their relative standing in this comparator group reflects performance. Indeed this type of measurement can be better than a forecast that was not much more than a guess. Organizations that have to meet certain thresholds in order to survive or to be viewed as successful will tend to use a future-oriented perspective when setting standards. Whichever perspective is used, there is the issue of a threshold, below which even base pay has not been earned and above which it is reasonable to reserve a portion of the bounty for those who made it happen.

An issue related to determining the award fund is the mix of base pay and variable compensation. Variable compensation can vary from nothing (an all-base-pay package) to everything (an all-variable-pay package), with most plans having a mix somewhere in between. This decision impacts the budgeting for both base pay and variable pay, as well as determining the makeup of the cost structure. The current organizational context should drive the overall mix decision, while the nature of different units and different occupational groups or jobs should establish the mix at the unit and individual level.

Formula for Allocating Funds

The second part of the allocation issue is how to allocate the funds generated to groups and/or individuals in the form of awards. Figure 14.1 provides the alternative approaches to fund allocation.

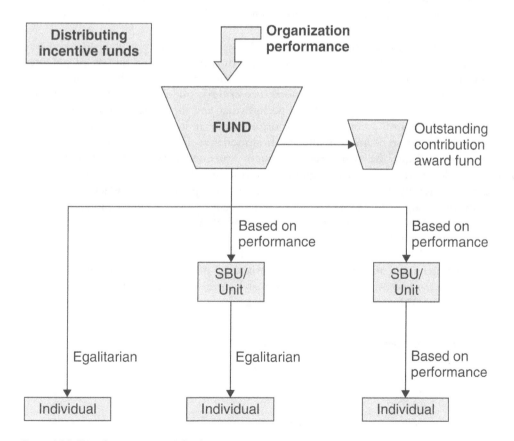

Figure 14.1 Distributing incentive funds

Some plans, such as cash profit-sharing plans, use an egalitarian distribution and award everyone the same percentage of base pay or the same dollar amount. Others will allocate the total fund to units, based on their relative performance, and then let the units allocate their funds to individuals (or prescribe that the allocation be on an equal percentage or dollar basis). Finally, an individual performance metric (e.g., performance appraisal rating) may be used to differentiate award size across individuals. One further variation of this approach is the "world series team share" method, which gives everyone their share assuming they showed up and did what was asked, as long as they performed individually at an acceptable level. This type of binary differentiation avoids people whose performance was not at least at a "fully meets expectations" level from receiving an additional award, for results achieved through the efforts of others.

One design feature that is useful is the addition of a "side fund," to be used for rewarding outstanding contributions by individuals or groups in periods when organizational performance does not produce an incentive fund. Those who produce results that make things less disastrous in a bad year will feel their performance went unrecognized. It is important to begin the creation of this fund at a high enough performance level, to ensure there is not a backlash from irritated investors. It is also important to ensure there is a sound process in place for evaluating the merit of contributions, lest the fund be used to placate those who are used to getting awards, no matter what organizational performance is. If the creation of this side fund is politically untenable, the use of cash awards tied to performance appraisal ratings may be acceptable.

It is helpful to formulate a model that addresses what variable pay awards are based on (organizational, unit and/or individual performance) and what the award potential is for all categories of employees. The most common practice is to base senior executive awards on organization-wide performance criteria, middle management awards on a combination of organization and unit performance and the awards of the remainder of eligible employees on a combination of organization, unit and individual performance. Table 14.1 shows an example of an allocation model; it should be noted that employees who do not fall into the managerial/professional category have the largest portion based on individual performance, although there can still be a "world series team share" binary approach, resulting in the same relative award for those performing satisfactorily.

The award targets are often tiered, with senior management having the highest variable pay award potential (expressed as a percentage of salary), reflecting their greater impact on performance and their ability to absorb more contingency in their direct compensation package. Table 14.2 illustrates the typical relationship between levels, with threshold, target and maximum awards specified as a percentage of base pay. The actual percentages vary widely by type of industry, organizational maturity and culture, but the relationship across levels is fairly typical.

Table 14.1 Basis for Determining Variable Pay Awards

Performance	Organizational	Group	Individual
Top management	100%	0%	0%
Middle management	50%	50%	0%
Professional/supervisory	25%	50%	25%
Other employees	25%	25%	50%

One way to base awards on multiple criteria is to create a matrix as shown in Table 14.3. This approach can be used to accommodate two goals or it can be used to combine organizational and unit performance determinants. For example, the vertical axis (labeled Goal 1) could be organizational performance and the horizontal axis (labeled Goal 2) could be unit performance. The same approach could be used to link unit and individual performance. A final modification would be to use all three levels, making individual performance a modifier that further revises the award indicated in the two-dimensional matrix, which would be based on both organizational and unit performance.

Once the funds available for incentives are determined, the basis for allocating awards to individuals must be decided upon. The alternatives for allocating awards to individuals are numerous, and each approach sends a different message:

- equal percentage of base pay rate;
- equal percentage of range midpoint;
- equal percentage of base pay rate up to a maximum;
- varied based on organizational level or grade level;
- equal dollars to each participant;
- equal dollars per hours worked in period;
- varied based on individual performance.

The objectives for the plan will help guide allocation. If the plan is intended to convey a shared destiny, it will be likely to award the same amount or same percentage of pay to each participant. If the plan is intended to differentially award based on contribution, the performance rating will be used to vary awards across individuals. For support personnel who are not exempt from the overtime pay regulations in the Fair Labor Standards Act, it is necessary to include any awards in the calculation of the base pay rate, for purposes of paying for overtime.

Table 14.2 Variable Pay Award Targets (Percentage of Base)

	Threshold	Target	Maximum
Top management	25%	50%	100%
Middle management	15%	30%	60%
Professional/supervisory	10%	20%	30%
Other employees	5%	10%	15%

Table 14.3 Variable Pay Awards: Two Objectives of Equal Weight

Goal 1 (e.g. Profit)	Goal 2 (e.g. Market Share)		
	Threshold	Target	Maximum
Maximum	100%	150%	200%
Target	50%	100%	150%
Threshold	25%	50%	100%

Form and Timing of Awards

Two maxims apply here: "Cash is not everything but it buys more than contingent future rewards" and "Sooner is better than later." The majority of variable pay plans deliver awards in the form of cash, although, as mentioned earlier, stock or other real property may be used. In some cases, non-financial recognition may be more appropriate. Perquisites (special advantages, such as cars, club memberships and the like) may also be used when they have status value or tax efficiencies associated with them. Unfortunately, perquisites have accumulated a bad image, and it might be more palatable to see advantages given to people who perform at high levels, rather than those who happen to have high pay rates. In the U.S., the taxation of perquisites has been altered to make them less of a tax avoidance tool.

The timing of awards becomes an issue when a plan covers a wide variety of occupations or the gamut from executives to operatives. For a production worker covered by a formula-based gainsharing plan, an entire year may not be an appropriate timeframe. More frequent measurement and reward (quarterly or monthly) may better fit the work cycle. The same may be true for direct sales personnel. On the other hand, for executives who may be responsible for planning, building and making operational a billion-dollar facility, it may be unnatural to try to measure and reward performance in a time period as short as one year. For this type of employee, a multiyear plan may make more sense, and measuring performance may be more accurate.

A final dimension of the timing issue is the option of either allowing an employee who would otherwise receive cash to defer the amount to sometime in the future or requiring them so to do. Some stock plans have a multi-year vesting period and some cash plans a multi-year measurement period. Some employees may value the option of voluntarily deferring awards to a time when they will no longer be working or to a time when triplets will start college simultaneously. Finally, some organizations allow deferrals of annual incentives to a time when the participants will require cash to exercise stock options, which enables the short- and long-term variable pay plans to be integrated. If participants sign an irrevocable election to defer, constructive receipt of income for taxation purposes may be avoided. These declarations must indicate that the participant does not know if an award will be received or what its amount may be, but if one is received it is to be deferred to some future date. In countries with tax laws that differ from those in the U.S. this election option might not exist or the conditions might differ.

Plan Implementation

An effective plan must "take" in the organization; that is, it must be accepted and must be viewed as adequate, appropriate, fair and competitive. The manner in which it is implemented will largely determine how well it will guide and motivate effort. The implementation plan starts with the initial design of the plan. If those who develop the plan (outsiders or insiders) do not have both the knowledge and the credibility required, the plan will not launch. Japanese organizations take a great deal of time to achieve consensus about issues like variable pay plan design—it is then a simple matter to gain acceptance, since all the right people were involved and had their say. U.S. organizations are criticized for moving quickly through design and then taking forever to force the plan into place, since they must prevail over the resistance inevitably forthcoming from detractors who did not have a say in the design process. In a culture like the one prevailing in the U.S., there is a tendency to reward moving quickly and bravely, and seeking broad-based participation is often viewed as weakness or indecision. The parties affected by the plan must accept the plan. But involvement does not mandate a democratic election, which could drag out indefinitely and end up being the camel that started out to be a horse, until a committee got involved.

Piloting a plan can give developers an opportunity to discover what they forgot. It is also a lower-risk way to launch a plan. However, there is always a danger of trying the plan out in one niche and then making the assumption that it will operate similarly in other parts of the organization, however different they may be. One of the techniques used to test the measures being used is to do a "dry run" behind the scenes to see how well the criteria can be measured and what resources will be required to do it well. And this should be done in each entity where the plan will be implemented, allowing for different results.

Communicating a plan and training those who will either play roles in its administration or be "consumers" (participants) are critical to implementing a plan. Too often, designers assume everyone will figure it out, which they do—each in their own way. And communication cannot be accomplished in 45-minute group meetings. One of the most effective ways to build understanding is to use scenarios that show how the plan will operate and how it will respond to changes. A simple four-page fold-over booklet can do much to explain the plan. The pages should answer the critical questions:

1   Why is the organization doing this? What does it want to accomplish?
2   How does it work?
3   How much can people get?
4   What specifically will happen and when?

Policies and procedures can also help enhance understanding, as can plan documents written to be understandable by those who did not complete law school. Training people who play roles is also critical, particularly managers who are expected to make decisions about how well individuals and units did and to what they are entitled. If there are deferrals or stock involved there will be a greater requirement for documenting the specifics, and it should be remembered that even if the plan is not fully committed to writing it is a verbal contract relative to those things that were said or even those hinted at. Finally, there should be a "sunset provision" that says the plan is good for a specific period (e.g., one year) and that at the end it will be evaluated and modified, left as it is or terminated. Too many plans went into old age strictly because of inertia, not because they worked.

The final step in plan implementation is to develop and communicate the "instrument panel" that will monitor the plan and evaluate its effectiveness. If this is not done at the start, the plan can be taking the organization in the wrong direction at high speed. Evaluation will be discussed in more detail in Chapter 15.

Plan Administration

The best-designed plan will fail if it is not administered effectively. The objectives for the plan and the type of plan will impact how a plan should be administered, and the design will largely prescribe the administrative policies. However, much can go wrong. Failure to continuously evaluate the continued appropriateness of a plan and not making the necessary modifications required by changes in the context will render a plan ineffective.

A variable pay plan must be aligned with the compensation strategy, which should be aligned with the human resource strategy. These strategies must also be consistent with the organizational strategy and its context. Therefore, a change in organizational context or strategy may signal the need to revise the human resource strategy and perhaps the compensation strategy. Variable pay is but one element of compensation and it must be kept in alignment with the other elements and remain consistent with the role the compensation strategy assigns it. This means that any variable pay plan must be a part of organizational strategic decision making, and those making decisions with long-range impact should be involved in variable pay plan design, communication, implementation, administration and evaluation.

The compensation strategy should provide direction to those charged with designing variable pay plans. It should answer the key question: what role variable pay will play in the total compensation package and what criteria will be used for evaluating its appropriateness and effectiveness on an ongoing basis. The variable pay plan design decisions should be guided by the compensation strategy, and the organizational culture should guide the communication and training necessary in order for a plan to succeed. The evaluation of plan effectiveness should be largely prescribed by the compensation strategy and the plan objectives.

Administrative Issues

Things happen—even things no one thought of. Variable pay plans are subject to challenge and litigation because they offer the promise of reward. Sales compensation suits are often found to be the most common type of civil suit in the U.S.; these plans tend to be much more specifically formula driven, although other types of variable pay plans may create the same kind of legal liability. The best way to make administrative decisions is to do so based on policies that were developed before the plan went into effect. Snap decisions can often fill the gap when rules are unclear but they then often become precedents that guide future action, even though they have not been thoroughly reviewed and adopted through consensus.

New hires and terminations during the year raise the question of eligibility for plan rewards and are probably the most common events requiring administrative action. There is no right answer to the questions that arise—only the best one for the organization at that time. For example, is someone hired six months into an annual plan eligible to get anything? Does someone who is fired on December 15 get left out of the annual plan that ends two weeks later? Death, disability and retirement decisions are usually clear, assuming the appropriate action is determined in advance, but what about leaves of absence? One critical issue for annual plans with quarterly or monthly interim payouts is whether everything earned that period is paid or if there should be some holdback for negative periods. Asking for refunds owing to a bad February after large payouts for a great January will hardly win over the hearts of participants, so this issue should be decided in advance, based at least partly on discussions with participants. For example, most gainsharing plans with monthly payouts hold back 25%, and the books are closed at the end of the year—with no refunds demanded if the holdback balance is not enough to cover a very bad yearend.

A key design decision with a major impact on how fair participants think the administration is when criteria and/or standards are changed. There are some who believe that once the plan is set no changes should occur. However, many incentive plans become outdated when unanticipated external events make meeting plan objectives automatic or impossible. Even though it seems reasonable to modify a plan to fit realities as they evolve, it is very hard to make this a two-way street. If something happens to make goal achievement harder, there will be a long line outside the plan administrator's office full of heart-rending stories. However, if something makes the plan easier, the lack of a line may alert the administrator to an unbalanced situation. That notwithstanding, a process for modifying a plan based on unanticipated external events should be established at the time of plan inception.

A legal issue arises when non-exempt employees are included in variable pay plans, particularly incentive plans with established criteria. The U.S. Fair Labor Standards Act (FLSA) prescribes that the base rate used for computing overtime pay must include non-discretionary incentive awards for non-exempt employees. This often necessitates the difficult re-computation of overtime earnings retrospectively. To avoid such an administrative disaster it is advisable to anticipate the requirement and to compute incentive awards on taxable earnings, or at least base pay plus overtime earnings. This should avoid the need for back computation, although it does present an additional expense which should be anticipated and planned for.

Evaluating Plan Effectiveness

As suggested earlier, if the evaluation criteria and processes are left until the end of the plan period it is much like saving the cost of ship radar and then trying to decide why it hit the rocks after it has sunk. The questions seem simple: Did the plan ask for the right results? Produce them? Did it ask for the right behaviors? Produce them? Did everyone understand the plan? Accept it? By developing a list of effectiveness criteria, measures and standards and by beginning to evaluate plan operation when it is launched, organizations can avoid salvaging wrecks. Interim results versus budget, trends in productivity and other analysis can diagnose difficulties and make it possible to do course corrections or to change standards before difficulties compound. Particularly in the first year of operation, it is critical to identify the refinements needed and to make them, before a payout is resentfully made. By continuously evaluating the plan, the organization can often limit changes to refinements and save a plan that otherwise would be cancelled at the end of its maiden voyage. More detail on plan evaluation will be provided in the next chapter.

Prerequisites for Variable Compensation Plan Success

If a plan is successful in facilitating the fulfillment of the organization's mission and meeting its objectives it will be viewed as a valuable tool for long-term viability and success. If it fits the culture and context, it is going to be consistent with the values and priorities of those who participate, making it acceptable to them. If the plan is consistent with the organization's structure and supports its strategy, it will become an integral part of the business plan. And if it is well integrated with the other elements of human resource strategy (staffing, development and performance management) it will assist in attracting and retaining the human capital the organization needs.

When Is a Plan Likely to Fail?

If the culture is one of entitlement, the pay-for-performance philosophy underlying variable pay will conflict with what employees expect and can be the source of dissension. If the economic environment is such that performance is largely dictated by outside factors (e.g., governmental regulation) it may be difficult to convince employees that they control their financial destiny. If good measures are hard to identify or get agreement about and/or if the organization does not have the required measurement mechanisms in place it will be difficult to convince employees that their performance can be fairly and consistently measured. If performance standards are viewed as being unrealistically high and therefore unattainable, employees will not be motivated to expend their best efforts, which would be thought to be fruitless. If the organization does not have the resources to afford variable pay the prospect of large rewards should not be made. Affordability of a plan is a critical part of a feasibility study, and multiple scenarios must be modeled in advance to ensure that the organization is happy to pay given alternative outcomes. If communication is poor or trust is lacking there is little chance for variable pay plan success. And finally, if the people who are the participants in a plan are not viewed as critical assets, who must contribute in order for the organization to succeed, there is no reason to consider adopting a plan.

What works is what fits a specific organization, or part of an organization, at a specific point in time. A well-designed plan also requires good implementation and administration, and it must be evaluated continuously to ensure it remains appropriate and effective.

Application of Principles: Chapter 14

A durable goods manufacturing organization has had a long history of hiring people and keeping them throughout their career. Base pay has been administered using a time-based step system and there have not been any variable pay programs other than an annual profit-sharing plan. At the end of the year executive management contributes to the profit-sharing plan fund based on a judgment of the organization's performance during the year, considering all factors. All employees receive a profit-sharing cash award that equals the same percentage of their base pay, computed by dividing the fund allocation by the payroll and shares of company stock the value of which is computed the same way. Several key executives are retiring and the new CEO and CFO have been hired from outside the organization, the first time that has happened. The two leaders wish to alter the compensation philosophy, strategy and programs so that individual and unit performance become the driving factor, rather than longevity. The CEO has told the CHRO that she wants a merit pay program for administering base pay, supplemented by organization, unit and individual cash incentive programs. Executive compensation should consist of base pay set at 90% of competitive base pay levels, short-term incentives that range from zero to well-above competitive levels and restricted stock programs limited to senior management personnel.

You have been retained by the CHRO to evaluate the new compensation philosophy and to develop a plan for reshaping programs. You are expected to anticipate any resistance by employees and provide direction as to how any resistance can be overcome. What are your concerns, if any, about this magnitude of change? Should everything be changed at once, for all employees? If not, develop a sequence and timeline for implementation. Early discussions with the CEO make it clear the destination is not negotiable but the path to get there is open.

Notes

1 Rynes, S., Gerhart, B. & Parks, L., "Performance Evaluation and Pay for Performance," *Journal of Applied Psychology*, 56 (2005), 571–600.
2 Graham-Moore, B. & Ross, T., *Gainsharing and Employee Involvement* (Washington, DC, Bureau of National Affairs, 1995).

Chapter 15

Evaluating Strategies and Administering Programs

Determining if strategies and programs are producing the desired results is a critical step in performance and rewards management. Yet few organizations conduct continuous, or even periodic, evaluations of effectiveness and continuing appropriateness of their strategies and programs. Programs running on autopilot can do a lot of damage if someone is not watching the instruments to determine if they are keeping the organization on the right course. At stake are cost-effectiveness, employee satisfaction and employee motivation.

The effectiveness of any program will be impacted by environmental factors. Given the rate of change experienced by many organizations today it is unlikely that programs in place for long periods will be as appropriate and effective as they were when first implemented. During the 1990s and 2003–08 the economy in the U.S. was healthy and the emphasis was on growth and finding and keeping critical talent. When intermittent downturns have occurred, organizations have shifted their emphasis to cost reduction, in order to maintain profit levels. Even though the principles used to guide performance and reward management often remained the same, the strategies varied, based on the criteria being used at the moment to define "performance." In many cases employees viewed the rapid and dramatic shifts as a sign of management indecision, as well as being out of their control. Executives are expected to scan the environment and adjust strategy so it remains a good fit to the current conditions and viable into the future. But the remainder of the workforce can be confused by changes in expectations and may become unwilling to take any initiative, preferring to wait for instructions. For these reasons it is critical for executive management to ensure not only that the strategy is adaptable to fit environmental change but that it remains continuously effective, given the realities.

This chapter will present models for evaluating current strategies and programs. Experience has shown that unless an evaluation model is fashioned when a strategy is formulated and programs are designed and implemented it is unlikely that enough attention will be paid to their effectiveness on an ongoing basis. The model presented in Figure 15.1 prescribes that rewards strategy be derived from the organizational strategy and HR strategy, to ensure a good fit to context. Then programs should be designed to support the rewards strategy, going through the design, communication and training, implementation and administration stages, with evaluation being started as soon as they are in place. But the model also suggests that the evaluation system should be developed as the program is being designed (the right-pointing arrow), so that the instruments for measuring effectiveness are in place when administration begins. The model also specifies that the results of program evaluation should be used to decide whether changes to the rewards strategy or program designed are needed.

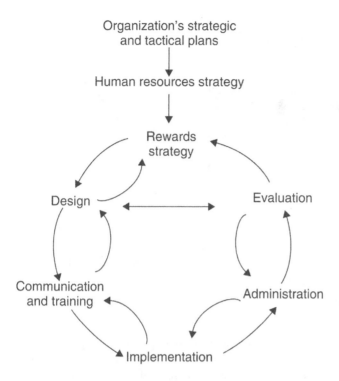

Organization's strategic
and tactical plans

Human resources strategy

Rewards
strategy

Design   Evaluation

Communication
and training   Administration

Implementation

Figure 15.1 Program management cycle

Without predetermined performance criteria, standards and measures it is difficult to evaluate a program, at least until things have gone so wrong that serious problems become obvious. All too often outside "firefighters" are brought in to deal with a raging inferno—a much more costly strategy than having a sound fire prevention program. After-the-fact remedies cannot undo the damage, and employees tend to be unforgiving when programs close to their hearts (or wallets) are declared to be defective.

Another issue that will be explored here is whether consideration should be given to variations from established policy, in order to fit individual situations. The chapters in Part II discussed fitting strategies and programs to different types of employees. This discussion will deal with varying policy for individuals who fall within the same function, the same occupation and even the same job.

Designing the "Instrument Panel" for Evaluating Programs

The balanced scorecard approach has been discussed often in earlier chapters. It is a tool that can act as an "instrument panel" for defining and measuring performance. In order for a scorecard to work the performance criteria, standards and measures must be designed in advance, hard-wired into the psyche of managing and continuously monitored so that effectiveness can be evaluated. The same principle holds true for a rewards program, such

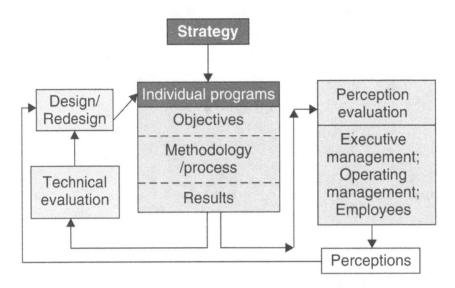

Figure 15.2 Evaluation model

as a new merit pay program. The gauges in the instrument panel each represent an objective of the program, translated into a performance measure. For example, one objective of a shift to pay for performance is to divert a larger share of the pay increase budget to better performers and a smaller share to poorer performers. A measure of current allocation (average increase related to performance rating) becomes a gauge reading on the evaluation instrument panel and results can be monitored.

Another category of measure used to evaluate program effectiveness is perceptions. What people believe to be the intent and/or reality is what is real to them. In the case of the merit pay program another measure may be the extent to which employees believe higher levels of performance result in larger pay adjustments. Perception can be compared to reality, giving an indication of gaps that exist. If both perceptions and actual results are positive it can be assumed that pay is being tied to performance, that the employees realize it and that they accept the results.

Figure 15.2 illustrates a model that can be used as the basis for developing an instrument panel for a specific organization.

Once program objectives have resulted in a design (method/process) the performance criteria, standards and measures that will be used to determine results can be formulated. Technical (actual results) audits are far more common than perceptions audits and therefore actual results often dominate evaluation activity. The focus on actual results is of course necessary, but often misperceptions can be the source of employee dissatisfaction, management misunderstanding and general frustration.

Table 15.1 presents the results of a perceptions audit relating to the distribution of performance ratings during the first cycle of a new program. What it demonstrates is that there are significant gaps between actual results and perceptions. The various parties at interest have different perceptions of what is happening, and this can be problematic. About the only good news is that the managers who did the ratings are closer to guessing the truth.

Table 15.1 Distribution of Performance Ratings: Actual and Perceived

Performance Rating	Actual Results	Executive Perceptions	Manager or Supervisor Perceptions	Employee Perceptions
Outstanding	22%	15%	20%	5%
Significantly exceeds standards	50%	25%	30%	10%
Fully meets standards	25%	45%	35%	60%
Does not fully meet standards	2%	10%	10%	15%
Unacceptable	1%	5%	5%	10%

The executive misperceptions can be very damaging to the careers of HR, the rating managers or both, once what is really happening is discovered. The performance appraisal program could be found to be at fault, but it is more likely that poor training or the absence of any monitoring of performance ratings is the source of the malfunction. It is critical for HR to detect this misalignment and to act on it, either to align executive perceptions with reality and/or to communicate to managers that ratings are out of line with expectations (if they are).

The employee misperceptions can also be the source of discontent. If an employee is rated "significantly exceeds," the belief will be that he or she is in the top 15% of the peer group and deserving of significant rewards. The reality that performance falls somewhere between the 77th and the 23rd percentile will no doubt result in a pay action that will be disappointing and viewed as unfair.

Whether the actual results are deemed to be good or bad will depend on the culture of the organization and management's philosophy. One further issue that should be addressed is the consistency or lack thereof across the organization, since problems may be occurring in specific functions, making them a bit easier to deal with.

Table 15.2 is the second part of this perception audit, which is to measure the degree to which pay actions are correlated to performance ratings. Once again, there are significant differences between the views of both the executives and the employees and what is actually happening.

The issues with these findings are many, both technical and perceptual. First, the actual results show little correlation between performance rating and pay adjustment. Given these average increases and the rating distribution in Table 15.1, the organization will have had to spend well over 6% of payroll and yet will have accomplished little differentiation

Table 15.2 Pay Actions Versus Performance Ratings: Actual and Perceived

Performance Rating	Actual Results	Executive Perceptions	Manager or Supervisor Perceptions	Employee Perceptions
Outstanding	7%	15%	9%	6%
Significantly exceeds standards	6%	9%	7%	5%
Fully meets standards	6%	5%	6%	4%
Does not fully meet standards	5%	1%	3%	3%
Unacceptable	2%	0%	0%	0%

between the highest and lowest level of performance. Most organizations would consider the program a failure.

Perception problems are also significant. Executive management believes pay is being adjusted based on performance and will probably not view the results as anything but a disaster. However, if there has been no history of paying for performance, it would probably be unrealistic to expect an overnight conversion to totally different behavior. If HR had been prudent enough to analyze the proposed ratings and adjustments prior to their being communicated to employees there would have been an opportunity to adjust the pattern. As mentioned earlier, conclusions based on overall averages may be premature; the problem may be with inconsistency across the organization. In any event, it would not be career enhancing for managers or HR if these increases became effective and executive management found out the truth only later.

The employee perceptions are also a large problem. Although they rightfully believe there is little difference between performing well and performing poorly, they also believe the organization is spending a lot less than it really is. It is one thing to be cheap but yet another to be spending lavishly and to be thought to be cheap. People act on their perceptions, and if you combine the employee beliefs about rating distributions and pay increase distributions they would assume the organization is spending less than 4% on increases. This clearly is not a winning combination for the organization: spending a lot and getting little credit.

Once an evaluation model has been built and objectives established for both actual and perceived results the organization is able to continuously monitor the gauges and to act to prevent year-end results such as those just offered as an example.

Evaluating Programs Using the Model

The evaluation of a base pay program will be used as an example of how the evaluation model can be applied in an audit. Other types of programs (benefits, incentives, etc.) will typically have different objectives and methods or processes and will therefore involve different effectiveness criteria, standards and measures. But the objectives are the same: 1) align program design with objectives; 2) develop both actual and perceptual measures to use in evaluating program performance; and 3) use the results to make changes to program design and/or to the perceptions of the parties at interest.

Program Objectives

The most common objectives for a base pay program are: 1) attract and retain required skills; 2) motivate high levels of performance; 3) administer programs efficiently and within established budgets; and 4) provide employees with a standard of living appropriate to their role in the organization. The attract–retain objective may be made more specific by stating that pay opportunity will be consistent with internal equity and external competitiveness and that individual pay rates will be based on performance and job mastery. However objectives are stated, it must be possible to test program performance against them to make evaluation meaningful.

The best test of a pay system's overall effectiveness is whether it produces the desired results. If the organization is able to get and keep the critical skills it needs to function and if the workforce performs well it is logical to infer that the pay system is working, or at least not impeding effectiveness. As compensation practitioners read about the new fad that has broken out in the field there is a temptation to try it, to see if it will improve performance. However, employees tend to control their enthusiasm for frequent pay system modifications, and in fact get testy if it seems the organization is floundering. It is therefore important to consider the impact of revising the pay program versus refining the existing program to increase its effectiveness.

There are two dimensions of program effectiveness: perceptions and realities. How employees will feel about programs and how they react to them will hinge on what employees believe about the programs (How fair is it? How competitive?). It is therefore important that those responsible for program administration do not respond to employee claims that they are not being paid fairly or competitively with "They are wrong." They may be, but it is critical that HR change their minds if this is the case, since perception is reality for an employee. Attitude surveys, focus groups and other forms of dialogue can help HR understand what the prevailing beliefs are and enable them to use training or improved communication.

If deficiencies are found when performing audits, it is important to acknowledge them, address them and communicate why any changes that are made are necessary. HR may wish to have people from outside the function do periodic audits, in order to dispel the suspicion that the designers of the programs are defensive about acknowledging inadequacies. A task force representing a horizontal slice of the organization can lend credibility to the evaluation process, and it may be advisable to involve people representing a vertical cross-section as well. Edward Lawler has been providing research results showing the adverse effects of pay secrecy for decades.[1] His research argues for opening up all policies and processes to public scrutiny, although individual pay rates and pay actions should still remain a matter between an employee and the organization. Sunshine kills a lot of viruses, and pay systems have too often been administered under a fog bank.

Given the legal and regulatory environment in the U.S., one of the major concerns about base pay administration is its impact on classes of employees. If audits find that one class of employee gets lower performance ratings and/or smaller increases even though the employees are similarly qualified and perform similarly, this may establish adverse impact and may require justification. If there are unexplained differences they should be investigated, regardless of the probability of legal action. Pay should be correlated to the value of the job or role, the mastery level and performance—nothing else. If this is not the case the policies and programs need examination. However, if females get lower performance ratings on average than males it may be due to actual differences in performance, so there should not be a premature assumption of discrimination. To accuse a manager of gender bias is a very serious indictment, especially if it is unwarranted. On the other hand, if the bias exists, even if it is unintentional, other steps need to be taken to ensure the end result of the system is equitable and consistent with policy. As mentioned earlier, perception is reality to employees and it is wise to ensure there is confidence in the administration of the pay program.

Program Methodology and Process

The elements of a base pay program are outlined below, with key questions provided that should be answered during an evaluation.

- *Pay policy*:

  - How are the labor markets within which the organization competes defined? Do they differ across occupations?
  - What should the competitive posture be relative to those markets? What is the actual competitive position?
  - What elements does the direct compensation package contain (base, variable) and what is the mix? Is it appropriate?
  - What does the organization base pay opportunity on: job held, results produced or qualifications—or a combination? Is the current approach appropriate?

- *Role definition and documentation*:

  - Are jobs well designed and documented?
  - Is documentation current and complete?
  - Do employees understand job requirements and expectations?

- *Pay structure*:

  - Is the process for grading jobs effective and efficient?
  - Is the process viewed as fair and is it efficient of resources?
  - Is the number of grades appropriate?
  - Are the grade assignments viewed as fair and appropriate?
  - Is the market pricing process appropriate?
  - Are pay ranges competitive?
  - Are pay ranges an appropriate width?
  - Is there a process for identifying changes to job responsibilities and requirements and adjusting grades or ranges as appropriate?
  - Is the pay structure adjusted each year consistent with market conditions?

- *Pay rate determination*:

  - Is the process that sets pay rates for new entrants appropriate?
  - Are pay adjustments based on the right criteria (e.g., performance, mastering skills, producing results)?
  - Are pay adjustments fair and appropriate?
  - Are pay adjustments non-discriminatory? If there is statistically significant adverse impact on a protected class, has the cause been identified and validated as appropriate?
  - Is there a credible appeal process available to employees?

- *Performance appraisal*:

  - Is performance appraisal based on job-related results and behaviors?
  - Are performance criteria, standards and measures defined in advance and communicated?
  - Are raters appropriately trained?
  - Are ratings non-discriminatory? If there is statistically significant adverse impact on a protected class, has the cause been identified and validated as appropriate?
  - Is there a credible appeal process available to employees?

- *Program administration*:
  - Do the program costs stay within the overall budget?
  - Is there consistency across the organization?
  - Is communication adequate to produce employee understanding?
  - Is there a need to reconsider methodology or process?

Determining the Business Impact of Program Modifications

An issue related to evaluation of program effectiveness is determining whether changes to programs will be good business decisions. All too often, HR makes the case for modifying a program to fix a problem without including the hard figures that determine if it is a good economic decision. The example of reducing turnover in a critical occupation will be used here, to demonstrate how the business case can be made, thereby putting the proposal in the primary language of the decision makers.

Fact: Turnover among software design engineers has been 25%, and this level of churn has had a negative impact on project performance and customer satisfaction. *Proposed action*: Increase the pay level of incumbents from market average ($80,000) to 10% above market average ($88,000). *Cost*: There are 100 incumbents: the annual cost of increased payroll is $800,000. *Projected benefit*: Turnover will drop from 25% to 15%, reducing the number of unwanted leavings by ten designers. For the purposes of this illustration let us assume it was determined that other organizations had experienced similar results after taking the same action and that the projected drop in unwanted turnover is believable.

Cascio provides costing models for use on issues such as turnover, absenteeism, work–life issues and the like, and his approach can be used to put benefits (cost avoidance in this case) into financial terms.[2] The decision makers must be able to determine average cost figures for events such as this, which would include:

- HR resources required to recruit a new employee;
- productivity lost in the unit;
- HR resources required to recruit a new employee;
- HR resources required to train a new employee.

These are not all the related costs, of course. Delays in product development, impact on customer satisfaction and other impacts will be difficult to estimate accurately, and this should be up to the management of the unit concerned. But management must be provided with hard figures on what the cost avoidance will be that is associated with losing and then replacing ten designers. There may also be a need to provide information on other outcomes that cannot be estimated in dollar terms, such as the need to pay new recruits more than even the $88,000 target, owing to labor market shortages, and the impact a premium would have on the equity perceptions of the software designers already on board. Certainly, these possible consequences need to be presented along with the expected costs—not to do so would underestimate the benefits associated with raising the pay levels. But it is likely the decision will turn primarily on the hard costs, and if they are not forthcoming then the proposal will have a lesser chance of acceptance.

Once the change has been implemented, results should be tracked. Although extenuating circumstances (e.g., competitors respond by raising pay levels 15%, the labor market tightens further, etc.) may intervene, it is important for actual benefits to be measured against estimated benefits and to make management aware of those results.

Performing Evaluations

The critical questions relating to program evaluations are: 1) How will they be done? 2) Who will do them? 3) What will the role of each party at interest be? The first question has been addressed. The issues concerning who should participate in evaluations and what the roles of the respective parties should be are too important not to discuss, however, so options will be presented here.

It is most common for human resources to be responsible for ensuring programs are effective and appropriate. However, since HR typically leads the design of programs and is held accountable for their performance it raises credibility questions if HR conducts evaluations. This is not to suggest that HR would knowingly misrepresent program performance, but rather that an all-HR evaluation team would bring an all-HR perspective to the process.

Having the internal audit function of the organization perform program evaluations certainly is a feasible option, especially if their scope includes operational audits, rather than strictly financial audits. Their role could be to establish the "What is actually happening?" portion of the picture, determining if managers are acting in a manner consistent with established policies and procedures. But it is unlikely that the auditors will have much to contribute to the "What should be?" question or "What do employees think is happening?" issue. If employee attitudes are to be surveyed using a structured questionnaire, auditors could perform this analysis, but increasingly perceptions are gained through focus groups and other interactive processes, and this may be outside the competence of an auditor.

One approach is to separate the evaluation process into an *audit*, which analyzes what is happening, a *perceptions evaluation*, which determines what people think is going on, and a *policy review*, which involves management and HR in determining if the program objectives or guiding principles need to change. The internal audit function could lead the first portion, HR (and perhaps employees themselves) could lead the second portion and HR and executive management could direct the third. HR is all too often the "rules police" anyway, and the auditing portion is where objectivity is most valued, so this approach removes some of the suspicion about bias from the evaluation.

Having the audit portion performed by a neutral party has been made even easier because of the technology that is now available. HR information systems provide a number of facts that can be used as diagnostics and that allow for objective evaluation. For example, compa-ratios (the ratio of current pay to some intended target, such as the midpoint) can be calculated for individuals, departments and classes of employee very easily. Calculating the compa-ratios by gender, race, age and even grade level can provide useful information for beginning a diagnosis of the workings of a pay program. If compa-ratios for minorities are found to be lower than those for other similarly situated people (same grade, same performance, same competence and same longevity), this can suggest potential inequities. A finding that there is statistically significant adverse impact on a protected class does not establish that something is wrong or that discrimination exists, but it can highlight the need to establish the causes and to determine what if anything needs to be done about it. The audit produces the indicators, but the further investigation should become the responsibility of HR, owing to the knowledge and skill of the function's staff. A finding that the compa-ratios increase as the grade level becomes higher does not in itself establish anything. It may be that higher market rates have forced pay levels up in the higher grades, and it may also be that there is more longevity among more senior-level professionals and managers. On the other hand, if performance ratings are shown to be higher as the grade level increases, this finding should be turned over to HR, to determine if the performance management system is understood and if it is being properly administered.

Inconsistency across functions is perhaps the most fertile ground for further expert investigation by HR. It may be that specific functions in short supply in the marketplace have been targeted to be paid higher in the ranges, to ensure those in critical occupations can be attracted and retained. Other occupations may have control points that are below range midpoints, because they are not critical to the performance of the organization's primary business. For example, if a hospital is paying RNs higher in the established pay ranges than they are accountants it may reflect a policy to divert funds to critical occupations, in order to deal with skill shortages. On the other hand, if the pattern does not coincide with a conscious policy it may be prudent to examine the causes further.

Chris Argyris has provided guidelines for evaluators that are both practical and sensible.[3] He contends evaluators should avoid taking the decisions away from the proper decision makers by providing complete, verifiable, unbiased information in a manner that leaves the decision to the designated party. The unbiased part is difficult, since posing alternative actions seems the natural outgrowth of evaluation. But if the evaluator narrows the range of options during the process of providing recommendations this may intrude on the decision maker's realm. A fine line indeed, but one that can be defined by having the decision makers clearly prescribe the type of information they require. If the evaluators are instructed to identify and analyze all options and to present the two or three deemed most appropriate this should be the product of the evaluation. On the other hand, it is always a good idea to document the rejected options, if only in an appendix, so the final decision maker can determine what was looked at and why certain options were rejected.

Another bias that can be dangerous is a bias in favor of change. Activity is often taken to demonstrate the evaluator is "proactive," "a change manager" or some other noble characteristic. But the most honest evaluation may result in a finding that a program is just fine. This is a hard conclusion to present, since resources have been expended and it is often felt something should come of it. Too often evaluators justify the effort by nit-picking on minor issues or leaping forward to changes that could be made that would make the program even better. If this is the charge it is the proper thing to do. But it should always be remembered that most employee populations have often had quite enough change, and tinkering with their pay program may not be the best way to increase their satisfaction levels. Overlooking defects in program operation is not suggested, but rather that things that are just fine should be found to be just fine.

Applying the Evaluation Results

The bottom line of any evaluation is what will be done as a result of the findings. More change does not automatically equate to an effective management response. And radical change is often disruptive, to be avoided unless it is deemed to be absolutely necessary and pressing in the short term.

Most programs atrophy over time and it may be better to manage a change effort to correct major alterations over time rather than to attempt immediate fixes. The most important tool for early diagnosis and gradual correction is to evaluate early and on a regular basis, so actual results and/or perceptions do not drift significantly off course. Fixing many small issues can often be easier than waiting until a major crisis is at hand. Programs that have become totally ineffective will become apparent to all parties, and there may be little choice but to put them out of their misery and to undergo a new program design and implementation. In addition to the resource consumption that takes place when a totally new program must be created, there should be concern about the impact the program failure will have on the reputation and future standing of HR and of management.

Modifications to programs, if done when needed, can be accepted as a normal evolution to keep the program aligned with the realities of the organizational context. They also can usually be accomplished without bringing in outside resources and without stirring up huge clouds of dust. Few employees can remain calm when programs close to their hearts and wallets are being substantially changed. And these upheavals will have a negative impact on the confidence level of employees that management knows what it is doing.

A Major Decision: Is Application of Policy Variable at the Individual Level?

The increased mobility of talent has made getting and keeping the people with the most critical skills more challenging. And the Generation X, Generation Y and Millennial cohorts have brought values to the workplace that have placed more pressure on management to accommodate their personal needs and preferences. Managers increasingly feel it necessary to argue for varying from established policies and practices, in order to get someone or keep someone they believe is critical to their function. They claim that other companies are paying more for specific critical skills and are making deals with individuals that include other rewards. They also complain that other managers have made deals that their employees are aware of and that they should be allowed to do the same thing. As the appeals mount up it appears every employee is critical and that they are all poised to leave for any of a hundred reasons, such as the need for more money, a need to work at home, a need to have a flexible work week, a need for better technology, a need for more staff, etc. Also, every outside candidate for employment seems to demand some deviation from some of the established policies and practices.

Even though this sounds like an unpleasant situation, it could be worse. Managers could be making the deals they deem appropriate without informing HR or senior management that the policies and practices are being applied in a way that is very different from what was intended. They could also be circumventing policies, by using contractors rather than hiring employees, and by cutting deals on compensation, work schedule and work assignment that are expedient in the short run and that get their department's work done.

No organization can totally avoid idiosyncratic deals that vary from established policy and administrative guidelines. In the book *I-deals*, Rousseau defines idiosyncratic deals as "voluntary, personalized agreements of a nonstandard nature negotiated between individual employees and their employers regarding terms that benefit each party."[4] In order to evaluate the impact of these agreements it is important to overcome the negative connotation often associated with the term "deal" (particularly in the U.S., where the term is used to describe special arrangements by district attorneys with criminals). The press of business makes some flexibility in applying policies necessary. But bad deals can result in inconsistencies that create inequities and even legal exposure. Inconsistencies between deals can result from: 1) poor decision making; 2) a lack of consistency between managers; or 3) a lack of consistency by the same managers over time. To avoid or remedy the damage that can be caused by inconsistency the organization must take the initiative to make the best of an imperfect situation.

There are numerous reasons for managers to vary from established policy. The pressure applied by employees who feel they have both a legitimate need and a right to accommodation is typically the most common reason given by managers. The things that cause employees to provide this pressure are the receipt of "better" offers from the outside, the discovery that they are paid inequitably relative to peers, finding "data" on the internet that shows them to be underpaid, or experiencing pressures in their private lives that necessitate accommodation in their work life. Initiating a request for varying from company policy may also be a way of testing how much the manager values the employee.

Managers also make deals that violate established policy owing to a poor understanding of what the policies are or an inadequate appreciation of the consequences of making such a deal. The fixes for a poor understanding are making policies explicit and communicating them broadly. Although policy manuals are generally not the most scintillating reading, it is a good investment to ensure managers and employees are fully informed about them. Too few new manager or new employee orientations focus on what the policies are, why they are what they are and what the consequences are of not adhering to policy. Many HR policies are mandated by law, although managers and employees may not be aware of that. Overtime pay provisions in the Fair Labor Standards Act are often violated by managers because they do "what makes sense" (e.g., get the work done this week and give some compensatory time off next week) rather than what the law prescribes. It is incumbent on the organization to explain that laws need not be convenient or make sense. They only have to be followed.

Yet another reason for "manager transgression" is that a manager is firmly convinced a policy is wrong or that it has been poorly implemented. They may be convinced that jobs are in the wrong grades in the pay structure. They may believe that market values gleaned through surveys are inappropriate, given the specific situation they are dealing with. And they may view salary increase budgets as more of a guideline than a constraint. If managers do not feel the pay ranges are equitable or competitive they are not going to feel bound to stay within the constraints contained in formal policies and procedures. Although the managers may accept that in general the policies can guide decisions, if they are being pressured to make an accommodation that might save a valued employee, the policies are likely to be trumped by the benefits associated with the expedient action.

Hiring

Another source of deals is the recruitment of outside candidates. People new to the organization are likely to have different employment conditions in their current employer (pay, work schedule, responsibilities and the like). A manager desperate to hire a candidate is likely to view their "must have" conditions as being reasonable—after all, the person already has adjusted his or her lifestyle to the current situation. But that same manager may have ruled out the same accommodations for existing employees, establishing a precedent. An example would be paying a new hire more than the pay range maximum. Another would be to make someone eligible for an incentive program that peers do not partici- pate in. This sets the stage for a deviation from policy or prior practice, necessitating an explanation to longer-service employees why someone who has not yet contributed to the organization is treated more favorably than those who have. Such a scenario seems to beg a complaint and create dissatisfaction.

Retention

Deals are also commonly made to attract or to retain critical-skill employees in short supply or to keep and satisfy top performers. The IT bubble in the late 1990s triggered a proliferation of deals to ensure critical skills were available. Making deals for top per- formers has a long history, both because the strong bargaining position of those who are contributing the most gives them power and because the company may wish to motivate others to perform as well. Larger salary increases, larger incentive awards, plum assignments and other rewards are commonly viewed as a legitimate way to treat highly valued employees. Some of these deals are consistent with established policy and practices. Organizations that publicly claim they pay for performance encourage managers to make

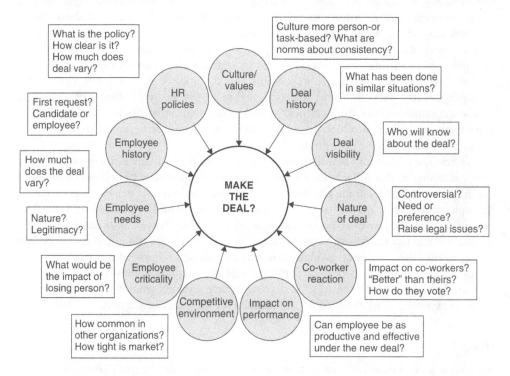

Figure 15.3 Evaluating idiosyncratic deals

these deals. Other preferences, such as overlooking shortcomings or rewarding people in a clandestine manner, may be done quietly by managers because they are not officially sanctioned by policies or practices.

Figure 15.3 illustrates all of the considerations that a manager should include in deciding whether to make a deal and what questions they should ask. If deals are evaluated using an appropriate decision-making structure, it will improve the quality and consistency of the deals that are made. The existence of a gestalt that can be used to frame decisions about individual deals can be a giant step towards improving consistency and making deals more acceptable to all parties at interest. Managers often unconsciously consider most or all of these factors, but by making them aware of all the potential consequences and by educating them about what to consider, the organization improves its chances of minimizing bad deals.

Managers also make deals because they want to have all employees view their employment conditions as fair. Equity theory provides a foundation for designing and administering HR programs in a manner that produces perceptions of "fair" treatment.[5] If employees feel worse off than those they compare to, the result is dissatisfaction. High levels of job dissatisfaction have been shown to increase turnover and absenteeism, a potentially disastrous result in today's competitive arena for talent.

Employees leaving the organization will tend to use their rewards package as the reason. Whether or not this is the real reason, it is easier for an exiting employee to cite pay as the reason for departure than it is to criticize the supervisor or other conditions. Perceptions of unfair pay relative to peers or others in the organization are certainly a common and legitimate cause for departure, as are perceptions of pay not being competitive with that of other organizations. Given the proliferation of survey data and the broad publication of data on average pay levels and average pay adjustments, an employee can easily find a data set that will support the case they wish to make. Rumors that employees who have left have received much higher pay are common. Rarely do ex-employees come back to report they are now making less, so the information received by employees is hardly balanced.

Sometimes, the underlying cause of dissatisfaction does turn out to be pay structures and/or pay rates. Some industries attempt to compete with lower levels of direct pay coupled with better-than-average benefit packages. Other organizations attempt to keep base pay levels somewhat below market to minimize fixed costs and use variable compensation programs to provide motivation to perform well.

During the last decade there has been significant turbulence in labor markets in the U.S., as well as in most developed and developing countries. Owing to the increased globalization of business and the increased competition for talent, the historical practice of mechanically adjusting pay structures upward to maintain competitiveness has come under fire. The late 1990s saw the competition for skilled IT personnel generate dramatic increases in market pay levels, particularly for those with network skills. Although organizations have historically varied their pay targets for specific occupations experiencing supply–demand imbalances, often creating inequities between new hires and longer-service employees, the dramatic inflation of market pay levels for IT strained their systems. Making the situation even worse, organizations were forced by economic constraints to pay the large premiums only to those with specific skills, creating significant differences between employees having the same job title. Horror stories about how this situation was mishandled have caused some to believe the days of orderly pay administration are over. They are not, but the angst caused by the proliferation of deals that seemed to violate accepted notions of what constituted fairness has left many employees cynical about how rewards are administered. If the belief that sustained high levels of performance are less important than being lucky enough to be in the right place with the right skills at the right time becomes widespread, organizations will suffer the loss of one of their most important motivational tools.

The Y2K debacle could have been managed better had there been a structure for making decisions that were explainable in terms of business necessity and that produced both flexibility and consistency. Consistency does not necessarily mean the same result for everyone. Consistently applying guiding principles may produce differences, but these differences can be explained in terms of business realities and can be demonstrated to be equitable. One way to provide a framework for making accommodations is to articulate and broadly communicate the guiding principles the organization wants managers to adhere to. For pay administration the most common principle is that each person's pay will be: 1) internally equitable; 2) externally competitive; and 3) administered appropriately. The organization then needs to "breathe life" into these principles by openly demonstrating that actions that are taken are consistent with them.

All factors impacting a decision should be considered prior to making the decision. If an employee is about to leave for substantially more money, the organization should consider the probable impact of matching the pay offer on the employee, on coworkers and on the organization. Counter-offers may violate a long-standing commitment to maintain equity among employees and cause morale problems with coworkers. Even worse, the action may precipitate feelings of inequity on the part of managers in other functions who now feel their people are not as valued. Much of the potential damage can be controlled by aggressive communication of the details of the situation, accompanied by an explanation of why the action makes sense from a business perspective. However, the willingness to make an exception sends a message about which skills are critical to the organization, and there will inevitably be some resentment on the part of those who do not fall in the "critical skills" category.

It is short-sighted not to explain to employees how the organization must compete for talent in the marketplace and what it needs to do to be competitive. It should be understood that those having skills that are central to the core capabilities of the organization and critical to its performance will enjoy a privileged status, and their attraction and retention will be given the highest priority. Explaining the realities of the business and the strategy may not make everyone happy but it will minimize the feeling that the decision is being made based on personal likes or in an arbitrary fashion. Professionals in occupations that are not central and critical to an organization should be able to accept reality. If they can they should attempt to find a place in an organization where their skills are critical. Public accounting firms will certainly value accounting skills highly and would rightly avoid alienating those who do the work that is at the heart of the business. A health care organization may be less concerned about accounting than about those occupations that are at the heart of its core activities. Paying more to specific occupations or skill sets is admittedly easier to explain than paying differently within an occupation. When a "deal" is made for one employee and not extended to others who have similar skills the need for an explanation becomes even greater. The perception that an individual benefits because of a friendship with the manager is perhaps the most difficult to deal with.

Organizations often cite mastery of job-critical skills and performance as the only two legitimate factors that contribute to pay level differences between employees within a classification. However, if an employee is viewed as a star by co-workers and if they feel their lives would be worse without that employee they may support actions to prevent the departure, even though these actions are outside policy and not available to them personally. And if the organization can make the decision in a manner that is consistent with the guiding principles that govern how it makes such decisions the outcome may be positive. Using the framework provided in Figure 15.3 can help to ensure all relevant factors are considered. Too few organizations have effective performance management systems that can justify differences in treatment based on contribution, but if that is the source of difficulty in making the right decision then the performance management system needs to be fixed.

Perhaps the most overlooked approach to building flexibility into rewards administration while retaining consistency and equity is the use of variable cost programs. Flexible ("cafeteria") benefits packages enable individuals to select from a menu those items that they value most highly relative to other options, while sending the message that everyone has the same total amount available to them. Similarly, the use of incentive pay programs to encourage and reward high levels of performance does not build the reward amount into base pay, thereby avoiding a fixed cost going forward. Even base pay administration can be modified to create temporary adjustments to rapidly changing market conditions. The use of variable "control points," while maintaining the established job grades and pay ranges, enables an organization to administer pay for specific occupations or skill sets in a way that responds to variations in market rates. For example, many organizations that recognized that the IT bubble in the late 1990s would be a temporary condition created "shadow ranges" that enabled them to hire at competitive levels and to grant competitive pay adjustments while retaining the flexibility to let the premiums added to the ranges disappear as the market for IT skills came back in line with that of other professional disciplines. Several organizations the author worked with during the late 1990s had premiums of 15% or more added to the range minimums, midpoints and maximums for about two years and then slowly phased out the premiums over the next two to three years. This approach enabled them to compete in the hot markets but also to avoid artificially upgrading the IT jobs or taking them out of the pay structure altogether. It also provided a basis for communicating that these actions were temporary responses to temporary market conditions and that they were prudent from a business perspective. Finally, it served to maintain internal equity.

Deals for Part-time and Seasonal Workers and Contractors

Charles Handy introduced a staffing model he called the "Shamrock organization."[6] There are three categories of employee in this model: 1) full-time core employees; 2) part-time or temporary employees; and 3) contractors. This approach has become widespread, owing to the necessity of matching staffing to continuously varying workloads and available resources. Having different categories of people working with each other raises several issues related to the terms and conditions accorded each category. Full-time core employees may feel their security is threatened by the use of contractors and part-timers or temps. Seeing others working under different arrangements makes the tenuous nature of their employment clear, since they may be replaced by these workers or may be forced to become one of them. If contractors are seen to be better paid, allowed to work more flexible schedules and assigned the "glamour" work an employee's satisfaction with their own conditions of employment are apt to diminish. Very few hiring managers factor in the potential impact on core employee satisfaction and productivity when developing a strategy for using flexible workers, and this is a major oversight. Although economics or work demands may mandate this approach it is prudent to understand all the implications.

The manner in which contractors are paid is a common source of resentment on the part of full-time employees. The author was in the office of an HR director in the late 1990s when an employee barged in, accusing the executive of "paying that hired gun 200 grand when I supervise her and make half as much." The employee had lunched with a new contractor working on converting the mainframe computer system to a network system and the contractor had told the employee she was being paid $100 per hour worked. The employee multiplied that by 2,080 hours and hence the "200 grand" figure. Although the HR director later admitted she almost had pointed out that the contractor did not have job security and was not eligible for benefits she had realized the folly of that approach. The security argument surely would have been scoffed at and the employee might have offered to sell her benefits back to the company for $25,000 per year. The issue here was internal equity between "outsiders" and those who are in it for the longer haul, and the Shamrock model creates contrasts that lend themselves to comparisons being made.

Organizations are constrained by legal and tax regulations when they decide how to compensate and manage contractors. The IRS has challenged contractor status more frequently and aggressively ever since the Microsoft court decision that resulted in huge fines and corrective action mandates. Making legal requirements known to all might help to moderate employee dissatisfaction with *how* contractors are paid, but may do little to address the *how much*. Market conditions might dictate a high rate of pay for a contractor with scarce skills, and it is possible that employees will accept pay level differences if they know what prevailing market rates are and if they accept that contractors are competent to do things they cannot do. There is also another approach—offer contractor status to employees. This must be done carefully, but rapid changes in the amount and type of work that must be done may suggest the need for a staffing model that utilizes flexible resources. The possible conversion of an employee's status should not be used as a threat, but it may be a better fit to the employee's needs and preferences if the conditions under which they would work as a contractor are acceptable. Another approach is to change the manner in which contractors are compensated. If the contractor is retained on a "fee for work delivered" basis it is possible to avoid an hourly rate basis. Motivation theory would predict that a contractor paid by the hour is motivated to do three things: 1) work as many hours as possible; 2) never get done; and 3) avoid training employees, lest a competitor be created. This makes the hourly pay approach a questionable strategy. There are also issues with part-time and temporary employees if they are paid an hourly rate that is higher than the rate at which full-time employees are paid.

Deals in Global Organizations

The issues associated with making decisions about individual deals become dramatically more complex when the workforce represents multiple national and ethnic cultures.

Whether cultural diversity is caused by people from different backgrounds working in the same country or due to a workforce dispersed across national borders the effect is the same. Different deals for different people or different situations is a concept accepted far more readily in some cultures than in others. The U.S. culture is strongly "universalistic" in nature, which mandates one set of rules for everyone.[7] Other more "particularistic" cultures (much of Asia, Latin America, Latin Europe and the Middle East) believe the particulars of the situation should dictate the need for variation. Who is involved can have a major impact on whether a deal is appropriate in these cultures. These significant differences in beliefs about what is fair and appropriate can cause a good deal of stress to the global organization. Americans often label hiring preferences extended to relatives or acquaintances as nepotism (not a good thing), while a Latin may think it the best approach. The Latin's underlying rationale is that scrutiny of the new hire by their family and social network will promote honesty and diligence. Pay levels and perceptions of performance may also be at least partially a function of who someone is in "ascriptive" cultures such as France, while in the U.S. the "achievement" culture mandates that rewards and career progress be based on what the person contributes, no matter who they are or where they went to school.

Deals in Public and Not-for-profit Sector Organizations

Rigidity in pay structures and pay administration policies is still prevalent in the U.S. public sector. Federal employee GS rules prescribe increases based mostly on time in grade and also that someone hired or promoted into a new job be paid at a specific step within the schedule. Sometimes, this inflexibility limits the ability to hire and/or retain highly skilled and mobile professionals who can negotiate a compensation package that is consistent with their market value and that reflects their performance. The rigidity can force a manager to attempt to attract or retain a valued individual by artificially upgrading the person to a level they cannot justify, thereby creating inequities with other employees. These end runs around the system are very difficult to control and to defend. It can be argued that there are benefits to tying pay level to longevity and by adhering to the rigid system managers may in fact avoid feelings of inequity on the part of other employees. But few managers will follow established policies and practices if they believe it will result in the loss of people who are critical to the performance of their unit (and to their own performance rating).

Deals in Start-ups

Organizations in their early life often do individual deals rather than formalizing policies. Often, this is a requirement in an environment when the organization has "one of everything": one finance person, one design engineer, etc. Since everyone's knowledge base and contribution is unique it is difficult to focus on consistency. However, since each deal sets a precedent, the realities of managing a larger organization in the future may force management to attempt to create order out of chaos. Often, the informal culture that people signed up for persists and resists standardization, no matter what the requirements of the business mandate. Therefore, the dilemma of consistency versus flexibility should be taken seriously by management in the early years, to ensure the balance between the two can be effectively and appropriately maintained to fit the realities faced in the future.

The continuous and dramatic changes occurring in the talent markets today place intense pressure on organizations to be flexible in how they administer programs within policy. The types of employer value propositions that sell to those with critical skills and who are mobile across organizations must include some flexibility and individualization. Yet every idiosyncratic deal that is made can create inequities relative to other employees, precedents for further variation from established policies and procedures and even exposure to legal liability.

The existence of a well-defined and broadly communicated decision-making structure can minimize the negative impacts of deals and in fact can improve the quality of the deals that must be made. The structure must prescribe consideration of how the deal will impact all parties at interest, including the individual, the organization and other employees. Guiding principles that are established formally and made public can provide a gestalt that managers can use to frame their decisions when they find it necessary to deviate from policies and practices. Employees are capable of understanding that market factors and business necessity can create the need for variation. Those who need flexibility in their own situation will appreciate the organization's willingness to attempt to make accommodations, while at the same time adhering to the values and principles that apply to all.

Application of Principles: Chapter 15

Select a "deal" relative to your conditions of employment you would like to make, or would have liked to have made in the past. Honestly appraise the arrangement using the model in this chapter (i.e., is it a necessity or just a preference for you? what would the impact be on the department? what would the cost be to the organization?). Consider the impact of your deal on the relative equity of conditions of employment if others did not receive the same accommodation. If you were the person asked to approve the deal would you? Why?

Notes

1 Lawler, E., *Pay and Organization Development* (Reading, MA, Addison-Wesley, 1981).
2 Cascio, W., *Costing Human Resources*, 4th ed. (Cincinnati, OH, South-Western, 2000).
3 Argyris, C., *Intervention Theory and Method* (Reading, MA, Addison-Wesley, 1970).
4 Rousseau, D., *I-deals* (Armonk, NY, M. E. Sharpe, 2005).
5 Lawler, E., *Pay and Organizational Effectiveness* (New York, McGraw-Hill, 1971).
6 Handy, C., *The Age of Unreason* (Boston, MA, Harvard University Press, 1989).
7 Trompenaars, F., *Managing People across Cultures* (Chichester, UK, Capstone, 2004).

Chapter 16

Sustainable Strategies

Facing into the Future

One of the realities organizations must face is that the environment within which they conduct their business has become more dynamic over the last few decades. This millennium has already seen the impact of Y2K, the economic downturns of 2000–02 and 2007–15. Many would argue that the cause of the downturn after 2000 was irrational exuberance and the causes of the second were irresponsible greed and poor regulation, rather than economic fundamentals. Whatever the cause, the downturns happened and organizations must cope. If, as evidence indicates, there will be dramatic swings in the economy for the foreseeable future, human resource management strategies must be sustainable into the future and not just a good fit to the present.

Compensation practitioners should be evaluating the fundamental makeup of the total rewards packages they provide to employees. Many organizations felt they had learned how to manage employee rewards in the sustained boom period of the 1990s and after the dotcom crash of 2000–02. That was until the economic crisis of 2007–08 materialized. After waging the "talent war," many of those responsible for developing rewards strategies were faced with a mandate to cut costs, without losing the talent they had acquired and that they would need in the future. Some rewards strategies work well when an organization is growing and prospering, but not so well when the economy turns down sharply. The challenge is finding a robust strategy that works well under any scenario that unfolds. The guiding principle of paying for performance has become even more critical, since organizations cannot afford to incur compensation expense without the results needed to provide the resources necessary to support the expense. Those responsible for formulating rewards strategies should be using scenario–planning tools to define possible futures based on environmental scanning and to ensure their strategies are robust, able to work reasonably well in any of the possible futures. Schwartz has defined scenarios as "tools for ordering one's perceptions about alternative future environments in which one's decisions might be played out." He believes them to be "a set of organized ways to dream effectively about our own future."[1] It is important to understand the nature of scenarios. They are not predictions, but vehicles for helping people learn. They do not merely extrapolate the trends of the present.[2]

Figure 16.1 is the outcome of a scenario–planning exercise in an oil and gas company that does exploration, drilling and distribution. The first part deals with the future faced by the business as it contemplates shifting emphasis from carbon fuels to alternative energy technology (AET). This is the result of strategic dialogues within executive management. The second part deals with strategies for building a workforce that will enable the organization to remain viable and to perform well in the future. This type of planning, however beneficial, is often difficult to begin and to sustain. When one's house is on fire there is little time for discussing fire prevention or insurance coverage. When there is no fire it is difficult to be enthusiastic about calling a consultant or insurance agent. When the economy turns down and/or the organization hits a bump in the road, all resources are aimed at dealing with the present conditions and with recovery. When the economy is booming the exercise does not seem urgent. But the old saying "If you continue to do what you have always done you will continue to get what you have always got" should be heeded. Without strategic dialogues, organizations will be condemned to putting out the fires as they happen, with little effort dedicated to controlling their destiny.

This type of planning requires a several-stage process: 1) identify key challenges; 2) define forces impacting outcomes; 3) rank challenges by their immediacy and impact on the organization; 4) conduct the strategic dialogues that produce the business scenarios; 5) evaluate how alternative human resource strategies will work under each of the scenarios; 6) select a strategy and evaluate its effectiveness continuously; and 7) adapt to changing conditions by altering the strategy as needed.

Scenario planning is critical for preparing for the future. It is not the answer to current challenges, however. Many organizations in early 2008 began engaging in large downsizings, viewing this as mandatory to remain viable given economic conditions. The average budgets for pay increases were reduced shortly after they had been established. A follow-up survey by WorldatWork conducted in December 2008 showed that the average budget fell from the 4% reported in mid-2008 in their annual survey to just over 3% in the special follow-up survey later that year.[3] The survey actually overstated the new budget due to a statistical anomaly. The comparison between the two years was calculated using the average budget set at the start of the year and the reported budget by participants in the special survey. But organizations cutting and freezing pay tended not to report in the special survey, since they are unlikely to expend the effort if they had no use for the resulting report. The true labor market movement had driven the average budget much lower than 3%. The number of organizations freezing base pay increases jumped from less than 3% to 10–15%. Over one-half of respondents indicated it was likely that cash incentive plans might not pay out at all or might pay out at much reduced levels. There was no data that measured how many organizations were changing their practices relative to stock-based programs, but it is likely that changes would be widespread. The association had published the survey for 20 years, providing data on what organizations projected as their budgets for the year just completed, what the expenditure actually was and projections for the following year. The special survey done in December 2008 was in response to the sudden collapse in the economy. The dramatic results illustrate how plans can shift in a few months as a result of external conditions. This further emphasized the need to adopt scenario-based tools to better anticipate changes and to formulate strategies for several futures.

A major opportunity was missed by many organizations during the boom periods of the 1990s and 2003–08. When resources were plentiful there was an opportunity to reward deserving employees generously. Most organizations did that. But *how* they did it is now coming back to haunt them. Those driving up fixed costs with large base pay increases set the stage for a real dilemma when resources became scarce. Since significant variable compensation opportunity is often limited to executives and managers, sales personnel and other key people, most direct compensation expense is in the form of

Results of Scenario Planning
Three Scenarios for an Oil and Gas Company's Business

Pessimistic Scenario

- Federal and state governments talk about the benefits of AET but do not take any substantive action to promote investment in AET.
- Recession of 2009 reduces spendable income and consumer confidence is very low.
- Oil price drops below historical levels and remains low.

Most Likely Scenario

- Federal and state governments provide modest tax breaks for the use of AET.
- Recession ceases to worsen and seems to be short- to medium-term in duration.
- Oil prices stabilize around historical levels.
- Consumer concerns about global warming increase their receptiveness to using AET.
- Consumer confidence recovers somewhat and people go back to prior spending levels.

Optimistic Scenario

- Government imposes significant taxes on carbon fuels and provides major tax breaks for those who adopt AET, making AET competitive with coal and oil.
- Economy responds to government stimulus and begins to rebound.
- Oil prices rise, owing to OPEC attempts to punish West for MENA region conflicts.
- Consumers get "fire in their bellies" about addressing global warming and carry their copy of *Hot, Flat and Crowded* with them everywhere.

Impact of Scenario Planing on Human Resource Planning

Impact of Shifting to AET on Workforce Viability

- Current workforce has adequate knowledge and skills to conduct current oil and gas business effectively, but is not prepared to engage in developing AET and using it.
- Skill shortages exist in the labor market for those with advanced knowledge of AET.
- Demand for AET skills will continue to increase, creating even greater shortages.
- Training current employees so they are competent in AET will require massive efforts that the current T&D function is unable to execute.
- Compensation levels for AET specialists have escalated rapidly and are 25% higher than those for current employees having traditional skills.

Alternative Strategies for Maintaining
Workforce Viability after Adopting AET

- Have AET development work done by contractors or outsource to full service provider.
- Recruit people with AET skills and pay them 115% of market rate, in order to get the best.
- Make training in AET available to current employees with the necessary education and experience to make them viable candidates for performing well in the new business; delay development until current employees are capable of doing the work.
- Retain contractors to oversee the development work and to train the existing workforce. Compensate contractors with project incentives that are based on three performance criteria: 1) productivity; 2) timely completion; 3) training existing employees to implement new technology.

Figure 16.1 Outcome of a scenario-planning exercise in an oil and gas company

base pay. And all of that base payroll is a fixed cost. This is not a recipe for success when revenues plunge. But making a significant portion of total direct compensation variable is certainly not a panacea, as discussed in earlier chapters. Employees finding it difficult to meet their expenses in 2009 because of reduced income will not feel much better if it is due to a justifiable shutdown in the profit- or performance-sharing plan. Their income is still reduced.

If downsizing seems to be the only feasible option, an organization should carefully consider what cost savings might actually be realized. Firing ten staff members earning an average of $50,000 per annum does not immediately save $500,000—it takes a full year to realize that amount. And those savings will be reduced by a number of required payments. The obligations relative to severance pay, accrued vacation and sick leave, pension obligations and other liabilities that will come due upon severance will add to immediate expenditures and must be paid earlier than the annual salary would have been. Increased unemployment compensation tax rates may result. Incurring these costs may be unwise if the downturn in revenues is not expected to last for an extended period. If downsizing is expected to improve profitability and/or productivity, the research done on the 2001–02 downturn should be considered. Cascio did an extensive evaluation of the impact of downsizings during that period and found that many of the outcomes were reduced morale and employee engagement, without the desired improvements in financial results.[4] A final consideration should be the potential increase in legal liability, owing to litigation that may be created as a result of downsizing. If the cuts have a statistically significant adverse impact on a protected class this could trigger discrimination suits. And angry people who believe they have nothing else to lose are more apt to initiate litigation.

Organizations should attempt to project whether a subsequent upturn in the economy will be likely to require staff additions, perhaps even before all the severance payments have been covered by reduced payroll costs. Some employee changes may be warranted, based on individual performance and on the organization's workforce needs going forward. If that is the case there should be steps taken to ensure unnecessary or underperforming employees are not added. Restarting a talent war to get the human capital required for future viability is a bad idea. Some organizations might find that having more work performed by outsiders will position them to constrain fixed costs better. If contractors, consultants and freelancers are used rather than additions to staff they represent controllable variable costs and do not inflate the fixed cost payroll. Chapter 11 discusses the use of outsiders in lieu of employees in greater detail.

No matter the other actions taken, today's environment is such that organizations should evaluate their rewards strategies and consider alternatives.

Alternative Rewards Strategies

There are a number of alternative actions that rewards strategists can consider to restructure the total rewards package. Immediate cost reduction is likely to be the favored result during economic downturns. Actions such as reducing base pay levels and freezing plan payouts are candidates for consideration. Freezing base pay levels and reducing incentive plan payouts are more moderate actions. And reducing benefit levels and/or increasing the employee share of benefits costs can help pare costs. However, these alternatives may not be sustainable over the long run, unless the major competitors are doing the same thing, since this strategy would cause the organization's pay levels to fall behind market levels. And waiting until a downturn occurs forces organizations to make decisions based on short-term needs, without a plan as to how to recover in the subsequent upturn.

A strategy that can be viable over the longer run is to revise how base pay and incentive plans are designed and how budgets and incentive funds are allocated. For example, salary increases for those at or above their pay range midpoint may be replaced by cash awards tied to performance. And over time it is possible to replace a portion of fixed cost base payroll with variable pay opportunity, by carving that opportunity out of what would have been base pay adjustments. This enables the organization to tie a larger portion of compensation expense to annual performance. Each of these actions should be subjected to a cost–benefit analysis before considering adoption. Combinations of these actions can change the composition of the total rewards package, as well as reducing workforce costs. But each of them constitutes a major intervention, and the need to develop a suitable process to use in implementing change is critical. Employees often do not fully understand why their rewards packages are what they are, and often misunderstand how programs actually work. And it is highly probable that they will be skeptical about major changes if the communication effort is not adequate. Initiating an extensive dialogue with employees can help to put all the cards on the table and to include employees in deliberations about how to best structure the rewards package, so that it provides the best result for the organization and the workforce.

If an organization is faced with an economic downturn and its cost structure is such that it must rely on reducing costs, there are a number of options, some of which can reposition it for the longer term. Table 16.1 summarizes the alternatives, their impact on the employer, their impact on employees and when they should best be utilized. Each of the alternatives will be explored.

Reducing base pay rates is a difficult action to take if employee morale and engagement are major concerns. Some employees will view a base pay reduction as a breach of contract, since they have established their standard of living based on the expectation that the base pay will always be there and that all changes to the rate will be increases. Many public sector organizations utilize time-based step systems to regulate base pay progression. The GS system, which covers a substantial portion of U.S. federal government employees, utilizes time-based step progression. Since step progression is written into policies it is very difficult to freeze progressions without policy changes and without challenges by those affected. The vast majority of private sector organizations use open ranges and merit pay systems, so in theory reductions to current base pay rates do not violate established policy. Certainly, an organization in danger of running out of cash may be forced to implement pay cuts. And executive pay cuts that are larger than those for other employees can promote a sense of fairness relative to sacrifice.

Replacing base payroll with variable pay opportunity is a high-impact strategy, but implementing it poses a considerable challenge. The most extreme approach is to lower base pay rates and to provide an incentive opportunity, which can result in even higher direct compensation levels if organizational performance exceeds a target. This may sound like a palatable offer, unless the employees realize that exceeding performance targets is a major (unachievable?) challenge, given the economic conditions that precipitated the strategy change in the first place. Certainly the dark side of this alternative is that if performance does not meet target the total direct income levels will decline. Most employees have obligations that are based on a certain income stream, and the prospect of an incentive payout does not ensure the mortgage is paid.

Table 16.1 Alternative Strategies for Reducing Workforce Costs

Alternative Action	Employee Impact	Employer Impact	When Appropriate
Reduce headcount	Loss of income; most severe	Immediate cost reduction, less costs of severance	Immediate cost reduction mandatory
Reduce base pay	Drop in income; impact on morale	Reduced payroll, beginning immediately	When only other option is firing people who will be needed in future
Freeze base pay	Income does not increase with inflation	Prevents further increase to fixed costs	Uncertain future; if it will not cause loss of critical skills
Split pay increase budget into increases and cash awards	Does not reduce income and good performers may prefer	Slows escalation of fixed cost payroll; may motivate better	When fixed costs must be controlled; more motivation needed
Replace future base pay increases with incentive potential	Positive for high performers; negative for poor performers	Enables restructuring of costs over time; ties costs to resources	When there is need to change strategy; when metrics are good
Replace cash awards with equity program	Impact based on market performance	Shifts funding to market	When stock price increase is possible
Increase employee participation in health care costs	Reduces net income; depends on current sharing formula	Saves growth in costs; depends on current sharing formula	When employee share is less than 25% of cost
Move from defined benefit to defined contribution plans	Increases investment return risk	Decreases investment return risk	When total rewards will be competitive
Tie contributions to defined contribution plans to performance	Increases focus on organization performance	Increases employee focus on performance; may impact morale	When performance is measurable and when formula is competitive

A more moderate approach is to freeze increases to base pay. This is an alteration to what employees have come to expect, but they certainly would prefer it if the only other alternative is base pay reductions. The problem with this approach is that it only impacts the growth in costs and does not provide a short-term reduction in costs. Another factor that must be considered is the impact of this strategy shift on turnover among those with critical skills and knowledge. This will depend largely on what other organizations do. Unfortunately, it is difficult to call all the competitors for critical skills and to ask them for detailed information on what they plan to do. So who goes first and what impact does the shift have on them? Base pay freezes could be accompanied by implementing a variable pay opportunity, to be realized if the organization is able to perform at a level that warrants the expense associated with incentive awards. The reception this approach will receive will depend on whether the employees believe the performance required is possible to achieve, and whether they can influence results. Another difficulty with freezing base pay rates is that it might not have any impact on costs for close to a full year. Most organizations use a single focal date to make salary adjustments, and if that date has already occurred the freeze option can be effective only the following year. Some organizations have "rolled back" increases, which can be viewed as a base pay reduction by employees. But it somehow seems more explainable than planned base pay reductions, if the economic conditions warranting the action are known to all and these conditions provide a credible justification.

One strategy that is being used by more organizations is to maintain the "merit pay" systems that are in place, but to consider both the current performance by an employee and the position of the current pay rate to the pay range when determining adjustments. If the organization believes that the initiation of a "two-dimensional guide chart" approach (described in Chapter 3) will be viewed as unfair by those paid in the upper portion of the range, it may help to make a small modification. Increases may be based only on performance but be calculated off the range midpoint, rather than the current rate of pay. This provides the same dollar increase to all of those in the same grade and performing at the same level. And since the midpoint represents the market rate for the job, this may be viewed as being fair. The pattern of increases can be modified if the organization wishes to allocate the available funds differently. For example, if further budget reductions are needed the increases for employees in the upper third of the range may be reduced or eliminated. This would save a significant amount only if there are many employees paid in that third. The reason for taking this approach is that these employees are already paid significantly above market levels. Those in the lower part of the range are below market and therefore the most susceptible to competitive offers. Another approach is to reduce increase amounts for "Fully Meets" employees and to utilize available funds to reward the best performers. When reducing costs, the general rule is to start by reducing pay adjustments for those paid high in the range and performing at low levels, and to reduce the adjustments for those paid lower in the range and performing at higher levels only as a last resort.

Yet another approach is to use guidelines that split the budget into base pay increases and cash awards, described in detail in Chapter 12. The advantages of the second approach are: 1) fixed cost payroll goes up more slowly; 2) cash awards are allocated in a more discriminating manner, increasing their motivational impact; and 3) it sends the message that one cannot go on "automatic pilot" once the pay rate reaches the upper part of the pay range, without reducing the rewards earned. If the organization wants to use all of the available funds for cash awards the guidelines can be modified to eliminate base pay increases altogether. And in organizations facing a cash flow crisis consideration might be given to replacing the cash awards with performance-based time-off awards or deferred incentives. One of the major benefits of this type of system is that separate incentive plans do not have to be designed, implemented and administered. Given the staff effort required to develop new incentive plans this can be a major consideration. Incentive plan design may be better delayed until the administrative resources exist. The use of this approach may be a major change, and communication is the key to building understanding and acceptance.

The decision to make variable compensation a larger part of the total direct compensation package will require considerable staff effort and extensive communication. This will be even more pronounced if eligibility is being extended to employees who were not eligible in the past. There is considerable guidance available in the literature about when and how to use variable compensation. But the organizational context will have a major impact on how programs should be designed and administered. Culture is one of the major factors determining whether incentives will be accepted and how well they will work. As mentioned earlier, if incentive plans are implemented to replace base pay that was reduced or frozen the employees may accept that something, even if uncertain, is better than a certain nothing. But using variable compensation for the first time or modifying the role it plays in direct compensation is a major step, and strategic issues must be considered:

- Is the organization going to stay with incentives?
- Is management willing to select and stand behind the metrics used to measure performance?
- Will the necessary training and communication be forthcoming, initially and on an ongoing basis?
- Will incentive plans measure and reward things that employees can impact?
- Will there be an adequate "line of sight," so employees see the connection between how well they perform and the metrics used to determine incentive awards?
- Will incentives be based on performance at the organization, unit or individual level, or a combination of them?

Another issue that must be considered if a portion of the budget for pay increases is to be split between base pay increases and cash awards. As has already been discussed the persistence of small budgets for a decade have strained the ability of organizations to move employees up into their range in a reasonable (and expected) timeframe. If less of the annual budget is going to be used for base pay adjustments this will further exacerbate the problem with slow movement within ranges. One of the ways to address this issue is to reduce the width of ranges to a level that is compatible with less base pay progression. Although employees might view this as a take away if the organization demonstrates that total direct income can be larger, albeit contingent on performance. Although top performers will prosper and lesser performers will perhaps realize a smaller award than they did before the organization might be willing to accept more differentiation (and displeasure by those not prospering) because it will be viewed positively by top contributors who are the people the organization is most concerned with keeping and motivating. On the other hand, if the culture is more egalitarian or collectivist dramatic differentiation may be viewed as inappropriate.

With regard to benefits programs, it is prudent to periodically examine all programs, what their objectives are, how they are designed and who pays for what. The cost of benefit programs has been rising in the U.S. at a rate that far outstrips direct compensation escalation over the last two decades. Many employers who had traditionally paid all or most of the costs associated with benefits programs have been attempting to deal with the cost escalation by increasing the share of the costs borne by employees, at least for health care coverage. Benefit surveys indicate that a reasonable and competitive employer–employee cost sharing is to have the employer pay 70–75% of health care costs. And the dramatic shift from defined benefit pension plans to defined contribution plans has resulted in employer plans that vary in their cost impact. For employers requiring employee contributions, the typical range of formulas is from those matching 100% of the first 6% of employee contributions, down to matching 50% of the first 3% of contributions. There are some employers who do not require an employee contribution and make the only contributions. It is surprising that only a very few plans have provisions that vary the employer match based on organizational performance (a.k.a. organizational ability to pay). It would seem prudent to set a floor level of contribution, such as 50% employer match, and then to increase the matching percentage if the annual performance warrants it. This is a way to make employer costs contingent on ability to pay. It is also a way to increase employee attention to how the organization is doing.

Very little appears in the literature questioning paid-time-off strategies used by most organizations. This is surprising, given the costs incurred by employers for this benefit. The philosophy behind current programs should be examined and alternatives considered. Vacation schedules that award the most time off to those closest to having a whole lot of time off (a.k.a. retirement) are questionable. Allowing vacation carryover seems to make little sense if the primary objective of providing vacations is to allow employees to experience a change in pace and to regenerate their energy stores. And using sick leave accrual formulas may increase the amount of leave taken, independent of the amount of actual illness. Pooling paid time off has become a more common practice, but allowing carryover still brings into question the objectives of time off. Public sector organizations tend to have much more generous time-off policies than private organizations, and one might question why that is necessary and whether it accomplishes anything other than raising taxpayer costs.

Decisions about benefit programs must also take into account what changes are being made in the direct compensation strategy. For example, raising employee contributions to health care costs while freezing or reducing base pay levels produces a double hit to employee income. The impact of doing both simultaneously may be thought by the organization (and employees) to be overly severe, forcing a choice between the two.

The use of equity-based plans to offset some of the current expense associated with base pay and benefit programs should also be considered. Since the equity markets can generate additional funds through stock price appreciation, without creating short-term expense for the organization, this can be a very effective way to compensate employees. However, many employees became shareholders for the first time during the 1990s and actually came to believe that 10–20% returns on investment were sustainable over the long run. The 2000–02 dotcom collapse was a major blow to the level of confidence in equities among those impacted. And the stock market chaos of 2008–09 no doubt made it more difficult for employers to offer stock options in lieu of more certain income sources, if they expected that employees would consider them to be an adequate replacement. Even restricted stock grants, which would have some future value unless the organization ceased to exist, would be a very hard sale.

Given these realities it seems the prudent rewards strategist will accept that there is no single approach that will deal with the turbulent environment and its impact on employees. However, it is within the powers of the strategist to make a case for beginning to reshape the total rewards package in a way that is sustainable.

Evaluating Future Workforce Viability

A prerequisite for organizational success is having a workforce that is qualified to do what needs to be done and that is motivated to perform at high levels. Yet far too few organizations plan adequately to ensure their workforce is viable for the long run. As members of the Baby Boom generation move through their career cycle in the United States, many organizations face significant losses of personnel during the coming decade. Experts differ in their opinions about the likelihood of worker shortages and the magnitude of those shortages, but it is prudent for every organization to evaluate whether it will face this issue and how extreme an impact it might have. Additionally, technology and environmental conditions are changing so rapidly that sustaining the competence of the existing workforce is another daunting challenge faced by organizations. Waiting until shortages of people with critical skills occur is irresponsible.

Several studies have shown that there is a critical need to do workforce planning. The Water Research Foundation did a study of the water utility industry in 2005 and concluded that: 1) more than 50% of the current workers will not be at their utility in ten years; 2) the supply of capable workers will be inadequate; and 3) utilities are grossly under-investing in training aimed at developing replacement workers. A Society of Human Resource Management study, also done in 2005, found that the majority of workers nationally 55 and older (20% of the workforce today and 30% in 2015) say they will not postpone retirement. The two findings may work together to produce the perfect storm: a large percentage of workers eligible to retire and intending to do so. As the ten years have passed those predictions were influenced by a huge economic downturn and poor equity market performance that may well have convinced employees to remain in employment longer so they could augment their savings for retirement.

A critical component of strategic human resource management is workforce planning. Figure 16.2 is a model that illustrates a typical workforce planning process. The component steps in the workforce planning process illustrated are:

1   Identify critical roles or occupations.
2   Determine the adequacy of the current workforce.
3   Identify gaps that exist today.
4   Project demand in one, two and five years.
5   Identify gaps that will exist in the future if no action is taken.
6   Define sources of additional people and ways in which people will be lost.
7   Develop a strategy to close gaps and ensure future workforce viability.

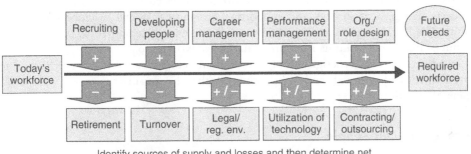

Identify sources of supply and losses and then determine net
gain or loss and whether net human capital will be adequate

Figure 16.2 Assessing workforce viability: today and against future requirements

It is important to differentiate workforce planning from replacement planning and succession planning. Replacement planning is used to identify qualified individuals who would replace specific individuals if they exit the organization or become incapacitated. It is very short-term in nature and serves the purpose of ensuring the organization can operate if unexpected personnel losses occur (e.g., pandemic outbreak, turnover, death or disability, etc.). Succession planning is more long-range and looks at aggregate supply and demand in a specific occupation or role (e.g., management development). Workforce planning as it is dealt with here is both short- and long-range and looks at external factors as well as internal factors that will impact the supply–demand balance in the workforce.

Figure 16.2 focuses on the various sources for replacing personnel (or growing the workforce) and the ways in which people are lost to the organization, at least for filling a particular role or occupation. The criticality of an occupation can certainly vary by organization, depending on what the core capabilities are. For example, a utility operating power plants or water treatment plants may identify control room operators as being critical to daily operations. Lacking adequate numbers of qualified people in specific roles could cause them to fail in their primary mission. On the other hand, administrative personnel with general skills may not be identified as critical. By focusing on critical skills, an organization can spend its resources ensuring its viability.

Once a critical skill is identified, the previously described process can be applied to that skill. An additional element in this model is the determination of how long it takes to bring a worker who is qualified to enter the role up to the minimum standard of performance in that role. If the organization finds that there will be a substantial gap between supply and demand in one to two years and it takes three to four years to develop an entrant it becomes apparent that a potential crisis already exists, since time is too short to train someone without the required skills. This was a common occurrence in the late 1990s when so many organizations tried to convert legacy IT systems to new client server network-based systems. They did not have the time to retrain their existing IT personnel because they had waited so long to face the issue and were forced into a very tight labor market to hire people or retain contractors. Some would argue that making projections into the future, as much as five years out, is sheer speculation, and indeed things can change. However, the option (not planning) is not viable. Besides, it is necessary to update the projections continuously, to reflect changes in the environment.

Once the planning is complete the organization is faced with developing a human resource management strategy and supporting programs that will produce the desired results. The key objectives are to attract the right people, develop people appropriately, maximize the supply of human resources, maximize workforce productivity, disseminate knowledge effectively, redesign the organization and employee roles, manage losses due to retirement and turnover, and outsource work that the organization is not able to do efficiently or effectively.

Attract the Right People

In order to ensure the organization is capable of competing for the available talent it is prudent to first define the "best fit" employee profile. The organization's culture, the competencies it determines are required to perform the roles and its rewards philosophy will all have an impact on the type of candidate the organization wishes to attract. This means that the organization must develop its "brand" as an employer and communicate what that means to potential candidates. It also requires that an honest value proposition be put forth so that those considering application know what to expect.

Research has shown that the best tool for preventing unwanted turnover in that critical first 6–18 months is the "realistic job preview,"[5] which entails providing a balanced picture of what is to be expected, including the potential negatives associated with the role and with the organization. By ensuring that the picture painted is accurate, the organization accomplishes two things: 1) the new employee is "vaccinated" against some of the inevitable negatives, preventing unpleasant surprises; and 2) the employment agreement is begun on an honest note.[6] How performance is defined, measured and rewarded is one of the most important conditions of employment to communicate. Finally, the organization must invest in a viable "onboarding" process that ensures new employees are smoothly transitioned into the workplace. If all of these requirements are not met the usual consequences are difficulty in recruiting and/or unacceptable losses through turnover.

Develop People Appropriately

The MIT study of the global auto industry conducted several years ago found that U.S. organizations invested far less in hiring new employees and in training new people than foreign organizations with U.S. operations.[7] That pattern appears to continue, according to further research. This may be due partly to the fact that U.S. accounting principles mandate treating training as a short-term expense (which reduces profits), while failing to credit the benefits as either assets or a source of future income. Yet most accept that training is necessary if people are to perform well. On-the-job training has been widely used, since it seems on the surface to be free. But the highly individualistic culture in many organizations breeds competitiveness for larger salary increases or bonuses and for promotions, which impedes the willingness of employees to share their knowledge with peers and to codify it in procedures. Additionally, in organizations subject to downsizing, employees often retreat into a protective mode, believing they compete for jobs. These realities are a significant obstacle to the dissemination of knowledge and to the application of best practices. They also make employee development more difficult, or at least more expensive, because of the additional need for formal training. Some of the resistance to sharing knowledge can be overcome by celebrating and rewarding those who make others more effective. As discussed in Chapters 2 and 12, adding "contribution to the effectiveness of others/the unit" as a factor to performance appraisals can help to show employees that this is valued.

Better career management can help reduce the need for formal training that requires people to be off the job. Much lost time can be avoided if career paths are well thought out and communicated and developmental assignments are used to allow employees to accumulate knowledge and skills while being productive. Career planning can also be a positive in retaining people, particularly those who have been entering the workforce during the last decade. Since the lifelong employment contract has expired, the "big two" for attracting and retaining Generation Xers, Generation Yers and Millennials have been: "Pay me well" and "Keep me marketable."

Maximize the Available Supply of Human Resources

Organizations that have experienced low levels of turnover often relax their recruitment efforts and/or lapse into using the same strategy for transitioning in new employees. If skill shortages are going to worsen, it is incumbent on organizations to become more proactive and innovative in developing sources of supply. Employee referrals are extremely effective if they are valued, recognized and rewarded. Identifying and developing non-traditional sources can also produce a high yield on investment. Alliances with educational institutions, job fairs, open houses and marketing campaigns can help to inform the outside world about opportunities.

Skilled trades personnel are becoming more difficult to find in many areas, and it may be necessary for organizations to band together to create training programs in technical schools. By demonstrating that there is an unfilled need, community colleges may be enticed into developing technical programs that provide additional qualified candidates, particularly if organizations support students with internships and the prospect of employment. In industries where females or minorities are underrepresented it may be possible to rethink recruiting strategies to reach this growing segment of the labor force.

Maximize Workforce Productivity

If people are made more productive it may take fewer of them to get the job done. Many organizations are shifting from seniority-based wages and salaries to performance-based pay and instituting incentive programs to provide a reason to increase performance. "What you measure and reward you most surely will get more of" is a concept supported by behavioral research. Although public and not-for-profit organizations still use incentive programs sparingly, the competition for people with the private sector and the benefits of offering incentives are beginning to increase the adoption of incentive programs. Investing in capital equipment and technology is another source of increased productivity. If skills are more expensive or unavailable, the economics of investing in technology may change and prove to be a good strategy. Also, redesigning work processes can take out unnecessary work and reduce staffing and timelines.

Disseminate Knowledge Effectively

Many organizations are investing in "knowledge management" programs that are designed to share best practices and critical information more widely and more efficiently. By promoting a sharing culture and recognizing contributions to the organization's knowledge, all employees can be made more effective and more likely to create and share new knowledge. Creating an internal "yellow pages" directory that refers people to documents or people knowledgeable in specific areas makes it easier for employees to deal with situations they have not faced before. It also makes it possible to recognize the experts as being valuable resources. It is advisable to invest in turning tacit knowledge (the know-how people carry around in their heads, often unaware of it) into explicit knowledge that is accessible by others. Databases that are coded by subject can supplement work procedures and manuals.

It is also necessary to create a culture that encourages informed emulation (called legal theft in one organization), which makes it clear that reusing practices is not the sign of someone who lacks imagination, but rather ingenuity in another form. Technology can be useful in dissemination, but just because people can share information does not guarantee they will, particularly if they believe it is not in their best interests. The culture of the organization is a major factor in encouraging or impeding dissemination.

Redesign the Organization and Employee Roles

Work design has a long history of success in positively impacting productivity and employee satisfaction. There is a rich literature in organizational design and in designing workplaces and work roles. Job enlargement (often called cross-training) can be a strategy for increasing productivity, since it produces a more flexible workforce that can be shifted to meet changing workloads. Job enrichment, which gives people more responsibility for their work, can also contribute to satisfaction and to fewer "handoffs" between people (e.g., having people handle quality control for the work they do).

There has been much discussion about the concept of a job becoming obsolete, but this varies across roles and workplaces. A model for effective role design should prescribe: 1) appropriate skill variety; 2) understanding why the work is important; 3) appropriate autonomy; and 4) continuous measurement and feedback. In cases where a given process must be adhered to (e.g., accounting) it is reasonable to assume jobs will continue to exist. Where people must jump from one activity or project to another there may be less focus on a specific list of tasks they are to perform and more on contributing to the desired results.

The use of work teams in place of individual jobs has become more prevalent where it makes more sense. But the use of teams should be limited to situations where the work process lends itself to this strategy and when there are people available who are capable of operating effectively as team members. Certainly, more work is being done in a project mode, and project management tools should be applied where appropriate.

Manage Losses Due to Retirement

For many organizations the biggest challenge will be replacing the retiring Boomers, particularly if they have spent all or most of their career with one employer. Some of the studies that have been done recently argue that Boomers do not intend to delay retirement, while others say they will never fully retire. This contradiction can be clarified only by carefully defining "retirement." If the employer has a defined benefit pension plan that enables employees to retire with full benefits when their age and years of service total 75 or more, it is reasonable to assume that some will exercise that right. And since U.S. laws limit the ability of some employees to continue to work for an employer while they are receiving pension benefits from that organization there are limitations with regard to the way in which they are retained after retirement.

It is possible to extend career management strategies beyond the time when an employee ceases to be a full-time, permanent employee. If an organization needs to train new personnel it could create a training contract with retiring employees to accomplish the training, in the capacity of consultant. Having a retiree spend one week a month or one day a week running a focused training program may allow the organization to utilize the retiree as a contractor and to accomplish what otherwise would have been a difficult challenge. Although mentoring and other on-the-job approaches can theoretically accomplish the same thing it is often found that daily work demands cause under-investment in training time, with dire consequences when the experienced person leaves.

Many organizations have created the ideal incentive for forcing out everyone eligible for retirement, no matter how badly they are needed or want to stay. Overly generous retirement plans, fully paid retiree health programs and other rewards for past service may provide more value to those who leave than those who stay. Employees who are eligible for full retirement at a fairly young age can begin to receive the income stream from the pension plan and move on to collect a second income from another organization. Defined contribution plans lend themselves to encouraging continued service more than defined benefit plans, since additional benefits will accrue beyond normal retirement. Also, those who are relatively secure financially are in a position to contribute more to these plans in their later years.

Manage Losses Due to Turnover

The most potent approach to ensuring a viable workforce into the future is to avoid losing any valued employees when it is inconvenient. Organizations with very low turnover of incumbents with critical skills and high performers will certainly have less of a challenge than those suffering large losses of these people. But since so many competitors will be likely to be facing the same challenges they will probably be doing their best to spoil the party by focusing on the organization's best people.

All of the approaches already mentioned will help to minimize dysfunctional turnover. Well-designed jobs in organizations with attractive cultures and generous rewards will certainly promote retention, as will career planning programs that invest in employees. The best strategy is to do all the things with a positive impact on turnover and avoid those with a negative impact. One of the rarest approaches to turnover is not giving up when someone leaves but to maintain "alumni relations." By making it clear in exit interviews that someone is welcome to knock on the door in the future and by periodically reminding them that this is still an option, organizations may find that losses can become future sources of supply. Although this book has focused on performance and rewards management, the manner in which an organization staffs, develops and manages its workforce will have a major impact on strategies and programs dealing with performance and rewards.

One of the most effective retention strategies is to aggressively communicate the value of the compensation and benefits package to employees. One of the tragedies for many organizations with generous employee benefits is that employees take them for granted and grossly underestimate the financial value of that which is provided. For example, most organizations would find that employees estimate the expenditure on benefits by the employer at something less than half of what it is. Further, if asked what the benefits would cost if they were acquired directly by the employee, the estimates would be far less than half of the true cost in most cases.

Failure to provide comprehensive individual employee benefits statements on a regular basis is usually a bad decision from a cost–benefit perspective, particularly since current technology has made providing them relatively easy and inexpensive. Another way to increase the perceived value of the benefits package is to compare what the organization provides with what is typically provided by other employers. This type of competitive analysis needs to be done periodically, to ensure that current trends towards limiting benefits and increasing the portion of total costs contributed by employees are recognized and that realistic values are placed on what is provided to employees. Organizations that do not require employees to contribute towards the cost of their health care will always experience resistance when beginning to charge employees even a nominal amount. But the noise level can be reduced if the economic necessity for these actions is clearly communicated and if the communication is accompanied by tangible comparisons to what is happening in other organizations.

There is another approach to benefits that can further increase the perceived value to employees. Providing a "flexible" package that enables individuals to pick from equal-value options gives them the freedom to choose those things with the most value and appeal to them. Pooling all types of time off, offering selection from a range of health care packages and ensuring employees understand how to create tax-free accounts to pay premiums and deductibles are all strategies that cost nothing except the time and attention of HR specialists knowledgeable about the options. Employees are intelligent enough to understand when programs make them better off by providing what they want at the best possible out-of-pocket cost. After all, the traditional "one size fits all" benefits package was designed for a career male employee with a wife and 2.1 children at home—almost certainly not the workforce profile existing in organizations today.

Outsource Work the Organization Cannot Do Efficiently or Effectively

Not all work performed by the organization needs to be performed by employees, which has been discussed throughout the book. Whether the full-blown "gig economy" will materialize and turn everyone into Bedouins is to be seen. Many organizations have been accustomed to contracting out large projects, such as building new infrastructure. However, most perform work that is ongoing with employees, either permanent full-time, part-time or seasonal. Organizations are increasingly finding that work not critical to their core capabilities can often be done better by other organizations specializing in that work. For example, it is unlikely that a hospital is going to be "world class" in IT, accounting, payroll and other administrative processes that are recurring and transactional in nature. This is true because the best qualified people in these fields will not aspire to work in a hospital, since they understand that the organization's primary mission is not closely related to what they do. Also, a hospital may not believe funding the development of the most advanced systems is prudent. Therefore, its employees will be unlikely to stay up with the "state of the art" in their field.

By working together, organizations could represent a viable business for an outsourcing provider and enjoy state-of-the-art systems and processes without each having to make the large investment in creating them on their own. For example a recommendation had been made to several utilities that they all contract to use the same advanced geographic mapping system offered by a software firm. Since the utilities did not have overlapping territories and did not compete with each other the idea was viewed positively. If they had been competitors attempting to gain a competitive advantage via their systems, this approach would have been rejected.

Alliances and joint ventures between multiple organizations have become more common in many industries: newspapers share distribution services and printing operations; organizations of all types use the same providers to process their payrolls. It is unlikely that organizations will outsource activities that are critical to success (e.g., customer service at Ritz-Carlton), but the current popularity of outsourcing demonstrates that it is not necessary to do some of the things organizations are doing if they will struggle to do them well and effectively. A last consideration is the culture, which is typically focused on core capabilities that produce competitive advantage. Having the most innovative and leading-edge administrative systems may be a low priority for an R&D organization, frustrating administrative professionals who are trained to make their work as good as it can be. This may create conflicts and lead to dissatisfaction and turnover.

Despite the uncertainties about whether there will be a shortage of workers in the near future and its magnitude, it is not wise to assume the organization will be able to deal with whatever happens. There have been shortages in some occupations for decades, often lasting as long as three to five years per crisis—the time it takes to replenish the supply. There will always be shortages for some organizations and for some critical skills, at least for short periods. The biggest mistake is not trying to plan for the future and waiting until the crisis is unarguably afoot. Turning to outside firms or freelancers can be a temporary antidote for critical shortages and may also avoid the need to staff up to levels not sustainable over the long haul just to meet a spike in demand.

Scenario planning should be applied to workforce planning. By looking into the future and formulating a "worst case," a "best case" and a "most likely" scenario, an organization can develop strategies that are reasonably robust when one of the possible futures becomes the present. This type of planning equips the organization to respond more quickly and appropriately because it has thought about its responses to a range of realities and has implemented processes and programs to help it deal with what occurs.

Better planning typically means fewer bad decisions are made. There is a principle that seems always to hold true: *in human resource planning if you run out of time all your best options are no longer available.* This is particularly true for workforce planning, since there are often no quick solutions to a labor shortage. Anticipating the future that is likely to materialize enables human resource planners to broaden their range of options. Some believe planning is useless when the environment is "permanent whitewater." Another school of thought believes planning is still critical, but that the type of planning done needs to change. Using the model presented in Figure 16.2 requires judgments to be made that are at best educated guesses, particularly when they are projected out for several years. But they accomplish the most important objective of all. They get the organization focused on what might occur and make workforce planning something that needs to become a daily part of management's activities. A final requirement is that workforce planning must be a continuous process. Today may not look much like what you projected it to be five years ago, given the rate of change. Therefore, each one-, two- and five-year projection must be refined as things change. Workforce planning is a daily part of effective human resource management. And even the best performance and rewards management strategies cannot motivate people who are not there.

Application of Principles: Chapter 16

Reflect on what is happening in the economy, society and in organizations and develop your pessimistic, optimistic and most likely scenarios for what the world of work will look like over the next decade. What should organizations do to ensure that they define, measure, manage and reward performance in a way that will be economically viable and sustainable and that will result in employee perceptions of equity, competitiveness and appropriateness?

What challenges will be faced when reshaping compensation philosophy and strategy in the manner you deem appropriate? How can those challenges be overcome?

Notes

1 Schwarz, P., *The Art of the Long View* (New York, Currency Doubleday, 1991).
2 Greene, R., "Scenario-based Rewards Planning," *ACA Journal* (Winter, 1997).
3 WorldatWork, *2008–2009 Salary Budget Survey* (Scottsdale, AZ, WorldatWork, 2008).
4 Cascio, Wayne, *Responsible Restructuring* (San Francisco, CA, Berrett-Koehler, 2002).
5 Cascio, W. & Aguinis, H., *Applied Psychology in Human Resource Management*, 6th ed. (Upper Saddle River, NJ, Pearson Prentice-Hall, 2005).
6 Cascio, W., *Costing Human Resources*, 4th ed. (Cincinnati, OH, South-Western, 2000).
7 Womack, J., Jones, D. & Roos, D., *The Machine that Changed the World* (New York, Rawson Associates, 1990).

Applying Analytics to Performance and Rewards Management

Understanding the concepts and techniques that can be used for acquiring and applying quantitative data and research findings is a critical area of competence for those responsible for managing performance and rewards. This appendix provides a basic understanding of the types of measures and how they can be acquired, analyzed and applied when making decisions.

Types of Quantitative Measures

Central Tendency Measures

Many statistical applications used in rewards management are aimed at finding "the number" out of a data set. Average rate is probably the most commonly sought value when using competitive market surveys. But when using an average, it is important to ask "average of what, calculated how?"

An example illustrating the importance of how a number is calculated: A survey reveals the average rate paid to all reporters in American newspapers is considerably higher than the average of the average rates paid by each newspaper reporting in the survey. Although this, on the surface, seems puzzling, there is a reason. Large metropolitan newspapers have more reporters than community papers and large newspapers pay more. The number calculated by adding pay rates of reporters and then dividing that total by the number of reporters is often called the "weighted average" or the "incumbent-weighted average"—called that because it provides equal weight to each reporter rate. The other number, calculated by adding the average pay rate reported by each newspaper and then dividing by the number of newspapers reporting, is called the "unweighted average" or the "company-weighted average"—called that because it provides equal weight to each newspaper.

No "right" answer exists as to which of these two averages an organization should use to set the targeted pay level for reporter jobs. The person selecting the measure of competitiveness must understand the statistics, understand the application, and have some labor-market knowledge, to make the right call.

Another measure indicating central tendency is the "median"— the middle rate in an array placed in ascending or descending order. For example, if seven rates are reported, the median rate is the fourth (from the top or from the bottom of the array placed in descending or ascending order by value). The median rate is determined by dividing the number of rates (n) plus one by two or

$$\text{Median rate} = \left[\frac{n+1}{2} \right]$$

in this case, the fourth rate in the array. As it is in the middle, the median is often considered the best rate to use to represent the competitive "going rate." Also, the median is less affected by extremely high or low rates than is the average (mean).

However, the median is also a distributional measure and an uneven distribution can cause nonsensical results. For example, if a survey reports seven monthly pay rates ($3,000, $3,100, $3,110, $3,125, $5,600, $5,800 and $5,900), the median is $3,125. The average is $4,234. Users should be concerned about *why* a big difference exists in the two clusters.

With four rates clustered around $3,100 and three clustered around $5,800, apparently a large difference of opinion exists about how this job should be paid. It could be argued that no "going rate" is determinable in this distribution. Was the job description too vague? Are newspapers reporting two levels of reporter into the single survey benchmark job? Does the sample consist of four small and three large newspapers?

This example illustrates that statistical measures may not produce a relevant answer, but only trigger examination of the measurements. Users must understand the nature of what is being measured and what does/does not make sense. Making sense of the data may require splitting the sample by newspaper size and/or refining the survey benchmark description to reflect skill/responsibility levels within a job family. The reality is sometimes survey results only provide a computed average, without information about the distribution of rates or the mix of organizations reporting those rates. In this case, if the surveyor decided to report the median it would be $3,125; if the average had been the choice, it would be $4,234. If the surveyor decided to report both, the knowledgeable user discovers something amiss in the sample and that further examination of the details (if available) was necessary. Regardless, the user should consider replacing the survey source with one compiled by parties who understood statistics and market surveys.

A third measure of central tendency exists . . . the mode. This is the rate with the highest incumbent count. It has little application in analyzing data relating to pay rates or other data involving the aggregation of discrete values.

Averages or medians can be used to compare two things as well. For example, most tourist books contain average monthly temperatures for destinations, to alert the traveler going to Chicago to pack either cotton shorts or down parkas, depending on the month. Averages and medians have wide application in pay administration as well.

When deciding whether the median or mean should be used as the "going rate," the user should be aware that the mean is usually higher, typically by 3% to 5% in large samples of pay rates in surveys. [Note: the author managed a survey of IT personnel that had over 2,000 organizations reporting on over 250,000 incumbents.] This difference is caused by the non-normal distribution of pay rates . . . the highest rates are often much further from the average or median than the lowest rates. The existence of a minimum wage impacts the distribution in hourly jobs by constraining how low rates can be, while no offsetting cap dictates how high they can be. As with selecting the type of average used, selecting between the median and the mean should be done based on which the practitioner feels is most appropriate. It is important though to ensure that once a measure is selected, it is used consistently in all related analyses.

Distribution Measures

Distribution measures are used to describe how individual values in a data array are distributed. The median (just described) is the most commonly used distributional measure.

Quartiles and percentiles are other useful distributional measures. *Quartiles* break a distribution into quarters, while *percentiles* break it into hundredths (terciles into thirds, deciles into tenths, etc.). If a student graduates in the second quartile of the class, it means that student's grade point average ranks below 50% to 75% of his or her classmates and above 25% to 50% of them.

Market surveys often report quartiles so the user knows generally how individual rates distribute between the lowest and the highest rate. The lowest and the highest rates are often outliers and useless to the user, but quartiles have a purpose. The quartiles enable the user to treat the "interquartile range" (range between the first and the third quartile) as the middle half of paid rates, and to use this as a test of competitiveness. A market median or a market average is a single point and it is known to those with market pricing expertise that these numbers are at best "accurate" within a band plus or minus a percentage (5–10% is commonly accepted). Given the reality that a computed point is probably subject to considerable error, an organization could adopt a philosophy that pay rates falling within a reasonable range should be considered to be competitive. This reduces employee perceptions that they are "underpaid" if they are not at least right at the market average rate.

The other distributional measurement tool is the frequency distribution (a.k.a., histogram). This tool is typically in the form of a table or chart and describes how individual values cluster in predetermined categories. Figure A1.1 shows the distribution of reported salaries across a series of predetermined brackets. The vertical height represents the number (or percentage) of rates falling within each bracket and provides a picture of the nature of the distribution.

Histogram's graphic nature enables us to see patterns not evident in a numeric table and a quick glance at the example indicates that this is not a normal distribution. It looks like two normal distributions side by side. This pattern is called a "bi-modal" distribution (two modes exist; one around 600 and another at the 750–800 bracket). An experienced survey analyzer would suspect that the job being surveyed is viewed as being two jobs by participating organizations, one with an average pay of about 600 and the other about 775. This is consistent with the discussion about the possibility that two levels of reporter should have been surveyed, rather than one, as participating organizations are making the distinction. A frequent surveyor error is to select the middle level of a job family to include in a survey, while omitting the other levels, in pursuit of "simplicity."

Participants want to be helpful and to report as much data as possible, so they squeeze the rates for entry-level people and for senior-level people into the one survey job, thereby producing an enormous range of reported rates. An experienced surveyor armed with individual pay rates can detect this problem by using a histogram to analyze each organization's rates, and then admit the mistake and refine the survey or ignore it. With the graphics built into the simplest analytical software, practitioners have the tools to evaluate data in this manner without much effort and expense. But to do this, HR practitioners must understand what they are looking for and what they are looking at.

For example, if one did not understand that professional/technical jobs are best represented as job families (jobs performing work of the same nature, but differentiated into levels of skill and responsibility), it would be easy to look at the data for the single job "Programmer" and be dismayed by the wide range of reported rates. Armed with a frequency distribution, the picture becomes clearer and the user could still use the overly combined data. By using the huge samples in the IT survey mentioned earlier, the author found that a family such as Programmer typically had either three or four modes and they were 12% to 15% apart, useful information for understanding how a pay structure for this family should look. Supported by knowledge of how participating company pay structures were constructed, it was possible to test the correctness of the number of levels within the job family defined in the survey. This type of analysis resulted in defining four levels in the Programmer family but only three levels in the Computer Operator family.

Relationship Measures

Relationship measures can be used to reflect the nature of relationships. The most common measure is *correlation*. For example, the weight of adult males is correlated to height (correcting for age). This does not suggest one thing *causes* the other, but only they tend to covary. The coefficient of correlation is a widely understood measure directly measuring the degree to which two factors covary: from 0 (no relationship) to 1.0 (perfect correlation).

The nature of the relationship between two or more variables can also explained by using *regression analysis*. Single factor regression is a technique attempting to explain one variable using one other variable. For example, a salary structure is typically built by relating the relative internal value of jobs to the competitive market averages for those jobs. If the point values for benchmark jobs, determined by using point-factor job evaluation plans, are used as the X axis values on a graph and the market averages for those same jobs are used as the Y axis values on a graph, the result is a *scattergram* showing the relationship between the two variables. Figure A1.2 illustrates the distribution of paired values for benchmark jobs.

Although the relationship is imperfect (it would be perfect if all Xs were on one straight diagonal line), it can be seen the relationship between market averages and point values is positive (the higher the points, the higher the market values) and probably could best be simply explained by drawing a straight line through the cluster, inclining as it went from left to right.

The single-factor linear name for this regression is derived from the fact that one factor (job evaluation points) explains another factor (salary). Software producing this chart also reports a coefficient of correlation enabling the user to determine what percentage of the variation in dollars is explained by the points. The number varies from 0.0 to 1.0 and for this type of application, the norm for acceptability probably ranges from .50 to .85.

If the relationship between points and salary is not linear, but rather some form of curve function, it requires the use of a nonlinear formula. This is frequently experienced when analyzing executive salaries, as the rate salaries increase is often faster than the rate at which points increase, creating an upward turning curve. Today's curve-fitting software selects the formula that produces the best fit between one variable and the other and provides a rank ordering of formulas based on how well they explain the relationship. It is prudent to test all data sets using such software, as operating under the assumption that a relationship is linear, forces it to be so, as that formula will be applied. And if a straight-line assumption is used on a non-linear data set, the results are distorted.

Unfortunately, in a complex world, one variable is often insufficient to explain another's behavior. In this case, one enters the world of multi-factor (multiple) regression analysis. If an organization is attempting to determine what best explains pay rates, it may use multi-factor regression to test various possibilities. If pay is entered as the variable to be explained, several variables might be entered as possible determinants. The range midpoint for the grade would be a leading contender. Time in job/grade might be another.

Performance rating might be another. If those three variables are entered and the multiple regression model results show that they explain 95 percent of the variation in pay rates, all is well. The contribution of each of these factors should also be examined, which is possible using the regression analysis output. It may be found on further examination that performance ratings add virtually no explanatory value and that grade level and longevity explain pay. This would be the time to take a hard look at the performance management and merit pay systems.

Another common application of multiple regression is to test the impact of HR programs on protected classes. Given today's legalistic environment, this is a good defensive technique, but it also is an opportunity to test for maladies such as racial bias or glass

Below 500	500–550	550–600	600–650	650–700	700–750	750–800	800–850	850–900	900–up
						X			
						X			
		X	X			X			
		X	X		X	X	X		
		X	X		X	X	X		
	X	X	X	X	X	X	X	X	
X	X	X	X	X	X	X	X	X	
X	X	X	X	X	X	X	X	X	X

Figure AI.I Frequency Distribution: Number of Weekly Salaries in Each Bracket

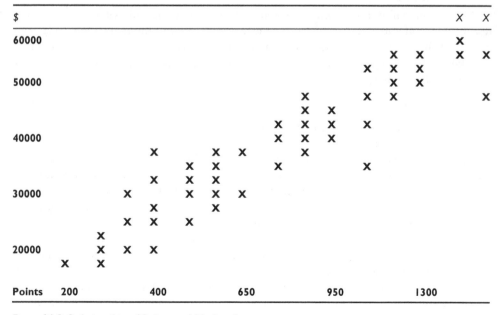

Figure AI.2 Relationship of Points and Market Averages

ceilings before trouble arises. In the previous example, the objective was to explain employee pay. If factors relating to age, gender and race were added to the equation, the results may provide more usable information.

As grade level, time in grade and performance are probably the ideal drivers of pay, one would hope to see no added factors have explanatory power. The regression would not indicate obstacles to career progression, however, as the assumption is that people are in the grade they should be (rather, as regression models do not make value judgments, this simply would not be measured). So if minorities, for example, were paid appropriately for the grade they were in, how long they had been there and their performance, the regression results would not tell us they should have been in higher grades if selection and advancement processes were operating in a bias-free manner.

Applying Research Findings

Research methodology is even more obscure to most HR practitioners than quantitative analysis methods. This is largely explainable by the fact that even entry-level research courses tend to first appear in university curriculum only at the Master's, and perhaps PhD level. But as the research being performed in areas directly related to the HR practitioner's world increased in value, it is unwise to remain uninformed about what makes sound research and how one can tell if it is prudent to act on reported results. When asked "is there any support for that or is that just an opinion?" by senior management, the total rewards practitioner recommending an action is well served by knowing the answer in advance. And support is not the opinion of a consultant or the results of an action reported in the literature, or even a proliferation of articles on how successful the adoption of an "X" program was. Recommendations based on high-quality research that is relevant to the issue is what practitioners should seek to support their proposals.

To determine if findings from a research study are believable and usable, there are two tests of that study: its internal validity and its external validity. Internal validity relates to how well the study was designed, consistent with the scientific method, and therefore whether the results can be believed. External validity relates to where, and under what conditions, the findings hold.

The classic test of internal validity addresses how well various threats to the veracity of the results were controlled for. For example, we assume HR proposes a hypothesis that if people were given more-responsible jobs, with appropriate amounts of latitude, that their job satisfaction would increase and that they would become more productive. One way to support that contention is to look to research results indicating the desired results occur when the proposed actions are taken. Such a study would be likely to have a longitudinal design . . . measure before and then after the treatment. If one could find one or more studies to support the hypothesis, the strength of one's conviction would be contingent on the confidence in the studies on two fronts.

First, were the studies designed in a manner controlling against threats to internal validity? Second, were the studies conducted in a context sufficiently similar to that of the subject organization so it is logical to assume the results would be similar? This requires some findings on external validity meaning that they would transfer to other contexts. What is important is to determine whether a similar result would be likely to occur in the context within which the practitioner means to take the action.

The internal validity threats include:

1   Events taking place during the study that might have caused the results (for example, benefits were improved during the time jobs were being enriched, positively impacting satisfaction).
2   Conducting the study when satisfaction is low relative to typical levels (for example, a layoff occurred before the study and morale is low enough that any change might be expected to improve satisfaction scores, particularly paying attention to employees and their needs).
3   Changes in the employee sample (For example, malcontents may have been encouraged to leave or chose to leave while the enrichment was going on and their satisfaction levels were among the lowest). Expectations as to what jobs and the workplace will be like after the study might have inflated job satisfaction on a temporary basis.
4   Satisfaction might have improved but there has been insufficient time to tell if this will positively affect productivity.

The threats to external validity are well known to those versed in sound benchmarking. A study that resulted in improved satisfaction and productivity in one organization might not translate to the same results in the organization embarking on a similar job enrichment program. The management style might differ from the organization(s) in the study (for example, supervisors might be more controlling and insecure about giving subordinates more latitude). The workforce might be from cultures that discourage employee initiative, which would be disrespectful of the supervisor. The workforce may lack the knowledge, skills and abilities to effectively perform the jobs in their enriched form. And so on.

The safest haven for the organization trying to determine if research supports the hypothesis they are putting forward is numbers. If numerous studies resulted in similar outcomes, the confidence level can be assumed to be higher. A *meta-analysis* is a study of multiple studies and can provide more confidence in research results. The reporting of these findings is often in research journals, which may be opaque to those untrained in research methodology. But an advisor with academic training can often locate, synthesize research findings and guide the organization in developing a hypothesis supported by research. The advisor should also be capable of ensuring the desired change to an HR program or practice is designed in a controlled fashion maximizing the likelihood of successful implementation.

Increasingly, HR research is being reported in books that are accessible to those lacking the training in research methodology. The SHRM Foundation supported a research program examining the role of HR in mergers and acquisitions and which factors seemed to explain success and failure. Watson-Wyatt developed three human-capital indices for measuring the effect of HR strategies and programs on shareholder value. The Gallup organization has developed an enormous database to explore factors influencing employee satisfaction and effectiveness. The Conference Board does in-depth research reports on current issues. Models for measuring the HR function's effectiveness have been developed and tested, and reported in several popular books.

Perhaps none of these research programs would meet the test of an academic research journal but the studies just cited meet the test of admissible evidence and provide practical guidance to practitioners. It is this type of practical guidance that can help HR be more "scientific" in its application of research and quantitative analysis methods.

A dangerous tendency is the inclination to believe evidence that is consistent with their currently held beliefs, while rejecting or avoiding evidence conflicting with their beliefs. Everyone is subject to this form of cognitive bias and professionals must make a conscious effort to remain open to research findings that bring into question the practices they have used with apparent success.

The behavioral research done during the past three or four decades has not demonstrated a strong causal link between employee satisfaction and motivation to perform at high levels. Even though this linkage seems to be consistent with common sense and with experience, the evidence is lacking. Evidence indicates that employee satisfaction positively influences absenteeism and turnover, however, so employee satisfaction is still a worthwhile goal. It is important for professionals to be clear about the effects satisfaction is shown to have, lest they mislead decision makers. Too many HR initiatives have produced positive results but have been viewed as failures as they did not produce the promised results. Research evidence can help guide HR to the correct path, but it is important not to try to force research to support desired results by stretching the conclusions it can support.

Although seeking employee opinions through surveys and other research techniques is a common approach to seeking understanding of how employees feel, it is also fraught with peril. As attitude surveys must frame questions in a technically sound manner for the results to be valid and actionable, this is not a technique to be undertaken by amateurs. A more fundamental concern is that sometimes results may not be actionable as what employees report and what they act on may differ. Ed Lawler, a renowned researcher, reported recently on an employee attitudes survey performed by colleagues and it concluded that the most-desired feature of the work environment (work-life balance) had no significant correlation with the desired outcomes (commitment to the organization and retention). Most attitude surveys would have looked at the high rating of work-life balance and assumed that achieving it would have the desired results. The survey pointed out, according to Lawler, that having people rank the importance of things that are likely to be at least somewhat important to everyone has limited value, unless the researcher is willing to go the extra mile and determine if providing these things had any tangible value.

Conclusion

Even in this complex world, there is still hope for the practitioner who does not have the inclination or the time to go back for a master's degree in statistics or a Ph.D., so sense can be made of the chaotic environment. Adequate published information enables one to gain adequate knowledge of research and quantitative analysis methods. Advanced software performs all statistical tests mentioned in this article without demanding that the user understand the underlying equations. Finally, an increasing number of researchers are making their results accessible to people without advanced training.

There is, however, a problem for practitioners that lack basic skills in this area. The "let's try it and see how it works" approach is too slow and too costly today. The effective practitioner will take the time to find out how it has worked or is apt to work by accessing research results and evaluating all relevant evidence. The effective practitioner will demand that data be turned into information and will be capable of examining the quality of that information as it applies to the context within which it will be used.

Defining and Evaluating Organizational Culture

The effectiveness of human resource management (HRM) strategies will be determined by how well they fit the organizational context and the characteristics of the workforce. The organizational context is to a great degree shaped by the culture(s) prevailing in the organization. Organizational culture has been described as the way in which an organization accomplishes internal integration and external adaptation.[1] Effective organizational cultures are strong, appropriate and adaptive,[2] and culture shapes the perceptions of those within it and impacts their behavior.[3] Culture filters perceptions and determines how factors such as external and internal realities are viewed and how they are dealt with. Culture also sets parameters for acceptable and preferred ways of achieving the organization's vision and mission. The criteria and standards used to select people, to develop them and to define, measure and reward performance must be accepted by all parties as being appropriate and as producing both fair processes and results. In order to meet this challenge HR practitioners must become knowledgeable about how to define and assess organizational culture and how to align HRM systems so they conform to the mandates of culture.

Organizational Culture

There are dramatic cultural differences between organizations, and the specific culture will have a major impact on who the organization employs, how it develops its employees, how performance is defined and measured and how its people are rewarded. What an organization intends to do is defined by its vision and mission, while culture determines how it might achieve it through a strategy and structure, both of which are influenced by the external and internal realities. Cultural anthropologists have studied cultures (societal, group and organizational) and have developed numerous models that can be used to define a culture. Organizational cultures are somewhat different from societal or national cultures, however, since they are imbedded within these larger cultures, and employees will have a foot in both of them.

Most organizations have spent considerable time talking about culture, but too often the result is confusion about what, if anything, was actually decided. Getting people to agree as to what the organization's culture *is*, what it *should be* and *how to reshape it* is the difficult part. Discussing culture by identifying salient characteristics does not define it, assess it and determine if modification is warranted. People who have spent extended periods in IBM, HP, Nordstrom, Walmart, Singapore Airlines or Southwest Airlines can tell you what behaviors will fly, as well as what the priorities are. Organizations in the same businesses and same geographic territories are often dramatically different in the way they define their values and preferred behaviors. But when one attempts to specifically define a culture or assess its effectiveness or identify what should be reshaped, the approach for doing so is generally unclear.

Figure A2.1 is a tool for defining, assessing and reshaping organizational culture. The factors used are taken from the cultural anthropology research and are tailored to fit a business organization. The instrument is intended to address the problem highlighted by a remark by Charles Hampden-Turner: "Organizational culture is like a chameleon—a creature of such variegated hues that, while everyone acknowledges its splendor, few can agree on its description." The process that most effectively operationalizes this model is one that evaluates what the culture *currently is* and then what the culture *should be* on each of the factors. Once those two scale points are identified significant *"is–should be" gaps* should be identified. For example, if an evaluator believes the organization currently is a "2" on the first factor but should be a "4" it suggests the current emphasis is too much on "making the numbers" and not enough on "satisfying the customer." A "1" is not better or worse than a "5" on a particular factor—just different.

A utility that has been a regulated monopoly for 50 years may have a focus on making budget and may seem relatively indifferent to customer satisfaction, since customers have no viable alternative. But an automaker in a very competitive industry with three times the capacity that demand would dictate would almost certainly have a different attitude about the importance of customer satisfaction. Where an organization is on this aspect of its culture may fit the realities of the past (monopolistic power) but current events (deregulation) may well alter the "should be" answer on this dimension from a singular focus on making the numbers to one of considering the customer. If the utility, after discovering the need to reshape its culture, begins to do so and then evaluates its human resource management strategies, it may find it needs to begin hiring different types of people, to train them differently, to measure their performance using different factors and to reward them for doing different things.

It would be useful for readers to evaluate their organization's culture on each of the 12 dimensions and to identify the significant gaps between what the culture is and what it should be. Once the gaps are identified the impact of closing them (or consequences of not doing so) should be evaluated and then compared to the resources required to accomplish this transition. This can provide an agenda for focusing efforts on reshaping those aspects of the culture that need to be changed.

For example: an assessment of a utility like the one just described identified the following gaps:

1 Performance must be defined as satisfying the customer while making the numbers.
2 The performance of the overall organization must be considered by managers when making decisions, rather than considering only how their unit will be impacted.
3 Managers must balance risk with costs when making decisions.
4 Employees must be viewed as assets to invest in, rather than a line item in the budget.
5 Pay levels and pay actions must be earned through performance, rather than being an entitlement that is based on time spent on the job.

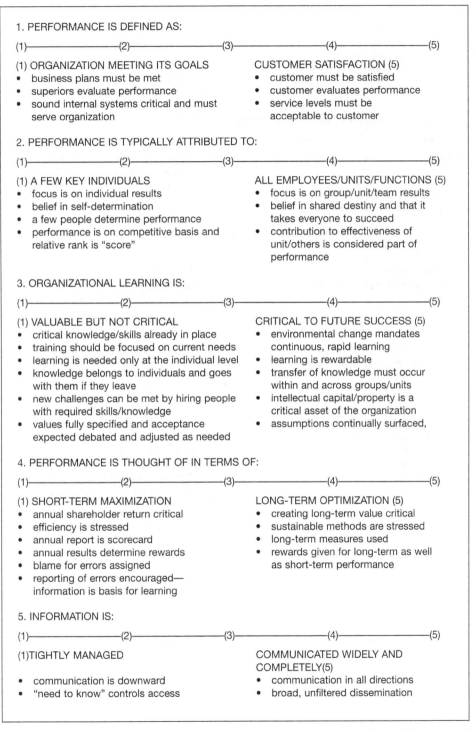

1. PERFORMANCE IS DEFINED AS:

(1)————————(2)————————————(3)————————————(4)————————(5)

(1) ORGANIZATION MEETING ITS GOALS
- business plans must be met
- superiors evaluate performance
- sound internal systems critical and must serve organization

CUSTOMER SATISFACTION (5)
- customer must be satisfied
- customer evaluates performance
- service levels must be acceptable to customer

2. PERFORMANCE IS TYPICALLY ATTRIBUTED TO:

(1)————————(2)————————————(3)————————————(4)————————(5)

(1) A FEW KEY INDIVIDUALS
- focus is on individual results
- belief in self-determination
- a few people determine performance
- performance is on competitive basis and relative rank is "score"

ALL EMPLOYEES/UNITS/FUNCTIONS (5)
- focus is on group/unit/team results
- belief in shared destiny and that it takes everyone to succeed
- contribution to effectiveness of unit/others is considered part of performance

3. ORGANIZATIONAL LEARNING IS:

(1)————————(2)————————————(3)————————————(4)————————(5)

(1) VALUABLE BUT NOT CRITICAL
- critical knowledge/skills already in place
- training should be focused on current needs
- learning is needed only at the individual level
- knowledge belongs to individuals and goes with them if they leave
- new challenges can be met by hiring people with required skills/knowledge
- values fully specified and acceptance expected debated and adjusted as needed

CRITICAL TO FUTURE SUCCESS (5)
- environmental change mandates continuous, rapid learning
- learning is rewardable
- transfer of knowledge must occur within and across groups/units
- intellectual capital/property is a critical asset of the organization
- assumptions continually surfaced,

4. PERFORMANCE IS THOUGHT OF IN TERMS OF:

(1)————————(2)————————————(3)————————————(4)————————(5)

(1) SHORT-TERM MAXIMIZATION
- annual shareholder return critical
- efficiency is stressed
- annual report is scorecard
- annual results determine rewards
- blame for errors assigned
- reporting of errors encouraged— information is basis for learning

LONG-TERM OPTIMIZATION (5)
- creating long-term value critical
- sustainable methods are stressed
- long-term measures used
- rewards given for long-term as well as short-term performance

5. INFORMATION IS:

(1)————————(2)————————————(3)————————————(4)————————(5)

(1)TIGHTLY MANAGED

- communication is downward
- "need to know" controls access

COMMUNICATED WIDELY AND COMPLETELY(5)
- communication in all directions
- broad, unfiltered dissemination

Figure A2.1 (continued)

(continued)

- generated/used by specialists
- policies/procedures provide direction
- too much information thought to confuse

- potentially created by anyone
- sharing is valued/rewarded
- individuals/groups given access to everything and are expected to decide on its value/use

6. MANAGERS ALLOCATE RESOURCES BASED PRINCIPALLY ON:

(1)————————(2)————————(3)————————(4)————————(5)

(1) IMPACT ON OWN UNIT'S PERFORMANCE
- units seen in competition
- contribution to overall organization not emphasized
- managers promote unit interests

IMPACT ON OVERALL PERFORMANCE (5)
- units share based on value added
- contribution to overall result is key
- managers balance interests of unit against interests of organization

7. THE OPERATIONAL PHILOSOPHY IS:

(1)————————(2)————————(3)————————(4)————————(5)

(1) MINIMUM RISK
- ensure adequate resources on hand at all times
- avoid shortages at all cost and minimize errors
- staff to meet workload peaks
- use only permanent workforce to provide critical skills/knowledge over time

BALANCED RISK (5)
- consider cost of resources when deciding what to have on hand
- plan to operate under conditions of shortages/limited supply
- staff to allow for slack but ensure levels are cost-effective
- ensure critical skills/knowledge are readily available

8. PLANNING IS:

(1)————————(2)————————(3)————————(4)————————(5)

(1) BASIC TO PRESCRIBING TACTICS
- future tactics determined
- plans changed only when required
- top-down planning process
- tactics linear/sequential
- plans internally driven
- leaders focused on results vs. plan

A TOOL FOR SETTING DIRECTION (5)
- focus on environmental scanning
- interactions determine direction
- bottom-up formulation of approach
- constant attention to possibilities
- plans dynamic and co-evolve with the environment
- leaders focused on preparedness for the unexpected

9. SOUND MANAGEMENT IS THOUGHT TO BE:

(1)————————(2)————————(3)————————(4)————————(5)

(1) CLOSE CONTROL/SPECIFIC DOWNWARD DIRECTION
- develop specific policies and procedures
- define specific work assignments
- make decisions at high level
- identify who produces results/failure and reward or punish accordingly
- focus on managing the known/expected
- deference is to rank

PROVIDING LEADERSHIP (5)
- articulate values, vision and culture
- identify objectives
- encourage initiative
- look for reasons for results/failure and use to improve performance
- prepare for managing unexpected
- deference is to expertise

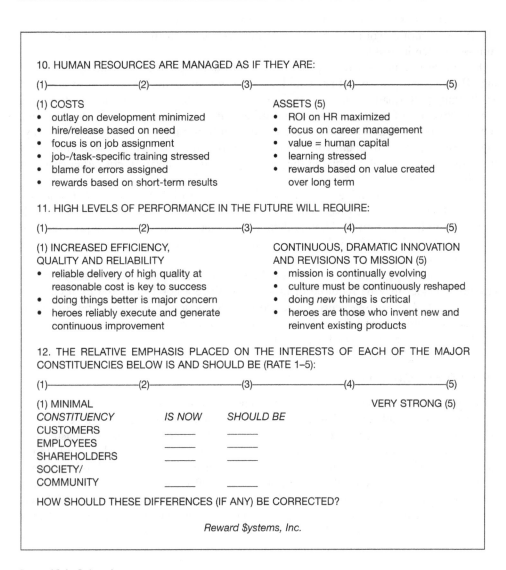

10. HUMAN RESOURCES ARE MANAGED AS IF THEY ARE:

(1)————————(2)————————————(3)————————————(4)————————(5)

(1) COSTS
- outlay on development minimized
- hire/release based on need
- focus is on job assignment
- job-/task-specific training stressed
- blame for errors assigned
- rewards based on short-term results

ASSETS (5)
- ROI on HR maximized
- focus on career management
- value = human capital
- learning stressed
- rewards based on value created over long term

11. HIGH LEVELS OF PERFORMANCE IN THE FUTURE WILL REQUIRE:

(1)————————(2)————————————(3)————————————(4)————————(5)

(1) INCREASED EFFICIENCY, QUALITY AND RELIABILITY
- reliable delivery of high quality at reasonable cost is key to success
- doing things better is major concern
- heroes reliably execute and generate continuous improvement

CONTINUOUS, DRAMATIC INNOVATION AND REVISIONS TO MISSION (5)
- mission is continually evolving
- culture must be continuously reshaped
- doing *new* things is critical
- heroes are those who invent new and reinvent existing products

12. THE RELATIVE EMPHASIS PLACED ON THE INTERESTS OF EACH OF THE MAJOR CONSTITUENCIES BELOW IS AND SHOULD BE (RATE 1–5):

(1)————————(2)————————————(3)————————————(4)————————(5)

(1) MINIMAL   VERY STRONG (5)

CONSTITUENCY	IS NOW	SHOULD BE
CUSTOMERS	____	____
EMPLOYEES	____	____
SHAREHOLDERS	____	____
SOCIETY/ COMMUNITY	____	____

HOW SHOULD THESE DIFFERENCES (IF ANY) BE CORRECTED?

Reward $ystems, Inc.

Figure A2.1 Cultural assessment instrument

These gaps were identified by administering the instrument to a cross-sectional (both vertical and horizontal) sampling of employees. The findings uncovered a number of undesirable realities. Departmental fiefdoms existed, causing managers to make their goals no matter what impact it had on other departments or the overall organization. Managers were indifferent to the costs of holding large inventories because they had been trained to avoid stockouts or other "failures." Investment in training was insufficient, since the costs of training went against each unit's budget and no credit was given for developing people, particularly for progression to greater responsibilities. Finally, pay adjustments equal to cost-of-living increases or increases in average wage levels (whichever was greater) were viewed as an entitlement and were given to everyone in the form of general increases and time-based step increases.

Employee and manager focus groups worked to develop recommendations for changing HRM systems in a way that would facilitate reshaping the culture. These included: 1) changing performance criteria to include satisfying customers and positively impacting the effectiveness of other employees and other units; 2) directing and funding training out of a corporate function and budget account; 3) hiring people experienced in satisfying customers; 4) teaching employees about the economics of the business and how they impacted results; and 5) modifying the base pay system to reward merit rather than just length of service.

The results of a cultural assessment and the changes to HRM strategy and programs prescribed will be unique to each specific culture. An assessment of another regulated utility might produce an entirely different definition of culture and/or different prescriptions. The example has been provided to illustrate the process but does not suggest an assessment by a utility would produce similar results.

The major theme of this book is that guiding principles should be established but that custom strategies may be required in order to produce a good fit to the local contexts within which different segments of the workforce function. For that reason, organizations should think about how well the culture they create fits different occupations and employees of different ages and stages of their careers.

Workforce Culture(s)

Each organization must consider the beliefs, values and priorities of its workforce to ensure its culture is compatible with what employees will accept. People bring different perspectives to the workplace, owing to occupational, generational and ethnic/national characteristics. This book suggests that how performance is defined, measured and rewarded should fit the guiding principles adopted by the organization but that strategies may need to be customized to fit different segments of the workforce. The emphasis in on the nature of the work performed and the context within which it is performed, but the mindset of employees must be considered as well. How people are trained, their age and experience and their ethnic/national background will predispose them to particular cultures, and organizations should take great care in ensuring their cultures are acceptable to their employees.

Workforces are increasingly diverse and this poses challenges when organizations attempt to gain acceptance for their cultures and their human resource management strategies. For example, merit pay programs emphasize individual performance. Employees from a country with a collectivist culture may view this focus on the individual as inappropriate. It is therefore incumbent on organizations to recognize cultural differences within their workforces, to respect that people are entitled to different views, and finally to reconcile the issues that these differences create.

Occupational Culture

Jokes are often made of the supposed "culture" of occupations such as actuaries, accountants and engineers. Stereotypes suggest that actuaries make subjective assumptions and then take seriously calculations based on those assumptions that are carried out to eight places past the decimal. Accountants have taken their share of the jabs as well, and recent events in U.S. firms could bring into question the way they do their work. Some would suggest that engineers will run an organization into bankruptcy trying to make a design perfect, rather than good enough. Much of this is silly but there is often a grain of truth in the proposition that extended formal training in a professional field or extensive work experience of any kind will have an impact on what people view as appropriate behavior. Indeed, most organizations determine the prevailing market pay levels for separate occupations and respond to them when administering their base pay programs. And many consider occupations when deciding on whether to make a group incentive eligible, as well as determining what type of plan (individual versus group) might be used.

Performance criteria can differ significantly across occupations as well. It is also prudent to ensure that performance is appropriately defined, measured and rewarded, based on the nature of work and duration of employment. How much differentiation in HRM strategies and programs there should be based on occupational characteristics will vary across industries and organizations within them.

Generational Culture

While advising a large research organization several years ago on a cultural change project the author attended a presentation by a consultant who had been retained to survey the views of the organization's young (Generation X) scientists. The presentation was to the senior management of the organization, and the key messages were: 1) get over your love affair with longevity; 2) engage these people in meaningful work from the start; 3) provide meaningful feedback continuously; 4) allow them to be self-reliant but reward them on what they accomplish; 5) worry less about the specific job they are doing and more about how they are developing; and 6) let them be in charge of their career. These suggestions are consistent with "modern management" tenets: delegation, appropriate autonomy, adequate feedback and performance-based rewards. But when the advice was compared to the HRM strategies and programs of the organization being described there were major conflicts.

The organization's staffing strategy was clear: "hire the best and brightest." Being a world leader in research made the organization attractive to this type of candidate and the fit was good—there was plenty of challenge for anyone. But on the hire date things began to unravel. The prevailing culture was "sit in the corner and watch—pay your dues." The consultant making the presentation pointed out that the scientists he had studied were a part of a generational cohort that had grown up with immediate feedback (computer games), had learned to be self-reliant (working parents) and had little fear of making a mistake. His point was that they did not understand the "pay your dues" concept and that if they did they would hate it. If that same message were to be delivered today it would be to Generation Y and Millennial Scientists. There is little evidence to suggest that the reaction would be any different than it was then.

The environmental realities that socialized these three latest cohorts make it prudent for them to take chances, develop their skills, stay marketable and get paid now for what is accomplished, rather than accepting delayed gratification. Part of staying marketable is working on new things and projects that provide stretch and growth. The only way that works is if there is continuous feedback on results and if direction is provided. Rewards should come at the time results are produced, since the employment contract was pretty much "I will stay as long as it is beneficial to both parties."

The contrast between expectations and the HRM programs in most organizations is striking. The approach to performance management is very often: "Go to work and we will get back to you at the end of the year to let you know how you did." Although many organizations provide interim reviews after three or six months to new hires this is usually a perfunctory exercise—and it is not repeated when someone changes roles. This hardly constitutes continuous, credible and relevant feedback.[4] The approach to compensation management is generally: "We will start you off slowly but if you perform well your rewards will come through large increases and promotions." This hardly fits someone who is deciding career moves on a continuous basis and who has figured out that a large salary increase takes an entire year to fully materialize.

Treating younger employees differently than older employees is fraught with peril—both legal and practical. But disregarding the changing characteristics of the pool of potential employees hardly seems wise either. Even if the research on the Boomer/Generation X/Generation Y/Millennial differences is disregarded, based on the belief that Boomers were also different when they were younger, it is still appropriate to reconsider HRM strategies if they are not working. The real question is whether it is smart to attempt to operate with an approach for only one group when the employment contract has been rewritten for everyone.

Research clearly shows it is folly to make performance appraisal a once-a-year, after the-fact blame allocation session, yet that is what it is in many organizations. The value of defined benefit pension plans approaches zero if few expect to be with the organization more than a couple of years—and defined contribution plans ask those who are not even thinking about saving for retirement to do so. Relying on base pay as the principal element in the compensation package means performance gets rewarded on a delayed basis, which makes newer employees paid lower in the range prime targets for competitors. These are all realities that need to be considered and incorporated into HRM strategy.

The skill shortages during the 1990s made organizations more receptive to changing their HRM strategies so that someone was sitting in all those cubicles doing the work. And the apparent contrast between the values and priorities of the new labor force entrants and those already there highlighted the misalignment between what people wanted and what they were being offered. If the Generation X versus Baby Boomers issue does no more than to prompt organizations to challenge the veracity of current practices as they relate to all employees then it has indeed served a noble purpose.

Millennials are prominent in those wishing to make their career a series of "gigs," which gives them control in how much they work, when, for who and how. As organizations use contractors it is not clear whether the seeming cultural differences are due to the age of the cohort or to the basis upon which they earn their living. Certainly not all Millennials value flexibility the same way and there are Traditionals who operate as contractors, as a way to keep busy or to augment retirement income. As a result, stereotypes are dangerous to make and organizations must inevitably consider the makeup of people at the individual level.

National/Ethnic Culture

The globalization that has occurred over the last several decades has resulted in work-forces that are diverse with respect to their national and ethnic backgrounds. Chapter 10 discusses the issues associated with performance and rewards management when a cultur-ally diverse workforce exists.

Accommodating Workforce Cultural Characteristics

Once an organization has defined and assessed its culture and performed a similar analysis of the culture(s) of its workforce it will certainly face paradoxes. One such paradox is due to the reality that subcultures exist in any organization, typically along functional, business unit or geographic lines. So although the organization may aspire to a single metaculture to provide alignment with its mission and desired values, it may need to deal with local adaptation. Perhaps the best that can be hoped for is localized adaptation that is consistent with global principles.

The amount of diversity in the typical workforce has increased dramatically over the last two decades. This is a healthy trend, since it is clear that a workforce must be at least as diverse as the environment it operates within if it is to understand that context. But that diversity breeds significant cultural variation between people, thereby creating pressure to accommodate those differences in the organization's HRM strategies and programs. Even an organization with a homogeneous product line, sold to a homogeneous customer base, delivered from a single location in a midsize Midwestern U.S. city faces this challenge. Globalization has brought the world to everyone's door, and periods of skill shortages demand that the recruiting territory be expanded beyond a 50-mile radius. This means that people will be imported, many of them bringing cultures (national, occupational, generational or all of these) to be dealt with.

As mentioned earlier, the degree to which an organization accommodates differences in the cultural orientations existing in the workforce is in many cases limited by law, by economics or by the organization's own culture. Trompenaars has pointed out that the U.S. culture is very high on a universalistic approach—the same set of rules for everyone.[5] This puts great pressure on those rules and how limiting they are. One of the most dramatic accommodations made during the 1980s and 1990s was the increased use of flexible benefits. This major change in the philosophy driving benefit design was largely attributable to the recognition that people with different needs valued benefits differently. It is in the best interests of any organization to derive the maximum amount of perceived value for every dollar spent, and the move to providing choice allowed organizations to increase that perceived value, since more people got what they really needed.

Creating flexible working schedules and allowing telecommuting have been other accommodations to the needs of specific employee groups—and even individuals.

Changing the base pay, incentive or performance management systems to accommodate cultural differences is much more difficult. Every difference created in these areas potentially creates a challenge about fairness—whether that challenge is addressed through the courts or directly with employees. On the other hand, if an incentive pool is created through a performance-sharing plan the option of letting employees choose how that pool is distributed may not be out of the question. If the vast majority of employees in an organizational unit or location prefer egalitarian distribution, what is gained by mandating individual awards be based on individual performance appraisal ratings? The objective, as with benefit costs, is to get the maximum perceived value from every dollar spent, so why not allow the Japan office to distribute the same dollar amount or percentage of pay to employees?

These are large issues and they relate to culture's impact on HRM strategies and programs. The organizational culture may prescribe one approach, while the workforce culture prescribes quite another. This is a challenge for the HR function to address.

Tools such as the cultural assessment instrument provided in Figure A2.1 can help with defining and assessing organizational culture. Research on workforce cultures can provide insight into how employees might react to specific HRM programs. Considering culture is a critical prerequisite for designing effective strategies and programs.

Notes

1 Schein, E., *Organizational Culture and Leadership* (San Francisco, CA, Jossey-Bass, 1992).
2 Kotter, J. & Heskett, J., *Corporate Culture and Performance* (New York, Free Press, 1992).
3 Greene, R., "Culturally Compatible Rewards Strategies," *ACA Journal* (Autumn, 1995).
4 Greene, R., "Contributing to Organizational Success through Performance Appraisal," paper on SHRM website, www.shrm.org.
5 Trompenaars, F., *Riding the Waves of Culture* (Burr Ridge, IL, Irwin, 1994).

Index

Locators in **bold** refer to tables, those in *italics* refer to figures

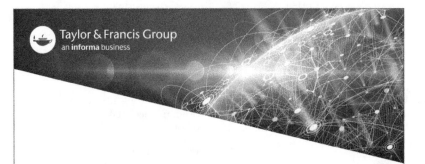